THE HORS D'OEUVRE BIBLE

THE HORS D'OEUVRE BIBLE

David Paul Larousse

John Wiley & Sons, Inc.

New York • Chichester • Brisbane • Toronto • Singapore

"The cook who has learnt the trick of making this exquisite
thing (fine pâté) has trouble keeping his hands off food.
Learn to leave things alone,
in their natural state.
They may taste even better that way."
—Hsiang Ju Lu and Tsuifeng Lin, *Chinese Gastronomy*

Publisher: Margaret K. Burns
Senior Editor: Claire Thompson
Photography: Marshall Gordon
Food Styling: Jeff Baggenstoss and D. P. Larousse
Prop Styling Consultation: Susan Neuer
Line Drawings: Carol Nunnelly
Canapé Schematics: José Luis Ayala

This text is printed on acid-free paper.

This publication is designed to provide accurate and authoritative information in regard to the subject matter covered. It is sold with the understanding that the publisher is not engaged in rendering professional services. If
legal, accounting, medical, psychological, or any other expert assistance is
required, the services of a competent professional person should be sought.

Library of Congress Cataloging-in-Publication Data:

Larousse, David Paul, 1949–
    The hors d'oeuvre bible / David Paul Larousse.
        p.   cm.
    Includes bibliographical references.
    ISBN 0-471-01312-9 (acid-free)
    1. Appetizers.   I. Title.
TX740.L33   1995
641.8'12—dc20   94-25399

Printed in the United States of America

10 9 8 7 6 5 4 3 2

CONTENTS

RECIPES

1 ANTIPASTI

2 CANAPÉS

Hot Dishes

SANDWICHES

3 TARTLETS AND BARQUETTES

TARTLETS

Cold Dishes

Hot Dishes

5 CROUSTADES, PASTRIES, AND PUFFS

CROUSTADES

Cold Dishes

Hot Dishes

PASTRIES

Cold Dishes

Hot Dishes

BOUCHÉES

6 PASTA AND PIZZA

7 EGGS AND CHEESE

8 FINFISH AND SHELLFISH

11 SALADS

SALAD SAUCES

Vinaigrette

Mayonnnaise

Mayonnaise Variations

VEGETABLE SALADS

FOREWORD

David Paul Larousse and I met in Newport, Rhode Island, during the summer of 1987. He had just returned from a winter working as chef de cuisine on a Caribbean-based yacht, and I was looking at a restaurant to lease.

"Are you working now?" I asked.

"I just started a job as a waiter but heard that this place was looking for a chef. I'm actually a writer, hoping to put another book together this summer."

Having been an innkeeper and a restaurateur for nearly two decades, I spoke his language. We shared notes and philosophies on the artistry that is an integral part of the culinary craft, particularly in the Garde Manger department. The passion that this chef and author felt for the craft was evident, not only in conversation, but also in his first book, on garnishing. He spoke of his travels—as a wandering chef, working in seasonal restaurants, and teaching. I shared stories of my own voyages, including a stint doing cooking demonstrations on the QE2.

From that first day in Newport, our friendship has grown into a fine and brotherly camaraderie. The following summer we proposed a radio show, "Food for Talk," to station WHJJ in Providence, Rhode Island, which I continue to host to this day. David returned to the other "city-by-the-bay," San Francisco, and continued writing and illustrating books and teaching culinary arts. No matter that the author knows his subject; in a market flooded with competition, it is only persistence that brings such achievement to date—five published works in the field. David's last book, *The Sauce Bible*, is the finest and most complete work on the subject I have ever seen.

This latest tome on the subject of hors d'oeuvres may be his best work to date. The French gave us hors d'oeuvres, the small dishes that are served "outside of the main course." David Paul Larousse has given us an expansive, gorgeously illustrated work on hors d'oeuvres, canapés, and contemporary small dishes. Without question, this informative and entertaining reference book will serve chefs, cooks, and culinary practitioners at all levels as a source of inspiration and instruction. Read it, and enjoy.

Peter Loring Pratt
Wyoming, Rhode Island

PREFACE

The term *hors d'oeuvre* covers a considerable area of appetizers, finger foods, small courses, first courses, and side dishes. There also exists a finite body of *classical hors d'oeuvres,* which, in Western civilization, dates back to the publication of *Le Viandier,* the first professional cookery book written in France. The author, Guillaume Tirel, better known as Taillevent (1310–1395), was in charge of the royal kitchens under King Charles V, and was a significant personality in the evolution of Western classical cuisine. And, while classical cuisine may be an endangered species in some parts of the world, understanding recipes and techniques that have stood the test of time is *essential* to the success of today's culinary professionals, for, in actual contemporary practice, the production of appetizers remains an ever-evolving area of culinary expression. Hence, the approach of this book has been to provide a synopsis of classical hors d'oeuvres, add a contemporary element, and provide the reader with an understanding of nuts-and-bolts techniques. Armed with this understanding, the culinary professional will then be prepared to develop his or her own unique style.

By definition, hors d'oeuvres should be small and delicate, visually appealing, and designed to be eaten with one's fingers or a small utensil. With this definition in mind, we tend to think of hors d'oeuvres solely as bite-size canapés passed among the guests at cocktail parties, both casual and formal. But if we consider the broader definition of any dish served outside the main course, then we can include a considerably larger body of dishes.

Hors d'oeuvres can be labor intensive. A great deal depends on a foodservice establishment's ability to devote the time and resources to the small dishes on its menu. The possible variations in style and substance are infinite. Yet in recent years the public, showing a preference for frequent dining, has spurred the growth of moderately priced cafés, bistros, trattorias, tapas bars, and trendy dim sum tearooms—places where one can dine frequently, well, and affordably. It is here that contemporary cooking styles have mingled with the tradition of classical small dishes, from both Eastern and Western cultures, and this has created some very innovative and engaging work.

The hors d'oeuvre dishes herein are gleaned from my own experience in the culinary trade. From the pages of a large, well-worn three-ring binder that was begun during my first year as a culinary student, I culled recipes, notes, and comments, recorded over a period of 22 years. Since only information deemed exceptional was entered into this journal, this final result represents the very best of all the years of working with some highly qualified chefs. One such experience was a one-year apprenticeship spent working with Peter Van Erp, then chef de cuisine at a rustic private hunt club in rural Dutchess County, New York. Van Erp had an incredible wealth of knowledge, and I consider that apprenticeship an initiation into the tradition of classical Western cuisine. The ubiquitous *Hors D'oeuvres Variées* on every Van Erp menu was where I really began to grasp the breadth of possibilities in this realm. His work, I believe, was on a par with that of the handful of world-class hotels and dining establishments around the world that still serve the elaborate and ornate dishes reminiscent of eighteenth-century haute cuisine and nineteenth-century *Belle Epoque.* Our early morning forays into the nearby woodlands of southeastern New York State, foraging for morels, chanterelles, MacIntosh apples, and fiddlehead ferns, which were later turned into small courses for our clientele, was a priceless experience. In the autumn months we worked with wild duck, partridge, pheasant, quail, and venison, brought into the kitchen still warm from the club members' hunting expeditions. It was as good as taking a trip back in time.

With contemporary interest in casual and frequent *grazing* in mind, and a focus on the all-important *presentation* of food, this book is intended to provide culinary practitioners with an opportunity to play with a host of colors, shapes, textures, and flavors. One particular area of hors d'oeuvres, specifically canapés—small, bite-size, open-faced sandwiches—may in fact be considered exquisite miniature works of art—*art on a cracker*. If readers glimpse the artistic possibilities of cooking as a result of working with this book, then writing it has been well worth the effort.

David Paul Larousse
San Francisco, California

ACKNOWLEDGMENTS

Special thanks to members of the photography team: Jeff Baggenstoss, student of the author, who performed invaluable service as both food-styling assistant and a significant member of the creative team during the photographing; Marshall Gordon, photographer, whose sense of humor was essential in maintaining a semblance of sanity during the photo shoots; and Susan Neuer, who supplied technical assistance and the loan of many props; and Delia Battista, Director of Student Services, and Lisa Romano, Librarian, Pennsylvania Institute of Culinary Arts, Pittsburgh, for assistance with research.

Thanks also to the following individuals for their contributions: Luc Brondel, former chef-instructor, Culinary Institute of America, Hyde Park, New York (Cream of Watercress Soup; Bouillabaisse); Rachel and Carolyn Collins, of Carolyn Collins Caviar, Chicago (see list of Specialty Suppliers), who supplied the caviar for the Caviar Fan; Mark Davis, garde manger instructor at California Culinary Academy, (recipe for Basic Crackers, assistance with canapé specifications, and loan of platter for Gravlax photograph); Peter Van Erp, former chef de cuisine, Dutchess Valley Club, Pawling, New York, currently chef-instructor, Brooklyn Community College, Brooklyn, New York (Braised Red Cabbage; Caponata, Dutchess Valley Style; Dutch Lentil Soup; Snails, Dutchess Valley Style; Gazpacho, Dutchess Valley Style; Pike Quenelles, Lobster Sauce); Dieter Faukner, chef-instructor, Culinary Institute of America (Oxtail Soup); Alan R. Gibson, director of research and development, and menu planning, Uno Restaurant Corporation, Boston (Asparagus, Vergé Sauce; Rhode Island Reds' Clam Chowder; Lobster Strudel, Tomato-Armagnac Sauce); Lars Kronmark, chef-instructor, California Culinary Academy (Acorn Squash Blintzes); Irwin Pirolt, chef-instructor, City College of San Francisco (Chicken Enchilada, Salsa Verde); Jackie Robert, chef-proprietor, Amelio's, San Francisco (Creamed Chicken Tenderloins with Pears and Belgian Endive); Albert Tordjman, chef-proprietor, The Flying Saucer, San Francisco (Florentine Pasta Rolls); Jasper White, chef-proprietor, Restaurant Jasper, Boston (Jasper Salad).

The following individuals, former students of the author, contributed a number of recipes to this book: Rob Brunst (California Grilled Quail and Watercress Salad); Johanna Carpo (Crostini with Prosciutto and Figs); David Gedney (Cheddar and Chicken Liver Canapés); Clarence George (Southwest Starburst, Polish Pieces); Brent Jones (Smoke and Puff, Shrimp in Heat); Kelly Jones (Spicy Shrimp on a Chip, Polenta Squares with Sun-Dried Tomato); Karletta Moniz (Asian Bird's Nest, Gorgonzola Bouchée); Paul Newman (Tuna & Grilled Eggplant Salad, Pacific Rim Style); Charles Olson (Grecian Morsels and Mexican Medallions); Joseph Ong (Thai-Style Chicken on Fried Wonton); Russell Young, (Broccoli on Onion Cracker).

INTRODUCTION:

Basic Preparations

*B*ecause this is not a book on fundamentals, it is understood that readers will possess an understanding of basic cooking techniques and processes. For this reason, not every minute detail or measurement is delineated. For example, most recipes call for *salt and pepper as needed*. This is standard procedure, since in actual practice foods are seasoned according to the taste of the individual preparing it. The following general notes are offered for clarification.

- Components of some dishes often taste better if prepared the day before they are used. Scientific explanation of this phenomenon dispels its mystery. In culinary nomenclature, however, we say that during the time in which a pesto, tomato sauce, vinaigrette, chutney, or other dish sits, the flavors of the ingredients have an opportunity to *marry*. If we accept the premise that food is a living thing, when we combine certain ingredients, cover them, place them in a safe place, close the door, and turn out the light, it is easier to understand why flavors and character improve during this *marrying* period.

- *Mise-en-place* is an important term in the culinary craft. In common parlance, the phrase means "A place for everything, and everything in its place." The concept is extremely important in commercial kitchens, where timing is critical. On the home front, in preparing a meal for friends and/or family, it means producing a well-planned meal smoothly, with minimum chaos.

- Nomenclature is difficult to pin down in the culinary world. One practitioner's *croûte* is another's *croustade,* one's *duchesse* is another's *éclair,* one's *caisse* is another's *bouchée,* and so on. We have endeavored to integrate classical and contemporary dishes and styles and to organize all dishes as logically as possible.

- A pastry thermometer is an essential tool, particularly in preparing certain doughs or deep-fried foods.

- Unless otherwise indicated, all recipes are designed for service to appoximately four persons.

- Cold food should always be served on *chilled plates,* hot food on *hot plates.*

- The paper wrapper around butter, which will always have some remnant of butter remaining on it, should be saved and used for numerous functions. It can be used to cover the top of a hot sauce, preventing a skin from forming on top. It can also be cut to size and placed on top of a ramekin or timbale in which a mousse is baked.

- Aspic, a crystal clear, highly flavored meat, fish, or poultry jelly, though commonly used in classical cookery, is not commonly found in contemporary North American cuisine, because savory jelly is not a taste Americans are accustomed to. Since it is an extremely satisfying and palatable addition to a dish, however, on occasion one may have the opportunity to prepare it. At such times, because the process for preparing it is complex, we recommend using the dried form. (For information on how to obtain this item, see the list of Specialty Suppliers on page 395.)

To prepare powdered aspic for coating cold dishes, heat some port, Madeira, or dry white wine, then stir in the powder (¼ cup powdered aspic to 3 cups hot liquid). Bring the aspic to a boil, then strain it through a fine sieve into a clean bowl. Set the bowl in an ice water bath and stir until the liquid cools down to a temperature of 110° F. Remove the aspic from the water bath and use as needed. If the aspic cools down to where it begins to jell, return the bowl to a pot of boiling water, heat until liquefied, then cool it down again in the ice water bath. For cutting into geometric shapes for use as a garnish, or mincing for use as a base, pour the hot aspic into a pan and allow it to set in the refrigerator. Then cut out shapes or dice as needed.

- At its best, the color and flavor of butter is directly related to the diet of the dairy animals from which it is made. In North America, butter tends to be created in a homogenous mass production, with little variations in character between regions. Unsalted butter is superior to the salted variety, since it is fresher and less adulterated (mostly with color and salt). There is a European-style butter available, mostly at the wholesale level. Soured heavy cream (past the due date on the package), though slightly sour-smelling, can be whipped until it curdles, then pressed through cheesecloth to remove the liquid. The resulting butter may have a slightly sourish flavor, but if this is not overpowering, the product is prefectly acceptable to use. This is an important trick to know, in terms of watching food costs.
- Cucumbers appear frequently in the recipes in this book, and hothouse cucumbers (also referred to as English cucumbers) are preferred for several reasons: they have very few seeds, making them highly functional as bouchées and socles; their skin is thinner, thus easier to digest, and is not coated with oil or paraffin, as are commercially produced varieties found in the supermarket.

- Flour, unless otherwise specified, refers to all-purpose flour.
- Green, red, white, and black peppercorns are all seeds of the genus *Piper nigrum,* in various degrees of their growth (respectively) or handling. Black pepper is created when picked in the late green stage and allowed to dry for several days. White pepper is black pepper soaked in water, then rubbed to remove the dark outer skin. In culinary usage, green peppercorns are often mashed into a paste, then spread on a steak and grilled. White pepper is used when the color of a dish is light and the dark specks of black pepper might suggest poor culinary hygiene. In such a case white pepper is more appropriate and, in fact, does have a slightly more refined flavor. Unless a recipe calls for white pepper, *pepper* indicates black pepper.

Pepper should always be ground as needed, not just for hygienic reasons, but for potency. Once ground, essential oils are released and flavor is diminished. We suggest two pepper mills— one for black pepper, one for white. In larger commercial operations, an electric spice or coffee grinder is sometimes used for grinding dried spices.

- Prepared mustard is nothing more than ground mustard seeds, simmered with wine, vinegar, and herbs. For the adventurous, a facsimile can be made as follows: 6 tablespoons crushed mustard seed, 4 tablespoons dry mustard, 3 teaspoons turmeric, 2 teaspoons minced tarragon leaves, ½ cup white wine vinegar, 6 tablespoons olive oil, and 2 pressed garlic cloves. Bring all the ingredients to a boil, allow to cool, and refrigerate until ready to use.
- A shallot is a mild member of the onion family, possessing a slight flavor of garlic. It is more easily digested than its relatives and is essential to the production of nearly all compound sauces and many other classical dishes. Its name is derived from Askalon, an ancient Eastern Mediterranean trading center, where it was a popular vegetable.
- When a dish calls for sour cream, it can be replaced with a domestic version of *crème fraîche,* a soured cream product commonly used in France and other European cuisines, possessing a higher fat content and a slightly different tartness. A facsimile can be made as follows: In a small, clean saucepan, combine 1 quart heavy cream, 1 cup plain full-fat yogurt, 1 cup buttermilk, 1 cup sour cream, and a pinch of salt. Heat to 100°F, then transfer to a clean stainless steel bowl. Cover with plastic wrap, and place in an oven over-

night (the heat from a pilot light provides sufficient heat to allow the culture to grow; in an electric oven, set the thermostat to the lowest possible setting for 2 hours, then turn off.) The next day, refrigerate the mixture for 24 hours, then remove the thickened part on top, using a slotted strainer, and use the remaining liquid part for the next batch. (By combining cream with yogurt, buttermilk, and sour cream, a fairly complex facsimile is created. Crème fraîche can also be made using cream and any one of the other ingredients, or any combination thereof.)

- Real vine-ripened tomatoes, while a real treat gastronomically (and agronomically), are not always available. When a dish calls for tomatoes, it is perfectly acceptable to use the canned variety, since they are often superior to the so-called fresh ones found in a supermarket, often grown on foreign soil, picked green, then exposed to some strange gas in order to facilitate their ripening. Cook's choice applies.

- Vinegar is more than just soured wine—it is a carefully fermented product, made with a mother, a special strain of bacteria that ingests alcohol and excretes acetic acid. Once you have tasted real vinegar, it is difficult to go back to the commercially produced distilled variety. (For a source of well-made vinegars, see the list of Specialty Suppliers.)

THE BASIC CUTS

For ease of understanding, we have used common nomenclature for the various cuts used throughout this book. The following list describes the more formal terminology and dimensions. It is important to note that the dimensions are approximate and will vary from kitchen to kitchen.

Potatoes	Les Pommes de Terre	
English	French	Description/Dimension
straw	paille	a thin ribbon
chip	chip	a thin uniform slice
waffle	gaufrette	a crisscrossed slice
matchstick	allumette	$\frac{1}{8} \times \frac{1}{8} \times 1\frac{1}{2}$ inches
French fries	frite	$\frac{1}{4} \times \frac{1}{4} \times 2$–$2\frac{1}{2}$ inches
steak fries	pont-neuf	$\frac{1}{2} \times \frac{1}{2} \times 3$ inches
medium dice	Parmentier	$\frac{1}{3}$–$\frac{1}{2}$-inch square
large dice	Carré	$\frac{1}{2}$–$\frac{3}{4}$-inch square
pea	pois	tiny ball or sphere ($\frac{1}{4}$-inch diameter)
noisette	noisette	a small ball or sphere ($\frac{1}{3}$-inch diameter)

Potatoes	Les Pommes de Terre	
English	*French*	*Description/Dimension*
Parisienne	Parisienne	a large ball or sphere (½–¾-inch diameter)
turned	tourné	7-sided oval
• small	château	1½ inches long
• medium	nature	2–2½ inches long
• large	fondante	2½–3 inches long

Vegetables	Les Legumes	
English	*French*	*Description/Dimension*
small dice	brunoise	⅛-inch square
medium dice	jardinière	¼-inch square
large dice	macedoine	⅓–1½ inches square
julienne	julienne	any variety of small rectangle
large julienne	batonnet	¼ × ¼ × 2–2½ inches
roughly cut	paysanne	a rough, unequal cut
thinly sliced	Vichy	a thin circular slice
turned	tourné	a 7-sided oval (1–2 inches long)
shredded	chiffonade	a thin ribbon, usually for green leafy vegetables

STOCKS

The French word for "stock" is *fond,* from the Latin *fundus,* meaning "bottom." This is a clear indicator of the importance of well-prepared stocks. According to *Hering's Dictionary of Classical and Modern Cookery,* "Good fonds and sauces are the foundation of fine cuisine. Their preparation is considered the most important business in every large kitchen."

Stocks are divided into two primary categories: brown stock *(fond brun),* in which the ingredients are roasted before they are simmered and prior to the addition of a tomato ingredient; and white stock *(fond blanc),* in which ingredients are not roasted.

Both white and brown stocks, when reduced, yield a dark glaze, though brown stock glaze will be a bit darker and thicker than white stocks. The choice of which variety of stock to reduce, will depend on its use.

The Elements of a Stock

- Nutritional: bones
- Aromatic: mirepoix (celery, carrots, onions) and bouquet garni (herbs and spices)
- Liquid: water, sometimes augmented with wine

General Guidelines for the Production of a Proper Stock

- Use quality ingredients.
- Wash ingredients well in cold water, and peel aromatics.
- Begin a stock with cold water.
- Perform the initial skimming before adding aromatics.
- When adding water to a simmering stock, use hot water.
- Skim regularly.
- Always simmer, never boil. (Simmering allows the natural clarifying processes to manifest, producing a rich, clear stock.)
- Simmer 4 hours minimum (for fish stock, 1 to 1½ hours).
- Strain, cool, and store properly.

COURT BOUILLON

1 gallon water
1 cup dry white wine
1 onion, peeled and quartered
1 bay leaf

1 bunch parsley stems, tied together with cotton string
1 lemon, peeled and quartered
1 tablespoon salt

- Bring all the ingredients to a boil. Turn down to a simmer, and poach fish, poultry, or meat items as needed.

———————————— • ————————————

Court bouillon is more a poaching medium than a stock. It is used to poach any food item that requires poaching. Additional ingredients can be added, in the way of aromatics or different wines, depending on the nature of the dish.

BROWN VEAL OR BEEF STOCK

(Fond Brun de Veau ou Boeuf)

6 pounds veal or beef shanks and knuckle bones, cut into 4-inch lengths
1 cup tomato paste
3 stalks celery, trimmed, rinsed, and roughly chopped

2 carrots, peeled, tops removed, and roughly cut
2 medium Spanish onions, peeled and roughly chopped
1 leek, green tops only, well rinsed and roughly chopped

2 gallons (approximately) cold water
1 garlic clove, crushed
2 bay leaves
3 sprigs fresh thyme

1 bunch parsley stems, trimmed, rinsed, and tied together
1 teaspoon black peppercorns, cracked
1 quart dry red wine

- Preheat an oven to 400°F.
- Wash the bones thoroughly in cold water. Place them in a roasting pan, and roast for 20 minutes. Remove from the oven, and spread a light coating of tomato paste over the bones, using a rubber spatula. Continue roasting another 15 to 20 minutes, or until golden brown.
- Remove the bones from the pan, and place into a stockpot that has been wiped out with a clean towel. Fill with cold water 4 inches above the highest bone, and place on a high flame. When the water just begins to boil, turn down to a simmer. Skim impurities from the top (albumen, fat, coagulated blood) and discard.
- Place the mirepoix and leek into the pan in which the bones roasted, and stir these ingredients with any fat remaining in the pan. Roast for 40 minutes, stirring occasionally, until the vegetables are well caramelized.
- Add the mirepoix and the bouquet garni to the simmering stock. Place the roasting pan over a high flame on the stove, add the dry red wine, and deglaze. Add this liquid to the simmering stock. Simmer 8 to 12 hours, skimming periodically as needed. Strain, cool, cover, label, and refrigerate.

ᛠHITE VEAL STOCK

(Fond Blanc de Veau)

5 pounds veal knuckle bones, cut into 3 or 4-inch pieces
5 pounds veal shank, cut into 3 or 4-inch pieces
2 stalks celery, trimmed, rinsed, and roughly chopped
2 carrots, peeled, tops removed, and roughly chopped

1 large Spanish onion, peeled and cut into eighths
2 bay leaves
3 sprigs fresh thyme
1 bunch parsley stems, trimmed, rinsed, and tied together
1 teaspoon white peppercorns, cracked
2 gallons (approximately) cold water

- Wash the bones thoroughly in cold water. Place them in a stockpot that has been wiped out with a clean towel. Fill with cold water 4 inches above the highest bone, and place on a high flame. When the water just begins to boil, turn down to a simmer. Skim impurities from the top (albumen, fat, coagulated blood) and discard.

- Add the mirepoix and the bouquet garni to the simmering stock. Place the roasting pan over a high flame on the stove, add the dry red wine, and deglaze. Add this liquid to the simmering stock. Simmer 4 to 8 hours, skimming periodically as needed. Strain, cool, cover, label, and refrigerate.

WHITE CHICKEN STOCK

(Fond Blanc de Volaille)

6 pounds fresh chicken bones, backs, necks, and wings
1 whole fresh chicken (optional)
2 gallons water
1 large Spanish onion, peeled and cut into eighths
1 large carrot, top removed, scrubbed, and roughly chopped
2 stalks celery, rinsed and roughly chopped
1 leek, green tops only, well rinsed and roughly chopped
2 bay leaves
3 sprigs fresh thyme
1 bunch parsley stems
1 teaspoon white peppercorns, cracked

- Rinse the bones (and whole chicken if used) thoroughly in cold water.

- Place the bones (and chicken) into a stockpot, and cover them with cold water (should be 3 to 4 inches above the highest bone). Heat over a high flame, just until the stock comes to a boil. Turn down to a simmer.

- Skim the top, removing, then discarding, fat and impurities.

- Add the vegetables, herbs, and spices.

- Simmer 1 hour, then lift out the whole chicken (if used), and set it aside to cool. Separate the meat from the skin and bones, reserving the meat for another dish, and return the skin and bones to the stockpot. Continue simmering, 6 to 8 hours, skimming off and discarding impurities periodically.

- Strain, cool, cover, label, and refrigerate.

———— • ————

The optional chicken is included for additional flavor. In commercial kitchen production, this step is appropriate if cold poached chicken is used in another dish.

The clear, savory broths found in the soups in Asian restaurants may be the result of the following technique. When the water first comes to a simmer, pour the contents of the pot into a colander, discarding the liquid. Rinse the bones again in cold water, then begin the stock all over again with fresh water. A stock made from bones rinsed in this manner will be clear and savory if it is carefully simmered throughout the remaining cooking time.

$\mathcal{B}$ROWN DUCK STOCK

(Fond Brun de Canard)

5 pounds of duck carcasses with giblets (excluding livers)
½ cup tomato paste
2 ribs celery, rinsed and roughly chopped
1 large carrot, peeled and roughly chopped
1 large Spanish onion, peeled and roughly chopped
1 leek, green tops only, well rinsed and roughly chopped

1 pint dry red wine
1 bay leaf
2 sprigs fresh thyme
1 sprig fresh rosemary
1 bunch parsley stems, trimmed, rinsed, and tied together
½ teaspoon black peppercorns, cracked
1½ gallons (approximately) cold water

- Preheat an oven to 400°F.
- Wash the bones thoroughly in cold water. Drain and dry. Place them in a roasting pan, and roast for 25 minutes. Remove from the oven, and spread a light coating of tomato paste over the bones, using a rubber spatula. Continue roasting another 20 to 30 minutes, or until well browned.
- Remove the bones from the pan, and place in a stockpot that has been wiped out with a clean towel. Fill with cold water 4 inches above the highest bone, and place on a high flame. When the water just begins to boil, turn down to a simmer. Skim impurities from the top (albumen, fat, coagulated blood) and discard.
- Pour off some of the excess fat from the roasting pan, saving for another use. Place the mirepoix and leeks in the pan from which the bones came, and stir these ingredients with any fat remaining in the pan. Roast for 40 minutes, stirring occasionally, until the vegetables are well caramelized.

....

Duck fat is particularly good used in roux, or in sautéing the vegetables for various soups, as well as in potato and rice dishes.

- Skim the simmering stock (duck will yield a considerable amount of fat), then add the mirepoix and the bouquet garni. Place the roasting pan over a high flame on the stove, add the dry red wine, and deglaze. Add this liquid to the simmering stock. Simmer 8 to 12 hours, skimming periodically as needed. Strain, cool, cover, label, and refrigerate.

$\mathcal{B}$ROWN GAME STOCK

(Fond Brun de Gibier)

5 pounds venison bones, cut into 3 or 4-inch pieces
1 pheasant, cut into
6 or 8 pieces
½ cup melted butter
a small piece of fat back, cut up into ½-inch cubes
½ cup tomato paste
2 ribs celery, rinsed and roughly chopped
2 carrots, peeled, tops removed, and roughly chopped
1 large Spanish onion, peeled and roughly chopped

1 leek, green tops only, well rinsed and roughly chopped
1 quart dry red wine
1 bay leaf
2 sprigs fresh thyme
2 sprigs fresh sage
1 bunch parsley stems, trimmed, rinsed, and tied together
½ teaspoon black peppercorns, cracked
2 whole cloves
10 juniper berries
1½ gallons (approximately) cold water

- Preheat an oven to 400°F.
- Wash the bones and pheasant thoroughly in cold water. Drain and dry. Place them in a roasting pan, and brush with the melted butter. Roast for 20 minutes. Remove from the oven, and spread a light coating of tomato paste over the bones and pheasant, using a rubber spatula. Continue roasting another 20 to 30 minutes, or until golden brown.
- Remove the bones and pheasant from the pan, and place in a stockpot that has been wiped out with a clean towel. Fill with cold water 4 inches above the highest bone, and place on a high flame. When the water just begins to boil, turn down to a simmer. Skim impurities from the top (albumen, fat, coagulated blood) and discard.
- Place the mirepoix and leeks into the pan in which the bones were roasted, and stir these ingredients with any fat remaining

The pheasant may be an extravagant addition, but it makes for an exceptionally well-flavored stock. The bones and carcasses from rabbit, partridge, or quail, if available, can also be used.

in the pan. Roast for 40 minutes, stirring occasionally, until the vegetables are well caramelized.

- Skim the simmering stock, then add the mirepoix and the bouquet garni. Place the roasting pan over a high flame on the stove, add the dry red wine, and deglaze. Add this liquid to the simmering stock. Simmer 8 to 12 hours, skimming periodically as needed. Strain, cool, cover, label, and refrigerate.

.... # *F*ISH STOCK

(Fond Blanc de Poisson)

3 tablespoons butter
1 Spanish onion, peeled and cut into eighths
1 stalk celery, roughly cut
1 leek, green top only, well rinsed and roughly cut
3 or 4 mushrooms, rinsed and roughly cut
10 pounds fresh white fish bones, cut into 3-inch lengths

1 cup dry white wine
1½ gallons cold water
the juice of 1 lemon
1 bay leaf
1 sprig fresh thyme
1 sprig fresh dill, rinsed and roughly chopped
1 bunch parsley stems, trimmed and rinsed
½ teaspoon white peppercorns, crushed

- Wash and soak the bones in cold water for 1 hour. Drain and rinse.
- Place the onions, celery, leek, and mushrooms in a stockpot with the butter. Cover, and sauté for 10 minutes over a medium flame, stirring occasionally. Add the bones, and sauté another 5 minutes.
- Add the wine, water, and lemon juice (the liquid should rise about 4 inches above the highest bone). Bring to a boil, then turn down to a simmer. Skim the impurities from the top and discard.
- Add the herbs and spices, and continue simmering for 1 to 1½ hours, skimming periodically. Strain, cool, cover, label, and refrigerate.

Meat Glaze (Glace de Viande)

A glaze is a 90% (or more) reduction of a stock. Any stock can be reduced to create a glaze, either brown or white. The only exception to this is fish stock, which requires clarification to produce a proper glaze. (This is discussed a little further on.) Though commercial kitchens produce large quantities of a single stock, which can then be made into a specific glaze, when working on a smaller scale at home, a stock made from several different nutritional components (varieties of bones), can also be reduced into a glaze. Glazes are used to fortify soups, stews, and sauces, or any dish where concentrated meat flavor is a welcome addition. They are one of the most important tools in a saucier's repertoire.

The word *glace* in French also means *mirror*, a linguistic connection to its reflecting qualities, which are amazingly effective, in spite of the fact that it turns into a dark brown, syrup as a result of the reduction. The commercial counterpart to glaze, is *base*, available in beef, chicken, clam, and lobster varieties, and used primarily in hotels and other large production houses, where time and labor cost prohibit the creation of natural glazes. These have a concentrated flavor of the food item they are made from, but they also include a high percentage of both salt and monosodium glutamate (MSG), and sometime other chemical preservatives. In the consumer market, *bouillon cubes* (bouillon is the noun form of the French verb *bouillir*, meaning "to boil.") are the home version of a concentrated stock base, and these too are made up of primarily salt and additives. Once consumers and those who pursue cooking as an avocation, learn the ease with which a good, flavorful stock can be made, they rarely return to the use of the cube.

When preparing a glaze, it is important to begin with a very clear stock. As it is reduced, minute solid particles in the stock that make up the flavor of the stock, become concentrated, and a clear stock is essential towards creating a smooth and flavorful glaze, without it burning or turning bitter. A clear stock can be achieved in two ways: (1) By the slow and careful simmering of the stock and (2) by clarifying the stock through a separate procedure undertaken after the first stock is made.

Glazes are also naturally salty, an indication of the amount of salt that is found naturally in the meats, fish, and aromatics that are used to create a glaze. It is for this reason, that stocks should not be salted.

To prepare a glaze, a stock is simply simmered until reduced by approximately half. It is then strained through a screen strainer (chinois mousseline) or several layers of muslin (cheesecloth), into a smaller vessel, and reduced by half again. (This second, smaller vessel, should be made of a heavy-gauge metal, which prevents the thickening stock from burning.) As the stock continues to reduce, it begins to thicken noticeably, as a result of the concentration of both gelatin, and the minute particles that give the stock its color and flavor. The reduction is continued, each time reducing by approximately half, then straining through a fine strainer into a smaller, heavy-gauge saucepan. Eventually, the glaze reaches a thick, dark, syrupy consistency, similar in appearance to molasses. It should then be transferred to small containers, preferably with securely fitting lids, cooled, then refrigerated or frozen. A glaze will keep for approximately one month under refrigeration. If any mold should form on the top surface, it can be scraped off and discarded, since the underlying glaze is so dense, that it will not be adversely affected by surface growths. The glazes can also be stored in the freezer, where they will keep for up to a year.

There is one exception to the production of a glaze, and that has to do with fish stock. While meat stocks, if simmered gently, yield a clear stock, fish are more difficult to produce clear on the first round. In order to create the best possible fish glaze, it is recommended that a fish stock be clarified.

CHAPTER 1

ANTIPASTI

*A*n *antipasto* is an appetizer of Italian origin, consisting of an assortment of roasted, smoked, and cured meats; cured fish and olives; tomatoes; grilled, roasted, or marinated vegetables; marinated hot peppers, capers, cheese, lettuce, and other ingredients; served with olive oil and vinegar.

We have come a long way from the iceberg lettuce, mortadella, salami, pepperoncini, tomato wedge, provolone cheese, and canned olive antipasto that was once the principal offering in most Italian-style restaurants from New York's Little Italy to San Francisco's North Beach district. Antipasto has evolved into the kind of dish that is at once more authentic to its Italian origins and the way we imagine it to be: passionate, multifaceted, full of color, flavor, and texture—and an expression of both a kitchen's style and the availability of local specialties.

There are no hard and fast rules on the how and what of antipasto. The options are wide, the possibilities infinite. At its best, antipasto provides an opportunity to express gusto and creativity with a Mediterranean flavor. One can discern the level of passion, expertise, and motivation of the staff within any kitchen simply by ordering this dish and perusing its contents. The presence of canned black olives is always a dead giveaway of a less-than-authentic antipasto. Sliced domestic provolone cheese may also raise concern, although alone it is not enough to red flag the entire dish. If one finds fresh buffalo mozzarella, shaved pecorino Romano, goat cheese rounds edged in herbs, or sliced pecorino, then the inclusion of the pedestrian provolone is acceptable.

Although there are no rules on the components of an antipasto, its style and presentation are important. By its very nature, antipasto is an earthier and more rustic approach to starter dishes, as compared with the more controlled style of classic canapés indicative of *haute cuisine*. For instance, it is at a formal dinner, where business or diplomatic matters of great financial or political gravity are the focus of the gathering, where we might find a menu of hors d'oeuvres, passed with abundant etiquette and decorum. Antipasto is the kind of dish one would find at a festive wedding, a raucous bachelor party, or a casual dinner with friends. The style of service, as well as the menu items at such a gathering, is more spontaneous, more informal.

A good antipasto features a variety of fresh, local ingredients and a balance of flavors, colors, and textures, but is not so overloaded that one cannot truly enjoy each component fully. Antipasto also offers an opportunity for a kitchen to use *quality* items remaining from other menus. For example, a kitchen may have a roasted veal tenderloin on one day's menu, which can be sliced cold the next day for an antipasto, accompanied by tuna mayonnaise *(Vitello Tonnato);* portioned ahi tuna steaks cut for an à la carte menu can be coated with pepper and herbs, sautéed medium-rare, then sliced very thin on the bias, accompanied by Rémoulade Sauce; asparagus peeled and blanched al dente for a banquet that canceled at the last minute can be dressed with olive oil, lemon juice, capers, and freshly ground pepper; rice pilaf can be served chilled, augmented with capers, garlic, sun-dried tomatoes, cilantro, olive oil, and vinegar.

There are also numerous ways in which an antipasto can be served: arranged on individual serving plates; brought to the dining patrons as ordered from a menu; offered in the salad bar mode, whereby patrons select their own dishes from a wide variety of offerings to fit their own taste (one can also request a food server to bring a selection of offerings to *his or her* own taste); or offered on a buffet table, arranged on a large platter or mirror. Many of the dishes presented in this chapter cross over into the area of salads and small vegetable dishes.

Whatever its design or service, antipasto represents a personal style. The palate of ingredients one works with includes those indigenous to the region of the Mediterranean Sea and reflects the styles of cookery from the cultures that have evolved in that region: southern Spanish and provincial French, ancient Roman and contemporary Italian, Corsican and Sicilian, Greek and Turkish, Tunisian and Moroccan. The ingredients are representative of this region of the world and are included here as a reflection of the style of the author.

Choosing from the vast array of ingredients, we can include up to five individual items from as many as three of each of the following eight categories for individual plate service, and increase that number for platter service, based on the number of guests it is intended for.

Type of Ingredient		Example
Meat		Sweet or spiced coppa, prosciutto, Parma ham, Genoa-style salami; beef, veal, or lamb
Poultry		Chicken, duck, or turkey breast
Fish		Anchovies, sardines, shrimp, tuna, mussels
Cheese	*Soft:*	goat cheese, provolone, fresh mozzarella, Gorgonzola
	Hard:	Asiago, Parmesan, pecorino
Vegetables	*Grilled:*	eggplant, zucchini, yellow squash
	Marinated:	artichoke hearts, mushrooms, patty pan squash, garbanzo beans, black beans, kidney beans
	Preserved:	pickled eggs; Calamata, Cailletier, Gaeta, Nafplion, Niçoise, and/or Nyons olives

The preserved meats (coppa, prosciutto, ham, salami), cheeses, grilled or marinated vegetables, and olives, are all served as is. Other ingredients (chicken, duck, turkey, shrimp, tuna, mussels, etc.) can be served poached, roasted, or grilled, depending on how they harmonize with the other elements of an antipasto presentation.

CHEESE

Although several varieties of cheese are often served on a large wooden board for buffet presentation, certain varieties of Italian origin can be included in an antipasto offering. Softer varieties are served in large-wedge form, accompanied by toasted baguette slices, or cut into smaller wedges and included as part of a small-dish offering. In a small-dish presentation, the cheese is sometimes accompanied by other elements; an example is buffalo mozzarella layered with sliced tomato and fresh basil leaves and drizzled with extra-virgin olive oil. (See color plate.) Harder cheese varieties are also sometimes served in small dishes, shaved paper-thin. Such options include the following:

Soft: Bel Paese, buffalo mozzarella, fontina, Gorgonzola, provolone, scarmorze, taleggio.
Hard: Asiago, Caciacavallo, Parmesan, pecorino (Romano and Sardo).

GRILLED OR ROASTED VEGETABLES

Vegetables take on a noble presence when seasoned with salt, pepper, and olive oil, then grilled or roasted. Some excellent examples follow:

*B*ELL PEPPERS

(Peperoni Arrosto)

2 green bell peppers
2 red bell peppers

2 yellow bell peppers
olive oil as needed

- Preheat an oven to 400°F.
- Rub the peppers with the olive oil. Place in a baking pan and roast until they begin to turn dark brown and black. Remove, place in a bowl, and cover with plastic wrap for 10 minutes (or wrap in a plastic bag). Tear the peppers open and carefully remove the skin from the flesh, discarding the skin, inner ribs,

and seeds. Serve dressed with olive oil and seasoned with salt and pepper.

———————————— • ————————————

The genus *Capsicum*, to which the pepper belongs, may be so called because it resembles a box (Latin *capsa*), which encloses its seeds. Another theory relates it to the Greek *capto*, meaning "I bite," because of the acrid and pungent flavor of some varieties. Peppers are native to South America and have been cultivated there for nearly 8,000 years. There are so many varieties of peppers—at least 300 known varieties—with so many different species and subspecies, that classification can become quite confusing. The simplest way is to divide peppers into two types, sweet and hot, and then explore regional varieties as one finds them. Leading cultivars of sweet peppers in the United States include Bellringer, Bell Boy, California Wonder, Merrimack Wonder, and Worldbeater.

*E*GGPLANT

(Melanzane Arrosto)

2 large eggplants, ends trimmed, cut into ½-inch thick slices, widthwise	salt, pepper, and olive oil as needed

• Sprinkle the eggplant slices lightly with salt, place in a colander or strainer, and let sit for 1 hour. Wipe excess salt off the eggplant, brush with olive oil, and sprinkle with pepper. Grill, broil, or sauté on both sides until golden brown. (See color plate.)

———————————— • ————————————

Although eggplant is an ancient fruit, native to India, it was unknown to the Greeks and Romans of antiquity and appeared in Europe via Africa only in the fourteenth century. It is virtually never eaten raw, probably because of a high content of *solanine*, a bitter, poisonous alkaloid once used to treat epilepsy. Cooking is believed to eliminate most of the solanine. Eggplant figures prominently in all Mediterranean cuisines, and significant dishes include Ratatouille from Provence, Imam Beyeldi *(swooping Imam)* from Turkey, Babaganoosh from Persia, and Eggplant Parmesan from Italy. Cultivated varieties include Barbentane, Naples Early Purple, Giant New York, Chinese, and Japanese.

FENNEL ROOT

(Finocchio Arrosto)

4 large fennel bulbs, trimmed of stems	salt, pepper, and olive oil as needed
pinch of salt	grated Parmesan cheese

- Slice the fennel along the widest width, into 4 pieces.
- Preheat an oven to 400°F.
- Brush both sides of the fennel slices lightly with olive oil, and season with salt and pepper. Arrange on a roasting pan, roast for 15 minutes, then turn over. Sprinkle each slice with Parmesan cheese and continue roasting another 15 minutes, or until golden brown. (See color plate.)

GARLIC

(Aglio Arrosto)

4 garlic bulbs	olive oil as needed

- Preheat an oven to 400°F.
- Remove excess skin from the exterior of the garlic bulbs. Brush liberally with olive oil, place on a pan, and roast for 30 to 40 minutes. Serve with hot baguette. Dining guests pull cloves off, squeeze out the garlic (which has turned into a lightly caramelized paste), and spread it on the hot bread.

    There are several ways to prepare roasted garlic. The cloves can be separated, peeled; tossed in olive oil, salt, and pepper; and roasted until golden brown. The cloves can also be peeled, skewered on bamboo skewers, oiled and seasoned, then grilled or roasted.

Garlic, *Allium Sativum*, is native to Central Asia and has been cultivated since the earliest days of agriculture. The Latin genus *Allium* is derived from the Celtic word *all*, meaning "hot" and "burning," in reference to the sensation it produces on the palate. The name *garlic* (from Old English *garleac*, Middle English *garlec*) means "spear leek," in reference to the plant's long spearlike green shoots. The culinary uses of garlic are well known in all cultures, but it is also well known for its health-maintaining properties. In *New England Cookery,* c.1808, author Lucy Emerson wrote: "Garlicks though used by the French, are better adapted to medicine than cookery." Still used today in the manufacture of pharmaceuticals, in its unaltered state garlic acts as a purgative, antiseptic, and expectorant. It stimulates digestive organs, regularizes the action of the liver and gallbladder, and is helpful for all intestinal infections. Garlic added to the diet, while one is traveling in foreign lands where parasite-laden food and drink are difficult to avoid, can help prevent illness.

The origin of the proverb "Garlic is as good as ten mothers" is unknown, though the properties and characteristics of garlic have been written about by many, including Aristophanes, Celsus, Charlemagne, Culpeper, Dioscorides, Gandhi, Henry IV, Herodotus, Hippocrates, La Fontaine, Mohammed, Pasteur, Pliny, Eleanor Roosevelt, and Virgil. The late Waverly Root, in his last tome *Food,* c.1980, wrote: "Garlic has been the vehicle in the United States of a self-reversing snobbery. Before I left America to live in Europe in 1927, you were looked down upon if you ate garlic, a food fit only for ditch diggers; when I returned in 1940, you were looked down on if you *didn't* eat it." In France, the presence of garlic is more of a regional phenomenon, scorned within the boundaries of *haute cuisine* and looked on askance by *cuisine bourgeois.* Generally, garlic reigns decisively south of the river Loire. In the east, it is referred to as "the truffle of Provence," and Aïoli, the garlicky mayonnaise from that region, is known as "the butter of Provence." Garlic is also a regional phenomenon in Italy, well known in Piedmont's *bagna cauda* ("hot bath"), but more prevalent in the south. Alexander Dumas wrote that the Greeks disliked garlic, which was erroneous. It was an important vegetable in ancient Greece and was eaten in its own right, not simply as a seasoning for something else.

⃟EEKS AND CARROTS

(Porri e Carote Arrosto)

4 medium leeks, white portion, root removed, split, and well washed

4 medium carrots, peeled, ends trimmed, cut in half widthwise, and split lengthwise

1 cup walnut halves

salt and pepper as needed

- Preheat an oven to 400°F.
- Coat the leeks and carrots well with the olive oil, and season lightly with salt and pepper. Place in a roasting pan and roast for 15 minutes. Add the walnuts, turn the vegetables, and roast another 15 minutes or until golden brown.

$\mathcal{O}$NIONS

(Cipolla Arrosto)

6 medium Spanish or Bermuda onions, peeled and halved olive oil, salt, and pepper to coat	½ cup olive oil ¼ cup red wine vinegar 2 tablespoons lemon juice 1 tablespoon Dijon-style mustard

- Preheat an oven to 400°F.
- Coat the onions with olive oil, and season with salt and pepper. Place in a roasting pan or cast-iron skillet, cut side down, and roast for 20 minutes. Turn the onions over, and continue roasting until well caramelized.
- Beat the olive oil, vinegar, lemon juice, and mustard together, and pour over the onions at service. (See color plate.)

$\mathcal{P}$OTATOES

(Patate Arrosto)

½ cup olive oil 1 medium onion, sliced lengthwise 2 garlic cloves, crushed	16 medium Red Bliss potatoes, scrubbed and cut in half 4 sprigs rosemary salt and pepper to taste

For a Roasted Potato Salad, toss the potatoes in a sauce consisting of ½ cup olive oil; ¼ cup basalmic vinegar; 3 garlic cloves, pressed; 2 tablespoons grainy mustard; 2 tablespoons minced chives, salt and white pepper.

- Preheat an oven to 400°F.
- Sauté the onion and garlic in the olive oil for several minutes. Add the remaining ingredients, coating everything with the oil. Place in the oven and roast for 30 minutes, or until the potatoes are tender.

*Z*UCCHINI

(Zucchini Arrosto)

4 large zucchini, rinsed,
ends trimmed, cut width-
wise, slightly on the bias,
into 1-inch pieces

salt, pepper, and olive oil as
needed

- Brush the zucchini pieces with olive oil, season lightly with salt and pepper, then grill, broil, or sauté on both sides until golden brown.

MARINATED VEGETABLES

*A*RTICHOKE HEARTS

(Carciofini Marinati)

1 pound small artichokes
the juice of 6 lemons

1 tablespoon salt
2 cups emulsified vinaigrette

- Prepare a water bath with about 2 quarts of water and half the lemon juice.
- Cut the bottom stems from the artichokes, and cut the tops off, leaving the artichokes approximately 1 to 1½ inches long. With a paring knife, cut away the dark outer leaves, leaving the light green inner heart. (See Figure 1.1.) Place immediately into the lemon bath.
- Bring 2 quarts of water, the remaining lemon juice, and the salt to a boil. Place the trimmed artichokes in the boiling water and cook for 10 minutes, or until tender. Drain, cool, and set aside.
- Cover the artichokes with the vinaigrette, and marinate several hours. (See color plate.)

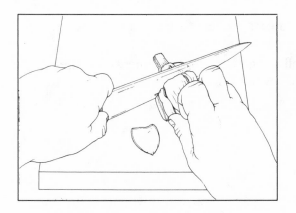

Slice off the bottom of the artichoke.

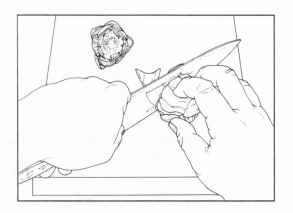

Slice off the top of the artichoke (artichoke should be approximately 1 to 1½-inches long).

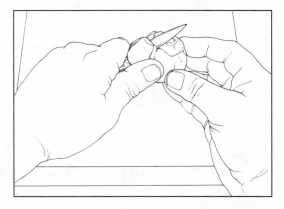

Trim around the bottom edge with a paring knife, removing the tough outer leaves.

Figure 1.1
Paring down an artichoke to the heart

🅑ELL PEPPERS WITH FONTINA

(Peperoni con Fontina)

1 cup olive oil
½ cup champagne vinegar
2 tablespoons water
2 garlic cloves
1 tablespoon Dijon-style
  mustard
2 tablespoons parsley,
  roughly chopped
2 tablespoons tarragon
  leaves, roughly chopped

2 tablespoons basil leaves,
  roughly chopped
salt and pepper to taste
2 green bell peppers, cut
  into medium dice
2 yellow bell peppers, cut
  into medium dice
1 cup Niçoise olives
1 cup Italian fontina, cut
  into ⅓-inch cubes

- Combine the oil, vinegar, water, garlic, mustard, herbs, salt, and pepper in a blender, and purée.
- Toss the pepper, olives, and Fontina together, pour the sauce over, and marinate several hours.

$\mathscr{B}$EETROOT

(Barbabietole Marinati)

6 medium beets
1 cup scallions, sliced very
   thin on the bias
¼ cup parsley, minced

¼ cup olive oil
1 cup champagne vinegar
salt and pepper to taste

- Place the beets in a roasting pan with about ½ inch of water in the bottom, and bake in a preheated 400°F oven for 45 minutes to 1 hour, or until tender. Remove and cool.
- Peel the beets and slice into ⅛-inch thick slices. Combine with the remaining ingredients, and marinate overnight.

$\mathscr{B}$LACK, GARBANZO, AND RED KIDNEY BEANS

(Fagioli Marinati)

1 cup each, black, garbanzo,
   and red kidney beans
2 cups olive oil
½ cup champagne vinegar
½ cup lime juice
2 jalapeño peppers, seeds removed and roughly
   chopped

½ cup cilantro leaves, well
   rinsed and dried
½ cup mint leaves, well
   rinsed and dried
½ teaspoon salt
½ teaspoon black pepper

- Purée sauce ingredients in a blender. Pour over each kind of beans (keep them separate) and marinate several hours. (See color plate.)

Bean varieties fall into three basic categories: French, or common string beans; faba, or broad beans; and lima beans.

The important status of beans in the ancient world may be found in the names of four prominent Roman families, whose names evolved from four varieties of legumes: Fabius (faba), Lentulus (lentil), Piso (pea), and Cicero (chick). Faba and lima, as well as some bean varieties normally found in their dried form (e.g., kidney beans), can also be consumed fresh. Other dried bean varieties include adzuki, black lentils, mung, navy, black-eyed peas (also cowpeas), chickpeas (also garbanzos), and pinto.

CARROTS WITH HERBS

(Carote Marinati con Erbes)

3 cups small carrots, peeled and cut on a sharp bias
1 bunch scallions, roots removed, cleaned, and cut on a sharp bias
1 tablespoon oregano leaves, roughly chopped
1 tablespoon sage leaves, roughly chopped

1 tablespoon fennel sprigs, roughly chopped
1 tablespoon flat-leaf parsley, roughly chopped
½ cup olive oil
½ cup balsamic vinegar
salt and white pepper to taste

- Blanch the carrots in boiling salted water until al dente (tender, but firm). Toss with the remaining ingredients, cover, and marinate for 4 hours.

Carrots (and parsnips), native to Afghanistan, were listed under *medicinal essences* by the ancient Greeks and Romans. There are many different varieties of carrot, cultivated as a food only since the sixteenth century. Our familiar orange variety, high in alpha-beta-gamma carotene, was developed in seventeenth-century Holland. In addition to beta carotene, which is transformed into vitamin A (one pound yields four-and-a-half times the minimum daily requirement), carrots contain vitamins B, C, E, and carbohydrates. Varieties include Goldinhart, Nantes Half-Long, Danvers Half-Long, Gold Pak, Burpee's Oxheart, Royal Chantenay, and Little Finger.

FENNEL WITH CUCUMBERS

(Finocchio e Centrioli Marinati)

1 cup olive oil
6 tablespoons rice vinegar
1 garlic clove, pressed
salt and pepper to taste
1 fennel bulb, trimmed and
  sliced very thin
⅓ English (hothouse)
  cucumber, sliced very thin

8 large radishes, trimmed,
  rinsed, and sliced very
  thin
1 small red onion, sliced
  very thin
1 bunch chives, minced
1 ripe tomato, cut into 12
  wedges

- Blanch the fennel slices in boiling salted water for 1 minute. Drain, rinse in cold water, and set aside.
- Beat the oil, vinegar, garlic, salt, and pepper together. Add cucumber, radish, and onion slices, cover, and marinate for 2 hours.
- Arrange the vegetables on a platter or individual plates, garnish with the tomato wedges, and sprinkle with the chopped chives.

FENNEL WITH ORANGES

(Finocchio e Arancia Marinati)

2 fennel bulbs, trimmed,
  rinsed, and sliced very
  thin
the segments of 4 oranges
the juice of 4 oranges
the juice of 1 lemon
2 shallots, minced

½ cup olive oil
3 tablespoons champagne
  vinegar
salt and white pepper to
  taste
4 sprigs fresh mint

- Marinate the fennel in the orange and lemon juice for 2 hours. Combine the shallots, oil, vinegar, salt, pepper, and ¼ cup of the juice marinade in a bowl, and blend. Arrange the fennel on a platter or individual serving plates. Top with the orange segments, some vinaigrette, and garnish with mint.

LEEKS

(Porri Marinati)

8 medium leeks, white part only (about 4 inches long)
water as needed
1 garlic clove, sliced
½ teaspoon salt
¾ cup olive oil

¼ cup red wine vinegar
½ teaspoon Dijon mustard
salt and pepper as needed
4 small lettuce leaves
4 wedges tomato
2 tablespoons chopped parsley

- Cut the root from the end of each leek. Split each leek in half, leaving it joined at the root end.
- Rinse thoroughly several times in cold water.
- Place the leeks in a saucepan and cover them with water. Add the garlic and ½ teaspoon salt. Cover and simmer for about 10 minutes, or until tender. Remove from the heat and drain thoroughly. When cool, complete the partial cut, separating each leek in half.
- Whip the olive oil, vinegar, mustard, and a pinch each of salt and pepper. Pour over the leeks, cover, and marinate in the refrigerator until ready to serve. Place 2 leeks on each individual plate on a base of lettuce. Top with some of the vinaigrette, garnish with a tomato wedge, and sprinkle with chopped parsley.

The leek is a member of the lily family and a relative to grasses. Cultivated in prehistory in their native Mediterranean region, leeks were spread across Europe by the Romans. According to legend, the Roman emperor Nero ate leek soup daily to make his voice sonorous and clear for delivering orations, and the last Briton king Cadwallader, in his victory over the Saxons in 640 A.D., instructed his Welsh army to wear leeks in their hats to distinguish them from the enemy. Cultivars include Monster of Carretan, Winter Paris, Rouen, Mezières, Giant of Verrières, and Broad London.

---

*L*ENTILS

(Lenticchie Marinati)

1 pound orange lentils
1 cup green bell pepper, medium dice
1 cup red onion, medium dice
2 cups diced tomatoes
1 cup fennel root, shaved very thin, and cut into julienne
the zest of one lemon

1 cup olive oil
¼ cup basalmic vinegar
¼ cup champagne vinegar
¼ cup water
2 dried red chile peppers, roughly chopped
4 garlic cloves
½ cup flat-leaf parsley leaves
salt and pepper to taste

- Pick through the lentils and remove any damaged beans. Pour about 1 quart boiling water over them to cover, and soak for 1 hour. Drain, place them in boiling salted water, and cook for 30 minutes, or until tender but still firm. Drain and set aside.
- Blanch the bell pepper and onion by dropping them into boiling water for 1 minute. Drain, and add to the lentils along with the tomatoes, fennel, and lemon zest.
- Place the remaining ingredients in a blender, and purée. Pour over the lentils and marinate 1 hour before serving.

*M*USHROOMS, GREEK STYLE

(Funghi alla Greca)

1 cup button mushrooms
1 cup shiitake mushrooms
1 cup chanterelle mushrooms
the juice of one lemon
1 package of fresh enoki mushrooms
¾ cup olive oil
¼ cup red wine
¼ cup white wine vinegar
salt and white pepper to taste

4 garlic cloves, crushed
1 shallot, thinly sliced
2 sprigs rosemary
2 sprigs thyme
2 sprigs oregano
1 bay leaf
8 Boston lettuce cups
4 red cabbage leaf cups
16 Belgian endive leaves
¼ cup chopped parsley

- Trim the very bottom portion of the stems of the button, shiitake, and chanterelle mushrooms, and discard. Rinse the mushrooms in cold water and lemon juice, and pat dry. Cut the shiitakes into julienne, and the chanterelles into ½-inch pieces.
- Combine all of the marinade ingredients in a saucepan and bring to a boil. Add all the mushrooms except the enoki, simmer for 1 minute, then turn off the fire and cool to room temperature. Cover and refrigerate overnight.
- Arrange the lettuce leaves on four individual plates, and place a cabbage leaf in the center of each. Arrange the marinated mushrooms in the cabbage leaves, garnish with the endive and enoki mushrooms, and top with chopped parsley.

Any variety of vegetable can be marinated Greek style (*à la Greque, alla Greca*), including artichoke hearts, carrots, fennel, pearl onions, and zucchini.

$\mathcal{M}$USHROOMS WITH LEMON

(Funghi al Limone e Olio)

1 pound fresh button mush-rooms	the zest of 1 lemon
½ cup lemon juice	1 bay leaf
½ cup olive oil	1 sprig thyme
3 garlic cloves, sliced thin	¼ cup parsley, minced
	salt and pepper to taste

- Rinse the mushrooms in a cold water bath, using about half the lemon juice. Drain the mushrooms, pat dry, and discard the bath.
- Place all of the ingredients except the parsley in a saucepan, bring to a boil, remove from the fire, cover, and allow to sit 1 hour. Add the parsley, cover, and marinate overnight.

There are thousands of varieties of mushrooms, mostly found in their natural (wild) state, though some varieties in recent years have been successfully cultivated. The Field Mushroom is the variety most often commercially available all year round. Others include Caesar's, Cépe, Chanterelle, Horn of Plenty, Parasol, Shiitake, Wood Ear, and Yellow Boletus.

ZUCCHINI WITH MINT

(Zucchini Marinati)

6 medium zucchini, ends removed and cut into spears
1 tablespoon salt
¾ cup olive oil

4 garlic cloves, sliced very thin
½ cup basalmic vinegar
¼ cup mint leaves, cut into chiffonade

- See Figure 1.2. Toss the zucchini with the salt, then place on absorbent paper for 30 minutes.
- Brush off as much of the salt as possible, then sauté the zucchini over high heat in ¼ cup of the olive oil until light brown. Add the garlic and cook for several minutes. Transfer the zucchini to a bowl or casserole dish.
- Pour the remaining ingredients over the zucchini, cover, and marinate for 4 hours.

Pumpkins and squash are of American origin, thriving in the arid climates of southwestern United States and northern Mexico. Some of the 25 better-known species have been cultivated for 9,000 years. Squash is easily hybridized, resulting in such a wide range of colors and forms that it is difficult to tell the varieties apart. Summer varieties—zucchini, yellow crookneck, golden, and patty pan—are eaten when young and soft. Winter varieties—acorn, banana, butternut, Hubbard (Ohio), Sea (Chioggia), Yokohama and chayote squashes, and American, Brazilian, and whale pumpkins—are allowed to mature into hard, starchy fruits that will keep for months. There are also ornamental varieties, such as turban squash, scallop and bottle gourds, and various hybrids.

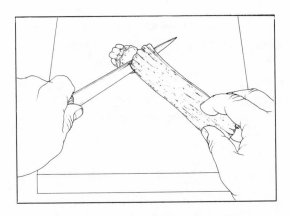

Slice and remove the ends of the zucchini or carrot.

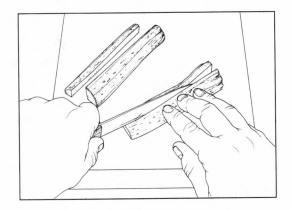

Cut into quarters, lengthwise.

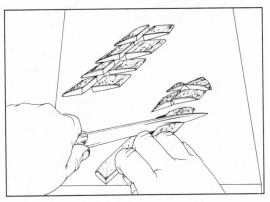

Cut into pieces, at roughly a 45-degree angle. (For uniformity, discard uneven end pieces.)

Figure 1.2
Cutting zucchini (or carrots) into spears

Cold Dishes

················ # ASPARAGUS WRAPPED IN PROSCIUTTO

(Asperagi con Prosciutto)

2 bunches medium-thick asparagus

1 pound prosciutto ham, sliced paper thin

- Remove the woody bottom of the asparagus (roughly the lower third), and discard. Peel approximately the lower three-quarters of the asparagus spears carefully, using a vegetable peeler. Blanch in boiling salted water, uncovered, for about 5 minutes until al dente. Drain, cool, and set aside.

- Roll a slice of prosciutto around each spear (you may wish to fold the slices in half lengthwise, so they do not cover the entire spear). Repeat until all the spears are wrapped. (See color plate.)

Asparagus is a member of the lily family and a relative of the grasses. Called *sparrow grass* in England until the eighteenth century, cultivated asparagus is derived from a wild form still commonly found in sandy places, woods, and along riverbanks in south-central Europe, western and central Asia, and northern Africa. Asparagus was well known in ancient Egypt, Greece, and Rome, and though its use in Europe during the Dark Ages seems to have diminished, it remained popular in Arab countries. Its use was renewed in Europe during the reign of the Sun King, Louis XIV. Today, commercial names of asparagus are derived from the origin of its cultivation: Argenteuil (considered to be the finest), purple Holland, German, Bassano del Grappa, Purple Genoa, and Mary Washington (United States). White asparagus is created by piling up soil around the spears toward the end of its cultivation, which blocks exposure to sunlight, thus preventing the development of green chlorophyll. Asparagus is unique in having no leaves, typically speaking, but *phylloclades*, which are clustered at the tip. It is expensive today because the shoots grow at different rates and must be harvested by hand.

ℋUMMUS

3 cups cooked garbanzo beans
1 cup sesame tahini
¼ cup olive oil
6 garlic cloves, pressed
the juice of 2 lemons
salt and white pepper to taste
pita bread cut into triangles, and toasted

- Combine the beans, sesami tahini, oil, garlic, and lemon juice in a food processor, and purée, using the pulse switch. Season to taste with the salt and pepper, and serve with toasted pita bread triangles.

ℳUSSELS CAPRICCIOSE

(Cozze Capricciose)

2 pounds fresh mussels
1 cup dry white wine
1 garlic clove, crushed
1 cup mayonnaise
2 tablespoons Dijon-style
  mustard

2 large Red Bliss or all-
  purpose potatoes
3 tablespoons chopped
  parsley

- Debeard the mussels, scrub and rinse well with cold water.
- Steam the mussels in the white wine and garlic until all the shells have opened.
- Strain the mussels, returning the liquid to the fire, and simmer until reduced to ¼ cup. Set aside to cool.
- Remove the mussels from the shells, set aside, and discard the shells.
- Place the potatoes, skin-on, in boiling salted water, and boil until tender but still slightly firm. Drain, peel, cut into ¼-inch slices, and set aside.
- Blend the mayonnaise, mustard, and reduced liquid until smooth. Blend in the mussels. Arrange on a serving plate, surrounded with the sliced potatoes, and sprinkled with chopped parsley.

𝒫ICKLED GARDEN VEGETABLES

2 cups assorted vegetables,
  cut into a variety of
  shapes (such as bell
  peppers, cucumbers, pearl
  onions, baby zucchini,
  yellow squash, patty pan
  squash, carrots,
  cauliflower, brussels
  sprouts, broccoli; cut in
  round slices, half circles,
  spheres, squares, triangles,
  on the bias, julienne, etc.)
1 tablespoon salt

3 cups champagne vinegar
1 cup water
1 teaspoon salt
½ cup sugar
¼ teaspoon whole cloves
1 teaspoon mustard seeds
1 teaspoon coriander seeds
1 teaspoon black pepper-
  corns
1 bay leaf
2 sprigs oregano
4 garlic cloves, crushed

- Place the vegetables in a colander, sprinkle with salt, and let sit for 3 hours.

- Combine the remaining ingredients in a saucepan, bring to a boil, and simmer for 5 minutes. Rinse the salted vegetables in cold water, and drain. Place the pickling brine over the vegetables, cool, cover, and refrigerate. Marinate 24 hours before serving.

$\mathscr{S}$HELLFISH FANTASIA

(Frutti de Mare Fantasia)

2 cups dry white wine
1 bay leaf
1 celery stalk
½ onion, peeled
1 bunch parsley stems, trimmed and tied together with cotton cord
12 large fresh oysters on the half shell
12 16–20 count shrimp, peeled and deveined

¾ cup mayonnaise
¼ cup medium-dry sherry (such as Amontillado)
2 tablespoons lemon juice
2 tablespoons Dijon-style mustard
2 tablespoons tomato purée
salt and white pepper to taste
½ cup parsley, finely minced
12 very thin lemon slices

- Bring the white wine, bay leaf, celery, onion, and parsley stems to a boil. Add the oysters (without shells) and shrimp, and bring to a boil. Cover, remove from the fire, and let sit 10 minutes. Drain, remove and discard the vegetables and herbs, and cool.

- Combine the mayonnaise, sherry, lemon juice, mustard, tomato purée, salt, and pepper, and blend thoroughly.

- Place an oyster, followed by a shrimp, on each of the oyster shells. Coat with the sauce, then place on a serving platter or plates. Sprinkle with chopped parsley, and garnish with lemon slices.

Hot Dishes

$\mathscr{A}$RTICHOKE HEARTS, ROMAN STYLE

(Carciofi alla Romana)

12 artichokes, stems intact
the juice of 3 lemons
1 cup dry bread crumbs

½ cup olive oil
¼ cup mashed anchovies
¼ cup chopped parsley

2 tablespoons capers,
    drained
6 garlic cloves, pressed

¼ cup chopped mint leaves
salt and pepper to taste

- Bring 1 quart of water, two-thirds of the lemon juice, and a little salt to a boil.
- Peel the artichokes down to the heart. Peel the stems, and remove the choke from the inside of the hearts. Blanch the artichokes in the boiling water for 5 minutes. Drain, cool, and set aside.
- Preheat an oven to 350°F.
- Combine the bread crumbs, oil, anchovies, parsley, capers, garlic, mint, salt, and pepper. Stuff the artichokes with this mixture, then place in a baking dish. Add the remaining lemon juice, along with a little water, and a dash of olive oil. Bake covered, 20 to 30 minutes, or until tender.

———————————— • ————————————

The artichoke is a *thistle* native to the Mediterranean and was well known to the ancients. The name is a corruption of the Arabic *al'qarshuf*. The Latin word *cynara* did not survive, though we know that name applied to a modern Italian aperitif made from this member of the daisy family. The edible parts are the fleshy bases of the leaves, the bottom, and the stem. The consumption of artichokes in the United States began in the nineteenth century when a band of Italian immigrants settled near Half Moon Bay, California, and planted a few hundred acres. In 1906 they made their first shipment to the East Coast. James Beard once wrote, "there is a great feeling among serious wine drinkers that artichokes spoil the flavor of fine wines and therefore should be forbidden at great dinners." Cultivars include Green Gold, Paris Green, Lyons Green, Venice (or Chioggia) Violet, Tuscany Violet, Provence Violet, Breton Stocky, and Roman.

ℬAGNA CAUDA

1 cup olive oil
4 garlic cloves
¼ cup anchovies, mashed
¼ cup capers

¼ cup Romano cheese,
    grated
freshly ground black pepper

- Purée all the ingredients in a blender, place in a saucepan, and heat slightly. Transfer to a chafing dish with warmer, and serve with freshly cut vegetables, such as red, orange, yellow, and green bell peppers, Belgian endive leaves and hearts, cucumber sticks, artichoke hearts and bottoms, and celery spears. (See color plate.)

————————————— • —————————————

Bagna Cauda means "hot bath," and is a Christmas specialty of Italy's Piedmont region. This dish often contains shaved white truffles, virtually impossible to find in the United States. Bagna Cauda is also accompanied by cardoons, relatives of the artichoke and similar in appearance to celery. If these are unavailable, simply substitute other vegetables, including artichoke hearts and celery.

*B*AKED STUFFED ROMA TOMATOES
(Pomodori Romana al Forno)

1 cup ground sausage meat
½ teaspoon fennel seed
3 garlic cloves, pressed
2 tablespoons chopped basil
½ cup ricotta cheese
½ cup grated mozzarella cheese
¼ cup grated Parmesan cheese
12 Roma tomatoes
1 baguette, sliced and toasted
1 bunch fresh watercress

- Sauté the sausage and fennel until fully cooked. Add the garlic and basil and cook a few more minutes. Remove from the fire, drain excess liquid, and cool.

- Slice a ¼-inch thick slice from the side of each tomato (lengthwise), and scoop out the pulp. (Save the scooped-out pulp for another use.)

- Preheat an oven to 400°F.

- Blend the sausage mixture and the cheeses together, then stuff the tomatoes. Place the tomato "lids" on, and bake for 10 to 15 minutes, or until the cheese is melted. Serve with the toasted baguette slices and fresh watercress.

————————————— • —————————————

In the late eighteenth century, a New York food importer claimed duty-free status for a shipment of tomatoes from the West Indies. He argued that since tomatoes were anatomically a fruit, then according to the import regulations of the day, they were not subject to import fees. The customs agent disagreed and imposed a 10% duty on the shipment, designated as vegetables. The case went as far as the New York Supreme Court, which decided in favor of the customs agency, on the grounds of traditional linguistic usage. Tomatoes, stated the majority, are "usually served at dinner, in, with, or after the soup, fish, or meat, which constitute the principal part of the repast, and not, like fruits, generally as dessert."

BROCCOLI WITH GORGONZOLA SAUCE

(Broccoli al Gorgonzola)

1 bunch fresh broccoli
1 garlic clove, crushed
2 tablespoons grated onion
2 cups milk
3 tablespoons clarified butter
3 tablespoons flour

1 cup heavy cream
1 cup Gorgonzola cheese, crumbled
salt and white pepper to taste

- Cut the broccoli into 1-inch flowerettes. Trim the stems, and slice ¼-inch thick on the bias.
- Heat the butter, and blend into a paste with the flour. In a heavy-gauge pan, heat the milk with the garlic and onion. Beat in the butter/flour paste, and simmer for 5 minutes, stirring continuously. Strain the sauce, return to the fire, add the cream and cheese, and simmer several minutes. Season to taste with salt and pepper, and set aside, keeping warm.
- Blanch the broccoli in boiling salted water, uncovered, until al dente (do not overcook). Drain, place on a platter or individual plates, and serve accompanied by the sauce.

CAPONATA, DUTCHESS VALLEY STYLE

½ cup olive oil
1 cup celery, cut into 1-inch julienne

1 cup carrots, cut into 1-inch julienne
2 cups onion, medium dice

1 cup cauliflower flowerettes
1 cup mushrooms, medium dice
1 cup green pepper, cut into 1-inch julienne
4 garlic cloves, crushed
½ cup tomato purée
1 cup dry white wine
1 pound bay scallops
½ pound 20–24 count shrimp, peeled and deveined

1 teaspoon minced basil
½ cup chopped parsley
salt and pepper to taste
½ cup green olives, pitted
½ cup Niçoise olives
¼ cup capers
8 anchovy fillets, diced
4 hard-boiled eggs, cut into 8 wedges each
½ cup chopped parsley

- Sauté the celery, carrots, onion, cauliflower, mushrooms, green pepper, and garlic in the olive oil. Add the tomato purée and wine, and blend. Add the seafood, basil, and ½ cup parsley, and season to taste with salt and pepper. Add the olives, capers, and anchovies, and blend thoroughly. Remove from the fire. Serve warm or chilled, decorated with the eggs and the remaining ½ cup parsley.

𝒞APONATA, FARMER'S STYLE

(Caponata alla Contadina)

6 large zucchini, cut into ½-inch pieces
½ cup olive oil
2 cups onion, ½-inch dice
1 cup celery, ½-inch dice
1 cup red bell pepper, ½-inch dice
6 garlic cloves, sliced

2 cups diced tomatoes
½ cup tomato purée
¼ cup capers, drained
¼ cup balsamic vinegar
½ cup coarsely chopped walnuts, toasted
salt and pepper to taste

- Sauté the zucchini in the olive oil until lightly browned. Add the onion, celery, pepper, and garlic, and continue cooking about 5 minutes. Add the remaining ingredients, except the nuts, and simmer 10 minutes. Season to taste, cool, cover, and refrigerate overnight. Serve at room temperature, garnished with the walnuts.

CAULIFLOWER AND FENNEL ROOT GRATIN

(Cavolfiore e Finocchi alla Panna)

1 small head cauliflower, cut
   into ½-inch flowerettes
2 fennel bulbs, trimmed, and
   cut into ¼-inch julienne
½ cup olive oil
1 cup onion, cut into fine
   julienne
1 garlic bulb, cloves peeled
   and sliced in half
   lengthwise

1 cup dry white wine
1 cup half-and-half cream
salt and white pepper to
   taste
½ cup dry bread crumbs
½ cup grated Parmesan
   cheese

- Preheat an oven to 400°F.
- Blanch the cauliflower and fennel in lightly salted boiling water, about 4 minutes. In a large pan, sauté the onion in the oil without coloring. Add the garlic, and cook briefly. Add the white wine, and reduce by half. Add the cream, cauliflower, and fennel, and blend thoroughly. Season to taste with salt and pepper, and remove from the fire.
- Lightly oil a deep 8-inch pie dish with olive oil. Place the mixture into the pan, and sprinkle with the bread crumbs and Parmesan cheese. Bake for 20 to 30 minutes, or until golden brown.

CAULIFLOWER WITH HERB SAUCE

(Cavolfiore al Pesto)

½ cup basil leaves
½ cup cilantro leaves
½ cup marjoram leaves
½ cup parsley
1 small tin anchovies

6 garlic cloves
1½ cups olive oil
salt and pepper to taste
1 head cauliflower
1 cup walnut pieces, toasted

- Combine the herbs, anchovies (with oil), garlic, oil, salt, and pepper in a blender, and purée. Cover and set aside.
- Remove the outer green leaves of the cauliflower, reserving for another use (soup, marinated salad, etc.). Using a paring knife,

carefully cut a funnel in the top center of the head, about 1½-inches round at the top and extending down about 3 inches (reserve this portion as well). Trim any blemishes from the head.

- Cook the cauliflower by steaming it in a small amount of water, covered, until the outer flowerettes are tender.

- Drain the cauliflower, place on a large plate or platter, pour the herb sauce into the cavity so that some of it drips down the sides. Sprinkle with toasted walnuts, and serve the remainder of the sauce on the side.

DEEP-FRIED CHEESE

(Formaggio Fritti)

For the Sauce

2 cups mixed herb leaves (such as basil, cilantro, oregano, parsley, and/or tarragon), rinsed and dried

¼ cup large capers
6 garlic cloves
1 cup olive oil
salt and pepper to taste

For the Fritters

1 pound Bel Paese, fontina, or mozzarella cheese (or combination), cut into 2 × ½ × ½-inch sticks
1 cup flour, seasoned with salt, pepper, and paprika

6 eggs, well beaten
4 cups dry bread crumbs
¼ cup mixed dried Italian herbs
1 quart vegetable oil
2 lemons, sliced and seeded

- Put the herbs, capers, garlic, and olive oil in a food processor and purée. Season to taste with salt and pepper, cover, and set aside.

- Heat the vegetable oil in a heavy-gauge pot to a temperature of 375°F, and preheat an oven to 375°F.

- Dust the cheese sticks with flour, dip into the eggs, then the bread crumbs blended with the dried herbs. Shake off excess crumbs, then dip into the egg a second time, and again into the bread crumbs. Be sure each piece is fully coated with bread crumbs.

- Shake off excess crumbs, and deep-fry the sticks until golden brown. Transfer to a pan lined with absorbent paper, and place into the oven to hold until all the cheese is fried. Serve garnished with the sliced lemon, accompanied by the herb sauce.

$\mathcal{D}$EEP-FRIED ZUCCHINI

(Zucchini Fritti)

4 medium zucchinis	1 teaspoon chopped marjoram
2 cups flour	1 teaspoon chopped parsley
1 teaspoon salt	vegetable oil as needed
½ teaspoon white pepper	2 lemons, cut into 8 wedges each
½ teaspoon paprika	12 parsley sprigs
3 eggs, well beaten	
2 cups dried bread crumbs	

- Cut the zucchini into 3-inch lengths, and cut each of these lengthwise into quarters. Slice and remove a ¼-inch wide piece of the center of the zucchini (the seeds), and discard. Cut the remaining piece into two or three sticks. Drop them into boiling water for 30 seconds, then drain well.
- Combine the salt, pepper, paprika, and flour, and toss the zucchini in this mixture, shaking off excess. Dip into the egg, allowing excess egg to drip off.
- Combine the bread crumbs and herbs, and toss the zucchini in this mixture, pressing it firmly onto each stick.
- Deep-fry in 375°F fat until golden brown. Drain on absorbent paper, and hold in a warm oven, if necessary, before serving. Serve garnished with parsley and lemon wedges, and with a mayonnaise-based sauce if desired.

$\mathcal{D}$EEP-FRIED ZUCCHINI FLOWERS

(Fiori di Zucchini Fritti)

1 cup milk	16 zucchini flowers
4 eggs, beaten	vegetable oil as needed
2 cups flour	

- Beat the flour into the milk and eggs until smooth. Heat the oil in a heavy-gauge deep-frying pan to 375°F.

- Gently open the flowers and remove the pistils. Dip the flowers into the batter, allowing excess to drip off. Fry until golden brown on all sides, place on absorbent paper, and sprinkle with a little salt.

······················ # ℰGGPLANT STUFFED WITH TOMATOES AND OLIVES

(Melanzane Ripiene con Pomodori e Olive)

4 small eggplants	2 tablespoons capers
1 tablespoon salt	½ cup dry bread crumbs
½ cup olive oil	¼ cup grated Parmesan
4 garlic cloves, pressed	cheese
½ cup scallions, finely diced	¼ cup parsley, minced
1 cup diced tomatoes	salt and pepper as needed
½ cup pitted Calamata olives	

- Cut the eggplants in half lengthwise, and cut out the inside pulp. Cut the pulp into large cubes, and sprinkle them and the interior of the eggplants with salt. Set the inverted halves and the cubes into the colander, and allow to sit for 30 minutes. Drop the eggplant into boiling water for 1 minute, then drain.
- Preheat an oven to 375°F.
- Sauté the garlic and scallions in the olive oil for several minutes. Add the tomatoes, olives, capers, half of the bread crumbs, half of the cheese, and the parsley. Blend well, season with salt and pepper, then set aside.
- Fill the eggplants with this mixture, and place in a baking pan. Sprinkle the tops with the remaining bread crumbs and cheese, and bake for 20 to 30 minutes.

———————————— • ————————————

It is not certain when the olive was first cultivated, but it may date back to the Minoan civilization (3000–1500 B.C.). In the Bible, Moses spoke of the olive tree on Mount Ararat, and Noah was brought an olive branch by a dove, Homer, Virgil, and Herodotus all wrote about the olive. Prior to the seventeenth century, olive oil was used for religious rites, as a cosmetic, and for lighting. Since then, production as a food has increased continuously. In the eighteenth century, Franciscan Jesuits brought the olive from Mexico to

California. Ninety-five to 98% of world production comes from the Mediterranean basin, with Spain and Italy competing for the lead. Olive oil extraction is a complex operation, resulting in several grades: generally, extra virgin, virgin, superfine, and pure. Raw olives are extremely bitter and must be processed to become edible. In California they are dipped into a solution of ferrous gluconate, treated with lye, rinsed, and packed in brine. In Greece, black olives are cured with salt, but green olives are processed by the (California) method.

FRIED POLENTA WITH CABBAGE

3 cups red cabbage, finely diced
4 cups chicken stock
¼ cup olive oil
½ teaspoon salt
½ teaspoon white pepper
1 cup yellow corn meal
½ cup grated Parmesan cheese
flour and olive oil as needed

- Blanch the cabbage in ½ gallon boiling, lightly salted water for 10 minutes. Drain and set aside.
- In a heavy-gauge pot, bring the chicken stock, olive oil, salt, and white pepper to a boil. Add the corn meal, stirring it in slowly to avoid lumping. Turn the fire down to very low and simmer for 5 minutes, stirring continuously. Add the drained cabbage and the cheese, blend thoroughly, and pour into a lightly oiled pan deep enough so that the polenta is roughly ½-inch thick. Cover, cool, then refrigerate overnight.
- Remove the polenta from the pan, and cut into 2-inch squares. Dust the squares with flour, and sauté in olive oil on both sides, until golden brown.

GARLIC AND RED BELL PEPPER CROSTINI

1 large sour baguette, cut into ½-inch slices
4 tablespoons unsalted butter, melted
½ cup olive oil
3 large red bell peppers
2 bulbs garlic, cloves separated
½ pound wedge of Parmesan, Romano, or other hard cheese
about 12 fresh basil leaves, cut into fine strips

- Combine ¼ cup olive oil with the butter, and brush the sliced baguette with this mixture. Put into a baking pan, and place in a 200°F oven, until golden brown and crisp. Set aside.
- Turn the oven up to 400°F. Rub the peppers with the remaining oil, place in a baking pan, and roast—along with the garlic—until very dark brown. Place the peppers in a bowl, cover with plastic wrap, and allow to sit 10 minutes. Separate the peel and seeds from the flesh of the peppers. Set the flesh aside, and discard what remains. Squeeze the garlic paste into a separate bowl.
- Spread the toasted baguette slices with the garlic paste, and place some of the basil on top of this. Top with a piece of bell pepper and a thin shaving of cheese. Place in the oven for about 5 minutes, then serve.

𝒢RILLED TOMATOES WITH ANCHOVIES

(Pomodori e Acciughe Gratinati)

3 large vine-ripened or beefsteak tomatoes	3 tablespoons basil leaves, chiffonade
1 small tin anchovy fillets	½ cup olive oil
2 tablespoons oregano leaves, minced	black pepper and grated Parmesan cheese as needed

- Remove the core from the top, and a thin slice from the bottom, of the tomatoes. Cut the tomatoes into 6 slices each, and arrange 3 slices in each of 6 ovenproof casserole dishes.
- Cut the anchovies in half lengthwise (reserve the oil they are packed in), then place an anchovy fillet crisscross fashion over each of the tomato slices. Drizzle the olive oil (and the oil from the anchovy tins) over the tomatoes, sprinkle with the herbs, black pepper, and grated cheese.
- Bake or broil the tomatoes until golden brown, and serve with toasted baguette slices.

𝒢RILLED TUNA WITH ONIONS

(Tonno con Cipolina)

1 large red onion, peeled, and sliced widthwise paper-thin	1 cup champagne vinegar
	½ cup water
	8 3-ounce slices of fresh tuna, lightly pounded

salt, pepper, and olive oil as
  needed
½ cup large capers, drained

1 lemon, cut into wedges
8 sprigs flat-leaf parsley

- Bring the vinegar and water to a boil, pour over the onions, and marinate 2 or more hours
- Brush the tuna steaks with olive oil, season with salt and pepper, then grill, broil, or sauté over very high heat, 1 minute on each side. Set aside.
- Arrange the tuna on a platter or individual plates. Arrange the marinated onions on top, sprinkle with capers, and garnish with lemon wedges and parsley sprigs.

$\mathscr{P}$OTATO AND ANCHOVY SALAD

(Insalata di Patate e Acciughe)

1 pound small Red Bliss
  potatoes
1 large red onion, peeled,
  and sliced paper-thin
1 cup Calamata olives, pitted
3 small tins anchovy fillets,
  finely diced

½ cup olive oil
½ cup basalmic vinegar
½ cup Italian parsley,
  roughly chopped
black pepper as needed

- Cook the potatoes in boiling salted water until tender. Drain, cool, then slice ¼-inch thick.
- Toss the potatoes, onion, olives, anchovies, oil, and vinegar together. Top with chopped parsley and freshly ground black pepper.

———————————— • ————————————

The potato, a relative of tobacco and the tomato, is indigenous to the southern United States and Central and South America. Hardy and easy to grow, it was cultivated by the Incas more than 4,000 years ago in mountainous areas. Its name comes from a Caribbean Indian name for sweet potato, *batata*. Until the late eighteenth century (about 1780), it was considered in France to cause leprosy.

Auguste-Antoine Parmentier (1737–1817), economist, pharmacist, and agronomist, was taken prisoner in 1761 by the Hanoverian (Prussian) army during the Seven Years' War. In the year he spent in prison, he subsisted solely on potatoes. Upon his return to Paris, convinced that they were a nutritional foodstuff, he went about changing public perception of potatoes. At a Versailles birthday reception for Louis XVI on August 25, 1785, he presented a bouquet of purple potato flowers to the king. The king slipped one flower into a buttonhole, gave several to Marie Antoinette to pin onto her corsage, and held out a third flower to Parmentier. The next morning everyone at court sported a potato flower in his or her buttonhole. Later, Parmentier hosted a dinner at his home, composed of 20 different potato dishes. (Among the guests was Benjamin Franklin.) One dinner guest suggested that Parmentier raise potatoes himself, and he did just that, in the open country around Sablons, with the field guarded by retired soldiers he had hired. Once the curiosity of local residents was piqued, he removed each of the four sentries, one by one, over a period of weeks. With the small plot left unguarded, his neighbors began surreptitiously to steal the potatoes for their own consumption, which is what Parmentier had intended all along. Numerous dishes subsequently created, made with or accompanied by potatoes, are still found on contemporary menus. Among them are Pommes Parmentier (large diced potatoes roasted in butter), Boeuf Hachis Parmentier (chopped beef topped with puréed potatoes, gratinéed), and Oeufs Parmentier (shirred eggs baked on a bed of cubed fried potatoes).

*R*OASTED ALMONDS WITH HERBS

2 cups whole raw almonds, shelled
¼ cup olive oil
½ teaspoon powdered cumin

3 sprigs rosemary, cut into 1-inch lengths
2 garlic cloves, crushed
salt to taste

- Preheat an oven to 350°F.
- Heat the olive oil, and toss the almonds, rosemary, and garlic in it. Sprinkle with the cumin and salt, and roast for about 30 minutes or until golden brown (stir every 10 minutes).

ROASTED BELL PEPPERS WITH GOAT CHEESE

(Peperoni al Formaggio)

2 large green, red, or yellow
  bell peppers
½ pound goat cheese
2 eggs
1 teaspoon minced basil
1 teaspoon minced cilantro

1 teaspoon minced tarragon
salt and pepper to taste
¼ cup grated Parmesan
  cheese
¼ cup plain dried bread
  crumbs

- Preheat an oven to 375°F.
- Split the peppers in half lengthwise, and remove the seeds and ribs. Blanch the pepper halves in boiling salted water for 30 seconds. Drain and pat dry.
- Blend the goat cheese, eggs, herbs, salt, and pepper together. Stuff the peppers with this mixture, smoothing out the top of each. Combine the bread crumbs and cheese, and sprinkle on top of the peppers. Bake for 15 to 20 minutes, or until the peppers are tender and the tops are lightly browned.

ROASTED BELL PEPPERS WITH RICE

(Peperoni al Riso)

¼ cup olive oil
1 medium onion, finely
  diced
6 garlic cloves, pressed
1½ cups plain white or
  arborio rice
2 sprigs oregano

3 cups chicken stock, hot
¼ cup basil leaves, cut into
  chiffonade
1 cup mozzarella cheese,
  grated
8 large red or green bell
  peppers

- Sauté the onions and garlic in the olive oil, without browning. Add the rice, and stir until the rice is well coated with the oil. Add the oregano and stock, blend thoroughly, season with salt and pepper. Cover, and cook over very low heat (or place into a 400°F oven) for 20 minutes. Remove from the stove (or oven), set aside, and cool.
- Preheat an oven to 375°F.

- Cut off the tops of the peppers and trim the bottoms minimally, so that they will stand up. Scoop out the seeds and ribs from the interior of the peppers and rinse thoroughly.
- Blend the basil and mozzarella cheese with the rice, and fill the peppers with the rice mixture. Put the tops on, and place in a baking pan or casserole. Pour a cup of hot water into the pan, and bake for 30 minutes or until the peppers are tender, but still standing.

$\mathcal{V}$EAL SCALLOPINE, TUNA MAYONNAISE

(Vitello Tonnato)

8 4-ounce veal cutlets, pounded thin
salt, pepper, and flour as needed
¼ cup olive oil
8 ounces fresh tuna fillet, roughly cut into 1-inch pieces
1 cup dry white wine
the juice of 1 lemon

1 bunch parsley stems
1 bay leaf
1½ cups mayonnaise
¼ cup lemon juice
½ cup large capers, drained
½ cup gherkins, small dice
¼ cup parsley, minced
salt and pepper to taste
2 lemons, sliced very thin
8 sprigs parsley

- Bring the wine, lemon juice, parsley stems, and bay leaf to a simmer. Add the tuna, cover, and simmer for 5 minutes. Remove from the fire, and allow to sit 5 minutes. Drain and set the tuna aside. When cool, rough mince.
- Season the veal with salt and pepper, and dust with flour. Sauté in the olive oil until golden brown on both sides. Remove to absorbent paper and set aside.
- Combine the mayonnaise, lemon juice, half the capers, half the gherkins, half the minced parsley, and the tuna, and blend thoroughly. Season to taste with salt and pepper.
- Arrange the veal on a serving platter or individual plates. Coat (nap) with the sauce, and sprinkle the top with the remaining capers, gherkins, and parsley, and garnish with the sliced lemon and parsley sprigs.

CHAPTER 2

CANAPÉS

A canapé is a slice of bread cut into any of various shapes and garnished. Cold canapés are served at buffets or lunches or with cocktails and aperitifs; hot canapés are served as entrées or used as foundations for various dishes. These dainty slices of bread, cut into assorted shapes, usually toasted, and decorated to be visually appealing are designed to be eaten with the fingers or a small utensil.

Traditional European canapés, primarily French in origin and under the heading of *classical cuisine,* are awkward in their style by today's standards. Many classical canapés, for example, are traditionally glazed with aspic, a crystal-clear highly gelatinous meat jelly. The function of aspic is to add flavor, to help guard against drying, and to add an attractive sheen. Aspic has not found common acceptance in North American cookery, since we are accustomed to clear jelly (read: Jell-O) having a sweet, as opposed to savory, taste. Nevertheless, classical canapés are important, because they form the body of work from which today's genre has evolved. In the real world of foodservice production, the use of classical canapés is limited, yet a knowledge of their composition is essential to understanding this type of hors d'oeuvres.

Canapés represent a unique area of expression for the culinary practitioner. They are miniature, visually creative, edible works, requiring meticulous attention to detail and design, and thus great patience and exact timing to produce. One may consider these bite-sized, open-faced, decorative sandwiches as "art on a cracker."

The crunch of a canapé is important. Foods that crunch when bitten into *stimulate* the appetite, whereas foods that are soft *satisfy* the appetite. The crunch should be the dominant texture, the soft a secondary texture. The function of a canapé is to stimulate appetites; thus it is acceptable to run out of canapés before dining guests' appetites are satisfied. In essence, their design should be simple and elegant—visually attractive but not overcomplex, while flavor and color should be harmonious and pleasing to the eye. In the creation of a canapé menu, with the intent to fulfill a client's expectations, we consider the socioeconomics of the client's group: where they live geographically, the kind of work they perform, their social customs and dress, the reason for their assembling.

Consider a sit-down dinner for 8,500 conventioneers, representing an American automobile dealership association. The first course consisted of a shellfish terrine with tomato coulis, each garnished with a crayfish from the Louisiana delta. Virtually every plate came back to the kitchen with the crayfish untouched—a perfect example of an upscale dish served to a clientele better acquainted with more common and easily recognized fare. And although a group hailing from a cosmopolitan city would understand and recognize beluga caviar and salmon tartar, a group of midwestern American ranchers would better understand steak tartar. Hence, we must consider the tastes, styles, and preferences of a given dining group.

COMPONENTS OF A CANAPÉ

A canapé consists of the following components: *base, adhesive, body,* and *garnish.*

Base Materials

Classical canapés are virtually all prepared on a base of toasted white, brioche, rye, or pumpernickel bread. It is essential that they be crunchy when bitten into. In contemporary practice other bases are often innovated—of polenta, wonton skin, small Red Bliss potatoes, phyllo, tortilla, small socles and even mushrooms, snow peas, zucchini, crookneck squash, cucumber, jicama, and daikon. If cucumber is used for a base, an English cucumber (also called a *hothouse* cucumber) is preferred because of its excellent crunch and absence of seeds.

Adhesives

Butter, compound butters, and pastes are important because they act as both an adhesive and a *moisture barrier* between the base and the body. This prevents moisture in the body ingredients from seeping into the crouton (base), making it soggy. Cream cheese is sometimes blended with butter, which is more palatable to contemporary tastes.

Body

The body of a canapé consists of various ingredients, including fish (herring, salmon), shellfish (lobster, shrimp), eggs (hard-boiled: sliced or sieved), meat (roasted beef fillet, sausages), poultry (grilled or poached chicken), game (venison, pheasant, quail), and vegetables (broccoli, bell pepper, radish). Odds and ends of food items are often used, but they *must* be made from premium products.

Garnish

The garnish adds a final touch of color, shape, and focal point to the finished piece. It may also function as an additional crunchy element, such as a toasted nut, slice of radish, or pâte à choux filigree. Most herbs do not hold up well as a garnish, with the exception of parsley and chive. Typical garnishes include asparagus, bell pepper, capers, caviar, cornichon, olive, and sieved hard-boiled egg.

CANAPÉ PRODUCTION

In commercial kitchens, canapé production for banquets and cocktail receptions can number several dozen or several hundred, or even as many as a thousand or more, per event. For this reason, it is essential that an efficient and well-organized *mise-en-place* be set up to expedite the production of these miniature artworks.

- All of the components of a given canapé should be fully prepared and ready to set in place before production is begun: the toasted bread sheets, the adhesive paste, the individual body components, and all garnishes.
- The bread used for canapé bases should ideally be purchased in *pullman* form—that is, unsliced. This bread can then be sliced into fairly large sheets, using a serrated knife (a serrated knife is engineered to cut bread and pastry and is never sharpened). Though difficult to cut evenly at first, with practice one can achieve a level of expertise in slicing these sheets uniformly. See Figure 2.1.
- When toasting the bread, timing is critical. The bread should be dry enough to have lost its pliability, though not so dry that it cracks when spread with the adhesive and cut into individual bases.

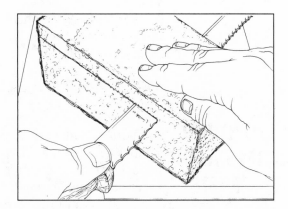

Hold the pullman loaf securely with one hand and, using a serrated blade, cut into ⅙ to ¼-inch thick slices. (While an electric slicer will cut more uniform slices, such a machine is not always available. For this reason, it is good to develop this skill, so that it can be used when needed. It is the same skill required of a pâtissier when squaring off baked rounds of génoise and other cakes.)

Figure 2.1
Slicing the pullman loaf

- After the bread has been toasted and cooled, it should be spread with the appropriate paste (adhesive). It can then be cut into individual bases. Uniformity is extremely important, and because these items are so small, any variation in size and shape is readily apparent.

- Although there are specific names and ingredients for canapés of the classical mode, there are no hard and fast rules for their design. This is where individual style and creativity come into play.

- The croutons in all of the classical canapés described in this chapter are toasted. This is what will give the canapés their appetite-stimulating crunch.

VISUAL APPEARANCE OF CANAPÉS

Size: Canapés should be small enough to be consumed in one or two bites (1½ to 2 inches); the base should be thick enough to grasp easily (⅙ inch).

Shape: Classical canapé bases have any of the following shapes: square, diamond (also called *lozenge*), rectangular, round, half circle, oval, and triangle. Other shapes, such as a crescent or a star, are sometimes innovated through the use of a variety of cutters.

Color: Canapés are ideally limited to four colors that harmonize well.

Texture: The base or one other component should be crisp, offering a resilient crunch (not soggy) when bitten into; the body should be smooth and tender.

Taste: The taste of a canapé should be a balance of savory, spicy, and tart, through the use of salt, pepper, herbs, and spices.

COMPOUND BUTTERS AND PASTES

Compound butters and pastes are used both as adhesives for canapés and as flavoring components. Compound butters are made primarily of butter combined with herbs and/or spices; pastes are more complex preparations, often including cream cheese in addition to herbs and spices. (The addition of cream cheese makes a paste a bit more palatable to contemporary tastes.) Compound butters also have two other functions: they are used to fortify the flavor of sauces by *mounting,* the colloquial term for beating pieces of plain or compound butter into a simmering sauce just before it is to be served; they are also used in place of sauces on certain grilled and fried foods, sliced from a wrapped cylinder of the particular butter preparation and placed on top of the grilled or fried item.

In canapé production, a paste or a compound butter is used as the *primary* adhesive because it acts as a *moisture barrier,* preventing the crisp crouton from becoming soggy. There is no limit to the number of compound butters and pastes that can be innovated. Compound butters alone are made with ingredients such as basil, blue cheese, caviar, chives, coriander, curry, edible flowers, roasted garlic, green vegetables, horseradish, lemon (juice and zest), mustard, paprika, pistachios, red bell pepper, saffron, salmon and shrimp (fresh or smoked), tarragon, thyme, tomato, truffle, walnuts, and wild mushrooms. Some examples follow.

Compound Butters

For the following recipes, whip all ingredients together thoroughly by hand, using soft (room temperature) butter, or in an electric mixer, using a paddle attachment. Shape into a cylinder, on baking parchment paper or wax paper, measuring approximately 1½ inches in diameter, and refrigerate until needed.

*A*LMOND BUTTER

(Beurre d'Amandes)

½ pound unsalted butter, soft
¾ cup slivered almonds

1 tablespoon cold water
salt and white pepper to taste

Almond butter is also used in the preparation of petits fours, cakes, and certain pastries.

- Toast the almonds on a baking sheet in a preheated 375°F oven, for 15 to 20 minutes, or until golden brown. Pound in a mortar, or put into a food processor, along with the water, and process. Whip the puréed almonds, butter, salt, and pepper, then wrap and store.

*A*NCHOVY BUTTER

(Beurre d'Anchois)

½ pound unsalted butter, soft
¼ cup anchovy fillets

1 tablespoon lemon juice
white pepper to taste

- Rinse the anchovies well in cold water. Pat dry, and mince very fine. Whip all the ingredients together, then wrap and store.

BASIL BUTTER

(Beurre de Basilic)

Basil butter is also excellent tossed with pasta.

½ pound unsalted butter, soft
1 cup fresh basil leaves, minced very fine

1 garlic clove, pressed
salt and white pepper to taste

BLUE CHEESE BUTTER

(Beurre de Fromage Bleu)

½ pound unsalted butter, soft
½ cup Maytag blue cheese

salt and white pepper to taste

CAVIAR BUTTER

(Beurre de Caviar)

Any good-quality fish roe can be used to make this butter—from beluga and osetra, two of the finest imported sturgeon caviars, to salmon, shad, trout, or whitefish roe.

½ pound unsalted butter, soft

¼ cup fine-quality caviar
pinch of white pepper

• Pound the caviar to a paste with a mortar and pestle. Whip along with the butter and pepper until thoroughly blended, then wrap and store.

CURRY BUTTER

(Beurre de Cari)

2 shallots, minced
½ cup dry white wine
the juice of 1 lemon
2 tablespoons curry powder
½ pound unsalted butter, soft

2 tablespoons cilantro, minced
salt and white pepper to taste

• Simmer the shallots, white wine, lemon juice, and curry powder until nearly dry. Set aside to cool. Whip all the ingredients together until thoroughly blended, then wrap and store as described.

The word *curry* is believed to be a corruption of *kari* or *karhi*, a southern Indian word for "sauce." Traditionally, however, curries evolved from a need to slow the spoilage of food in a hot climate. By experimenting with different spice combinations, blends were created that inhibited spoilage.

Within India (a nation of 15 major languages and 1,600 dialects) curry blends vary, as much as tomato sauces among the families of Sicily or barbecue marinades in the regions of southeastern United States. Among the herbs and spices used in curry blends are anise, cardamom, chile pepper, cinnamon, clove, coriander, cumin, fennel, fenugreek, garlic, ginger, lemon grass, mace, mustard, nutmeg, onion, saffron, tamarind, and turmeric.

GREEN BUTTER

(Beurre Vert)

1 large bunch of parsley, stems removed, well rinsed, and dried	½ pound unsalted butter, soft salt and white pepper to taste

- Roughly chop the parsley in a food processor, and then finely mince manually. Wrap in a double layer of muslin, and squeeze all the juice out. Whip this juice along with the remaining ingredients until thoroughly blended, then wrap and store as described.

HORSERADISH BUTTER

(Beurre de Raifort)

¼ cup grated fresh horseradish root ¼ cup dry white wine	½ pound unsalted butter, soft salt and white pepper to taste

If fresh horseradish root is unavailable, substitute prepared horseradish, squeezing out excess juice before adding.

- Simmer the horseradish and wine until nearly dry. Whip all the ingredients together until thoroughly blended, then wrap and store.

ℒEMON BUTTER

(Beurre de Citron)

the zest and juice of
  1 lemon
½ pound unsalted butter,
  soft

salt and white pepper to
  taste

- Blanch the lemon zest in lightly salted boiling water for 5 minutes. Drain and dry. Whip all the ingredients together until thoroughly blended, then wrap and store.

ℳAÎTRE D'HÔTEL BUTTER

(Beurre de Maître d'Hôtel)

½ pound unsalted butter,
  soft
3 tablespoons parsley,
  minced

2 tablespoons lemon juice
salt and white pepper to
  taste

- Whip all the ingredients together until thoroughly blended, then wrap and store.

ℳUSTARD-THYME BUTTER

(Beurre de Moutarde et Thym)

½ pound unsalted butter,
  soft
2 tablespoons fresh thyme
  leaves, minced

3 tablespoons Dijon-style
  mustard
salt and white pepper to
  taste

- Whip all the ingredients together until thoroughly blended, then wrap and store.

𝒫IEDMONT BUTTER

(Beurre Piémontaise)

½ pound unsalted butter,
  soft
½ cup Parmesan cheese,
  grated
the zest of 1 lemon

pinch of freshly grated
  nutmeg
salt and white pepper to
  taste

- Whip all the ingredients together until thoroughly blended, then wrap and store.

ℛOASTED GARLIC AND HERB BUTTER

3 garlic bulbs, cloves separated
olive oil as needed
½ pound unsalted butter, soft

⅓ cup minced fine herbs (e.g., basil, tarragon, parsley, cilantro, oregano, and/or thyme)
salt and white pepper to taste

- Preheat an oven to 375°F. Lightly coat the garlic cloves with olive oil. Place on a roasting pan, and roast for 45 minutes to 1 hour. Remove and allow to cool.
- Squeeze the garlic from the roasted cloves into a bowl. Whip this along with the remaining ingredients until thoroughly blended, then wrap and store.

ℐAFFRON BUTTER

(Beurre de Safran)

1 shallot, minced
1 garlic clove, minced
1 cup dry white wine
½ teaspoon saffron
1 bay leaf

1 sprig thyme
salt and white pepper to taste
¾ cup unsalted butter, soft

- Place all the ingredients, except the butter, into a saucepan. Simmer until reduced to approximately 3 tablespoons. Remove the bay leaf and thyme, and discard. Whip the reduction along with the remaining ingredients until thoroughly blended, then wrap and store as described.

ℐARDINE BUTTER

(Beurre de Sardine)

½ pound unsalted butter, soft
½ cup skinless, boneless sardines, drained of oil

salt and white pepper to taste

- Whip all the ingredients together until thoroughly blended, then wrap and store.

⎝TOMATO-CORIANDER BUTTER

¼ pound unsalted butter,
   soft
½ cup tomato, peeled,
   seeded, and diced small

2 tablespoons fresh cilantro
   leaves, minced
1 tablespoon dry white wine
salt and white pepper to
   taste

- Whip all the ingredients together until thoroughly blended, then wrap and store.

⎝TUNA BUTTER

(Beurre de Thon)

½ pound unsalted butter,
   soft

½ cup poached fresh tuna,
   drained, chilled, and finely minced

- Whip all the ingredients together until thoroughly blended, then wrap and store.

⎝WINE MERCHANT BUTTER

(Beurre au Marchand de Vin)

1 shallot, minced
1 cup dry red wine
1 cup rich brown beef or
   veal stock, or consommé
1 tablespoon parsley, minced

½ pound unsalted butter,
   soft
salt and white pepper to
   taste

- Simmer the shallot and wine until reduced by half. Add the stock or consommé, and continue reducing until two tablespoons of liquid remain. Whip the reduction along with the remaining ingredients until thoroughly blended, then wrap and store as described.

Pastes

In the recipes that follow, unless otherwise indicated, blend all ingredients together thoroughly, cover, and refrigerate until needed.

⎝ASIAN-STYLE PASTE

1 cup cream cheese
1 tablespoon wasabi
1 tablespoon grated gingerroot

1 tablespoon oyster sauce
2 tablespoons soy sauce

Cheddar Cheese Paste

½ pound cream cheese
½ pound unsalted butter
1 pound grated sharp cheddar cheese
2 tablespoons prepared horseradish, squeezed dry

1 teaspoon dry mustard, dissolved in 2 tablespoons white Worcestershire sauce
2 tablespoons beer
salt and white pepper to taste

Chicken Liver Paste

½ pound chicken livers, trimmed of connecting membranes and coarsely chopped
¼ pound unsalted butter
1 medium onion, coarsely chopped

3 cloves garlic, crushed
¾ cup mushrooms, coarsely chopped
¼ cup brandy
pinch of nutmeg
salt and pepper to taste
¼ pound unsalted butter

- Sauté the livers in half the butter until pink in the center. Remove with a slotted spoon and set aside. Sauté the onions over medium heat, stirring continuously for 10 minutes, without coloring. Add the garlic and mushrooms, and sauté another 5 minutes. Add the brandy and deglaze, then add the nutmeg.

- Transfer the livers, onion, garlic, mushrooms, and remaining butter to a food processor, and purée. Press through a screen sieve, using a rubber spatula. Season to taste with salt and pepper. Allow to cool, then blend thoroughly with the remaining butter. Cover and refrigerate until ready to use.

Egg Yolk Paste

½ cup unsalted butter
½ cup cream cheese
16 hard-boiled egg yolks, sieved
3 tablespoons mayonnaise
2 tablespoons white Worcestershire sauce

1 tablespoon Dijon-style mustard
1 tablespoon Tabasco sauce
salt and white pepper to taste

$\mathcal{E}$GGPLANT PASTE

(Mock Caviar)

2 eggplants, about 1 pound
  each
6 large garlic cloves, skin on
  the juice of 2 lemons

3 tablespoons olive oil
3 tablespoons chopped flat-
  leaf parsley
salt and pepper to taste

- Preheat an oven to 425°F.
- Split the eggplants lengthwise, coat the cut surface with olive oil, place on a baking sheet along with the garlic, and bake for 30 to 40 minutes, or until tender. Remove and allow to cool.
- Scoop out the pulp and place in a food processor. Squeeze out the garlic and add, along with the remaining ingredients. Pulse until smooth.

$\mathcal{J}$ALAPEÑO PASTE

6 jalapeño peppers finely
  minced
2 tablespoons olive oil

1 cup cream cheese
salt and white pepper to
  taste

- Rub the peppers with the olive oil, and roast in a preheated oven at 400°F for about 30 minutes, or until they begin to turn dark brown. Remove to an airtight container (e.g., jar, plastic bag, covered bowl), and leave them for 15 minutes. Remove the peppers, and separate the flesh from the seeds and skin. Discard the skin and seeds, and mash the flesh with a fork. Blend this paste into the cream cheese, and season to taste with salt and white pepper.

$\mathcal{O}$LIVE AND ANCHOVY PASTE, PROVENCE STYLE

(Purée d'Olives à la Provençale)

2 cups Calamata olives,
  pitted
¼ cup anchovy fillets, with
  packing oil
6 garlic cloves
¼ cup brandy
¼ cup olive oil

2 tablespoons Worcestershire
  sauce
¼ teaspoon black pepper
2 tablespoons chopped
  parsley
1 teaspoon thyme leaves,
  minced

- Purée all ingredients in a food processor, or pound with a mortar and pestle. Cover and refrigerate until ready to use.

*O*LIVE PASTE

(Tapenade)

1 cup Calamata olives, pitted	1 tablespoon lemon juice
2 garlic cloves	¼ cup olive oil
½ teaspoon grated lemon zest	black pepper to taste

- Purée all ingredients in a food processor, or mince very finely with a knife and press through a fine sieve. Refrigerate until needed.

*R*OASTED GARLIC PASTE

1 garlic bulb	½ cup cream cheese
2 tablespoons olive oil	salt and white pepper as needed
¼ pound unsalted butter, soft	

- Preheat an oven to 375°F.
- Break up the garlic bulb into cloves, discarding excess skin. Toss the cloves in the olive oil, place in a roasting pan, and roast for 30 to 40 minutes. Remove, and set aside to cool.
- Squeeze out the soft garlic from the cloves and mash thoroughly with a fork. Add the cream cheese and butter, blend thoroughly, and season to taste with salt and white pepper.

*S*ALSA VERDE PASTE

4 tomatillos, skin removed, roughly chopped	½ teaspoon ground cumin
2 jalapeño peppers	½ cup water
1 cup cilantro leaves, roughly chopped	1 cup goat cheese
	salt and white pepper to taste

- Simmer all the ingredients, except the goat cheese, in a small noncorrosive saucepan, until soft. Continue simmering until the mixture becomes a fairly dry paste.
- Allow to cool, then combine with the goat cheese and blend thoroughly. Season to taste with salt and pepper.

Sardine Paste

½ pound cream cheese
½ pound unsalted butter
2 to 3 tines boneless, skinless sardines, drained and
  mashed

2 tablespoons Tabasco
salt and pepper to taste

- Blend all ingredients together until smooth. Season to taste with salt and pepper.

Tuna Paste

½ pound cream cheese
½ pound unsalted butter
1 pound fresh tuna, poached
  and finely ground

2 tablespoons Tabasco
salt and pepper to taste

- Blend all ingredients together until smooth. Season to taste with salt and pepper.

Cold Dishes

Admiral Canapés
(Canapés à l'Amiral)

Oval crouton spread with shrimp butter, topped with a poached shrimp, garnished with lobster coral (lobster eggs).

Alberta Canapés
(Canapés à l'Alberta)

Square crouton spread with anchovy butter, crisscross of sliced smoked salmon, garnished with beets and Maître d'Hôtel Butter.

Alladin Canapés
(Canapés à l'Alladin)

Half-circle-shaped crouton spread with stockfish paste, garnished with mango chutney.

Alsacian Canapés
(Canapés à l'Alsacienne; also Imperial Canapés)

Round crouton spread with butter, topped with a slice of goose liver (or goose liver mousse), garnished with a slice of truffle, glazed with Madeira aspic.

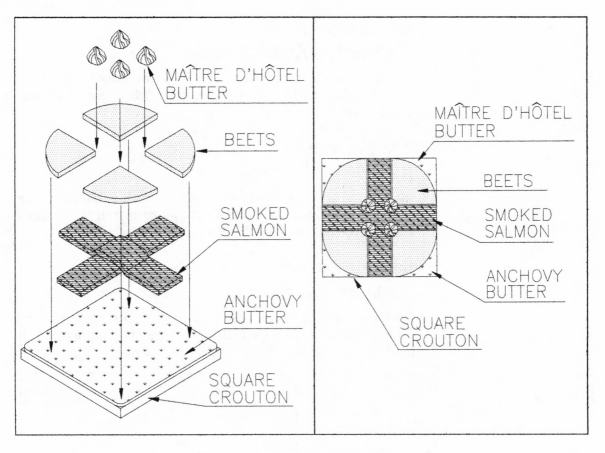

MAÎTRE D'HÔTEL BUTTER

BEETS

SMOKED SALMON

ANCHOVY BUTTER

SQUARE CROUTON

Alberta Canapé

Truffles are members of the botanical family *Funghi*, which also includes mushrooms and morels. They are unique in that they produce their fruiting bodies underground and have a symbiotic relationship with trees such as beech, hazelnut, oak, poplar, and willow. The white truffle (Alba truffle) is found in the Piedmont and Emilia regions of Italy. The black truffle (Périgord truffle) is found primarily in the Dordogne region of southwestern France and in parts of Spain, Germany, and Italy. The French production of truffles today is about one-tenth of what it was a century ago, because of the loss of forest lands and overharvesting. Their scarcity, combined with the labor required to locate these truffles, explains their exorbitant cost.

Anchovy Toasts
(Pain Grillé aux Anchois)

Crouton spread with dry mustard–cayenne pepper butter, topped with a crisscross of anchovy fillets, garnished with sieved hardboiled egg, chopped parsley, and sliced lemon (quarters).

Andalusian Canapés
(Canapés à l'Andalousienne)

Crouton spread with butter, topped with thin-sliced shrimp and anchovy fillets, coated with mayonnaise collée, garnished with green pepper.

Aurora Canapés
(Canapés à l'Aurore)

Round crouton cut from sliced brioche, spread with butter paste, topped with thin-sliced smoked salmon, garnished with a small circle of cooked beet, spinkled with sieved egg yolk.

Beatrice Canapés
(Canapés à la Beatrice)

Oval crouton spread with chervil butter, topped with two very thin slices of dried sausage with a thin slice of hard-boiled egg in between, garnished with dots of tomato butter.

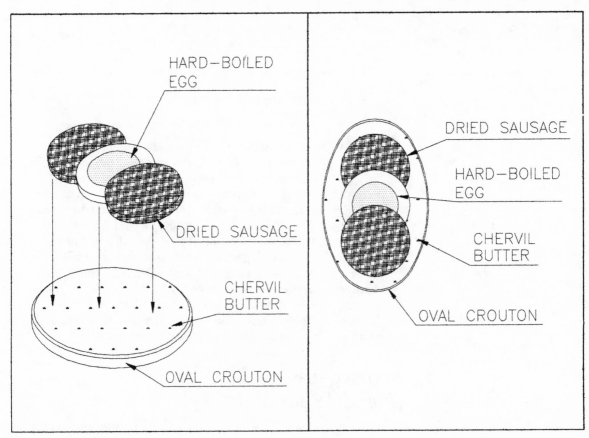

Beatrice Canapé

Beaulieu Canapés
(Canapés à la Beaulieu)

Round crouton spread with butter or basic paste, topped with a small wedge of seeded and skinned tomato, seasoned with salt and pepper, garnished with a half black olive.

Belle de Lauris Canapés
(Canapés à la Belle de Lauris)

Square crouton spread with asparagus butter, topped with a thin slice of poached chicken breast, coated with asparagus collée, decorated with asparagus tips.

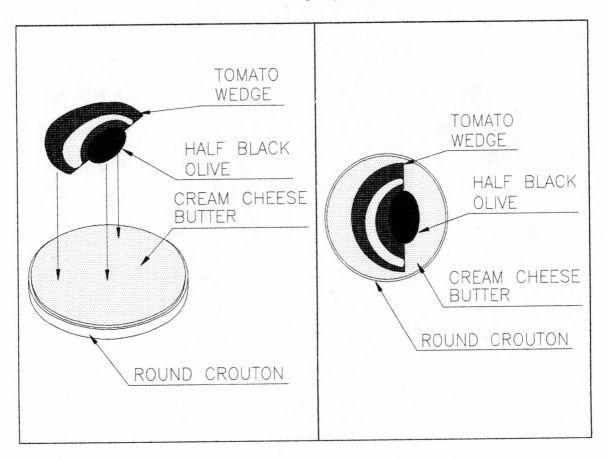

Beaulieu Canapé

Bordeaux Canapés
(Canapés à la Bordelaise)

Oval crouton spread with shallot butter, topped with two thin slices of shiitake mushrooms with a thin slice of ham in between.

Brillat-Savarin Canapés
(Canapés à la Brillat-Savarin)

Oval crouton spread with crayfish butter, topped with poached crayfish tails split in half, garnished with a small piece of truffle.

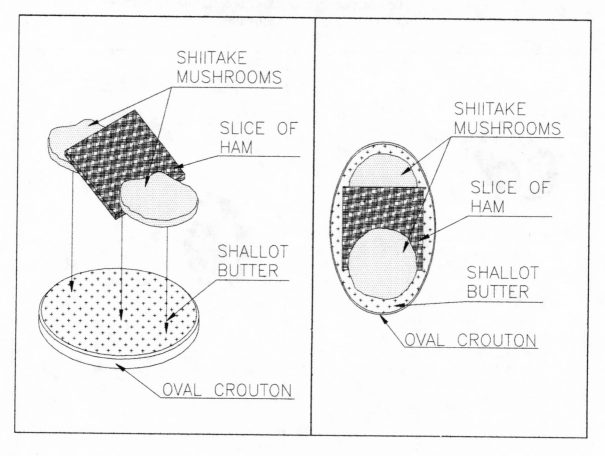

Bordeaux Canapé

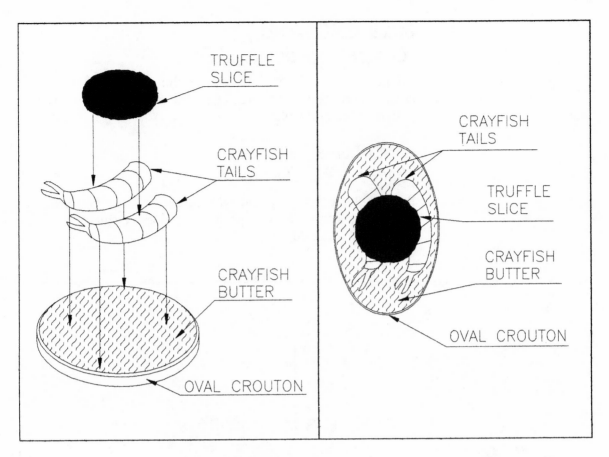

Brillat-Savarin Canapé

Jean Anthelme Brillat-Savarin (1755–1826), statesman, gourmand, musician, and author of *Le Physioligie du Goût* (The Physiology of Taste), first published in 1825. Though the first edition did not bear the name of the author, the book was fairly successful and is still in print today. During the Revolution, Brillat-Savarin fled France to escape the Tribunal, first to Switzerland and, later, to America, where he played the violin on the streets of Philadelphia in order to survive.

Buttercup Canapés
(Canapés à la Bouton d'Or)

Round crouton spread with watercress butter, topped with watercress leaves, garnished with egg yolk paste piped in a lattice pattern. (See color plate.)

Cambacérès Canapés
(Canapés Cambacérès)

Rectangular crouton spread with butter or basic paste, topped with thin-sliced seeded and peeled cucumber marinated in lemon vinaigrette (drained).

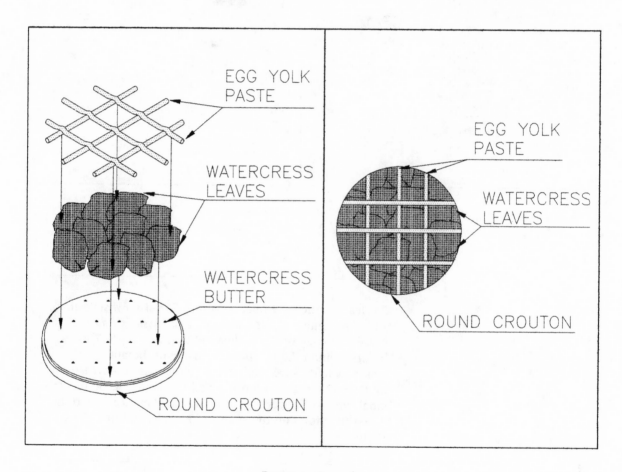

Buttercup Canapé

Capuchin Canapés
(Canapés à la Capucine)

Round rye bread crouton spread with mayonnaise, one-half covered with sieved hard-boiled egg yolks, the other half covered with caviar, garnished with a small shrimp in the center.

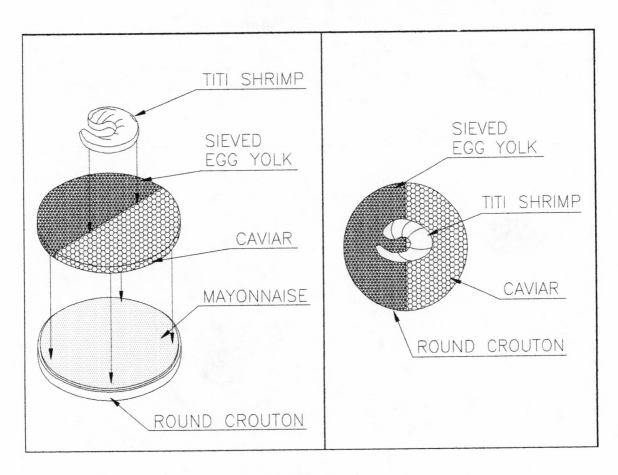

Capuchin Canapé

Truffles are an intriguing food, fabled for centuries for their mystical and aphrodisiac qualities. Brillat-Savarin called them "the diamonds of cookery"; in Italian, they are called *perle dela cucina*—"pearls of the kitchen"; the Roman satirist Juvenal told the Libyans in the first century A.D., "Keep your wheat, and send us your truffles."

Cardinal Canapés
(Canapés à la Cardinale)

Round crouton spread with mayonnaise topped with a slice of lobster tail, garnished with a slice of truffle.

Chantereine Canapés
(Canapés à la Chantereine)

Triangular-shaped crouton spread with butter, half spread with ham mousse and garnished with a small circle of hard-boiled egg, the other half spread with chicken mousse and garnished with a small round of truffle.

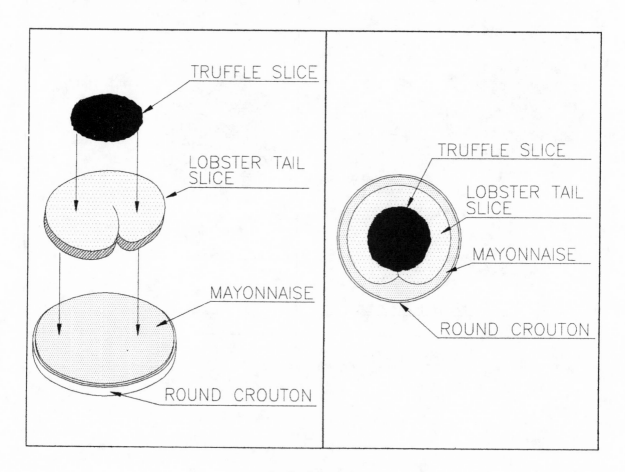

Cardinal Canapé

Claire Canapés
(Canapés à la Claire)

Rectangular pumpernickel crouton spread with lemon butter, topped with alternating thin-sliced strips of smoked salmon and caviar.

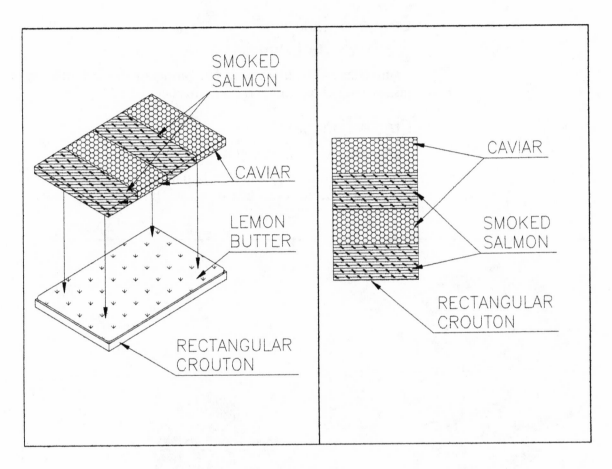

Claire Canapé

Collioure Canapés
(Canapés à la Collioure)

Diamond-shaped crouton spread with anchovy butter, topped with anchovy fillets (crisscross or lattice pattern), garnished with miniature tomato balls.

Coquelin Canapés
(Canapés de Coquelin)

Crouton spread with anchovy and Parmesan cheese butter, garnished with chopped gherkins and capers.

Creole Canapés
(Canapés à la Creole)

Rectangular crouton spread with butter, topped with a thin slice of Gruyère cheese, garnished with two thin slices of banana.

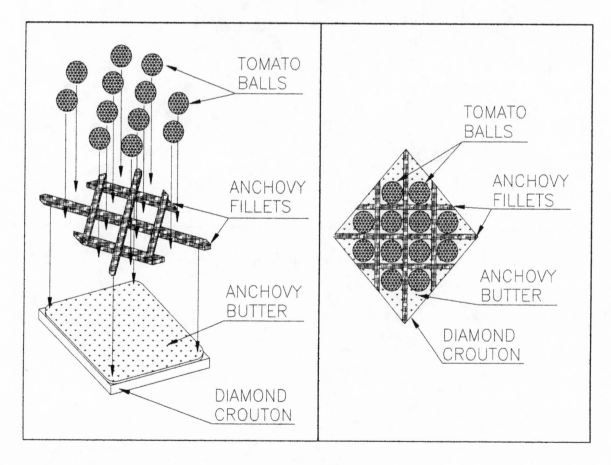

Collioure Canapé

Danish Canapés
(Canapés à la Danoise)

Square rye bread crouton spread with horseradish butter, topped with alternating strips of sliced smoked salmon and herring, garnished with chives and caviar.

Derby Canapés
(Canapés à la Derby)

Crouton spread with ham paste, garnished with chopped toasted walnuts.

Domino Canapés
(Canapés à la Domino)

Rectangular crouton spread with butter or plain paste, topped with a thin slice of poached chicken breast, glazed with mayonnaise collée, decorated with small dots of truffle to resemble a domino. (See color plate.)

———————— • ————————

The word *truffle* is derived from the Spanish *trufa* or the Italian *treffere*, both meaning "deceit," probably a reference to the fact that this variety of wild mushroom grows just underneath the surface of the ground and is thus difficult to locate. Because humans do not possess a keen olfactory sense, we must elicit help. In Sardinia goats are employed to track down truffles, bear cubs have been used in Russia, and pigs and specially trained dogs in Europe. Pigs are the true experts, however. German researchers recently discovered in truffles a musky chemical that is also secreted in a male pig's saliva, which prompts mating behavior. When the pig's sharp nose detects that aroma from under the ground (both pigs and dogs can detect it from as far away as 50 yards), it sends the creature into a lustful frenzy and it must be held back to prevent it from eating the truffle.

Douarnen Canapés
(Canapés à la Douarnenez)

Rectangular pumpernickel crouton spread with basic butter paste, topped with skinless and boneless sardines, garnished with a small seedless and skinless lemon segment.

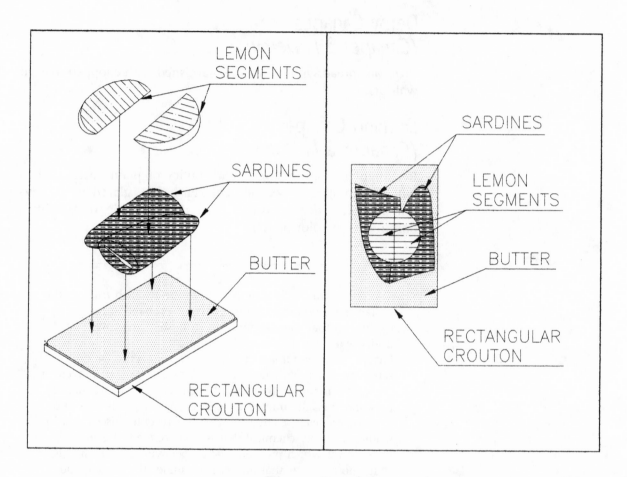

Douarnen Canapé

Dutch Canapés
(Canapés à la Hollandaise)

Rectangular or square crouton spread with caviar butter, topped with thin-sliced pickled herring, garnished with sieved egg yolks and minced chives.

French Canapés
(Canapés à la Française)

Rectangular crouton spread with anchovy butter, topped with a sardine (slightly flattened), coated with rémoulade collée, edged with chopped parsley.

Gâtine Canapés
(Canapés à la Gâtinais)

Triangular crouton spread with butter, chicken liver pâté, garnished with tarragon leaves, glazed with aspic.

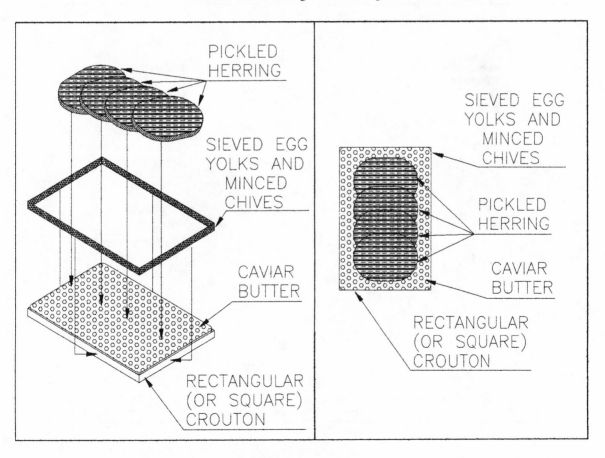

Dutch Canapé

Gedeon Canapés
(Canapés à la Gedeon)

Rectangular crouton spread lightly with butter, followed by liver paste, topped with crisscrossed strips of roasted duck breast.

Gourmet Canapés
(Canapés à la Gourmet)

Oval crouton spread with goose liver butter, topped with a thin slice of poached chicken breast, garnished with chopped truffles, glazed with Madeira aspic.

Grenoble Canapés
(Canapés à la Grenobloise)

Round crouton spread with walnut butter, topped with a thin slice of Gruyère cheese, garnished with a toasted walnut.

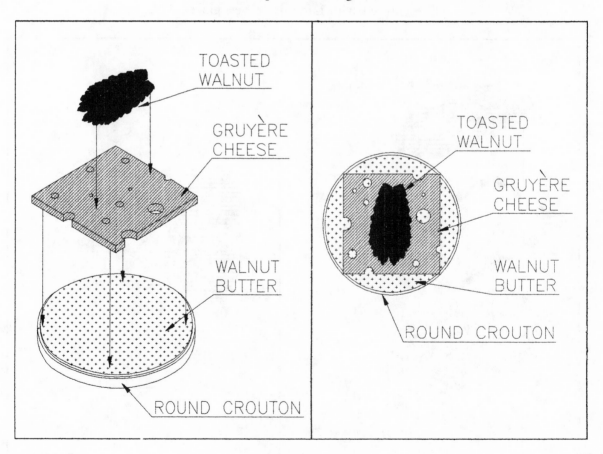

Grenoble Canapé

Hamburg Canapés
(Canapés à la Hamburgoise)

Rectangular rye bread crouton spread with butter, topped with a thin slice of smoked meat, garnished with a small gherkin fan.

Harlequin Canapés
(Canapés à l'Arlequin)

A general term for a style of croutons cut into diamonds or rectangles, spread with horseradish, mustard, paprika, tomato, or watercress butter, topped with finely chopped ham, chicken, smoked or pickled tongue, edged with minced parsley, attractively decorated with hard-boiled eggs, radishes, truffles, olives, or other garnish.

Helvetian Canapés
(Canapés à la Helvetia)

Rectangular pumpernickel crouton spread with a paste made of ½ cup butter, ½ cup grated Gruyère or Emmenthaler cheese, 2 sieved hard-boiled egg yolks, 1 tablespoon grated celery root, 3 tablespoons heavy cream, salt, and white pepper.

Hungarian Canapés
(Canapés à la Hongroise)

Round or oval croutons spread with paprika butter, topped with chicken paste, garnished with strips of red and green bell peppers.

Imperial Canapés
(Canapés à la Monseigneur)

Rectangular crouton spread with anchovy butter, topped with a thin slice of grilled tuna, garnished with anchovy butter.

Indian Canapés
(Canapés à l'Indienne)

Crouton spread with curry butter, topped with chopped hard-boiled egg yolks, garnished with mango chutney.

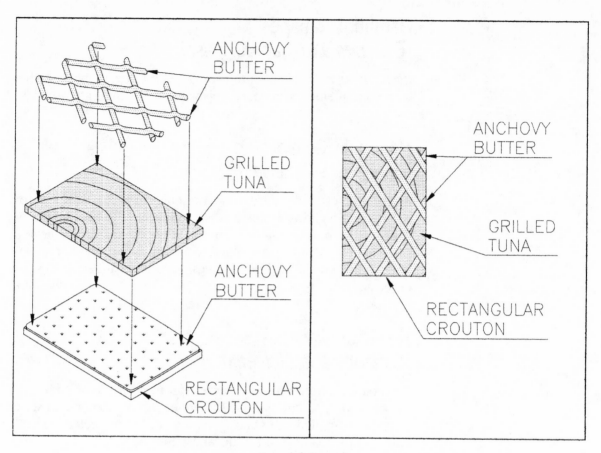

Imperial Canapé

Jodler Canapés
(Canapés à la Jodler)

Round pumpernickel crouton spread with butter or basic paste, covered with grated radish, topped with a square of Swiss cheese, garnished with finely chopped toasted peanuts.

Joinville Canapés
(Canapés Joinville)

Round crouton spread with shrimp butter, edged with minced hard-boiled egg, topped with titi shrimp, garnished with a small (unsalted) butter curl.

La Fayette Canapés
(Canapés La Fayette)

Rectangular crouton spread with butter or basic paste, topped with a slice of boiled lobster, coated with lobster collée, garnished with truffle, glazed with aspic.

Laguipière Canapés
(Canapés à la Languipière)

Diamond-shaped brioche crouton spread with truffle butter, edged with minced truffle and minced smoked tongue, topped with thin-sliced chicken breast.

Lily-of-the-Valley Canapés
(Canapés Belle Muguette)

Oval crouton spread with tarragon butter, topped with a lengthwise slice of hard-boiled egg, decorated with tarragon leaves and tiny round cutouts of egg white, glazed with aspic.

Livonian Canapés
(Canapés à la Livonienne)

The Granny Smith apple brings a nice crunch to Livonian canapés, and should be dipped in lemon juice and drained before using, to prevent browning.

Rectangular pumpernickel crouton spread with horseradish butter, edged in chopped chives, topped with slivers of pickled herring alternating with thin julienne of tart apple.

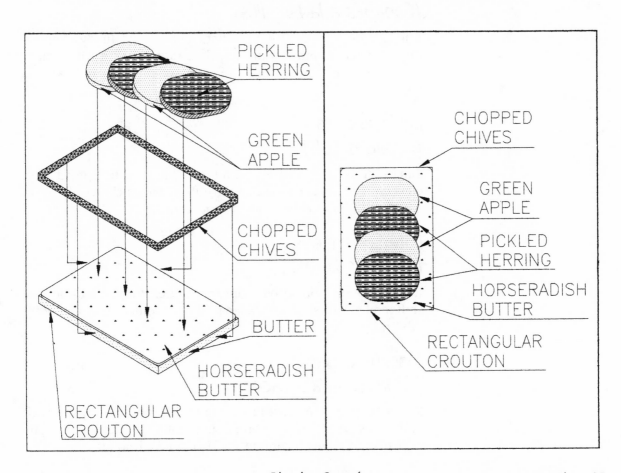

Livonian Canapé

Lothringian Canapés
(Canapés à la Lorraine)

Square crouton spread with butter, topped with chicken paste blended with minced beef tongue, glazed with aspic.

Lucca Canapés
(Canapés à la Lucca)

Oval crouton spread with butter, topped with a raw or poached oyster, garnished with caviar.

Lucille Canapés
(Canapés à la Lucille)

Oval crouton spread with butter, topped with minced beef tongue, garnished with a thin slice of poached chicken breast, glazed with aspic.

Lucullus Canapés
(Canapés à la Lucullus)

Round crouton spread with butter, topped with finely chopped raw beef tenderloin (tartare), with a raw oyster in the center, garnished with caviar and a segment of seedless and skinless lemon.

Lulli Canapés
(Canapés Lulli)

Square crouton spread with butter or basic paste, spread with chicken mousse, garnished with truffle or pâte à choux filigree in the shape of a G cleff (musical notation).

Lutetia Canapés
(Canapés Lutetia)

Round crouton spread with mustard butter, topped with lettuce chiffonade, garnished with a small slice of tomato seasoned with salt and pepper.

Mascot Canapés
(Canapés à la Mascot)

Rectangular crouton spread with green herb butter, topped with thin slices of artichoke bottom marinated in vinaigrette, garnished with a small noisette (ball) of cooked potato.

Mexican Canapés
(Canapés à la Mexicaine)

Crouton spread with butter, topped with minced sardines and anchovies, then with a slice of hard-boiled egg, garnished with red bell pepper.

Monselet Canapés
(Canapés à la Monselet)

Oval crouton spread with egg yolk paste, edged with minced truffle, topped alternately with thin-sliced poached chicken breast and smoked tongue, garnished with a small thin slice of truffle.

Charles Pierre Monselet (1825–1888), journalist and author, was known for his witty style in writing on gastronomic matters. He collaborated with many well-known writers of his day (including Alexander Dumas) on *La Cuisinière Poétique*, published in 1859. He also published a gastronomic newsletter—*Le Gourmet*, later changed to *Almanach des Gourmands*—off and on between 1861 and 1870. A gourmand of some distinction, Monselet was known to many of the finest restaurants of his day and had a number of dishes named after him, nearly all including some form of truffle.

Mont-Bry was a pseudonym used by Prosper Montagné, and denotes dishes created by or for him. His best-known work, first published in 1938, is the still-published *Larousse Gastronomique* (no relation to this author).

Mont-Bry Canapés
(Canapés à la Mont-Bry)

Rectangular brioche crouton spread with herring butter, edged with chopped egg yolk, garnished with alternating strips of herring, cooked beet, and gherkins.

Monte Carlo Canapés
(Canapés à la Monte Carlo)

Crouton spread with goose liver paste, garnished with chopped hard-boiled egg.

Moscow Canapés
(Canapés à la Moscovite)

Square pumpernickel crouton spread with horseradish butter, decorated with a border of lobster butter, filled with caviar, garnished with a poached shrimp.

Nantes Canapés
(Canapés à la Nantaise)

Oval crouton spread with sardine butter, topped with skinless and boneless sardines, garnished with sardine butter.

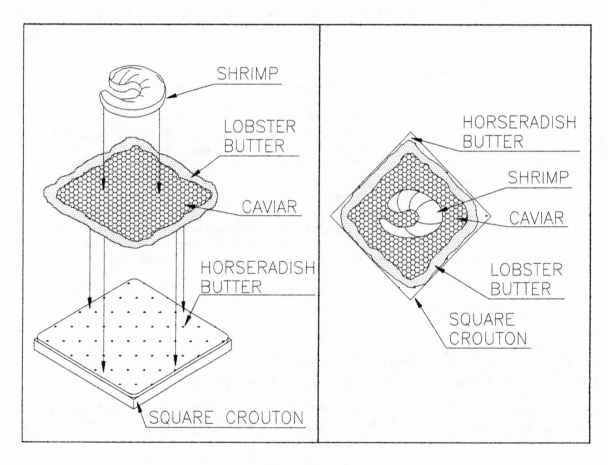

Moscow Canapé

Netherlands Canapés
(Canapés à la Néerland)

Oval crouton spread with mustard butter, topped with a large mussel poached in white wine, garnished with finely diced celery (brunoise) marinated in mustard vinaigrette.

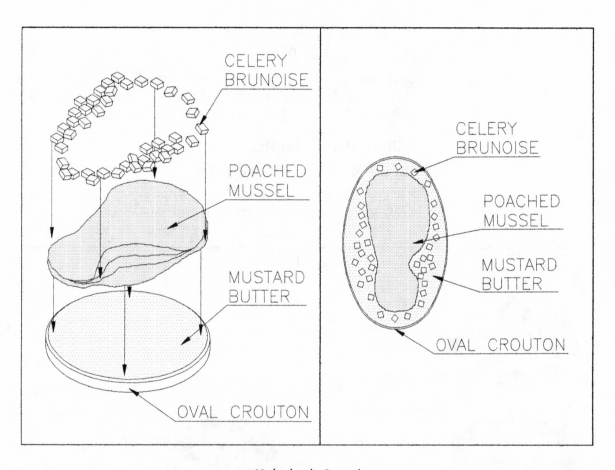

CELERY BRUNOISE

POACHED MUSSEL

MUSTARD BUTTER

OVAL CROUTON

CELERY BRUNOISE

POACHED MUSSEL

MUSTARD BUTTER

OVAL CROUTON

Netherlands Canapé

Nice Canapés
(Canapés à la Niçoise)

Round crouton spread with anchovy butter, topped with a thin slice of tomato, a split anchovy fillet crisscrossed on top, a slice of olive in each of the four sections, garnished with chopped parsley.

Ninon Canapés
(Canapés à la Ninon)

Oval crouton spread with green vegetable butter, topped with alternating thin-sliced poached chicken breast and ham, garnished with a small thin slice of truffle.

Norwegian Canapés
(Canapés à la Norvégienne)

Rectangular rye bread crouton spread with butter, topped with strips of anchovy fillets, garnished with horseradish butter.

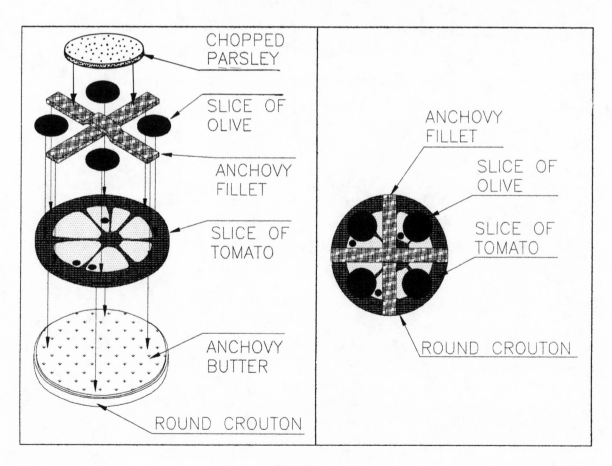

Nice Canapé

Ogourzi Canapés
(Canapés à l'Ogourzi)

Rectangular rye bread crouton spread with butter or basic paste, topped with a drained salad of paper-thin sliced seedless and skinless cucumber marinated in dill and sour cream, garnished with a sprig of dill.

Ondine Canapés
(Canapés à la Ondine)

Diamond-shaped crouton spread with tarragon butter, topped with a piece of sole poached in white wine, coated with tarragon-and-fish-flavored mayonnaise collée, garnished with tarragon leaves.

Oriental Canapés
(Canapés à l'Orientale)

Triangular crouton, spread with butter or basic paste, topped with a thin slice of poached chicken breast, coated with tomato and saffron flavored collée, garnished with roasted red bell pepper (or pimento) cut into a crescent and a star.

Otero Canapés
(Canapés à l'Otero)

Round crouton spread with butter, topped with caviar and a raw or poached oyster, coated with rémoulade collée.

Paris Canapés
(Canapés à la Parisienne)

Rectangular crouton, spread with chervil butter, topped with thin-sliced poached chicken breast, coated with mayonnaise collée, garnished with a small slice of truffle and tarragon leaves.

Pellaprat Canapés
(Canapés à la Pellaprat)

Round crouton spread with watercress butter, edged with watercress butter, spread with salmon mousse.

Ogourzi (or Agourzi) is also a salad made of the same ingredients (see Chapter 11, "Salads").

Henri Paul Pellaprat (1869–1950), a chef and pâtissier of considerable repute, worked under Casimir Moisson at the celebrated Maison Dorée in Paris (1840–1902), eventually taking over as chef. He is the author of *L'Art Culinarie Moderne*, first published in 1935, then published in 1966 and 1971 under the title *The Great Book of French Cuisine*.

Phileas Gilbert Canapés
(Canapés à la Phileas Gilbert)

Round crouton, spread with shrimp-cayenne butter, topped with a slice of poached turbot fillet, glazed with fish collée, garnished with truffle, glazed with aspic.

———————————— • ————————————

Turbot is a large white-fleshed fish, similar in appearance to a large flounder, found in the North Atlantic and the Mediterranean. That it has been gastronomically prized for centuries is indicated by the fact that there exists a large poaching vessel fabricated in the shape of the turbot, known as a *turbotière*. Its gastronomic importance is also indicated by a considerable body of elaborate recipes for its preparation. Any variety of flounder is the best substitute for turbot.

Phocaean Canapés
(Canapés à la Phocaea)

Round crouton spread with lemon butter, topped with red mullet salpicon (baked in olive oil and lemon), garnished with tomato concassé.

Pompadour Canapés
(Canapés à la Pompadour)

Oval or round crouton spread with butter or basic paste, topped with a thin slice of poached chicken breast, coated with tomato collée, garnished with a sprig of chervil (or parsley) and miniature circles of tomato.

———————————— • ————————————

Numerous dishes, designated "Pompadour style" are named after Jeanne Antoinette Poisson (1721–1764), mistress of Louis XV, king of France, who conferred on her the title Marquise de Pompadour. Among these dishes were Suprême de Volaille en Bellevue; Noisettes de Mouton Pompadour; Pavés de Riz, Pompadour, and Atteraux Pompadour à l'Abricot.

———— • ————

Phileas Gilbert (1857–1942) worked with many great chefs, notably August Escoffier and Prosper Montagné. He penned numerous books and articles, assisted Escoffier in writing his *Guide Culinaire*, and contributed a short preface to *Larousse Gastronomique* (removed from the 1988 edition).

———— • ————

Phocaea was an ancient city in what was known as Ionia, circa 1100 B.C., located in a group of islands situated between southern Italy and western Greece.

Salpicon is a fairly broad term, referring to any meat, fish, poultry, game, or vegetable, cut into fairly small dice and cooked by stewing or braising.

Princess Canapés
(Canapés à la Princesse)

Round crouton spread with butter, topped with a slice of poached chicken breast, then crisscrossed with anchovy fillets, garnished with a slice of hard-boiled egg, sprinkled with minced chives. (See color plate.)

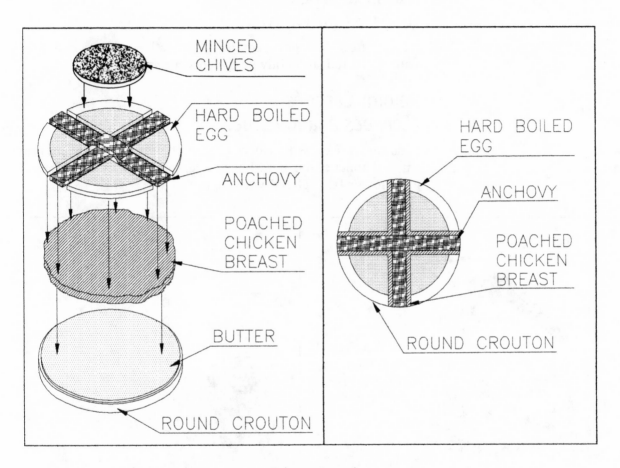

Princess Canapé

Prosper Montagné Canapés
(Canapés à la Prosper Montagné)

Oval crouton spread with tomato butter, topped with a thin slice of roasted turkey breast, garnished with roasted red bell pepper or pimento.

Radish Canapés
(Canapés au Radis)

Slice of fresh baguette (untoasted) spread with butter, topped with sliced radish, lightly seasoned with salt.

Reform Canapés
(Canapés à la Réforme)

Crouton spread with anchovy butter, topped with minced smoked tongue and hard-boiled egg, garnished with a slice of gherkin (or fan), glazed with aspic.

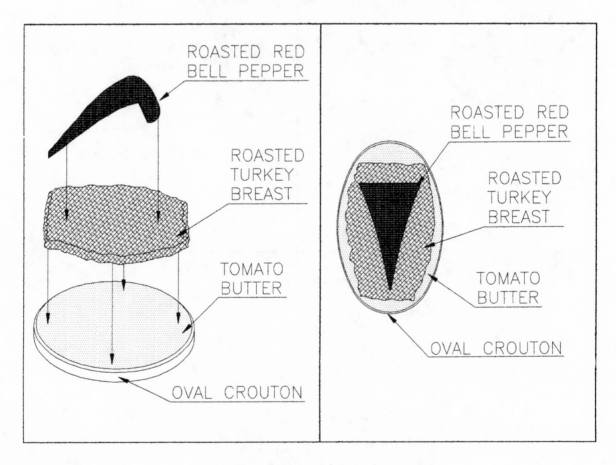

Prosper Montagné Canapé

Souvaroff Canapés
(Canapés à la Souvaroff)

Square pumpernickel crouton, spread with goose liver paste, topped with a thin slice of roast pheasant, garnished with truffle, glazed with aspic.

Spanish Canapés
(Canapés à l'Espagnole)

Rectangular or oval crouton spread with cayenne butter, topped with a sheet of cooked egg, garnished with a little finely diced tomato concassé in the center.

To prepare an egg sheet: Beat very well, 2 eggs and a little salt and pepper. Pour into a hot pan with some oil, and cook on both sides until light brown. Drain on absorbent paper, then cut to the exact size of the croutons.

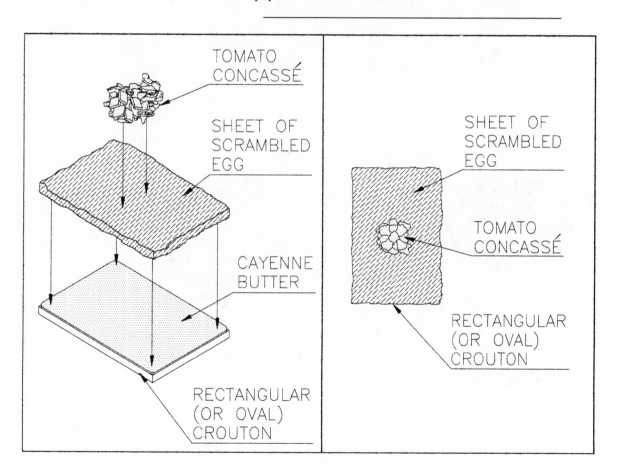

Spanish Canapé

Spring Canapés
(Canapés aux Printinière)

Slice of baguette or white bread (untoasted) spread with parsley butter, topped with chopped watercress, garnished with a slice of hard-boiled egg.

Sultan Canapés
(Canapés à la Sultane)

Crouton spread with anchovy butter, topped with chopped lobster meat, coated with mayonnaise collée blended with minced lettuce, garnished with chopped red bell peppers.

Swedish Canapés
(Canapés à la Suédoise)

A general term for rye bread canapés, toasted and untoasted, spread with anchovy butter, topped with various ingredients—

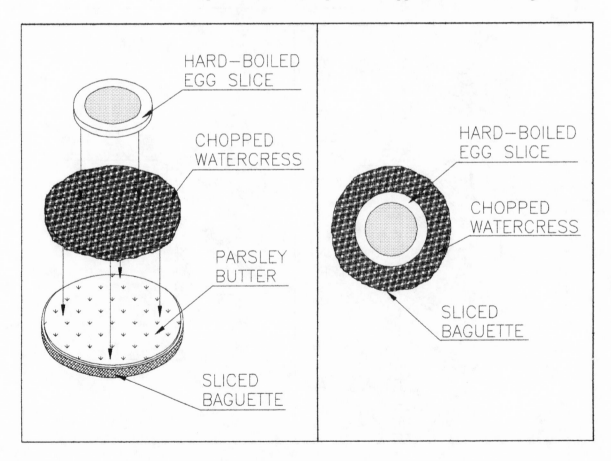

Spring Canapé

anchovies, smoked salmon, herring, eggs, lobster, shrimp, oysters, ham, and so forth—attractively decorated. (See color plate.)

Tartar Canapés
(Canapés à la Tartare)

Square or rectangular rye bread (untoasted) spread with butter, topped with ground lean beef seasoned with salt and pepper, garnished with chopped onions and gherkins.

Turbigo Canapés
(Canapés à la Turbigo)

Crouton spread with butter, topped with chopped shrimp, coated with seasoned tomato purée, garnished with diced pickles and diced cooked celery root.

Véron Canapés
(Canapés à la Véron)

Square pumpernickel crouton spread with horseradish butter, edged with a mixture of chopped egg yolks and chopped parsley, topped with very thin slices of Bayonne ham. (See color plate.)

Westphalian Ham Canapés
(Canapés à la Westphalienne)

Crouton spread with horseradish butter, topped with a thin slice of dry-cured ham, glazed with aspic.

Simple ham and sausage canapés can be made from any variety of ham, and then take on the name of the ham or sausage used. Typical variations include Ardennes, Arlesian, Bayonne, Berry, Parma, Virginia, or York ham; Arles, Calabrese, Chipolata, Cognac, or Lyons sausage.

Windsor Canapés
(Canapés à la Windsor)

Crouton spread with chicken paste mixed with chopped tongue, ham, and dry mustard, garnished with gherkins and capers, glazed with aspic.

· · · · · · · · · · · · · · · · · · ·
*B*ASIC CRACKER RECIPE

2¼ cups flour
2 tablespoons sugar
2 teaspoons baking powder
1 teaspoon salt
¼ cup vegetable oil
¼ cup milk

1 egg, beaten
2 teaspoons finely minced herbs or ground spices, as needed (fennel, caraway seed, cracked black pepper, paprika, saffron, etc.)

- Blend the dry ingredients together. Add the oil, milk, egg, and herbs or spices. Knead together until smooth, and allow to rest 30 minutes.
- Preheat an oven to 350°F.
- Roll out the dough on a floured board, and cut into various shapes. Bake for 15 minutes, or until the edges brown.

———————————— • ————————————

Homemade crackers are excellent bases for canapés, both because of their crunch, and because of the option to season them and cut them in any way desired. They can also be made a day or two ahead.

Artichoke Bottoms with Garden Vegetables

Trim canned artichoke bottoms into uniform circles, using a round pastry cutter, and flatten the bottom. Drop into boiling lemon water for 15 seconds, drain, and cool. Pipe in ½ teaspoon cream cheese blended with chopped herbs (e.g., parsley, cilantro, tarragon), and garnish with four different varieties of blanched vegetables, such as a broccoli flowerette, a carrot noisette, a half slice of radish, and a yellow turnip noisette.

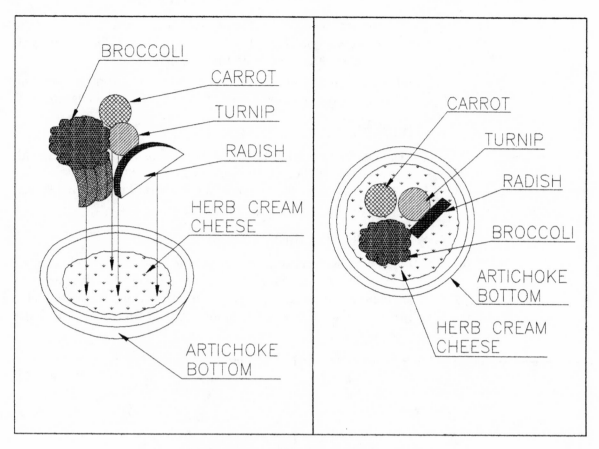

Artichoke Bottom with Garden Vegetables Canapé

✑SIAN BIRD'S NEST

1 cup titi shrimp
¼ cup celery cut into very fine dice (brunoise)
¼ cup scallion, finely minced
½ cup rice wine vinegar
2 tablespoons grated ginger-root

2 tablespoons minced cilantro leaves
2 tablespoon soy sauce
48 2-inch square pieces of wonton skin
peanut oil as needed
½ cup chopped roasted peanuts
24 cilantro leaves

- Marinate the shrimp, celery, scallion, vinegar, ginger, minced cilantro, and soy sauce for 2 hours.

- Brush the insides of a miniature muffin pan with oil. Preheat an oven to 375°F.

- Brush one square of wonton with water, and press a second square on top, so that the corners do not line up. Press this square into an oiled muffin pan cavity, and brush the top of the wonton with oil. Repeat with all the wontons, bake until golden brown, then set aside to cool.

- Drain the marinated shrimp, and divide up among the wonton bases. Garnish each with chopped peanuts and a cilantro leaf.

Beef Janna

Rectangular crouton, spread with horseradish butter, topped with a slice of roasted beef tenderloin, garnished with a rosette of blue cheese and cream cheese paste, a cornichon fan, and watercress leaf.

Broccoli on Onion Cracker

Prepare a basic cracker recipe, with the addition of finely minced onion lightly sautéed and drained. Spread the cracker with jalapeño cream cheese, top with a small broccoli flowerette lightly blanched in boiling salted water, and garnish with pâte à choux filigree.

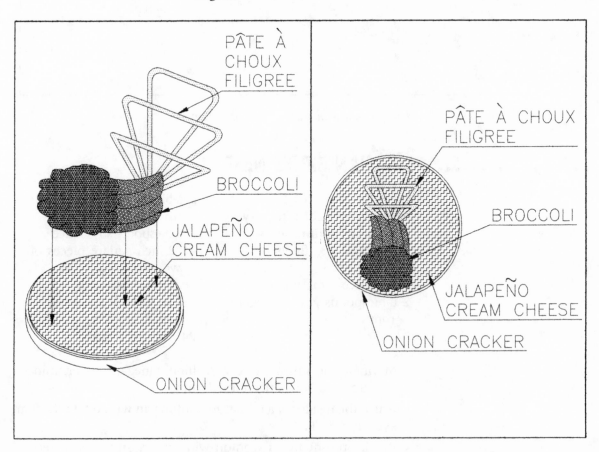

Broccoli on Onion Cracker Canapé

Pâte à Choux Filigree

½ cup milk
½ cup water
pinch of salt
¼ pound unsalted butter,
  cut up

1½ cups all-purpose flour,
  sieved
6 eggs

- Bring the milk, water, salt, and butter to a simmer in a noncaustic pan. When the butter is melted, add the flour and stir until completely blended. Continue stirring over medium heat, until the paste comes away from the side of the pan. Remove from the fire.

- Add the eggs, one at a time, blending in each one completely before adding the next. Allow to cool, then fill a small pastry bag or parchment cone fitted with a No. 1 round tube. Pipe out in small filigree designs, no longer than 1-inch, on a baking sheet covered with parchment paper. Bake at 350°F 10 to 15 minutes, or until golden brown. Remove and set aside to cool.

*B*RUSCHETTA MEDITERRANEAN STYLE

1 large ripe tomato
1 medium green bell pepper
3 garlic cloves, pressed
3 tablespoons olive oil
2 tablespoons parsley,
  minced
salt and pepper to taste

1 sweet baguette, sliced
  ¼-inch thick on a sharp
  bias
unsalted butter as needed
thinly sliced Virginia or
  Bayonne ham
Calamata olives

- Peel the tomato and cut into small dice, discarding excess seeds. Cut the green pepper into small dice. Combine the tomato, pepper, garlic, oil, parsley, salt, and pepper, toss thoroughly, and marinate several hours.

- Brush the baguette slices with olive oil, toast on both sides, and allow to cool. Spread each crouton lightly with butter, and top each with a slice of ham, trimmed to fit the crouton.

- Drain the tomato/pepper mixture of excess moisture, and place a half teaspoonful on top of each slice of the ham. Garnish with a slice of black olive.

Cajun Shrimp Canapés

Round cayenne pepper cracker, spread with jalapeño cream cheese paste. Dust peeled deveined shrimp with Cajun spice blend, sauté briefly in a hot pan, cool, then place on top of the jalapeño spread. Garnish with cream cheese and cilantro leaf.

Camembert and Apple Canapés

Round crouton spread with butter, topped with a large rosette made with 2 parts Camembert cheese mashed with 1 part cream cheese, garnished with a half red grape and a small wedge of apple dipped in lemon juice.

Cheddar and Chicken Liver Canapés

Prepare a basic cracker recipe with the addition of grated cheddar cheese. Spread cracker with cashew butter mixed with a little minced onion sautéed in oil until lightly caramelized then seasoned with a little basalmic vinegar. Pipe out a rosette of chicken liver paste blended with cream cheese on top of this, add a dollop of sour cream, garnish with a toasted cashew nut.

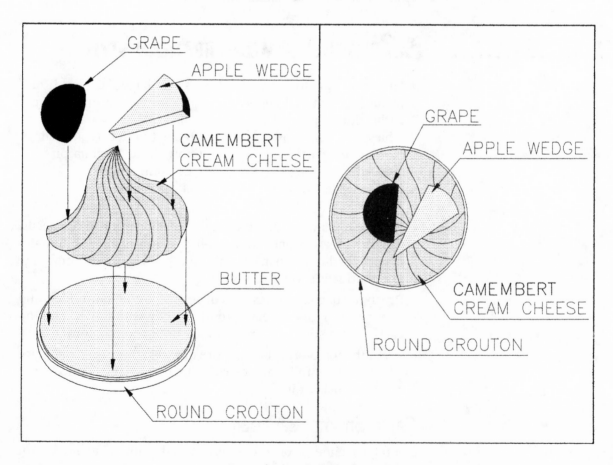

Camembert and Apple Canapé

Crostini with Prosciutto and Figs

Rectangular crouton spread with herb butter, topped with a paper-thin slice of prosciutto, garnished with a small dollop of marscapone cheese and two wedges of fresh figs (Calmyra or Black Mission).

Flower Blossom Canapés

Rectangular crouton, spread with nasturtium blossom (or other variety) butter, topped with radishes sliced paper thin, garnished with a dot of the butter and a piece of chive.

———————————— • ————————————

Nasturtium vegetable soup, a favorite of President Dwight D. Eisenhower, contains an herbal type of penicillin and a considerable amount of vitamin C. Flowers used in the kitchen should be purchased at a market, where they are certain to have been grown specifically for consumption. *Never* use flowers for cooking unless they are specified for such use, because they may have been chemically sprayed. Moreover, some flowers are poisonous (e.g., azalea, daffodil, oleander, poinsettia, and wisteria). Edible varieties include apple blossoms, chrysanthemums, marigolds, nasturtium, pansies, tulips, violets, and zucchini.

In Japan and China, chrysanthemums are believed to increase longevity, make teeth grow again, and turn white hair black. In France, pansy oil is still rubbed on eyelids to induce love at first sight. And medieval philosopher Albertus Magnus wrote that gathering violets during the final quarter of the moon would cause all one's wishes to come true.

Foie Gras Parfait

A round crouton spread with butter, topped with a large rosette of cooked fresh or canned goose liver mashed into a smooth paste with cream cheese and seasoned with fresh herbs, garnished with a dot of cream cheese and a slice of cornichon.

Gaufrette Potato, Russian Style

Using a potato mandolin, slice peeled potatoes into ¼-inch thick gaufrettes. Deep-fry until golden brown and drain well. Place on top of round cracker spread with cream cheese paste, top with a mixture of minced shallots caramelized in olive oil, cooled, and blended with sour cream, cream cheese, salt, and white pepper. Garnish with caviar and a chive spear.

Gorgonzola Bouchée

Pâte à choux bouchée filled with a mixture of equal parts Gorgonzola cheese, cream cheese, and butter, blended into a smooth paste, garnished with a half slice of seedless grape and a toasted walnut.

To prepare a pâte à choux bouchée, prepare the paste described in the recipe on page 101 (filigree). Pipe out balls of the paste, about ¾-inch in diameter, using a no. 5 or no. 6 round pastry tube. Bake at 375°F, until puffed up and golden brown.

Grecian Morsels

Diamond-shaped crouton spread with a thin layer of olive tapenade, garnished with a half cherry tomato that is scooped out and filled with feta cheese blended into a paste with garlic, oregano, and black pepper.

Greek Tomato Canapés

Round crouton spread with goat cheese, topped with a slice of Roma tomato, then a mixture of crumbled feta cheese, goat cheese, basil, olive oil, and garlic, garnished with a small wedge of Calamata olive.

Grilled Chicken on Fried Wontons

Wonton skin brushed lightly with water, folded diagonally twice into a triangle, then deep-fried and drained; spread with a thin layer of wasabi-flavored cream cheese, topped with a slice of grilled chicken breast, garnished with pickled gingerroot and a cilantro leaf.

Ham Cornets

Cut thin-sliced ham into 1½-inch circles, and make an incision from the center to the edge. Roll into a cone shape, and fill with cream cheese flavored with Dijon-style mustard and tarragon. Spread a round crouton with a thin layer of the same spread, place the cornet on top, and garnish with a small wedge of pineapple.

Jicama and Chorizo Canapés

Spread a ¼-inch thick slice of jicama, cut into a star, with a paste make from goat cheese and salsa verde (see recipe earlier in this chapter). Top with a slice of chorizo, garnish with a red pepper spear.

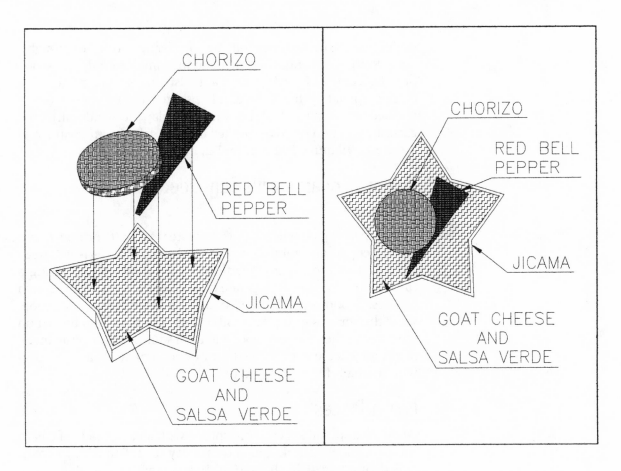

Jicama and Chorizo Canapé

Mexican Medallions

A dill-flavored round cracker, spread with cream cheese blended with tequila and minced cilantro, topped with a slice of Mexican-style Gravlax rolled into a rose, garnished with a dollop of sour cream and a cilantro leaf.

Mushroom and Chicken Liver Canapés

Remove the stems of medium mushrooms (about 1½-inch wide caps), and blanch the caps in white wine and lemon juice. Drain and cool. Stuff with basic chicken liver paste, and garnish with an asparagus tip blanched al dente, and a sprig of chervil or parsley.

Polenta Bouchée Southwest Style

Prepare a seasoned polenta (3 parts water to 1 part cornmeal, salt and white pepper), and pour into a ¾-inch deep half sheet pan to slightly overflowing. Even off the top, using a ruler or straight-edge. Refrigerate until cold, then cut into small rounds and scoop out the center of each, using a Parisienne scoop. Place on a cracker spread with adhesive, fill with guacamole (ripe avocado mashed with minced garlic, tomato, jalapeño, and salt), and garnish with two strips of smoked duck, a dab of sour cream, and a sprig of cilantro. See Figure 2.2.

Polenta Squares with Sun-Dried Tomato

Prepare a seasoned polenta (3 parts water to 1 part cornmeal, salt, white pepper, and minced herbs), and pour into a ¾-inch deep half sheet pan to slightly overflowing. Even off the top, using a ruler or straightedge. Refrigerate until cold, then cut into 1½-inch squares. Scoop out each square, using a small Parisienne scoop, sauté the squares in hot olive oil or butter until golden brown on the bottom, then allow to cool. Fill each square with a paste made of cream cheese and minced sun-dried tomatoes, and garnish with a small dot of basil pesto.

Polish Pieces

Square pumpernickel crouton, spread with a paste made of cream cheese, drained sauerkraut, and caraway seed. Top with a slice of grilled or sautéed kielbasa (Polish-style sausage), a dot of the cream cheese, and garnish with a diamond-shaped piece of red onion.

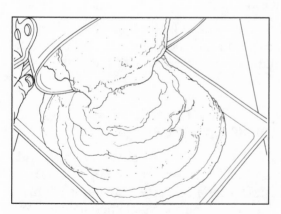

Rinse a baking pan with cold water, leaving it slightly wet, then pour in the hot cooked polenta.

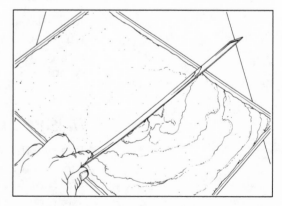

Even off the polenta by sliding a straightedge across the top edge of the pan (discard the excess that spills over the sides).

Figure 2.2
Filling a pan with polenta

Prosciutto and Fennel Points

Triangular crouton, spread with garlic and basalmic vinegar cream cheese paste, topped with a paper-thin slice of prosciutto, garnished with a dot of the paste and a piece of paper-thin shaved and briefly blanched fennel root.

Prosciutto and Melon Canapés

Baguette crouton spread with pistachio butter, topped with paper-thin prosciutto folded into a small fan, topped with a dot of cream cheese, garnished with a melon ball.

Roast Duck Canapés

Round crouton spread with orange butter, topped with a slice of roasted duck breast, garnished with orange segments and sprinkled with chopped toasted pistachios.

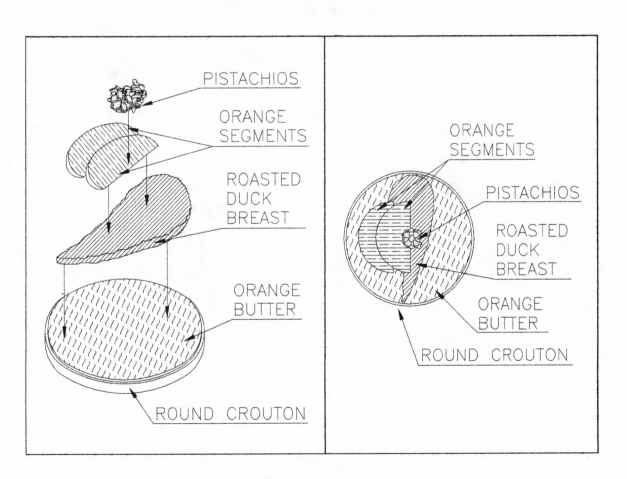

Roast Duck Canapé

Roquefort Cheese Bouchées

Fill a small bouchée with a paste made of 1 part Roquefort cheese mashed with 1 part butter, garnish with sliced radish and a sprig of parsley. See Figure 2.3.

Salmon Tartar Canapés

Spread a large slice of toasted pullman pumpernickel with butter. Top with a layer of finely minced raw salmon, seasoned with lemon juice, salt, white pepper, and dill. Cut into squares or diamonds, and garnish with a red onion triangle and poached lemon zest. (See color plate.)

Shrimp in Heat

Cucumber bouchée cut on a vertical bias, filled with wasabi-flavored cocktail sauce, filled with a shrimp poached on a bamboo skewer (so that it remains straight), tail left on, and garnish with radish sprouts.

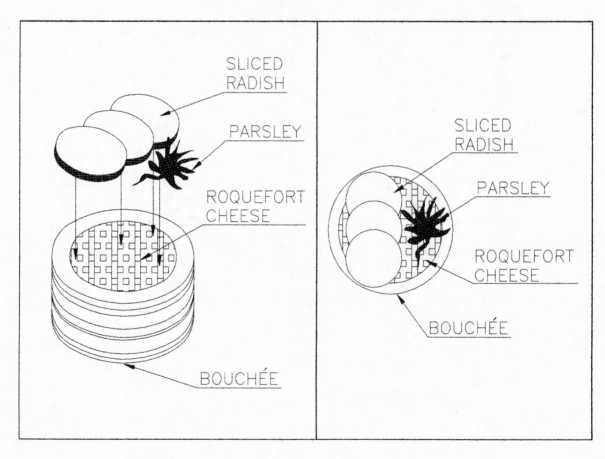

Roquefort Cheese Bouchée Canapé

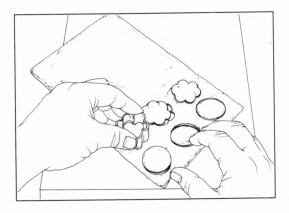

Punch out small rounds of puff pastry, using round or floral-shaped cutters.

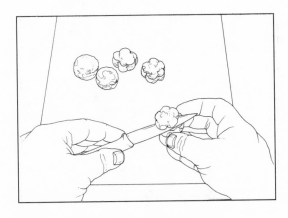

After baking, slice off the tops.

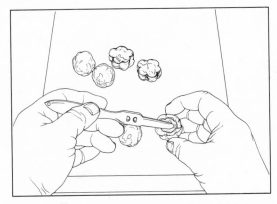

Press down the interior of each bouchée, then fill as required.

Figure 2.3
Making a puff pastry bouchée

Smoke and Puff

Cucumber bouchée filled with a paste made of smoked salmon, dill, and cream cheese, garnished with a salmon egg and a sprig of dill. See Figure 2.4.

Smoked Salmon Roulade

Lay very thin slices of smoked salmon, slightly overlapping, onto a sheet of plastic wrap or parchment paper. Place a sheet of nori on top of this, and spread a very thin layer of dill cream cheese, allowing a ½-inch border. Roll tightly, wrap in plastic, and freeze. Slice ¼-inch thick, place onto a round crouton spread with butter, and garnish with a sprig of dill.

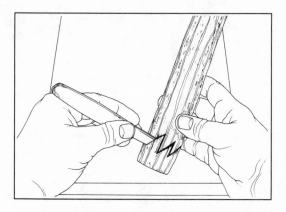

Cut a zigzag into a hothouse (English) cucumber, then cut into approximately 1-inch segments.

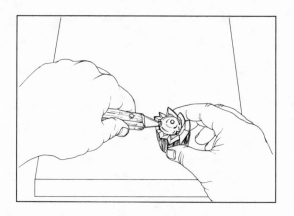

Scoop out the interior, using the small end of a Parisienne scoop, and fill as required.

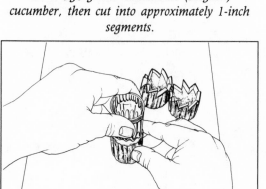

Punch out the interior of a cucumber segment, using a floral cutter (discard the skin).

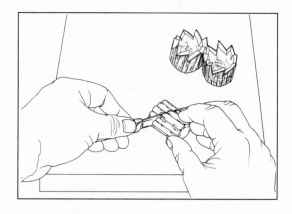

Cut each segment in half, on the bias (see first variety shown for comparison).

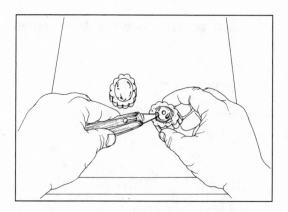

Scoop out each segment, and fill as required.

Figure 2.4
Cutting two varieties of cucumber bouchée

Smoked Chicken Mousse Bouchées

Prepare a mousse with finely chopped or ground smoked chicken, cream cheese, and Dijon-style mustard. Pipe into a puff pastry bouchée, and garnish with a wedge of quail egg, toasted walnut half, and a sprig of chervil.

Snow Peas Stuffed with Roquefort Cheese

Remove the very ends of snow peas, removing the thin strand of fiber from each side as you snap off the ends. Carefully open one side of each snow pea, and pipe in a paste of Roquefort cheese mashed with cream cheese. Garnish with carrot curls.

Southwest Starburst

Remove the tops from miniature patty pan squash, scoop out, blanch briefly in boiling salted water, drain, and cool. Spread a round crouton with cayenne pepper paste, top with the squash, and fill with salsa fresca (tomato, green pepper, red onion, cilantro, and lime juice).

Spicy Shrimp on a Chip

Cut flour tortillas into 1½-inch circles, sauté or deep fry until golden brown, drain, and cool. Spread with jalapeño cream cheese paste (see recipe for Jalapeño Paste, page 66), top with a small grilled shrimp, and garnish with the cream cheese paste, cilantro leaf, and a red pepper spear.

Swedish Cucumber Canapés

Small skinless English cucumber bouchée, filled with a little mustard-dill sauce, topped with a rolled rosette of Gravlax, garnished with a sprig of dill.

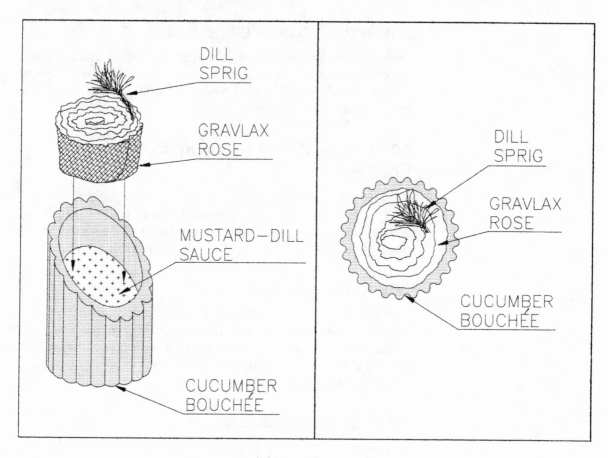

Swedish Cucumber Canapé

$\mathcal{T}$HAI-STYLE CHICKEN ON FRIED WONTON

2 8-ounce chicken breasts,
  pounded thin
2 tablespoons curry powder
¼ cup coconut milk
2 garlic cloves, pressed
2 tablespoons hot chili oil
salt as needed

24 wonton skins
oil as needed
1½ cups peanut butter
¼ cup coconut milk
3 tablespoons hot chili oil
2 scallions

- Marinate the chicken in the curry powder, ¼ cup of coconut milk, garlic, 2 tablespoons of hot chili oil, and salt for several hours.

- Brush the wonton skins with water, fold in half, and cut each into 2 triangles. Sauté or deep fry until golden brown, drain, and cool.

- Drain the chicken, and grill or sauté.

- Make a paste with the peanut butter, ¼ cup of coconut milk, and 3 tablespoons of hot chili oil. Spread a little of this paste on each wonton, and top with a slice of the grilled chicken. Top the chicken with a rosette of the peanut butter mixture, and garnish with a slice of scallion cut on the bias.

𝒯UNA CARPACCIO ON TOAST POINTS

6 ounces fresh, boneless ahi tuna, sliced paper-thin (see note in left margin)
¼ cup Kimberly champagne vinegar
1 tablespoon sherry vinegar
2 tablespoons olive oil
1 tablespoon fresh tarragon leaves, minced

salt and pepper to taste
4 large slices white bread
unsalted butter as needed
1 head bibb lettuce, separated into 16 leaf cups
1 small red bell pepper, cut into very fine, uniform julienne

The most efficient way to slice tuna is to wrap it securely in parchment paper and aluminum foil, and freeze. When needed, peel back the wrapping, slice paper thin with an electric slicer, and place directly on a serving plate. It will thaw out in minutes and can then be garnished for service.

- Combine the vinegars, oil, tarragon, salt, and pepper. Beat together, pour over the sliced tuna, cover, and marinate in the refrigerator for 3 hours.
- Toast the bread, allow to cool, then spread with a light coating of butter. Trim the crusts and cut into 16 uniform triangles.
- Place a lettuce cup on each triangle. Top with a piece of sliced tuna, and garnish with the julienned pepper.

Hot Dishes

Hot canapés are not a heated version of cold canapés. They are a separate category of hot appetizers given the name canapé because of the base of toasted bread. It is also important to note that there is a fine line between dishes considered *hot canapés* and those termed *croûtes* or *croustades* (crusts). Technically, a canapé, whether hot or cold, is served on a slice of trimmed, toasted bread; croûtes and croustades are served on a thicker slice of bread that has been scooped out, forming a cavity, then toasted. In practice, the terms are interchangeable.

The only criterion for hot canapés that is the same for cold, is that the base should be trimmed and toasted. Unless otherwise specified, the bread used for the base is basic white bread. The size of the base depends on the size of the serving dish; the shape of the base is usually square; the garnish, if not specified, is open to creative expression; and an adhesive is unnecessary. Hot canapés are ideally served in individual ovenproof dishes as an appetizer at a sit-down or formal dinner, or buffet style, served from a larger vessel at a buffet table to each dining guest's plate. Some excellent varieties follow.

Andalusian Canapés
(Canapés à l'Andalousienne)

Round crouton toasted, spread with anchovy butter, topped with a medium boiled onion hollowed out, filled with a mixture of caviar and minced hard-boiled egg, topped with bread crumbs mixed with melted butter and ground pepper, and baked until brown.

Basel Canapés
(Canapés à la Bâloise)

2 cups chopped onion, simmered in 1 cup half-and-half or heavy cream until soft; puréed in a food processor, seasoned with salt and white pepper, poured over a toasted crouton, topped with a thick-slice of Gruyère cheese, and baked.

Bayonne Canapés
(Canapés à la Bayonnaise)

Toasted crouton topped with chopped ham bound in Madeira sauce, sprinkled with grated Parmesan cheese, and baked.

Bernese Canapés
(Canapés à la Bernoise)

Toasted crouton topped with chopped ham bound in cream sauce, covered with a slice of Gruyère cheese, and baked.

Bresse Canapés
(Canapés à la Bressane)

Toasted crouton topped with slices of fried or grilled ham, topped with sautéed chicken livers and mushrooms, drizzled with brown butter (*beurre noisette*).

Bristol Canapés
(Canapés à la Bristol)

Toasted crouton topped with slices of fried or grilled ham, slices of poached beef marrow, garnished with a large grilled or broiled mushroom cap and chopped parsley.

Broiled Sardines
(Sardines Grillée)

Toasted crouton topped with sardine fillets, drizzled with melted butter, baked until hot.

Charles V Canapés
(Canapés à la Charles V)

Thick toasted crouton, hollowed out slightly, filled with poached carp, shad, or other fish roe, topped with cheese soufflé mixture (recipe follows), baked until golden brown.

Basic Cheese Soufflé

3 tablespoons unsalted
    butter
6 tablespoons flour
1 cup milk, hot
4 large egg yolks

¾ cup grated Gruyère and/
    or Parmesan cheese
5 large egg whites, beaten to
    a stiff peak

- Melt the butter, and blend in the flour. Cook several minutes, stirring continuously without browning. Add the hot milk and stir until completely blended. Simmer while stirring continuously, until very thick. Set aside, and allow to cool, about 15 minutes.
- Add the cheese, and blend thoroughly.
- Add the yolks one at a time, and beat in thoroughly. Add half the beaten whites, and fold in gently, using a rubber spatula. Add the remaining white, and fold in.
- Pour over the designated dish, and bake in a preheated 375°F oven until puffed up and golden brown.

Deviled Sardines
(Sardines à la Diable)

Toasted crouton spread with mustard-cayenne butter, topped with sardine fillets, and baked until hot.

Diana Canapés
(Canapés à la Diana)

Toasted buttered crouton, topped with crisp bacon and sautéed chicken livers, garnished with chopped parsley.

Dutch Canapés
(Canapés à la Hollandaise)

Round toasted buttered crouton, topped with scrambled eggs mixed with smoked haddock, drizzled with melted butter.

Florence Canapés
(Canapé à la Florentine)

Toasted crouton topped with a mixture of chopped spinach blended with Mornay sauce, sprinkled with Parmesan cheese and browned.

Forest Mushroom Canapés
(Canapés à la Forestière)

Rectangular rye bread crouton brushed with butter, topped with assorted wild mushrooms (cépe, chanterelle, morel, oyster, shiitake, etc.) sautéed in butter and bound with a little Madeira sauce, topped with a large grilled mushroom cap.

Game Canapés
(Canapés de Gibier)

Round toasted crouton, spread with finely chopped game and mushrooms bound in Madeira sauce, garnished with sliced truffles.

•

With the addition of a cheese soufflé mixture on top of the cheese, this dish becomes a Swiss Cheese Talmouse (*Talmouse de Fromage*).

Gruyère Canapés
(Canapés au Fromage de Gruyère)

Cut four equal squares of puff pastry, and brush two of them with egg wash. Place some grated Gruyère cheese on top, then the second square. Brush the tops with egg wash, and bake until puffed up and golden brown.

Hungarian Sardines
(Canapés à la Hongroise)

Sardines mashed with sautéed diced onion and paprika, spread on a toasted crouton, topped with Hungarian sauce (chicken velouté flavored with beef or veal glaze, finished with sour cream and white wine), baked, and sprinkled with paprika.

Ivanhoe Canapés
(Canapés à la Ivanhoe)

Round toasted crouton, spread with a paste of ground smoked haddock and butter, topped with a large grilled or broiled mushroom cap, and baked.

Mushroom Canapés
(Canapés aux Champignons)

Round toasted croutons, topped with diced mushrooms sautéed in butter, sprinkled with Parmesan cheese, and baked.

Oyster Canapés
(Canapés à la Belleclaire)

Toasted buttered crouton, covered with a slice of grilled or sautéed ham, followed by sautéed sliced mushrooms, topped by one or two breaded and deep-fried oysters, and garnished with a sprig of fried parsley.

Provence Canapés
(Canapés à la Provençale)

Toasted baguette slice, spread with olive tapenade, topped with a piece of roasted red bell pepper, then a slice of mozzarella, sprinkled with grated cheese, and glazed. (See color plate.)

Sardines with Cheese
(Sardines au Fromage)

Toasted crouton covered with sardines, topped with Parmesan cheese soufflé mixture, and baked until golden brown.

Scotch Woodcock

Toasted buttered crouton, spread with soft scrambled eggs, garnished with a crisscross of anchovy and capers. (See color plate.)

Strasbourg Canapés
(Canapés à la Strasbourgeoise)

Round buttered toasted crouton, topped with a slice of apple sautéed in butter, a slice of sautéed foie gras, and a second slice of sautéed apple. (See color plate.)

Victoria Canapés
(Canapés à la Victoria)

Crouton topped with a salpicon of finely diced lobster, truffle, and mushrooms, bound in a very thick béchamel sauce, topped with fine dry bread crumbs moistened with clarified butter, and baked until golden brown.

Wild Mushroom Canapés
(Canapés à la Forestière)

Toasted crouton, topped with wild mushrooms bound with Madeira sauce, baked, garnished with a fluted (decorated) mushroom, and sprinkled with chopped parsley. (See color plate.)

SANDWICHES The sandwich was named after John Montagu, the fourth earl of Sandwich (1718–1792). These edible concoctions were prepared for him so that the inveterate gambler could remain at the gaming table without interruptions for meals. (The Bookmaker Canapé described in this section is reportedly the original sandwich ordered by Montagu.)

The argument against the sandwich is best recounted in the words of Henri Charpentier, in his 1934 autobiography, *Life à la Henri*. In it he shares the words of Jean Camous, his mentor: "A man should always see what he eats. It is true that the eyes and the nose give the signals for the release of the chemical fluids which are secreted in the body by an intelligence of tremendous significance in the philosophy of a chef." In essence, Camous was speaking of a physiological mechanism in the human body, by which the visual perception of a food item is as significant as the actual ingestion of the food. *People eat with their eyes first* is the axiom culinary professionals adhere to in our time. If a food item *looks* good (appetizing), it follows that it will also *taste* good.

Bayonne Canapés
(Canapés à la Bayonnaise)

Two rectangular pieces of white bread, spread with parsley butter, and filled with very thin slices of Bayonne-style ham.

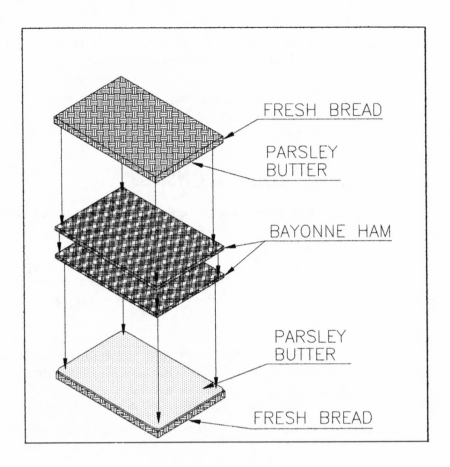

FRESH BREAD

PARSLEY BUTTER

BAYONNE HAM

PARSLEY BUTTER

FRESH BREAD

Bayonne Canapé

Bookmaker Canapés
(Canapés à la Bookmaker)

Two rectangular croutons spread with butter, with a thin slice of rare beef tenderloin, seasoned with prepared mustard and prepared horseradish placed between them.

*C*ALIFORNIA SANDWICH

8 slices 9-grain bread,
  toasted
½ cup mayonnaise
¾ cup low-fat yogurt
12 thin slices Monterey Jack
  cheese
1 large ripe Haas avocado,
  peeled, and cut into 16
  wedges

1 cup alfalfa sprouts
2 large vine-ripened tomatoes, sliced thin
8 raw carrot sticks
8 raw celery sticks
8 raw cucumber sticks,
  peeled and seeded

- Blend the mayonnaise and yogurt together. Spread on one side of each of the toasted bread slices.
- Arrange the cheese, avocado, sprouts, and tomatoes (evenly divided) on four slices of bread. Top each with a second slice of bread, and cut in half. Serve with carrot, celery, and cucumber sticks.

.... # *C*ROQUE MONSIEUR

8 ½-inch thick slices fresh white bread
unsalted butter (soft) as needed
12 ounces Gruyère cheese, sliced very thin

12 ounces ham, sliced very thin
6 eggs, well beaten
2 cups (approximately) clarified butter
8 sprigs watercress

- Preheat an oven to 350°F.
- Spread a light coating of butter on one side of each slice of bread. Top each of four slices with 1½ ounces of cheese, then 3 ounces of ham, followed by 1½ ounces of cheese. Place the remaining slices of bread, butter side down, on top of these.
- Trim the crusts from each sandwich, and place in the egg wash for 2 or 3 minutes, coating the bread thoroughly. Wipe off excess egg.
- Place about ½ inch of butter in a heavy-gauge sauté pan or cast-iron skillet, and heat over medium flame. Sauté the sandwiches in the butter until golden brown on both sides. Transfer to the oven, and bake for 5 minutes. Cut the sandwiches in half, and serve garnished with the watercress and a side dish of cole slaw or another marinated salad. (See color plate.)

———————————— • ————————————

The Croque Monsieur sandwich is believed to have been created at a Parisian café in the early 1900s. The word *croque* simply means "crunch," and variations include Croque à la Brandade, made with Brandade de Morue—a paste fashioned from salt cod, oil, garlic, and lemon—and sliced tomato; Croque Jeune-Fille, substituting the ham with sliced chicken breast, and the Gruyère with Gouda; Croque Madame, a Croque Monsieur served with a baked egg on top; Croque Marin, substituting the ham with thinly sliced shellfish; and Croque Monte Cristo, a triple-decker sandwich made with turkey, ham, and cheese.

$\mathcal{M}$OZZARELLA EN CARROZZA

For the Sauce

2 tablespoons unsalted butter
½ small tin anchovy fillets,
minced

2 tablespoons parsley,
minced
¼ cup capers, drained
the juice of 1 lemon

For the Sandwich

1 fat loaf Italian bread
(minimum 3½ inches in
diameter)
1 pound mozzarella cheese,
sliced ¼-inch thick

5 eggs, beaten with ¼ cup
milk
1 cup milk
dry bread crumbs as needed
vegetable oil as needed

- Combine the sauce ingredients, and simmer for 3 minutes. Set aside, keeping warm.
- Slice the bread into ½-inch thick slices, and using a cookie cutter, cut them into 3-inch circles. Cut the sliced mozzarella into 2½-inch circles.
- Place a slice of cheese between 2 slices of bread. Dip the edges in milk, and pinch together securely. Dip the entire sandwich including the edges, in the beaten egg, brush off any excess egg, then coat with bread crumbs. Refrigerate for ½ hour.
- Heat ½-inch deep oil to a temperature of 375°F. Fry the sandwiches to golden brown on both sides. Place on absorbent paper, and put into the oven until all the sandwiches are fried. Serve accompanied by the anchovy sauce.

$\mathcal{P}$EANUT BUTTER AND JELLY CLUB SANDWICH

12 slices whole wheat bread,
toasted
unsalted butter as needed
2 cups chunky peanut butter
1 cup Zinfandel grape jelly
1 large banana, peeled, and
sliced very thin
1 cup low-fat yogurt

¾ cup dried currants,
soaked in hot water
6 green seedless grapes
6 red seedless grapes
1 Granny Smith apple, cut
into 12 wedges, and
sprinkled with lemon
juice
8 large sprigs of mint

- Spread one side of the bread lightly with the butter. Spread the peanut butter onto four slices of bread. Top with the jelly, then place another slice of bread, butter side down, on top of this.
- Spread the yogurt on the second slice of bread. Top with the drained currants and the sliced banana. Place the final slice of bread on top of the banana, buttered side down.
- Trim the crusts on all four sides. Run a toothpick through each grape, and put four of these into each sandwich. Cut each sandwich into quarters, stand up on its outside edge, and serve garnished with fresh mint and sliced apple.

·················· ℛEUBEN GRILL

2 slices rye bread
¼ cup Thousand Island
  dressing
4 ounces corned beef, sliced

2 slices Swiss cheese
¼ cup sauerkraut
½ cup clarified butter

- Brush one side of both slices of rye bread with clarified butter. Spread the dressing on the other side. Top one slice (dressing side) with corned beef, the sauerkraut, and the cheese. Top with the other slice of bread, dressing side down.
- In a sauté pan, or on a hot griddle top, brown the sandwich on both sides in the remaining clarified butter. Place in a preheated 375°F oven for 10 minutes. Remove from the oven, cut in half, and serve, garnished appropriately.

················· 𝒮PINACH AND CUCUMBER PITA SANDWICH

¼ cup olive oil
6 garlic cloves, pressed
1 bunch spinach, stemmed,
  and well rinsed
the juice of 1 lemon
¼ cup fresh mint, cut into a
  fine julienne
12 ounces low-fat plain
  yogurt

1 small cucumber, peeled
  and seeded, and sliced
  thin
salt, pepper, and ground
  cumin to taste
4 pitas
¼ cup sesame seeds, toasted

- Sauté the garlic briefly in the olive oil, without browning. Set aside.

- Blanch the spinach in a small amount of boiling salted water for several minutes. Drain, squeeze dry, and finely chop.
- Combine the oil, garlic, spinach, lemon, mint, yogurt, salt, pepper, and cumin, and blend thoroughly.
- Cut the pitas in half and toast in a moderate oven for 10 minutes. Stuff the pitas with the filling and the cucumber, and sprinkle with sesame seeds.

CHAPTER 3

TARTLETS AND BARQUETTES

tartlet is a small open pie, filled with various fillings. A barquette is a small open pastry in the shape of a boat.

Like canapés, tartlets and barquettes provide the chef an opportunity to create miniature works of edible art. There are a considerable number of bite-sized pastries in the hors d'oeuvres arena that bear the names of persons, places, events, or styles of creation. Tartlets and barquettes may also be specific garnishes for larger dishes (for example, Chicken Nantua—barquettes filled with hot crayfish tail ragout; Chicken Demi-Deuil—barquettes filled with hot sweetbread, mushroom, and truffle salpico; Fillet of Beef, Colbert—tartlets filled with baby vegetables, glazed with aspic).

The forms for baking tartlets and barquettes vary considerably in size, and come with straight or fluted sides. For the purposes of compiling this book, the author's preference for tartlets is the fluted variety, measuring 4 inches in diameter at the top and 3 inches at the bottom; for barquettes, straight sides, 4 inches long at the top, and 2¾ inches at the bottom. There are also sets of small pastry forms with many special shapes (diamond, elliptical, square, triangular, etc.). Although a classical barquette is oval shaped and pointed at both ends, and a tartlet is usually round, these other shapes can be used as inspiration and creativity warrant.

After the tartlet and barquette forms are filled with short pastry, they are generally baked blind (empty) before being filled. When the filling is savory, they are served hot or cold, as hors d'oeuvres or as a garnish to a larger dish. When the filling is sweet (for dessert), they are generally served cold. Unless a dish specifies a particular filling, there is no limit to the kinds of fillings one can innovate.

· · · · · · · · · · · · · · · · · · ·   𝒟OUGH I

1¼ cups all-purpose flour
½ cup (1 stick) unsalted butter, cut into ¼-inch pieces

pinch of salt
4 tablespoons ice water

- Combine the flour, butter, and salt in a bowl, and rub together until the mixture has the consistency of coarse meal. Add the water, and press together into a large ball. (Add additional water or flour if necessary; avoid overworking.) Wrap airtight, and allow to rest 30 minutes.

- Preheat an oven to 400°F.

- Roll the dough out on a lightly floured board, to a thickness of approximately ⅛ inch. Cut out a piece of dough about ½-inch larger than the form it will fill. Brush the interior of the form lightly with oil or clarified butter. Brush off excess flour from the underside of the dough, and set into the form. Trim the dough even with the edges of the form. Dock the entire bottom surface of the dough by piercing it all over with the tines of a fork. Take a second form, exactly the same as the first, and press it down onto the dough. Bake for 10 to 15 minutes, or until golden brown.

- Allow the pastries to cool for 10 minutes. Remove the top form, then invert the pastry, and carefully remove. Set aside until needed, or fill with appropriate filling, and reheat or refrigerate, depending on the recipe.

The second tartlet/barquette form pressed into the dough of the first helps to make an even pastry and to keep the dough from puffing up. Dried beans are used to prevent the dough from puffing up on large tart and pie shells.

If they are used daily, baking forms are not washed after every use. They are simply wiped out. Thus they become *seasoned*, and do not need to be greased every time they are used.

𝒟OUGH II

1 cup all-purpose flour
¼ teaspoon salt
4 tablespoons unsalted
  butter (½ stick), cut into
  ¼-inch pieces

1 egg yolk
¼ cup sour cream
ice water as needed (about 3
  tablespoons)

Ice water is very cold, but does not have ice in it. The coldness of the water is important in making a good short dough.

- Combine the flour, butter, and salt in a bowl, and rub together until the mixture has the consistency of coarse meal. Add the water, and press together into a large ball. (Add additional water or flour if necessary; avoid overworking.) Wrap airtight, and allow to rest for 30 minutes until ready to use.

- Follow directions for baking as described in the recipe for Dough I.

TARTLETS

Cold Dishes

················ # *A*NCHOVY TARTLETS

(Tartelettes d'Anchois)

2 small tins anchovy fillets
½ pound cream cheese
2 tablespoons parsley, minced
2 tablespoons tarragon, minced
1 garlic clove, pressed

2 tablespoons lemon juice
4 hard-boiled eggs, yolks and whites pressed separately through a sieve
8 baked tartlet shells
8 small parsley sprigs

- Drain the oil from the anchovies, and reserve for another use. Separate 8 well-shaped fillets, split them in half lengthwise, and set aside.
- Mash the remaining anchovies, using a fork, into a smooth paste. Add the cream cheese, herbs, garlic, and lemon juice, and blend thoroughly. Spread this paste into the 8 tartlet shells. Garnish each with the sieved yolks and whites, then with a split anchovy placed crisscross on top of the egg, and a small sprig of parsley in the center.

················ # *R*OMANOFF TARTLETS

(Tartelettes à la Romanov)

¼ cup unsalted butter
¼ cup cream cheese
3 tablespoons anchovy paste
2 tablespoons minced chives
½ cup bowfin or sturgeon caviar

½ cup salmon caviar
12 baked tartlet shells
4 ounces smoked salmon, sliced very thin
¼ cup sour cream
12 chive spears

- Combine the butter, cream cheese, anchovy paste, and chives, and blend into a smooth paste. Spread this paste on the inside bottoms of the tartlet shells.

- Carefully place the bowfin (or sturgeon) caviar along one side of the tartlet, covering one-third of the butter/anchovy paste. Repeat on the opposite side of the tartlet, using the salmon caviar. Cover the remaining one-third area (in the center of the tartlet) with a slice of smoked salmon. Garnish with a dollop of sour cream and a chive spear.

Spring Tartlets
(Tartelettes à la Printinière)

Tartlet shell, baked, filled with an attractive composition of poached baby vegetables (such as squash, turnip, carrot, broccoli flowerettes, asparagus tips, etc.), and glazed with aspic.

Hot Dishes

Agnès Sorel Tartlets
(Tartelettes à l'Agnès Sorel)

Tartlet shell, baked, filled with minced chicken breast and truffle bound with cream sauce (or reduced cream), garnished with small circles of thin-sliced beef tongue.

Alsatian Onion Tartlets
(Tartelettes à l'Alsacienne)

Tartlet shell baked, filled with finely diced and sautéed onion, topped with heavy cream beaten with eggs, seasoned with salt, pepper, and nutmeg, and baked until golden brown. (See color plate.)

Andalusian Tartlets
(Tartelettes à l'Andalousienne)

Tartlet shell baked, filled with rice pilaf made with bell peppers, tomatoes, and garlic, garnished with green and black olives. (See color plate.)

....

CHICKEN AND MUSHROOM TARTLETS
(Tartelettes de Volaille et Champignon)

2 tablespoons unsalted butter	1 cup mushrooms, finely diced
1 shallot, minced	2 tablespoons lemon juice

1 tablespoon tarragon,
  minced
1½ cups poached chicken
  breast, finely diced
¾ cup cream sauce, hot

2 egg yolks
12 baked tartlet shells
½ cup grated Parmesan
  cheese

- Preheat an oven to 400°F.
- Sauté the shallot in the butter for several minutes. Add the mushrooms, and sauté several more minutes. Add the lemon juice and tarragon, and simmer until nearly dry. Remove from the fire and set aside.
- Combine the mushrooms, chicken, and cream sauce, and blend thoroughly. Temper the egg yolks into this mixture, then spoon into the shells. Place on a baking pan, sprinkle with grated cheese, and bake for 10 minutes, or until the cheese is hot and melted.

CURRIED SHRIMP TARTLETS

(Tartelettes à la Rajah)

2 tablespoons unsalted
  butter
1 shallot, minced
¼ cup scallions, finely diced
½ teaspoon ginger root,
  grated
2 tablespoons dry white
  wine

1 tablespoon curry powder
1½ cups cooked shrimp,
  finely diced
¾ cup cream sauce
12 tartlet shells, baked
12 small mushroom caps,
  poached in white wine

- Preheat an oven to 400°F.
- Sauté the shallot and scallions in the butter for several minutes. Add the ginger, wine, and curry, and cook several minutes. Remove from the fire.
- Combine the sautéed ingredients with the cream sauce and the shrimp, and blend thoroughly. Spoon the mixture into the tartlet shells, bake until hot and bubbly, and serve each topped with a mushroom cap. (See color plate.)

Finnan Haddie Tartlets
(Tartelettes à l'Aigrefin Fumé)

Tartlet shell, baked, filled with flaked smoked haddock bound with hot curry sauce, baked.

Florence Tartlets
(Tartelettes à la Florentine)

Tartlet shell, baked, filled with finely minced spinach bound with béchamel sauce (or reduced cream), topped with a slice of hard-boiled egg, and baked until hot (crisscrossed dough strips in photo are creative addition). (See color plate.)

GOAT CHEESE TARTLETS WITH FINE HERBS

(Tartelettes au Chèvre avec Fine Herbes)

3 tablespoons butter
8 ounces goat cheese
4 ounces cream cheese
4 ounces sour cream
salt and white pepper to taste
1 teaspoon minced chives
1 teaspoon minced tarragon leaves
1 teaspoon minced cilantro leaves
4 eggs
16 tartlet shells, baked
16 4-inch long chive spears

- Preheat an oven to 375°F.
- Combine the butter, goat cheese, cream cheese, sour cream, herbs, salt, and pepper in a stainless steel or glass bowl, and cream, using an electric mixer. Add the eggs, one at a time, and continue beating until completely incorporated. Transfer this mixture to the tartlet shells, place on a baking sheet, and bake for 10 to 15 minutes, or until golden brown. Serve garnished with the chives.

Marquise Tartlets
(Tartelettes à la Marquise)

Tartlet shell lined with puff pastry, filled with grated Gruyère cheese, topped with cream sauce, and baked until golden brown.

MILAN TARTLETS

(Tartelettes à la Milanaise)

3 tablespoons olive oil
½ cup mushrooms, finely diced
3 garlic cloves, pressed
2 tablespoons basil leaves, minced
½ cup ham, finely diced

½ cup prosciutto, paper-thin and finely diced
½ cup grated pecorino cheese

½ cup small ditalini, cooked and drained
½ cup tomato purée
salt and pepper to taste
12 baked tartlet shells

- Preheat an oven to 400°F.
- Sauté the mushrooms in the olive oil. Add the garlic and basil, cook briefly, and remove from the fire.
- Combine the mushrooms, ham, prosciutto, cheese, ditalini, tomato purée, salt, and pepper. Spoon into the tartlet shells, and bake until hot and bubbly.

MUSHROOM AND TOMATO TARTLETS

(Tartelettes aux Champignons et Tomates)

4 tablespoons unsalted butter
1 shallot, minced
1 pound mushrooms, small dice
2 garlic cloves, pressed
½ cup diced tomatoes
1 tablespoon tomato paste

4 anchovy fillets, mashed
pinch of fresh thyme
salt, pepper, and nutmeg to taste
3 eggs
1 cup heavy cream
12 tartlet shells, baked

- Preheat an oven to 375°F.
- Sauté the shallot and mushrooms in the butter. Add the garlic and tomato ingredients, and simmer until almost dry. Blend in the anchovy and thyme, and season to taste. Set aside.
- Beat the eggs and cream together. Divide the mushroom mixture among the tartlets, then transfer the tartlets to a baking sheet. Fill each with the cream mixture, and bake for 20 minutes, or until the custard is firm.

ONION TARTLETS

(Tartelettes à l'Oignon)

2 bacon slices, finely diced
2 tablespoons unsalted butter
1 cup onion, finely diced

2 tablespoons chopped parsley
2 tablespoons chopped chives

2 tablespoon chopped tarragon

1 cup heavy cream

3 eggs

salt and white pepper to taste

pinch of nutmeg

12 tartlet shells, baked

- Preheat an oven to 350°F.
- Sauté the bacon until brown and crispy. Drain off the fat, add the butter and the onions, and sauté 5 minutes without coloring. Add the herbs and seasoning, blend, remove from the fire, and allow to cool.
- Beat the cream and eggs together. Divide the onion mixture among the tartlet shells, and pour in the cream mixture. Bake in a baking pan for 30 to 40 minutes, or until golden brown on top.

𝒫ARIS TARTLETS

(Tartelettes à la Parisienne)

3 tablespoons butter

1 shallot, minced

1 cup mushrooms, medium dice

¼ cup dry white wine

2 cup tomatoes, diced and drained

1 tablespoon parsley, minced

1 tablespoon tarragon, minced

salt and pepper to taste

12 tartlet shells, baked

½ cup grated Parmesan cheese

½ cup grated Gruyère cheese

- Sauté the shallot in the butter for several minutes. Add the mushrooms, and cook another 5 minutes. Add the white wine, and simmer until nearly dry. Add the tomatoes, herbs, salt, and pepper, cook several minutes, then remove from the fire.
- Preheat an oven to 400°F.
- Fill the tartlet shells with the mixture, sprinkle with the cheeses, and bake for 15 minutes or until hot and bubbly.

Provence Tartlets
(Tartelettes à la Provençale)

Follow the recipe for Paris Tartlets, substituting olive oil for the butter, and basil for the tarragon. (See color plate.)

$\mathcal{A}$ntipasti   from left to right: Asparagus Wrapped in Prosciutto (p. 35); calamata olives; sliced Roma tomatoes with anchovies; Broiled Eggplant (p. 22); Roasted Red Onions (p. 25); Marinated Artichoke Hearts (p. 26); Fennel Root (p. 23) and grilled yellow squash (see p. 26); buffalo mozzarella and roasted red bell pepper with basil leaves and Nafplion olives (p. 21); Garbanzo and Red Kidney Beans (p. 28); toasted foccacia (upper right)

Canapés (Cold)   from left to right: *Salmon Tartar (p. 108); Buttercup (p. 74); Domino (p. 79); Princess (p. 93); Véron (p. 97)*

𝒯artlets (Hot) clockwise from bottom right: *Andalouse* (p. 130); *Welsh* (p. 135); *Alsatian* (p. 130); *Provence* (followed by second Alsatian) (p. 134); *Florence* (p. 132); *Curried Shrimp* (center) (p. 131)

$\mathcal{C}$anapés (Hot) clockwise from bottom left: *Scotch Woodcock (pp. 117, 242); Epicurean Croustades (p. 172); Wild Mushroom Canapés (p. 118); Strasbourg Canapés (p. 117); Provence Canapés (p. 117)*

*B*arquettes (Cold) from top to bottom: *Greek (p. 137); Bigorre (p. 136); Northern (p. 138); Romanoff (p. 138); Norma (p. 138)*

*E*ggs (Cold)   clockwise from bottom left: *Stuffed Eggs, Felix* (p. 230); *Eggs Casino* (p. 228); *Stuffed Eggs, Florist Style* (p. 231); *Stuffed Eggs, California* (p. 230); *Eggs in Aspic* (center) (p. 228)

Vegetable Hors d'Oeuvre (Cold) clockwise from top left: *California Apples* (p. 329); *Vegetables Vinaigrette* (p. 337); *Celery Stuffed with Roquefort* (p. 330); *Beetroot Squares* (p. 328); *Cucumbers, Danish Style* (p. 331) or *Danish Barquettes* (p. 137); *Leeks Vinaigrette* (center) (p. 335)

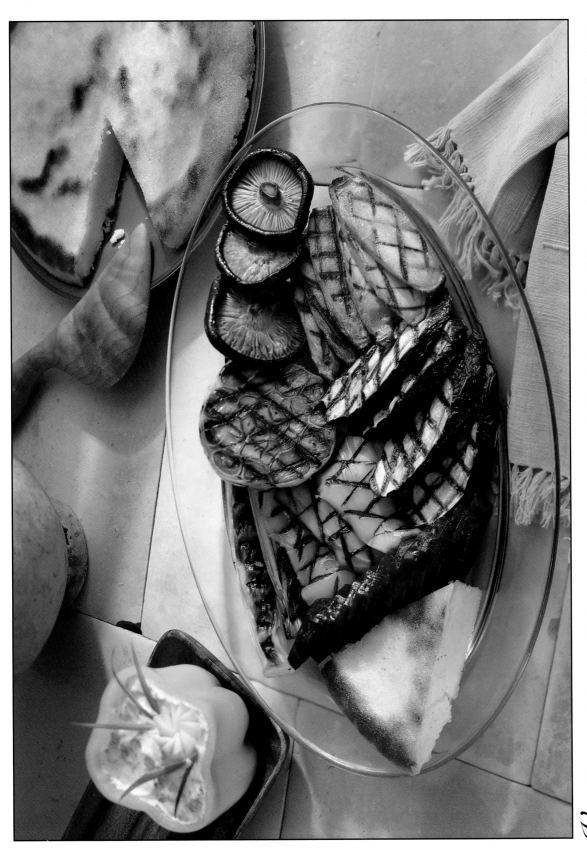

$\mathcal{V}$egetable Hors d'Oeuvre (Hot)   Grilled Vegetables California Style (from left to right) (p. 344): sun-dried tomato aioli (in hollowed-out yellow bell pepper); baked polenta (wedge); sliced roasted beets; grilled leeks (top edge); grilled yellow bell pepper; grilled zucchini; grilled half garlic bulb; grilled carrots; grilled shiitake mushrooms

Tomatoes (Cold, Stuffed)   left to right: *Oysters, Borchardt Style* (p. 272); *Tomatoes, Polish Style* (p. 380); *Tomatoes, Lucullus Style* (p. 379); *Tomatoes, Monaco Style* (p. 380); *Tomatoes, Waldorf Style* (p. 369)

Salads clockwise from bottom center: *Alexander (p. 360); Paris (p. 375); Hearts of Palm, Carnelian (p. 364); Bagration (p. 361); Pretty Helen (p. 366); Dutch (p. 372)*

Sausage Tartlets

(Tartelettes au Saucisse)

2 tablespoons unsalted butter	salt and pepper to taste
½ cup onion, small dice	12 tartlet shells, baked
½ cup green pepper, small dice	½ cup grated Parmesan cheese
½ pound ground pork sausage	½ cup grated Gruyère cheese

- Preheat an oven to 400°F.
- Sauté the onion and pepper in the butter. Add the sausage and fully cook. Season to taste with salt and pepper.
- Fill the tartlet shells with this mixture, top with the cheeses, and bake until they are hot and the cheese is melted.

Rumanian Cheese Tartlets
(Tartelettes de Fromage à la Roumaine)

Pipe a ⅓-inch deep layer of Gougère (see recipe for "Gougère" in Chapter 5, "Croustades, Pastries, and Puffs") into unbaked tartlet shells, top with additional grated Gruyère cheese, and bake in a preheated 375°F oven for 25 to 35 minutes, or until golden brown.

Welsh Tartlets

(Tartelettes à la Gallois)

1 cup leeks, white part only, well rinsed and cut into small dice	salt, white pepper, and nutmeg to taste
¾ cup cream sauce, warm	1 large green leek leaf
2 egg yolks	12 tartlet shells, baked
	clarified butter as needed

- Blanch the leeks in boiling lightly salted water until tender. Drain, cool, and set aside.
- Preheat an oven to 375°F.
- Beat the yolks into the cream sauce, and adjust seasoning. Add the leeks, and blend thoroughly. Divide this mixture among the tartlet shells.

- Blanch the leek leaf in boiling salted water, drain, cool, and cut into long ⅛-inch wide strips. Arrange them in a lattice (criss-cross) pattern on the tartlets, trim the edges, brush with butter, and bake until hot and bubbly. (See color plate.)

BARQUETTES

Cold Dishes

··················

*A*URORA BARQUETTES
(Barquettes à l'Aurora)

½ cup mayonnaise
1 tablespoon tomato paste
3 tablespoons champagne vinegar
1 teaspoon anchovy paste
¼ cup carrots, cut into fine dice
¼ cup green beans, cut into fine dice
¼ cup potatoes, cut into fine dice
¼ cup rutabagas, cut into fine dice

¼ cup black olives, cut into fine dice
¼ cup capers, drained
1 teaspoon basil, minced
1 teaspoon oregano, minced
1 teaspoon parsley, minced
salt and pepper to taste
12 baked barquette shells
2 hard-boiled eggs, yolks and whites sieved separately

- Blanch the vegetables separately, in boiling salted water, until al dente. Set aside to cool.
- Blend the mayonnaise, tomato paste, vinegar, and anchovy paste together until smooth. Add the vegetables and herbs, blend thoroughly, and season with salt and pepper. Marinate at least 2 hours.
- Fill the barquette shells with the salad and garnish with the sieved hard-boiled egg.

Bigorre Barquettes
(Barquettes à la Bigorre)

Barquette shell, baked, spread with tarragon butter, topped with a slice of poached salmon (cut to size), decorated with tarragon leaves, and glazed with aspic. (See color plate.)

Caledonian Barquettes
(Barquettes à la Calédonie)

Barquette shell, baked, filled dome-shaped with ham mousse, covered with a thin slice of ham, decorated with blanched leek leaves, small diamond-shaped slices of truffle, and hard-boiled egg white, glazed with aspic.

Danish Barquettes
(Barquettes à la Danoise)

Cut small rectangular boats measuring approximately 2 inches long by 1 inch wide, from a hothouse cucumber. (See Figure 3.1.) Prepare a mousse with finely ground smoked salmon and smoked herring, minced hard-boiled eggs, and cream cheese, seasoned with prepared horseradish squeezed dry. Fill the boats with the mousse, and garnish with chopped egg whites, sieved yolks, and a cucumber loop (optional). (See color plate.)

Greek Barquettes
(Barquettes à la Greque)

Barquette shell, baked, filled with a salad consisting of assorted vegetables (such as bell pepper, carrot, radish, rutabaga, zucchini) cut out with a pea scoop (noisette) or cut into small dice (brunoise), blanched al dente, and marinated in a Greek-style vinaigrette. (See color plate.)

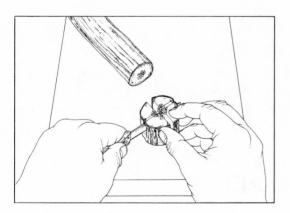

Cut a hothouse or standard cucumber into 1½-inch segments. Cut each segment lengthwise into quarters.

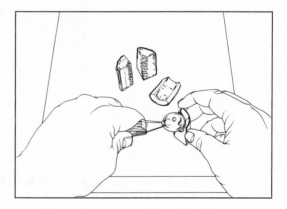

Scoop out the interior of each quarter, using a spoon or a Parisienne scoop.

Figure 3.1
Cutting a cucumber barquette

Indian Barquettes
(Barquettes à l'Indienne)

Barquette shell baked, filled with a little rice pilaf, followed by ground or finely minced chicken and ham bound in curry mayonnaise, garnished with sliced hard-boiled egg and chopped parsley.

Mirabeau Barquettes
(Barquettes à la Mirabeau)

Barquette shell baked, filled with chopped hard-boiled egg bound with anchovy butter, garnished with anchovy fillet.

Norma Barquettes
(Barquettes à la Norma)

Barquette shell baked, filled with finely ground tuna salad, garnished with sieved hard-boiled egg, caviar, chives, and lemon (lemon omitted from photo). (See color plate.)

Northern Barquettes
(Barquettes du Norde)

Barquette shell baked, filled with finely diced chicken salad, garnished with asparagus tips and a small slice of truffle. (See color plate.)

Romanoff Barquettes
(Barquettes à la Romanov)

Barquette shell baked, filled with a finely diced egg salad, covered with a slice of smoked salmon, garnished with sour cream and caviar. (See color plate. The filigree trellis shown is a creative addition).

················· # 𝓡USSIAN BARQUETTES

(Barquettes à la Russe)

For the Dough

3 ounces cream cheese, soft   1 cup flour
4 ounces butter, soft   pinch of salt

For the Filling

2 tablespoons unsalted
  butter
2 shallots, minced
1 cup sour cream
salt and white pepper to
  taste

2 ounces osetra or sevruga
  caviar
12 pâte à choux trellises
12 chive sprigs

• Combine the dough ingredients until they form a smooth paste. Allow to rest 30 minutes. Roll out, fill the shells, and bake, as described at the beginning of this chapter.

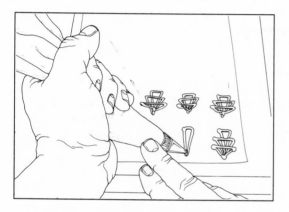

Fit a pastry bag with a No. 1 round tip, and fill the bag with pâte à choux (puff paste).

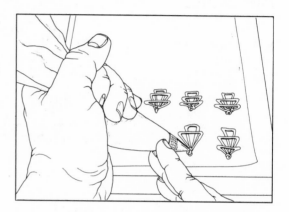

Pipe out small geometric patterns onto parchment paper, building up the filigree trellises in three stages.

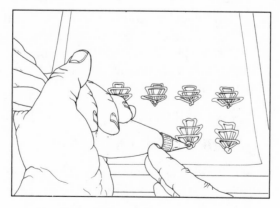

Bake until golden brown, then gently remove from the paper, set aside, and use for garnishing canapés, barquettes, tartlettes, and so forth.

Figure 3.2
Piping filigree trellises

- Sauté the shallots in the butter. Remove from the fire, and allow to cool. Blend the shallots, sour cream, salt, and pepper together. Fill the barquette shells with this mixture. Garnish each with a little caviar, a trellis, and a sprig of chive.

Varsovian Barquettes
(Barquettes à la Varsovienne)

Barquette shell baked, filled with a salad composed of finely diced cooked beets, sour gherkins, and hard-boiled egg whites, garnished with caviar and sieved egg yolks.

Hot Dishes

· · · · · · · · · · · · · · · · · ·

ENGLISH BARQUETTES

(Barquettes à l'Anglaise)

1 tablespoon unsalted butter	1 tablespoon parsley, minced
1 shallot, minced	1 cup béchamel sauce, hot
¾ cup ham, finely diced	½ cup grated sharp cheddar
3 tablespoons gherkins, finely diced	cheese
	16 barquette shells

- Preheat an oven to 400°F.
- Sauté the shallot in the butter for several minutes. Add the ham, gherkins, and parsley, and sauté several more minutes. Remove from the fire and set aside.
- Combine the sautéed ingredients and half of the cheese with the béchamel sauce, and blend thoroughly. Spoon this mixture into the shells, and top with some of the cheddar cheese. Place in a baking pan, and bake for 10 minutes, or until the cheese is hot and melted.

Lobster Barquettes
(Barquettes à l'Américaine)

Barquette shell baked, filled with finely diced cooked lobster bound in American sauce, garnished with a small piece of lobster.

Mussel Barquettes, Saffron Sauce

(Barquettes aux Moules et Safran)

20 barquette shells
1 shallot, minced
1 cup dry white wine
1 sprig thyme
24 large mussels, debearded
   and well rinsed
pinch of saffron

1 cup leeks, white part only,
   finely diced
1 cup heavy cream
salt and white pepper as
   needed
¼ cup minced chives

- Steam the mussels, covered, in the shallots, wine, and thyme, until all the shells are open. Remove the mussels from the shells, set aside, and discard the shells.

- Add the saffron and leeks to the wine broth, and simmer until almost dry. Add the cream and reduce by half. Add the mussels to this sauce, and season to taste with salt and white pepper.

- Place one mussel in each barquette shell, and top with a little sauce. Heat in the oven for several minutes and sprinkle with the chives.

Oyster Barquettes
(Barquettes des Huîtres)

Barquette shell baked, filled with a poached oyster, coated with cream sauce, sprinkled with grated cheese, and glazed under the broiler.

Shad Roe Barquettes
(Barquettes au Caviar d'Alose)

Barquette shell baked, filled with finely chopped cooked shad roe, bound with cream sauce, sprinkled with Parmesan cheese, and glazed under the broiler.

CHAPTER 4

SOUPS

*C*HICKEN BOUILLON, SPRING STYLE

(Bouillon de Volaille, Printinière)

For the Bouillon

6 pounds fresh chicken bones, backs, necks, and wings
1 whole fresh chicken, cut into 8 pieces
2 gallons water
1 large onion, peeled and coarsely chopped
1 large carrot, peeled, top removed, and coarsely chopped

2 celery stalks, coarsely chopped
1 leek, well rinsed and coarsely chopped
2 bay leaves
3 sprigs thyme
1 bunch parsley stems
1 teaspoon white peppercorns, crushed

For the Garnish

2 cups assorted vegetables (celery, carrot, leek, zucchini, turnip, sweet potato, etc.), cut into fine

julienne measuring 1 × ¼ × ¼ inches, and blanched in lightly salted boiling water

- Rinse the bones and chicken thoroughly in cold water. Place in a stockpot, and cover with enough water so that it is 4 inches above the highest bone. Bring the stock to a boil, drain and discard the liquid, and rinse the bones and chicken again in cold water.

- In a clean stockpot, cover the bones again with cold water, 4 inches above the highest bone, and bring to a simmer. Skim the top of the stock, removing the fat and foam. Add the aromatics (herbs), simmer *very gently* for 1 hour, then remove the whole chicken. When cool, remove the meat from the chicken, cover, and refrigerate for another use. Return the bones of the chicken to the stock, and continue simmering another 3 to 5 hours, skimming fat and impurities from the top periodically. Strain, adjust seasoning with salt, white pepper, and, if necessary, a little chicken glaze. Serve garnished with the julienned vegetables.

———————— • ————————

A bouillon is technically any stock made with meat in addition to bones, hence the inclusion of a whole chicken. It is a very clear broth, clarified through a *natural clarifying process*. The initial boiling and rewashing of the nutritional element (bones and meat) is a trick learned from a Cantonese cook many years ago, which effectively cleans the bones and meat. There will still remain enough naturally occurring albumen (in the bones, meat, and vegetables) for the clarifying process to take place. The subsequent slow, gentle simmering is also of *utmost importance*, since it allows the albumen to act as a clarifying agent. A more extreme clarifying process is employed in preparing consommé, in which egg whites, meat, and aromatics are added as additional clarifying agents.

---

*C*ONSOMMÉ WITH RUBY PORT

6 large egg whites
1 tablespoon kosher salt
1 pound lean ground veal or beef
1 celery stalk, coarsely chopped
1 small leek, well rinsed and coarsely chopped
1 carrot, peeled, top removed, and coarsely chopped
1 garlic clove, crushed
½ teaspoon black peppercorns, crushed

2 sprigs thyme
1 sprig rosemary
1 bay leaf
2 ripe tomatoes, coarsely chopped
3 quarts cold rich brown veal or beef stock
½ cup Ruby Port wine
1 cup mixed vegetables, cut into a very fine dice (brunoise) and blanched (such as celery, carrot, leek, zucchini, sweet potato, etc.)

- In a large bowl, whip the egg whites and salt until frothy. Add all the remaining ingredients except the stock, wine, and vegetables, and blend thoroughly.

- Place the stock in a large heavy-gauge pot, and blend in the above ingredients combined with egg whites. Over maximum heat, stir continuously, until the stock mixture reaches a temperature of approximately 150°F. Turn the fire down low, and allow the brew to simmer *very gently* for 1 hour.

- With a perforated spoon, very carefully lift out a section of the *raft*, and discard. From this opening, gently ladle out the broth, and strain through 4 layers of cheesecloth. Discard any remaining raft.

- Lay a piece of paper towel on the top of the broth, then remove and discard. Continue this process until all of the fat that sits on top of the broth is gone.
- Bring the soup back to a boil, add the port wine, adjust seasoning with salt, and serve garnished with the diced vegetables.

---•---

Consommé is a *mechanically*, as opposed to *naturally*, clarified broth. The initial continuous stirring step is extremely important. The egg whites will sit on the bottom of the cold stock and burn if the soup is not stirred. (There is no rescuing a consommé if this happens.) As the temperature rises, the egg whites and the aromatics will begin to rise and form a raft on the top of the soup, which is part of the clarifying process. At 190°F the broth will simmer, and the convection movement of the stock will move it through the raft as the egg whites slowly coagulate, effectively removing the impurities from the stock. This yields a crystal-clear broth, the earmark of a fine consommé. It takes practice to execute a consommé, and any culinary practitioner who has learned this dish has surely burned at least one,—which at least provides a better understanding of the technique.

DUTCH LENTIL SOUP

For the Stock

2 veal shanks
2 pork knuckles
1 onion, peeled and coarsely chopped
1 carrot, peeled and coarsely chopped
1 stalk celery, coarsely chopped

1 large leek, green tops only, well rinsed and coarsely chopped
1 bay leaf
1 teaspoon black peppercorns, crushed
1 bunch parsley stems, rinsed and trimmed
2 sprigs thyme
2 quarts water

For the Soup

1½ cups green lentils, culled and rinsed

½ cup olive oil
1 medium onion, peeled and cut into medium dice

1 large carrot, peeled and
   cut into medium dice
2 stalks celery, peeled and
   cut into medium dice

1 leek, white part only,
   rinsed, root removed, and
   cut into medium dice
1 large potato, peeled and
   cut into medium dice

—————— • ——————

Leftover lentil soup can be
reheated, puréed, and served
with sliced cooked sausage
or croutons for a second
service.

- Simmer the stock ingredients 4 hours. Strain, reserving stock.
  Remove the meat from the shanks and knuckles, coarsely chop,
  and reserve.
- Sauté the vegetables in the oil for 5 minutes. Add the lentils,
  and cook several minutes. Add the stock and meat, and simmer
  about 30 minutes until the lentils are fully cooked. Adjust
  seasoning with salt and pepper.

CREAMED SOUPS

*C*REAM OF ASPARAGUS SOUP

(Potage Crème d'Asperge)

1 pound fat asparagus
6 tablespoons unsalted butter
1 shallot, finely chopped
1 small onion, finely
   chopped
1 bay leaf
pinch of nutmeg

6 tablespoons flour
3 cups chicken stock, hot
1 cup heavy cream
salt and white pepper to
   taste
4 baguette croutons
2 tablespoons sour cream
4 sprigs fresh chervil

- Trim the woody ends from the bottom of the asparagus, and
  discard. Peel the remaining spears, reserving the peels. Cut
  these spears in half, and finely chop the bottom halves. Cut the
  top halves into 1/4-inch pieces, blanch in lightly salted boiling
  water, and set aside.
- Sauté the shallot, onion, bay leaf, peelings, and finely chopped
  asparagus in the butter. Add the nutmeg and flour, blend well,
  and cook 5 minutes without browning. Add the hot stock,
  blend thoroughly, and simmer 30 minutes. Purée in a blender
  or food processor, strain, and return to the fire. Add the cream
  and the blanched asparagus pieces, and adjust seasoning with
  salt and white pepper. Spread the croutons with the sour
  cream, top with a sprig of chervil, and serve on top of the soup.

CREAM OF CALIFORNIA LETTUCE SOUP

(Potage Crème de Laitue)

4 tablespoons olive oil
1 shallot, minced
1 bunch parsley stems, minced
the outside leaves of 1 large or 2 small heads of romaine lettuce
3 tablespoons flour
salt and pepper as needed

4 cups chicken stock, hot
¾ cup heavy cream or half-and-half
4 baguette slices, toasted
4 tablespoons sour cream or crème fraîche
¼ cup romaine lettuce, cut into very fine julienne

- Sauté the shallot in the olive oil a couple of minutes—do not brown. Add the lettuce leaves and parsley, cover, and sweat for 5 minutes. Add the flour, blend thoroughly, and cook for roughly 5 minutes, stirring continuously.
- Add the chicken stock, and blend thoroughly. Season to taste with salt and pepper. Simmer for 30 minutes.
- Transfer to a blender or food processor, and purée. Return to the fire, add the cream and bring to a simmer.
- Spread each of the baguette slices with a tablespoon of sour cream. Ladle the soup into soup plates or bowls, and top with a crouton, sprinkled with the julienned lettuce.

Virtually any vegetable can be turned into a creamed and puréed soup, using the recipe for Cream of California Lettuce Soup. These include broccoli, cauliflower, celery, fennel, leek, zucchini, and so forth.

CREAM OF SORREL SOUP

(Potage Crème de Germiny)

1 pound sorrel, well rinsed, dried, and roughly chopped
1 quart rich, clear chicken stock
5 egg yolks

1 cup heavy cream
½ cup crème fraîche or sour cream
4 baguette croutons
salt and white pepper to taste

- Simmer the sorrel in the stock for 10 minutes. Remove to a blender or food processor and purée. Return to the stove, and adjust seasoning with salt and white pepper.
- Beat the yolks and cream thoroughly. Pour the hot stock slowly into this mixture, while beating continuously. When half of the stock has been incorporated, stir this into the remaining stock.

Bring to a simmer, while stirring continuously, then remove from the heat (do not allow to boil).

- Serve the soup in hot bowls, topped with a crouton spread with the crème fraîche or sour cream.

Sorrel, also known as sour grass, has an intense tartness in its raw state, because of a high content of oxalic acid. When cooked, this tartness is considerably toned down. In the twentieth century sorrel is no longer cultivated on a large scale, which makes it difficult to find. It is, however, easy to grow and is considered an important dish on any fine-dining menu. In France, shad is prepared with a stuffing of puréed sorrel, and the oxalic acid reputedly softens the bones of that fish so that they can be easily eaten right along with the flesh. This soup was innovated by Adolphe Duglére at the Café Anglais in Paris during his reign as chef in the late 1860s.

CREAM OF WATERCRESS SOUP

(Potage Crème de Cresson)

3 bunches watercress
4 medium leeks, white part only, well rinsed, and roughly chopped
¼ pound unsalted butter
½ gallon chicken stock, hot

2½ pounds potatoes, peeled, and coarsely chopped
1 pint heavy cream
salt and white pepper to taste
1 cup plain white bread croutons

- Remove the leaves from 1 bunch of watercress, and set aside. Coarsely chop the remaining watercress, and sweat with the leeks and butter for 5 minutes. Add the stock and potatoes, and simmer until the potatoes are completely soft. Purée in a food processor or blender, and return to the fire. Add the cream and season to taste. Garnish with the croutons and watercress leaves.

Several wild forms of cress were known to the ancient Greeks and Romans. Charlemagne ordered it cultivated during the eighth century, and its juice was used as an ingredient in the medieval verjuice (unfermented grape juice). Louis IX (king of France, 1226–1270), overcome with thirst while hunting on a hot summer day, was handed a bunch of watercress to eat, which revived and refreshed him. As a result, to this day the coat of arms for the city of Veron bears three bunches of watercress. In the fourteenth century, Taillevent (Guillaume Tirel, 1310–1395), as chef to Charles VI, on a dinner menu in honor of the Compte de la Marche, served watercress alone as the fourth course, with the following qualifier: "Watercress, served alone, to refresh the mouth." Alexander Dumas considered it to be the healthiest of the fine herbs. Though originally brought to North America in cultivated form from Eurasia, watercress now grows wild in every state, including Hawaii and Alaska. It thrives in damp places and at high altitudes and, with the longest season of any salad plant, in temperate climates it can be found in clear-running streams all year round.

$\mathcal{K}$ESÄKEITTO

(Finnish Vegetable Soup)

½ cup string beans, cut into ¼-inch dice

½ cup carrots, cut into ¼-inch dice

½ cup cauliflower, cut into small buds

½ cup potatoes, cut into ¼-inch dice

½ cup radishes, cut into ¼-inch dice

½ pound fresh spinach, well rinsed and roughly chopped

3 tablespoons unsalted butter, kneaded with 4 tablespoons flour

1 cup heavy cream

1 egg yolk

½ pound titi shrimp

salt and white pepper to taste

2 tablespoons chopped dill

- Bring 3 cups of lightly salted water to a boil. Blanch the string beans, carrots, cauliflower, and potatoes, separately, until each is al dente (the potatoes should be cooked until tender).

- Beat the flour and butter paste into the remaining liquid, and simmer 10 minutes. Strain, and return to the fire. Add the blanched vegetables, radishes, spinach, and shrimp, and simmer about 5 minutes.

This soup can also be served chilled.

- Beat the cream and egg, then temper into the soup by slowly adding the hot soup to the cream and beating in. Return this mixture to the soup, and simmer for 3 minutes.
- Adjust seasoning, then serve garnished with the dill.

PUMPKIN AND GINGER SOUP

1 medium pumpkin, quartered, seeds and webbing removed
2 tablespoons unsalted butter
1 small onion, coarsely chopped
1 small carrot, coarsely chopped
2 celery ribs, coarsely chopped
2 tablespoons grated ginger
1 bay leaf
2 cups chicken stock, hot
1 cup heavy cream
salt and white pepper to taste
1 cup filberts, finely ground

- Preheat an oven to 350°F. Place the pumpkin, flesh side up, in a baking pan, with ¼ cup of water in each piece. Bake for about 1 hour, or until the pumpkin flesh is soft. Scoop out the pumpkin flesh, and set aside.
- Sauté the onion, carrot, and celery in the butter for several minutes. Add the ginger and bay leaf, and sauté briefly. Add the stock and the pumpkin, and simmer for 20 minutes, stirring frequently, then add the cream.
- Transfer to a food processor or blender, and purée. Return to the fire, bring to a boil, season to taste with salt and pepper, and add the filberts.

SWEET POTATO AND LEEK SOUP

3 tablespoons unsalted butter
5 medium leeks, white part only, roots removed, medium diced, and well rinsed
4 cups sweet potatoes, medium diced
3 quarts chicken stock
2 cups heavy cream
salt and pepper to taste

- Sweat the leeks in the butter over medium heat for 10 minutes. Add the potatoes, cook briefly, then add the chicken stock. Simmer until the potatoes are tender. Transfer about one-third of the soup, along with the leeks and potatoes, and purée in a food processor. Return this to the remainder of the soup, add the cream, and season to taste.

———————————— • ————————————

Commonly known in Italy as "American potato," but unrelated to the true potato or the yam, the sweet potato is a member of the morning glory family. Though introduced to Europe from the Americas by Columbus, it is believed to have originated in Asia, particularly Indochina, since it is an important economic crop there. It has a remarkably high sugar content of 3–6%, which increases during storage at warm temperatures. The sweet potato provides more calories, minerals, and vitamin A than a white potato, but less protein. What are called yams in the United States are actually a variety of sweet potato. Related to grasses and lilies, yams were cultivated in Asia as early as 8000 B.C.

PURÉED SOUPS

.... ## SPLIT PEA SOUP

6 strips bacon, finely diced
1 medium onion, coarsely chopped
1 medium carrot, coarsely chopped
2 celery ribs, coarsely chopped
1 bay leaf

2 cups green or yellow split peas, culled and rinsed
2 quarts chicken stock, hot
1 ham bone
1 cup finely diced ham
1 cup croutons
salt and pepper to taste

- Render the bacon in a heavy-gauge soup pot, over medium heat, until golden brown. Add the vegetables and bay leaf, and continue cooking, covered, for 10 minutes. Add the peas, and blend well. Add the chicken stock and ham bone, and simmer until the peas are very soft.

- Remove the ham bone and bay leaf, and purée in a food processor or blender. Return to the fire, add the ham, and season with salt and pepper. Serve garnished with the croutons.

WHITE BEAN AND ESCAROLE SOUP

1 cup dried navy (white)
  beans
½ cup olive oil
1 small onion, medium
  diced
1 small carrot, peeled and
  medium diced
2 celery ribs, medium diced
1 small white turnip,
  medium diced
1 garlic bulb, cloves peeled
  and sliced

½ cup dry white wine
4 sprigs thyme
2 bay leaves
3 quarts chicken stock
6 tablespoons unsalted
  butter
1 small head escarole,
  trimmed, well rinsed, and
  cut into 1-inch pieces
salt and pepper to taste

- Cull the beans, rinse several times in cold water, cover with water, and allow to sit overnight.

- Drain the beans, place them in 2 quarts lightly salted boiling water, and simmer until tender. Drain, then purée half of the beans in a blender or food processor, along with 1 quart of the chicken stock.

- Sweat the vegetables in the olive oil over medium heat for 10 minutes. Add the wine, herbs, remaining chicken stock, puréed beans, and whole beans, and simmer another 10 minutes. Sauté the escarole in the butter for several minutes, then add to the soup. Remove the thyme and bay leaf, and season to taste with salt and pepper.

BISQUES AND CHOWDERS

CIOPPINO

For the Rouille

16 baguette croutons
4 garlic cloves, pressed
2 egg yolks
2 tablespoons tomato paste
¼ teaspoon cayenne pepper

1 cup olive oil
salt to taste
⅓ cup mashed potato
the juice of 1 lemon

For the Cioppino

¼ cup olive oil
½ cup onions, cut into
  julienne

½ cup carrots, cut into
  julienne

½ cup leeks, cut into
  julienne
½ cup fennel root, cut into
  julienne
2 garlic cloves, pressed
2 cups dry champagne
1 cup tomatoes, diced
3 cups clear fish stock
2 pinches saffron threads
1 zest of half an orange
salt and white pepper as
  needed

1 fresh raw Dungeness crab,
  cut up into roughly
  1-inch pieces
8 16–20 count shrimp, in
  the shell
12 littleneck or Manila
  clams, well scrubbed
8 mussels, debearded and
  well rinsed
½ pound squid, cut into
  ½-inch rings
¼ cup parsley, chopped

- Pound the garlic, egg yolks, tomato paste, salt, pepper, and potato into a smooth paste, using a mortar and pestle. Pour in the olive oil in a slow, steady stream, interspersing it with the lemon juice. Set aside.

- Sauté the vegetables and garlic in the olive oil, covered, over medium heat for 10 minutes, stirring frequently. Add the champagne, tomatoes, stock, saffron, and orange zest, and simmer another 10 minutes. Season to taste with salt and white pepper.

- Add the seafood, and simmer until the clams and mussels open (6 to 8 minutes). Top with the chopped parsley, and serve with the baguette slices spread with the rouille.

*L*OBSTER BISQUE

2 1-pound lobsters
¼ cup olive oil
1 medium onion, coarsely
  chopped
1 medium carrot, peeled and
  coarsely chopped
1 celery stalk, coarsely
  chopped
1 leek, white part only, well
  rinsed and coarsely
  chopped
6 parsley sprigs
1 bay leaf

1 tablespoon paprika
2 tablespoons tomato paste
¼ cup brandy
¼ cup dry white wine
1 tablespoon flour kneaded
  together with . . .
2 tablespoons unsalted
  butter
1 quart heavy cream
salt and white pepper to
  taste
¼ cup amontillado (semi-
  dry) sherry

- Stun the lobsters by piercing them through the head with a knife, at the center point just about a half-inch behind the eyes.

Cut up the lobsters as follows: each claw cut in half; arms split; body quartered; tail cut in half. (When cutting, place a pan under the cutting board, so that any juices that run out of the lobster can be added to the vegetables during the sweating.)

- Sauté the lobster pieces in the oil, until the shells are bright red (about 6 minutes). Remove the lobster with a slotted spoon, crack the shells, remove the meat, cut into ¼-inch pieces. Crack all of the lobster shells into smaller pieces, and return them to the pan.

- Add the vegetables, herbs, tomato paste, and paprika, and sweat. Add the brandy, stand back from the stove, and carefully ignite. Extinguish with the white wine.

- Add the butter and flour paste, and blend thoroughly. Add the cream, and simmer until reduced by half. Purée in a blender or food processor, return to the stove, bring to a simmer, and season to taste with salt and pepper. Add the lobster, and finish with the sherry.

Be *very careful* when igniting the brandy. Always stand back and away from the pan, tipping it up to use the cooking fire to ignite. If using an electric range, hold a match cautiously just over the edge of the pan.

New England Clam Chowder

A *chaudière* was a large cast-iron soup kettle (*chaud* means "hot") that eighteenth-century French immigrants brought with them to New England. Their Yankee versions of Mediterranean fish stews, such as bouillabaisse and bourride, which they prepared in these big kettles, eventually came to be called chowders, a corruption of the French term.

¼ cup fat back, small dice
¼ cup bacon, small dice
1 medium onion, medium dice
1 celery stalk, medium dice
1 bay leaf
1 teaspoon fresh thyme leaves
salt and pepper to taste

1 tablespoon flour
1 quart clam juice
2 cups clams, finely chopped
1½ cups potatoes, medium dice
2 cups half-and-half cream
1 tablespoon white Worcestershire sauce

- Render the fat back and bacon until light brown. Add the vegetables, herbs, salt, and pepper, and sweat for 5 minutes.

- Blend in the flour, and cook for 3 minutes, stirring continuously. Add the clam juice and blend thoroughly. Add the remaining ingredients and simmer until the potatoes are tender, then season to taste with salt and pepper.

RHODE ISLAND REDS' CLAM CHOWDER

¼ pound unsalted butter
1 medium onion, medium dice
1 celery stalk, medium dice
1 medium carrot, peeled, medium dice
2 garlic cloves, pressed
½ cup fennel root, medium dice
1 teaspoon fresh thyme leaves
6 stalks dill, tied together with cotton twine

1 cup tomato, peeled, medium dice
1 cup potatoes, medium dice
1 tablespoon Worcestershire sauce
5 cups clam juice
2 cups clams, finely chopped
1 tablespoon minced dill
salt and white pepper to taste
4 4-inch round French or kaiser rolls

- Sweat the onion, celery, carrot, garlic, and herbs in the butter for 10 minutes.
- Preheat an oven to 400°F. Slice a lid off the top of each roll and reserve. Scoop out the inside of the rolls, discarding the inside and reserving the scooped-out rolls. Bake for about 10 minutes, or until toasted and golden brown.
- Combine the tomato, potatoes, Worcestershire, clam juice, and clams, and simmer until the potatoes are tender. Add the dill, and adjust seasoning with salt and pepper.
- Serve the piping hot soup in the toasted rolls, with the lids on, in a wide soup plate.

This soup was created in 1975 by Alan R. Gibson, in honor of the Rhode Island Reds, a semiprofessional hockey team.

CORN CHOWDER

4 slices bacon, finely diced
2 tablespoon unsalted butter
1 medium onion, finely diced
1 celery rib, finely diced
2 cups whole kernel corn

1½ cups potatoes, cut into ¼-inch dice
4 cups chicken stock
1 cup heavy cream
salt and white pepper to taste

- Render the bacon until brown and crispy. Pour off excess fat, add the butter, onion, and celery, and sauté for 5 minutes.

Add the corn, and blend. Add the potatoes and stock, and simmer until the potatoes are tender. Add the cream and season to taste with salt and pepper. Place a third of the soup in a food processor or blender, and purée. Return the puréed portion to the pot, bring to a boil, and serve.

•

Margaret Visser, in her book *Much Depends on Dinner,* terms corn "the driving wheel of Western civilization." Corn is a native of South America and an integral part of ancient cultures there. Today there is not a single product in a North American supermarket that has not been touched in some way by corn, whether in the form of starch, sugar, or caramel color. These include fresh meat and poultry, frozen meat and fish, soft drinks, puddings, canned food, all cartons and packaging, margarine, candy, ketchup, ice cream, soft drinks, beer, gin, vodka, baby food, jams, pickles, adhesives, toothpaste, cosmetics, detergents, and so forth. Cultivars include Sugar and Gold, Buttercorn, Butter and Sugar, Gold Mine, Sunchief, Golden Cross Bantam, White Jewel, and Silver Queen. Eastern Sunburst and White Cloud are two varieties grown for popcorn.

*B*ILLY BI

2 pounds mussels, scrubbed, rinsed, and debearded
2 cups dry white wine
1 medium onion, small dice
2 shallots, finely chopped
1 bunch parsley stems, tied together with cotton twine
¼ teaspoon salt
¼ teaspoon black pepper
pinch of cayenne pepper
1 bay leaf
2 cups heavy cream
3 egg yolks
4 tablespoons unsalted butter, cut into ½-inch pieces

This unique soup was reputedly created for William B. Leeds, the "tinplate tycoon," at Maxim's in Paris.

- Steam the mussels with the wine, vegetables, herbs, and spices 8 to 10 minutes, or until all the mussels are open. Remove the mussels and set aside. Strain the liquid, place in a saucepan, and bring to a simmer.

- Beat the cream and egg yolks together, and temper into the soup by pouring about half the hot soup slowly into the cream while continuously beating. Beat this back into the hot soup along with the butter, bring just to a simmer, and serve over the steamed mussels.

MUSSEL CHOWDER

2 pounds mussels, scrubbed, rinsed, and debearded
1 cup dry white wine
1 medium onion, small dice
2 garlic cloves, pressed
1 pinch saffron
3 cups tomatoes, diced

2 cups fish stock
1 cup clam juice
3 cups potatoes, cut into ¼-inch dice
salt and pepper to taste
2 tablespoons unsalted butter

- Steam the mussels and the white wine 8 to 10 minutes, or until all the mussels are open. Remove the mussels and set aside. Add all the remaining ingredients, except the butter, and simmer until the potatoes are tender. Return the mussels to the soup, and garnish with a piece of butter.

REGIONAL AND INTERNATIONAL SOUPS

BOUILLABAISSE

For the Stock

¼ pound unsalted butter
5 pounds whitefish bones (sole, flounder, halibut), cut into 2-inch pieces
1 1½-pound lobster
2 cups mirepoix, finely chopped

1 bay leaf
1 teaspoon white peppercorns, crushed
2 sprigs thyme
1 bunch parsley stems
2 cups dry white wine

For the Rouille

16 baguette croutons
4 garlic cloves, pressed
2 egg yolks
2 tablespoons tomato paste

salt and white pepper to taste
⅓ cup mashed potato
the juice of 1 lemon
1 cup olive oil

For the Soup

½ cup olive oil
1 pound each of five varieties of fish, as available (e.g., cod, conger, sea bass, eel, mackerel, red snapper)

1 large onion, medium dice
1 large leek, well rinsed, medium dice
4 garlic cloves, crushed
1 small fennel bulb, cut into strips

2 pinches saffron
the rind of ½ orange
2 cups diced tomatoes
1 bay leaf
2 sprigs thyme

1 bunch parsley stems, tied
  together with cotton
  twine
¼ cup chopped parsley

- Detach the claws and tail from the lobster. Split the tail in half, crack the claws, and set aside. Cut the body up into four pieces.
- Sweat the fish bones, lobster body, mirepoix, herbs, and spices in the butter. Add the white wine and enough water to rise above the fish by 2 inches. Simmer for 45 minutes, then strain, reserving the stock.
- Pound the garlic, egg yolks, tomato paste, salt, pepper, and potato into a smooth paste, using a mortar and pestle. Pour in the olive oil in a slow, steady stream, interspersing it with the lemon juice. Set aside.
- Sauté the fish and lobster in the olive oil for 5 minutes. Remove with a slotted spoon, and set aside. Add the remaining vegetables, herbs, and spices, and sauté for 5 minutes. Add the fish stock, lobster, and fish, and boil rapidly for 10 minutes. Adjust seasoning with salt and pepper.
- Ladle the soup into wide soup plates, and top with chopped parsley. Spread the croutons with the rouille, and serve alongside the soup.

The word *bouillabaisse* is derived from the French *bouillir* (to boil) and *abattre* (to lay down). "Boil and settle" (down) is an old Provence colloquial command for the fish to calm down after the dish was boiled. The resulting brew, a specialty of coastal southern France, is intended to be busy (with ingredients) and cloudy (from the boiling), reflective of the passionate nature of Mediterranean-French cookery and the hearty nature of this dish.

GERMAN BEER SOUP

(Soupe d'Allemande à la Bière)

3 tablespoons unsalted
  butter
1 garlic clove, crushed
2 thin slices gingerroot
3 tablespoons flour
2 cups beer
2 cups chicken stock
2 egg yolks

½ cup beer
1 teaspoon sugar
the zest of ½ lemon
¼ teaspoon freshly grated
  nutmeg
12 toasted baguette slices
salt and white pepper

- Sauté the garlic and ginger in the butter for several minutes. Remove the garlic and ginger, and discard.
- Add the flour, blend thoroughly, and cook several minutes, stirring continuously.
- Add 2 cups of beer and the stock, and blend well.

- Beat the egg yolks, ½ cup of beer, and sugar, and temper into the soup. Add the lemon and nutmeg, season to taste with salt and white pepper, and serve with the toasted baguette.

Minestrone, Malta Style

(Minestrone Maltaise)

½ cup olive oil
1 large onion, medium dice
2 celery stalks, medium dice
1 large carrot, medium dice
1 cup red cabbage, medium dice
1 cup white cabbage, medium dice
½ cup yellow split peas

¼ cup tomato purée
2 quarts chicken stock
1 cup potatoes, medium dice
1 cup small cauliflower flowerettes
salt and pepper to taste
4 eggs
1 cup small-curd cottage cheese

- Sauté the onion, celery, carrot, and cabbage in the olive oil, covered, over medium heat, stirring frequently. Add the split peas, tomato purée, and stock, blend thoroughly, and simmer about 20 minutes. Add the potatoes, and simmer another 15 minutes. Add the cauliflower, and simmer until the yellow split peas and cauliflower are tender.
- Combine the eggs and cottage cheese, and temper into the soup. Adjust seasoning with salt and pepper.

Just as *tortelloni* is larger than *tortelli* and *panettone* is larger than *pane*, *minestrone* is larger and richer than *minestra*, which means "to serve, to dish out" (see *minister*).

Minestrone provides a creative opportunity and is often made according to availability of local ingredients. One approach to making this soup is that it should have one ingredient from each of the following categories: aromatic vegetables, dried vegetables, fresh vegetables, seasoning vegetables, pasta, and meat.

Onion Soup, Gratinée

4 tablespoons unsalted butter

12 medium onions, halved, core removed, sliced lengthwise ¼-inch thick

2 garlic cloves, pressed
2 tablespoons toasted flour
1 bay leaf
¼ cup dry sherry

3 pints brown stock
salt and pepper to taste
4 3-inch round croutons
1 cup Gruyère cheese, grated

- Sauté the onions and the garlic in the butter, stirring frequently, until they are lightly caramelized throughout. Add the flour and blend thoroughly. Add the bay leaf and sherry, and deglaze. Add the stock, and simmer for 30 minutes, skimming the top of foam and other impurities. Season to taste with salt and pepper.
- Ladle the soup into ovenproof crocks, and place a crouton on top of each. Sprinkle with the cheese, and melt under the broiler.

Flour can be toasted by sprinkling it on a baking sheet, placing it into a 375°F oven until it turns light brown, then sifting. This adds color, flavor, and body to the soup.

The brown stock is generally made from beef and/or veal bones, though a brown chicken stock can also be used.

If a broiler is unavailable, the cheese on the croutons can be melted in the oven, then placed on top of the soup.

*O*XTAIL SOUP

(Potage Queue de Boeuf)

1 oxtail, cut into 1-inch pieces
1 cup mirepoix, finely chopped
8 tablespoons unsalted butter
¾ cup flour, toasted
1 cup dry red wine
1 cup tomato purée

2 quarts water
2 sprigs thyme
1 bay leaf
½ teaspoon black peppercorns, crushed
1 bunch parsley stems
2 cups mushrooms, medium dice
salt and pepper to taste

- Preheat an oven to 400°F. Place the oxtail in a roasting pan, and roast for 30 minutes. Add the mirepoix, turn down the oven to 375°F, and continue roasting another 30 minutes.
- Remove the oxtail and mirepoix with a slotted spoon, and

transfer to a heavy-gauge stockpot. Put 6 tablespoons of the butter and the flour into the roasting pan, place over a medium flame, and blend thoroughly. Add the red wine, and blend. Add the tomato purée and water and blend, then transfer to the stockpot. (Use additional wine to completely deglaze the pan, then add it to the stockpot.) Add the herbs and spices, and simmer for 2 hours.

- Sauté the mushrooms in the remaining butter, and set aside.
- Remove the oxtails, pull and reserve the meat from them, and discard the bones. Cut up the meat into ¼-inch pieces.
- Simmer the soup, skimming the top, under desired thickness is achieved. Adjust seasoning with salt and pepper. Add the mushrooms and meat, and serve.

$\mathscr{P}$HILADELPHIA PEPPER POT

Tripe is the lining of the stomach of a cow, pig, or sheep and has been appreciated in many cultures since both Athenaeus and Homer praised it in ancient Greece. Rich in protein and gelatin, tripe requires long cooking to make it palatable and considerable seasoning to make it tasty. One of the best-known classic preparations of tripe is *Tripes à la Mode de Caen,* in which the tripe is cooked in an earthenware dish for 10 to 12 hours and flavored with Normandy's apple brandy, Calvados.

1 pound tripe, cut into 1-inch squares	4 ounces beef suet, very finely minced
1 veal knuckle	2 large onions, medium diced
1 small onion, halved	2 green jalapeño peppers, finely diced
1 bouquet garni (leek, parsley stems, thyme, and bay leaf, tied with cotton twine)	½ cup flour
2 quarts water	2 cups potatoes, medium diced

- Bring the tripe, veal, onion, bouquet garni, and water to a simmer, and cook for 2½ hours. Discard the onion and bouquet garni. Separate any meat from the veal knuckle, leaving the meat in the broth and discarding the knuckle.
- Render the suet without coloring. Add the onions and sweat. Add the peppers, and cook a few more minutes. Blend in the flour, and cook several minutes, stirring continuously. Add the stock, and blend. Add the potatoes, and simmer until tender. Season to taste with salt and pepper.

$\mathscr{P}$ISTOU SOUP

(Soupe au Pistou)

1 quart chicken stock, hot	2 large potatoes, peeled, and cut into ¼ dice
½ pound green beans, cut into ¼-inch dice	

¾ cup cooked white navy
  beans
2 fresh, ripe tomatoes,
  peeled and diced
2 small zucchini, cut into
  ¼-inch dice

½ cup vermicelli, broken
  into 1-inch pieces
½ cup basil pesto
salt and white pepper as
  needed
grated Parmesan cheese as
  needed

In Provence dialect, *pistou* means "pesto" (from the Latin *pestare*, meaning "to pound") and refers to the basil, garlic, and olive oil paste well known in Italian cuisine.

• Simmer the green beans, potatoes, navy beans, tomatoes, zucchini, and vermicelli in the stock until the vermicelli and potatoes are tender. Beat in the pesto, and adjust seasoning with salt and pepper. Serve accompanied with the grated cheese.

CHILLED SOUPS

Cold soups are not very popular in contemporary American cuisine, probably because of our high-speed culture that prefers to get on with the main event—the entrée—as opposed to lingering over spoonfuls of chilled savory soup. There are, however, several included here, inasmuch as dining styles have changed considerably in recent years. These are worthy of preparation for the occasional palate that can appreciate them.

*A*VOCADO SOUP, CHAMPAGNE

2 cups milk
1 cup fresh white bread
  crumbs
4 large ripe Haas avocados,
  peeled and seeded
1 quart dry champagne

the juice of 1 lemon
salt to taste
½ teaspoon mace
1 cup heavy cream, whipped
4 sprigs of mint

• Soak the bread in the milk for 1 hour. Place in a blender or food processor with 1 avocado and 1 cup of champagne, and purée. Transfer to another bowl.
• Purée the remaining avocados, interspersing the champagne and lemon juice. Blend all ingredients, and season with salt and mace. Fold in half the whipped cream, then serve garnished with a dollop of whipped cream and a sprig of mint.

GAZPACHO, DUTCHESS VALLEY STYLE

2 cups vine-ripened toma-
toes, peeled, cored,
seeded, and coarsely
chopped
½ cup green pepper, seeded
and coarsely chopped
½ cup cucumber, peeled,
seeded, and coarsely
chopped
½ cup onion, peeled and
coarsely chopped
2 stalks celery, peeled and
coarsely chopped
4 garlic cloves, coarsely
chopped

½ cup tomato purée
¼ cup tarragon vinegar
½ cup rich beef stock or
consommé
2 tablespoons olive oil
½ cup tomato juice
salt and white pepper to
taste
¼ cup each, finely diced red
bell pepper, green bell
pepper, avocado, and
cucumber
¼ cup small plain white
bread croutons
2 tablespoons minced chives

- Place all of the ingredients except the diced vegetables, croutons, and chives, into a blender or food processor, and purée.
Season to taste with salt and pepper. Marinate at least 12 hours.
- Serve in individual chilled bowls, garnished with the diced
vegetables, croutons, and chives.

GAZPACHO, ADALUSIAN STYLE

¼ cup olive oil
4 garlic cloves
1 small cucumber, peeled
and seeded
1 medium green pepper
1 quart diced tomato
2 fresh vine-ripened tomatoes, peeled, and cut into
fine dice
2 tablespoons Worcestershire
sauce
¼ teaspoon ground cumin

salt and cayenne pepper to
taste
1 small, stale hard roll, finely chopped, and soaked in
1 cup water and ½ cup
white wine vinegar
1 pint half-and-half cream
2 egg yolks
1 cup plain croutons
2 tablespoons chopped
parsley

- Cut a portion of the cucumber and the green pepper into fine
dice, enough to yield ¼ cup each.

- Purée all of the remaining ingredients (except the croutons and parsley) in a blender or food processor. Adjust seasoning, and garnish with the croutons and chopped parsley.

𝒦ÆNEMÆLKSKOLSKÅL

3 egg yolks
½ cup sugar
the juice of 1 lemon
1 quart buttermilk
the zest of 1 orange and
   1 lemon

1 cup fresh white bread
   croutons
2 tablespoons sugar
4 tablespoons unsalted
   butter
4 sprigs fresh mint

Kænemælkskolskål (pronounced: canner-mal-*skole-skal*), Swedish buttermilk soup, is translated as follows: *Kæne,* to churn from butter; *mælk,* made from milk; *skol,* cold; *skål,* bowl.

- Whip the eggs and sugar until thick and lemon yellow. Beat in the lemon juice, then blend in the buttermilk.
- Blanch the zest briefly in boiling water, drain, then add to the buttermilk mixture. Chill until ready to serve.
- Toss the croutons in the sugar, then sauté in butter until golden brown. Refrigerate until well chilled.
- Serve the soup in chilled cups, garnished with croutons and mint.

CHAPTER 5

CROUSTADES, PASTRIES, AND PUFFS

CROUSTADES

Technically, a *croustade* is a thick slice of bread or a small roll, hollowed out, brushed with butter, then baked until brown and crispy. A croustade can also be a case made of puff pastry, phyllo dough, Duchesse potatoes, pasta, polenta, or rice, baked, removed from the mold, then filled with any of innumerable fillings—from salpicons and stews, to vegetables and purées of various sorts—then heated again and served. Although these are usually served hot, they are on occasion served cold or at room temperature, depending on the specific dish. This is a very elegant way of serving a dish and opens a whole genre of creative possibilities. Some traditional croustades are presented here. (See Figures 5.1 and 5.2.)

Though croustades are generally brushed with butter before being baked to golden brown, it is acceptable to toast a croustade without the butter so as to minimize dietary fat.

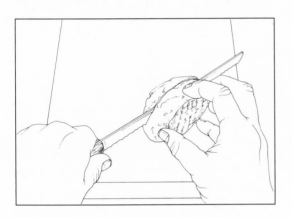

Slice the top off of a small hard roll.

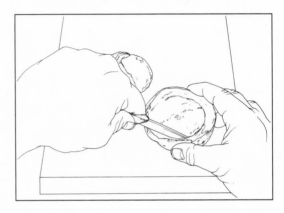

Score the inside of the roll with a paring knife.

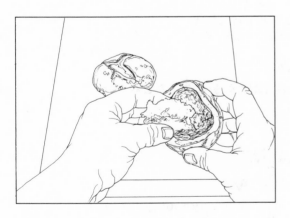

Pull out the dough from the interior of the roll.

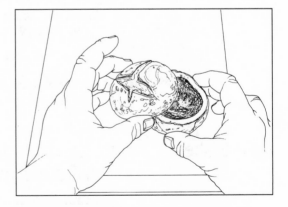

Brush the interior lightly with clarified butter, bake until golden brown, fill with appropriate filling, and set the top in place.

Figure 5.1
Creating a croustade from a roll

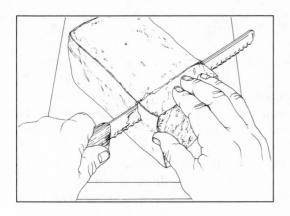

Cut a 1½ to 2-inch thick slice of bread from a pullman loaf.

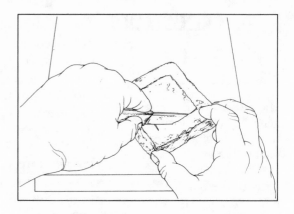

Score the inside of the bread slice, about half-way down, leaving a ½-inch wide border at the edges.

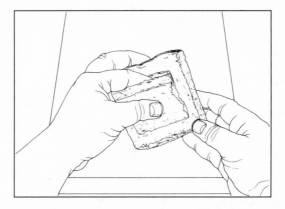

Carefully remove the interior bread, leaving a clean cavity. Brush with clarified butter, bake until golden brown, and fill as required.

Figure 5.2
Creating a croustade from a thick slice of bread

Cold Dishes

Casanova Croustades
(*Croûtes au Casanova*)

Croustade filled with celeriac (celery root) julienne, truffles, and hard-boiled egg, bound with mayonnaise.

Goose Liver Croustades
(*Croûtes au Foie Gras*)

Croustade filled with goose liver purée, glazed with Madeira aspic.

Indian Croustades
(Croûtes à l'Indienne)

Croustade filled with chilled curried rice pilaf mixed with diced shrimp, chutney, and parsley, garnished with diced hard-boiled egg yolks and whites.

Romanoff Croustades
(Croûtes au Romanov)

Croustade filled with a fine purée of tuna fish moistened with mayonnaise, garnished with chopped pistachio nuts.

Rosamond Croustades
(Croûtes au Rosamond)

Croustade filled with tomato salad (diced peeled tomatoes, scallion, basil, olive oil, garlic, salt, and pepper), garnished with anchovy fillets and hard-boiled eggs. (See color plate.)

Spanish Croustades
(Croûtes à l'Espagnole)

Croustade spread with anchovy butter, filled with hard-boiled egg salad seasoned with anchovies and bound with tartar sauce, garnished with green olives.

Tzarina Croustades
(Croûtes à la Czarine)

Croustade filled with onion paste (puréed onions and cream cooked down until thick, then cooled) seasoned with anchovy paste, garnished with caviar.

Victoria Rolls
(Petits Pains Victoria)

A croustade made from a small dinner roll, filled with any shellfish (lobster, crab, crayfish), poultry (chicken, game), or meat (beef, pork, lamb) salad, bound with mayonnaise-based or vinaigrette sauce.

Hot Dishes

Charles V Croustades
(Croûtes à la Charles V)

A thick, square slice of bread or small roll hollowed out, lightly buttered and baked until crispy and brown, filled with poached fish roe (carp, shad), coated with cheese soufflé and baked.

DuBarry Croustades
(Croûtes à la DuBarry)

A thick, square slice of bread or small roll hollowed out, lightly buttered and baked until crispy and brown, filled with small cauliflower flowerettes, bound in cream sauce with an egg white beaten to a stiff peak folded in, topped with grated Gruyère and dry bread crumbs moistened with butter, and baked.

Épicurean Croustades
(Croûtes à l'Épicurienne)

A thick, square slice of bread or small roll hollowed out, lightly buttered and baked until crispy and brown, filled with creamed spinach (cooked and chopped), mixed anchovies, and capers, garnished with hard boiled eggs. (Can also be served cold.) (See color plate.)

Eureka Croustades
(Croûtes à l'Eureka)

A thick, square slice of bread or small roll, hollowed out, lightly buttered and baked until crispy and brown, filled with mushroom soufflé, garnished with diced anchovies, and baked.

———————————— • ————————————

Mushroom Soufflé for Eureka Croustades

For the Duxelle

1 tablespoon unsalted butter	½ cup dry white wine
1 shallot, minced	salt and white pepper to taste
1 cup fresh mushrooms, rinsed	

- Sauté the shallot and the mushrooms in the butter for several minutes. Add the white wine, simmer briefly, then remove to a food processor and purée. Return to the pan and continue simmering until dry. Season to taste with salt and white pepper.

For the Soufflé

1/4 cup unsalted butter
1/2 cup + 1 tablespoon flour (9 tablespoons)
1 cup hot milk or chicken stock
salt and white pepper to taste
5 egg yolks
1/2 cup mushroom duxelle (dry)

1/4 cup anchovies, finely diced
7 egg whites, beaten to soft peak
4 to 6 hard-crust rolls, tops removed, and inside bread scooped out (reserve for bread crumbs)

- Cook the butter and flour in a pan for about 5 minutes, without browning. Add the milk or stock, and simmer several minutes, stirring continuously. Remove from the fire, season lightly with salt and pepper, and allow to cool.
- Preheat an oven to 400°F.
- Add the egg yolks, one at a time, blending each one in before adding the next. Add the duxelle and anchovies, and blend thoroughly. Brush the rolls lightly with butter.
- Beat the egg whites to a soft peak. Fold in half the beaten whites, using a rubber spatula. Fold in the second half of the whites. Fill the buttered rolls nearly to the top with the soufflé mixture, and bake 25 to 30 minutes, or until golden brown. Serve immediately.

The traditional soufflé recipe for these croustades is made with milk. Chicken (or veal stock) will work just as well and is included for those who prefer to avoid dairy foods.

Florentine Croustades
(Croûtes à la Florentine)

A thick, square slice of bread or small roll hollowed out, lightly buttered and baked until crispy and brown, filled with finely chopped cooked spinach bound with crème fraîche (or sour cream), sprinkled with Gruyère cheese and dry bread crumbs moistened with butter, and baked.

Goose Liver Croustades
(Croûtes à la Landaise)

A thick, square slice of bread, lightly buttered and toasted, topped with sliced goose liver (foie gras) sautéed briefly in a hot pan, topped with cream sauce, sprinkled with grated cheese, and glazed.

MUSHROOM CROUSTADE

(Pasticcio di Funghi Ovoli)

1 loaf plain white bread
olive oil as needed
6 garlic cloves
2½ pounds mushrooms,
  sliced
2 tablespoons chopped sage
  leaves

2 tablespoon chopped
  parsley
salt and pepper to taste
6 large eggs
1 cup rich chicken stock

- Trim the bread of crusts, and brush one side of each bread slice lightly with olive oil. Line a metal bread pan with the bread, the oiled side touching the pan, cutting the bread slices so that a solid lining is formed.

- Preheat an oven to 375°F.

- Sauté the garlic and mushrooms in about ½ cup olive oil, allowing excess moisture to evaporate. Add the herbs and season with salt and pepper. Set aside to cool.

- Beat the eggs with the stock. When the mushrooms have cooled, blend in the egg mixture, and place into the bread form. Seal the top completely with bread slices, oiled side up. Bake for 45 minutes, or until the bread is golden brown. Allow to rest 15 minutes, invert onto a serving platter, slice and serve.

PASTRIES

Carolines and *duchesses* (eclairs and puffs) are all prepared with *choux* paste *(pâte à choux)*, but are different in shape and size: carolines are 3-inch long miniature eclairs; duchesses are 1-inch round puffs. A caroline is a miniature form of the more familiar eclair, the 4- to 6-inch treat filled with pastry cream and glazed with chocolate. A duchesse is a 1-inch round miniature version of the cream puff, the 3-inch round puff filled with pastry cream and dusted with powdered sugar. The basic recipe follows:

PÂTE À CHOUX

1 cup water
1 cup milk
10 tablespoons unsalted butter, cut into 1-inch pieces

pinch of salt
2¼ cups flour
6 eggs

- Bring the water, milk, butter, and salt to a boil in a noncorrosive pan. When the butter has melted, add the flour and blend thoroughly until it forms a ball of paste that comes away from the side of the pan (add a little additional flour if necessary). Continue stirring and cooking for several minutes, without browning. Remove from the fire.
- When the paste has cooled slightly, add the eggs, one at a time, and stir until completely incorporated.
- Scoop the paste out of the pan with a rubber spatula, and place in a pastry bag fitted with a No. 5 or No. 6 round tip. Pipe out on a lightly greased pan, with about 1½ inches between each piece to allow for expansion. Bake in a preheated 350°F oven for 15 minutes, or until golden brown.

———————————— • ————————————

Choux is also the French term for "cabbage," and its application to this pastry reflects its appearance when baked—it looks like a little cabbage.

Puff pastry dough (*pâte feuilletée,* or *feuilletage*) is unique among pastry doughs, believed to have been invented in the seventeenth century by Feuillet, a pastry cook in service to the house of Condé. Another theory holds that it was developed in ancient Greece, which is quite possible, given the similarity of certain Greek dishes made with phyllo dough. Spanakopita and baklava, for example, though prepared in a different way, yield a product with a texture similar to puff pastry. It is, however, unique, not only in the way it is created, but also in the inclusion of butter, not commonly prevalent in Mediterranean cookery.

A Napoleon, a dessert made with sheets of puff pastry, is termed *mille-feuille* in French, which means "thousand leaves." By the repeated folding and rolling, folding and rolling of this dough, literally more than a thousand layers of flour and butter are created. (The recipe that follows yields 2,187 layers of butter and flour.) The final dough is rolled out to a thickness of ⅛ inch, then baked. The butter in the dough melts; the water in the butter boils, producing steam; and that steam pushes up the minute layers of dough. This process renders an incredibly flaky and delectable pastry.

Puff pastry is used to prepare hundreds of different dishes, both savory and sweet, from pastry shells *(bouchées)* and cheese straws *(allumettes)* to Napoleons *(mille-feuille,* both savory and sweet) and Elephant Ear cookies *(Palmiers).*

.... $\mathcal{P}$UFF PASTRY DOUGH

(Pâte Feuilletée)

1 pound flour	1 pound unsalted butter, soft
pinch of salt	1 tablespoon flour
1 cup cold water	

- Combine 1 pound of flour, salt, and water, and knead well into a smooth, elastic dough (adjust quantities as necessary). Set aside and allow to rest for 30 minutes.
- Knead the butter and 1 tablespoon of flour into a smooth paste.
- Roll the dough out into a square, roughly 8 inches on each side, and of even thickness. Spread the butter in the center of the dough, allowing roughly a 2-inch border between the butter and the edge of the dough.
- Bring each corner up into the center of the butter, completely enclosing the butter. The edges of the dough, when the corners are brought up, should overlap each other slightly.
- Roll the dough out into a rectangle, measuring roughly 22 inches long, and 8 inches wide. Fold up the dough in thirds, and roll out again into a rectangle. Fold up into thirds, make a small indentation in the top with 2 fingers, and refrigerate for 15 minutes.
- Roll the dough out again into a rectangle, fold up, mark with 3 fingers, and refrigerate.
- Repeat this process 3 more times, for a total of 6 turns. Refrigerate the dough until ready to use. (See Figure 5.3.)

Cold Dishes

Pompadour Puffs
(Petit Napoleon à la Pompadour)

A 3 × 12-inch sheet of baked puff pastry spread with cream cheese, topped with thin-sliced ham, topped with another sheet of baked puff pastry, a second layer of cheese and ham, and a third sheet of baked puff pastry. Trim all four edges square, slice widthwise at 1-inch intervals, and garnish with cream cheese and herbs. (See color plate.)

Queen Puffs
(Petit Napoleon à la Reine)

A 3 × 12-inch sheet of baked puff pastry spread with a purée of finely minced cooked chicken breast blended with cream cheese,

These small puffs, served cold, are nearly identical to Dartois puffs, which are served hot.

. . . .

topped with another sheet of baked puff pastry, a second layer of chicken paste, and a third sheet of baked puff pastry. Trim all four edges square, slice widthwise at 1-inch intervals, and garnish with cream cheese and a toasted pecan. (See color plate.)

ℬLUE CHEESE NAPOLEON

1 pound puff pastry (or 2
   sheets frozen puff pastry)
2 eggs, beaten
1 pound blue cheese
½ cup sour cream
¾ pound cream cheese, soft
2 ripe Bosc or d'Anjou pears

½ cup sour cream, beaten
   until runny
½ cup pistachio nuts,
   toasted and finely
   chopped
1 small bunch fresh mint

- Preheat an oven to 375°F.
- Roll out the pastry to a thickness of ⅛ inch. Cut into three sheets, measuring approximately 4 × 10 inches. Brush them with the beaten eggs, dock them (gently poke the dough with the tines of a fork), place on a lightly buttered baking sheet, and bake for 15 minutes or until golden brown. Remove and set aside.
- Beat the blue cheese with the cream cheese and sour cream, until smooth.
- Peel the pears, cut in half lengthwise, cut out the cores, and cut into ¼-inch thick slices.
- Spread one sheet of puff pastry with the cheese mixture, then top with a layer of pear. Coat another sheet with cheese, and place over the pears, cheese side down. Coat the top side of this second sheet with the cheese mixture, and top with pears. Spread a third sheet with the cheese mixture, and place on top of the pears, cheese side down. Press down gently.
- Trim the four edges of the pastry, using a serrated knife, then cut widthwise at 1-inch intervals. Drizzle the sour cream over the top, and garnish with the nuts and a sprig of mint.

Hot Dishes

. . . .

𝒜CORN SQUASH BLINTZES

3 large eggs
1 cup milk
1 teaspoon sugar

pinch of salt
1⅓ cups flour
¼ cup clarified butter

2 large acorn squash
3 tablespoons unsalted
  butter
3 tablespoons brown sugar

salt, white pepper, and
  nutmeg to taste
butter as needed
1 cup sour cream

- Combine the eggs, milk, sugar, and salt, and beat thoroughly. Add the flour, and beat continuously until smooth. Add the clarified butter, and set aside.
- Preheat an oven to 375°F.
- Cut the squash in half widthwise, scoop out the seeds, fill the cavity with a little water, and bake until the flesh is tender. Remove from the oven, pour off any water left, and allow to cool.
- Scoop out the flesh, and place in a bowl with 3 tablespoons of butter, the sugar, salt, pepper, and nutmeg. Mash with a fork, adjust seasoning, and set aside.
- Place an 8-inch nonstick sauté pan over medium heat. Add 1 tablespoon butter. When the butter foams, add enough batter to coat the bottom of the pan. When lightly browned, flip, brown the second side, then set aside. Continue until all the batter is used up.
- Place several tablespoons of the squash, slightly off-center, in each of the blintzes in a rectangular shape, roughly 4 × 2 inches. Fold the side of the blintz closest to the squash, over the squash. Fold the ends of the blintz in, then roll up like a small envelope.
- In the same sauté pan, melt a tablespoon of butter, and lightly brown the blintzes on both sides. Hold in a low oven until all the blintzes are browned. Serve with sour cream.

*A*SPARAGUS IN PUFF PASTRY, GREENSBORO STYLE

1 sheet puff pastry,
  8 × 8 × ⅛ inches
2 eggs, beaten
24 asparagus spears,
  trimmed to 5 inches and
  peeled
3 shallots, minced

1½ cups dry white wine
½ cup white wine vinegar
¾ cup unsalted butter
salt and white pepper to
  taste
1 lemon, sliced very thin
4 sprigs parsley

- Preheat an oven to 375°F.

- Cut the puff pastry into 8 4 × 2-inch rectangles. Brush with egg wash, place on a baking pan, and bake 10 to 15 minutes, or until golden brown. Remove and set aside.
- Simmer the shallots, wine, and vinegar until reduced by three-fourths. Add the butter, and beat in until fully incorporated. Season to taste and set aside, keeping warm.
- Blanch the asparagus in boiling salted water until al dente. Drain.
- Place a piece of pastry on each of four serving plates. Top with 6 asparagus spears, and ladle about 2 ounces of sauce on top. Place another piece of pastry on top, and garnish with the lemon and parsley.

This dish was prepared by the author and served to Mr. and Mrs. Edwin Thrower and guests at their home in Greensboro, North Carolina, in May 1985.

BOUCHÉES

Bouchées are small pastry cases, generally round, 3 to 4 inches in diameter, though they can be cut into different shapes (such as diamond, oval, square, and rectangle). They are always made from puff pastry *(pâte feuilletée)*, and can be prepared two different ways: first, puff pastry may be rolled out to a thickness of ¼ inch, cut into a circle, and scored ½ inch inside the outside edge (creating a border ½-inch wide). When the pastry is baked, a lid can be lifted out where it was scored. A second and more efficient way is to roll the pastry out to a thickness of ¼ inch, cut the shape desired, brush with egg wash, then place a second piece of dough the same size and shape, with a center area cut out. When baked, a concave center area is automatically created. (See Figure 5.3.)

Bake bouchées on a lightly buttered pan, in a preheated 375°F oven until puffed up and golden brown. There are dozens of different fillings for bouchées, which can be served as small dishes, luncheon main courses, or as a specified garnish for a larger dish. All of the examples that follow are round, unless otherwise indicated.

Bouchée, Ambassadress Style
(Bouchée à l'Ambassadrice)

Filled with diced lamb sweetbreads, asparagus tips, and minced truffles, bound in Supreme Sauce.

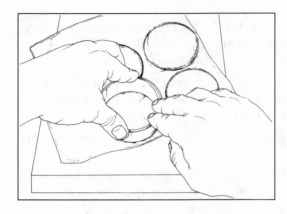
Cut out 3 to 4-inch circles of puff paste.

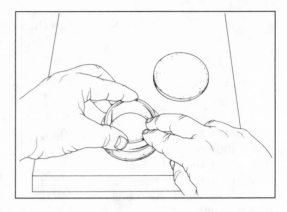
Cut out a smaller interior circle, leaving an approximately ¼-inch wide circle.

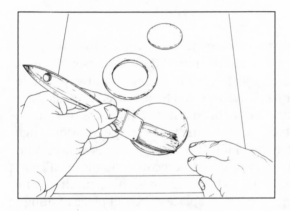
Brush the larger circle with egg wash.

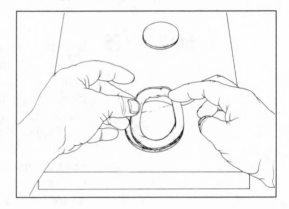
Place the cutout circle around the edge of the full circle, brush with egg wash, and bake until golden brown.

Figure 5.3
Preparing a bouchée (puff pastry shell)

Bouchée, American Style
(Bouchée à l'Américaine)

Filled with diced lobster bound in American (Lobster) Sauce, topped with a slice of lobster.

Bouchée, Bresse Style
(Bouchée à la Bressane)

Oval shaped, filled with diced sautéed chicken livers and mushrooms bound with Duxelles Sauce.

Bouchée, Don Juan Style
(Bouchée à la Don Juan)

Filled with diced cooked chicken breast, mushrooms, and truffles, bound with demi-glaze.

Bouchée, Dutch Style
(Bouchée à la Hollandaise)

Oval shaped, filled with smoked salmon bound with Dutch Sauce (hollandaise), topped with a poached oyster.

Bouchée, Flower Girl Style
(Bouchée à la Bouquetière)

Filled with diced vegetables bound with Supreme Sauce, topped with a round slice of carrot on top (also known as Bouchée à la Printinière).

Bouchée, Hungarian Style
(Bouchée à la Hongroise)

Filled with finely minced ham bound with Paprika Sauce (demi-glaze seasoned with paprika and onions).

Bouchée, Hunter Style
(Bouchée à la Chasseur)

Filled with diced game and mushrooms, bound with a game demi-glaze.

Bouchée, Indian Style
(Bouchée à l'Indienne)

Filled with a base of rice, followed by diced fish or chicken bound in a curry flavored velouté, garnished with sieved (or a slice of) hard-boiled egg.

Bouchée, Mascot Style
(Bouchée à la Mascot)

Filled with diced chicken, artichoke bottoms, and truffles, bound with a demi-glaze flavored with a white wine reduction (such as Bercy Sauce).

Bouchée, Metternich Style
(Bouchée à la Metternich)

Filled with diced chicken and truffles bound with cream sauce, garnished with truffle.

Bouchée, Milan Style
(Bouchée à la Milanaise)

Filled with ditalini, tongue, mushrooms, and truffles, bound with tomato sauce.

Bouchée, Mirabeau Style
(Bouchée à la Mirabeau)

Filled with flaked cooked sole, bound with cream sauce finished with anchovy butter, garnished with a green olive.

Bouchée, Princess Style
(Bouchée à la Princesse)

Filled with diced chicken, asparagus tips, and truffles, bound with German Sauce (velouté flavored with mushrooms and lemon, finished with cream and egg yolk).

Bouchée, Russian Style
(Bouchée à la Russe)

Filled with diced poached sturgeon bound in Smitane Sauce (velouté with onions, finished with sour cream), garnished with hard-boiled egg.

Bouchée, Souvaroff Style
(Bouchée à la Souvaroff)

Filled with veal sweetbreads, diced cucumber, poached chicken, and artichoke bottoms, bound with German Sauce.

Bouchée, Vatel Style
(Bouchée à la Vatel)

Square-shaped, filled with diced poached chicken and goose liver, bound with Supreme Sauce.

Cheese Straws
(Allumettes au Fromage)

Puff pastry sheet brushed with water, sprinkled with grated cheese, folded over, cut into strips, strips twisted, then baked, and served warm. See Figure 5.4.

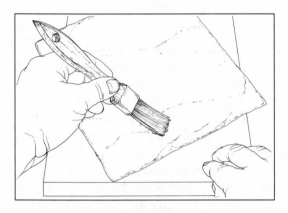

Brush a sheet of puff pastry with clarified butter, and sprinkle evenly with grated Parmesan cheese.

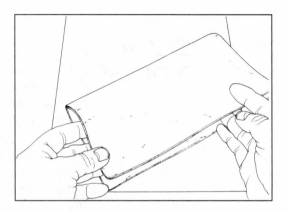

Fold the sheet over in half, and press gently together.

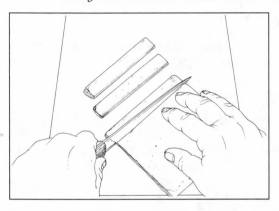

Brush the dough with egg wash, and cut into ½-inch wide slices.

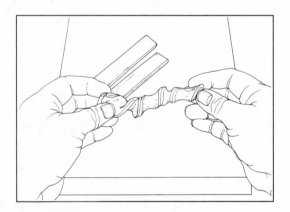

Twist each slice, place on a parchment paper-lined pan, and bake until golden brown.

Figure 5.4
Making allumettes

Variations include Anchovy Straws (*Allumette d'Anchois*, spread with minced anchovies), Caprice (*Allumettes Caprice*, minced chicken, tongue, and truffles), Caviar Straws (*Allumettes au Caviar*), and Salmon Straws (*Allumettes au Salmon*, salmon mousse or flaked poached salmon). (See color plate.)

CRESCENTS (RISSOLES)

Rissoles are puff paste crescents stuffed with various fillings, then baked or deep-fried. To cut out crescents, roll out puff pastry to a thickness of ⅛ inch. Beginning at the bottom edge of the dough, cut out a half circle, using a large (4-inch) circle cutter (this first piece is scrap). Make a second cut roughly 2 inches from the first cut edge. Repeat these cuts until there are an even number of crescent-shaped pieces of dough. Brush two pieces of dough with egg wash, then place a small amount of filling in the center of one piece. Place the second piece on top, and press the edges together. Brush with egg wash, and bake or deep-fry at 375°F until golden brown. See Figure 5.5.

Crescents, Bresse Style (Rissoles à la Bressane)

Filled with finely minced and sautéed chicken livers and mushrooms, bound with a little thick chicken velouté.

Crescents, Norman Style (Rissoles à la Normande)

Filled with finely minced cooked mussels, oysters, shrimp, and mushrooms, bound with a little thick creamed fish velouté.

Crescents with Vegetables (Rissoles à la Bouquetière)

Filled with finely diced cooked vegetables, including asparagus tips, bound in a little thick cream sauce.

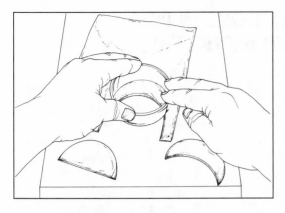

Cut out crescent-shaped pieces of puff pastry, 1½ to 2-inches wide, using a 4-inch round cutter.

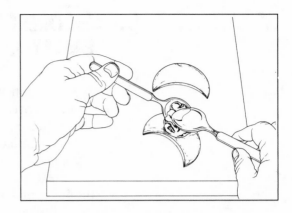

Brush the edges of one crescent with egg wash, and place the required filling in the center.

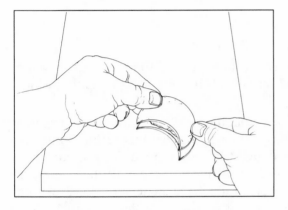

Place a second crescent on top.

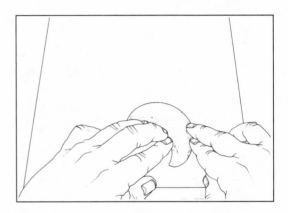

Press the edges together firmly. (Quantity of filling is important; too much, and it can ooze out.)

Figure 5.5
Preparing a rissole (puff pastry crescent)

Dartois Pastry
(Mille Feuille à la d'Artois)

Roll out some puff pastry dough, and cut into an even number of long strips measuring roughly 3 × 12 inches. Spread with some finely ground and seasoned meat, poultry, game, or fish, bound with a little brown, velouté, cream, or tomato sauce (depending on the type of filling), top with a second sheet, brush with egg wash, and bake until golden brown. Allow to cool slightly, then cut widthwise into 1-inch wide strips, and serve.

*F*OREST MUSHROOMS IN PUFF PASTRY, ROASTED GARLIC SAUCE

1 pound puff pastry dough
  (or 2 frozen sheets)
1 egg, beaten
2 cups of mixed wild mushrooms (chanterelles,
  morels, shiitakes, oyster)
the juice of 1 lemon
¼ cup olive oil
2 garlic bulbs
¼ teaspoon thyme leaves

¼ teaspoon oregano leaves
½ cup very rich demi-glaze
  (brown sauce)
2 garlic cloves, pressed
olive oil as needed
1 cup dry white wine
1 shallot, minced
2 cups heavy cream
salt and pepper to taste
8 sprigs watercress

- Preheat an oven to 375°F.
- Rinse the mushrooms in cold water and the lemon juice. Wrap in paper towels, and set aside. When dry, cut them into ¼-inch pieces.
- Roll out the puff pastry dough on a lightly floured surface, to a thickness of ⅛ inch. Cut out 8 rectangles, measuring about 3 × 4 inches. (Wrap the dough trimmings in plastic and refrigerate or freeze for other uses.) Brush 4 of these with the egg wash, then set each of the remaining 4 rectangles on top. Brush off excess flour, coat with egg wash, and transfer the pastries to a lightly buttered baking sheet. Bake for 15 to 20 minutes, or until golden brown. Remove and set aside.
- Remove excess papery skin from the outside of the garlic bulbs. Rub with olive oil and roast for 45 minutes. Remove from the oven, allow to cool, then squeeze the garlic out, clove by clove, and set aside.
- Sauté the mushrooms in the olive oil for several minutes. Add the pressed garlic cloves and herbs, and continue sautéing. Add the demi-glaze, blend thoroughly, and set aside.
- Simmer the wine and the shallot, and reduce by three-fourths. Add the garlic paste and the cream, and simmer until desired thickness is achieved. Season to taste with salt and pepper.
- Split the pastry croustades in half horizontally. Put the mushroom mixture into the bottom half of each croustade, place the other half on top, and heat briefly in the oven. Place on a serving plate, lift up the pastry lid, and ladle a little of the sauce onto the mushrooms. Serve garnished with watercress.

Mushrooms are part of the vegetable family known as *fungi*, further subdivided into the categories of *morels, mushrooms,* and *truffles*. There are thousands of varieties of mushrooms, all of which are related to molds and yeasts, that are among our most primitive foods. The rich, meaty flavor of fungi and their ability to intensify the flavor of foods they accompany is largely due to an abnormally high content of glutamic acid, which makes them a natural version of monosodium glutamate (MSG). Glutamic acid opens the taste buds, which is why MSG functions as a flavor enhancer.

The availability of wild mushrooms varies according to geographical region and season. Some varieties, now cultivated commercially, are easier to locate. The ubiquitous off-white mushroom found in supermarkets year round is a cultivated variety variously referred to as *Parisienne* or field mushrooms. In the absence of the wild varieties, whether foraged for in their natural setting or cultivated commercially, the ordinary supermarket variety can be used in their stead.

$\mathscr{P}$OTATO DUMPLINGS, ROMAN STYLE

(Gnocchi di Patate alla Romana)

For the Dumplings

1 pound potatoes, peeled
1¼ to 1½ cups high-gluten flour
½ teaspoon salt

1 egg
1 egg yolk
white pepper and nutmeg to taste

For the Sauce

½ cup olive oil
1 cup onion, medium dice
4 cloves garlic, pressed
1½ cups diced tomatoes

3 ounces unsalted butter
salt and pepper to taste
grated Romano cheese

- Boil the potatoes in lightly salted water until tender. Drain thoroughly.
- Mash the potatoes with a ricer or food mill. Add the remaining dumpling ingredients, and blend into a smooth dough. (The amount of flour will depend on the moisture content of the

potatoes.) Roll out the dough on a floured board, into cylinders about ¾-inch thick. Cut into 1-inch lengths and roll gently with a fork, leaving a ribbed pattern. Allow to rest 30 minutes.

- Cook the gnocchi in lightly salted boiling water 6 to 8 minutes, or until fully cooked. Drain and set aside.

- Sauté the onion in the olive oil for 5 minutes. Add the garlic, then the tomatoes. Beat in the butter, and season to taste with salt and pepper. Serve over the gnocchi, topped with freshly grated cheese and black pepper.

SPINACH DUMPLINGS, FLORENCE STYLE

(Gnocchi alla Florentina)

For the Dumplings

1 pound fresh spinach, rinsed and stemmed	2 tablespoons unsalted butter
2 cups milk	½ cup grated Parmesan cheese
1 cup semolina flour	
¼ teaspoon salt	1 egg
	2 egg yolks

For the Sauce

2 tablespoons butter, kneaded into a paste with 2 tablespoons flour	salt and white pepper to taste
4 cups milk, hot	½ cup grated Parmesan cheese

- Steam the spinach in a little water for several minutes. Drain, squeeze dry, and purée in a food processor, or chop very fine by hand. Set aside.

- Heat the milk, and stir in the salt and semolina, while stirring continuously. Simmer for about 7 minutes, stirring continuously, then blend in the spinach, butter, cheese, and eggs. Set aside and allow to cool.

- Preheat an oven to 375°F.

- Beat the butter/flour paste into the hot milk, and simmer for several minutes, stirring continuously. Season to taste with salt and pepper.

- Scoop out heaping tablespoonfuls of the dumpling mixture, shape into round dumplings in the palm of your hand (moistened with water), then transfer to buttered casserole dishes. Ladle a small amount of the sauce over the dumplings, top with grated cheese, and bake about 25 minutes.

SPINACH PIE, GREEK STYLE

(Spanakopita)

¼ cup olive oil
1 cup onion, finely diced
2 pounds spinach, well
   rinsed, stems removed
¼ cup chopped dill
2 cups feta cheese, crumbled

6 eggs, beaten
salt, pepper, and nutmeg to
   taste
16 sheets phyllo dough
clarified butter as needed
   (about 1 cup)

- Sauté the onion in the oil, without coloring. Set aside.
- Cook the spinach in a small amount of water, covered, for about 2 minutes. Drain and squeeze dry. Coarsely chop the spinach and place in a large bowl.
- Add the onion, dill, feta, eggs, salt, pepper, and nutmeg, and blend thoroughly. Set aside.
- Preheat an oven to 350°F.
- Lightly butter the bottom of a baking dish that is slightly smaller than the sheets of phyllo dough. Place 1 sheet of phyllo into the pan, with a third of the sheet extending outside the edge of the pan. Lightly brush this sheet with butter, then place another sheet on top, extending outside a second side of the pan. Brush with butter, and continue laying in phyllo, until there are 8 sheets of phyllo, with two overlapping flaps on each of the four sides of the pan.
- Spread half of the spinach mixture in an even layer over the phyllo. Top with 4 sheets of phyllo, directly over the spinach, lightly buttering each sheet before placing on the next. Spread the remaining spinach on top of this, and turn the 4 overlapping flaps of dough onto the tart. Cover with the remaining 4 sheets of dough. Brush the top with butter, and bake for 30 to 40 minutes, or until the top is golden brown.
- Remove from the oven and allow to rest 10 minutes. Cut the pie into squares or diamond-shaped pieces (lozenges) and serve.

QUESADILLA, CALIFORNIA STYLE

For the Salsa

½ tablespoons radish, finely diced

½ tablespoons red onion, finely diced

3 scallions, finely sliced

½ tablespoons fresh cilantro leaves, minced

1 teaspoon jalapeño pepper, minced

the juice of 8 limes

salt to taste

For the Quesadilla

8 flour tortillas

2 cups grated Monterey Jack cheese

½ cup cilantro, minced

½ cup pickled jalapeño peppers, finely chopped

oil as needed

- Combine all the salsa ingredients in a stainless steel bowl. Cover, refrigerate, and marinate for at least 1 hour.
- Brush a griddle top on medium fire with the oil, and place 4 of the tortillas on it. Divide the cheese, cilantro, and peppers among the tortillas, in that order, spreading them within 1 inch of the edges of the tortillas. Top each with one of the remaining tortillas.
- When the bottom tortilla is light brown, flip the whole thing, and brown the second side. Cut into 8 pie slices and serve with the salsa.

PUFFS

Cold Dishes

LOBSTER PUFFS

(Duchesses à la Cardinale)

12 duchesse shells

¾ cup cooked lobster, small dice

¼ cup celery, small dice

¼ cup scallions, small dice

1 teaspoon tarragon, minced

1 teaspoon parsley, minced

¼ cup mayonnaise

2 tablespoons lemon juice

salt and white pepper to taste

½ cup mayonnaise

2 tablespoons tomato paste

warm liquid aspic as needed

Giocchini Antonio Rossini (1792–1868), the prolific opera composer and gastronome, is credited with creating a dish at Café Anglais in Paris. Rossini had become bored with usual menu and gave his waiter instructions for a dish he innovated on the spot. The waiter replied, "Never would I dare to offer a thing as . . . as unpresentable." "Well! Arrange not to let it be seen—*Tourne le dos*, (turn the [your] back.)" Thus was created *Tournedos Rossini*, a medallion of beef filet, sautéed, topped with a slice of goose liver, and served with Périgord sauce (brown truffle sauce).

Under the heading of puffs, made from pâte à choux, are Carolines, 2- to 3-inch-long puffs (similar to a miniature éclair), and Duchesses, 1½ to 2-inch round puffs.

Hot Dishes

- Combine the lobster, celery, scallions, herbs, ¼ cup mayonnaise, lemon juice, salt, and pepper.
- Slice the top off the duchesse shells and scoop out the interiors. Fill with the lobster salad, then set aside.
- Blend ½ cup mayonnaise, tomato paste, and enough aspic to make a smooth, thick collée. Place the pastry tops on a wire rack, and coat with the collée. Refrigerate until set, and recoat if necessary.
- Place the tops onto the stuffed pastries and serve.

Murat Puffs
(Carolines à la Murat)

A duchesse shell, filled with a purée of artichoke bottoms blended with cream cheese and herbs, glazed with mayonnaise collée, decorated with herbs, and glazed with aspic. (See color plate.)

Rossini Puffs
(Duchesses à la Rossini)

A duchesse shell, filled with a purée of goose liver and minced truffles, glazed with demi-glaze and aspic.

Sultan Puffs
(Carolines à la Sultane)

A duchesse shell filled with chicken mousse, glazed with chicken chaud-froid, garnished with chopped pistachios. (See color plate.)

Swedish Anchovy Puffs
(Duchesses à la Suédoise)

A duchesse shell, top removed, filled with a paste made with anchovies, butter, cream cheese, and chopped parsley, top glazed with aspic, covered with sieved egg yolks.

𝒞HEESE SOUFFLÉ

2 ounces butter	5 egg yolks
2 ounces flour	6 ounces Gruyère cheese, grated
10 ounces milk, hot	

7 egg whites

butter, flour, and grated Parmesan cheese as needed

- Knead the butter and flour together into a smooth paste. Beat this into the hot milk, and place over a medium flame. Simmer about 8 minutes, stirring continuously. Remove from the fire, and allow to cool.
- Coat the inside of 4 soufflé ramekins with butter. Dust with a combination of flour and Parmesan cheese. Refrigerate until ready to use.
- Preheat an oven to 400°F.
- Add the egg yolks to the milk mixture, one at a time, blending each one in before adding the next.
- Beat the egg whites to a soft peak. Blend the Gruyère cheese thoroughly into the milk mixture. Fold in half the beaten whites, using a rubber spatula. Fold in the second half of the whites. Fill the ramekins three-quarters full, and bake 25 to 30 minutes, or until the soufflés are golden brown. Serve immediately.

———— • ————

The word *soufflé* is the past participle of the French verb *souffler*, meaning "to whisper, to blow, to breathe"—an indication of the dish's well-known fragility. Successfully preparing a soufflé may be the quintessential culinary challenge. This eighteenth-century relative of *genoise* (a light sponge cake) must be baked at a temperature high enough to set the proteins in the egg, yet low enough to heat the interior without burning the exterior. The unsure culinarian is wise to keep a spectacular backup dish on hand.

This was Peter Van Erp's recipe, a dish we prepared frequently during my apprenticeship with him. It is not a very difficult dish to prepare, but there are some important points to remember.
- Be sure to allow the milk mixture to cool before adding the yolks.
- Beat the whites in a grease-free bowl, otherwise they will not rise properly.
- When folding in the egg whites, be sure the first half is completely incorporated before adding the second half.
- Make sure the ramekins are completely coated with butter, especially the top inside edge.
- When pouring the mixture into the ramekins, do not allow any vestige of it to adhere above on the inside edge of the ramekins. In other words, they must be filled very cleanly.
- The soufflés should be served directly from the oven to the table. Timing is critical.

*G*OUGÈRE

2 cups water
½ pound unsalted butter
½ teaspoon salt
3 cups flour, sifted

¼ teaspoon white pepper
10 large eggs
2 cups Gruyère cheese, grated

- Bring the water, butter, and salt to a boil. Add the flour, and stir until completely blended and the paste pulls away from the side of the pot (add additional flour if necessary). Remove from the fire.
- Add the pepper and the eggs, one at a time. Blend in each egg completely before adding the next. Add the cheese, and blend.
- Preheat an oven to 375°F.
- Moisten hands and a tablespoon with water, then scoop out small egg-sized pieces, shape into smooth spheres, and place on a lightly buttered baking sheet. Bake for about 20 minutes, or until golden brown.

To prepare Samurai Fritters, substitute the cheese with an equal amount of diced lobster, shrimp, and crab meat, sautéed in peanut oil with a few dried chile peppers (removed afterward), seasoned with grated ginger and a few drops of soy sauce. (See color plate.)

---

*N*EAPOLITAN POLENTA PUFFS

3 pints of water
½ teaspoon salt
2 cups yellow cornmeal
¾ cup grated Parmesan cheese
12 ½-inch square cubes of Gruyère or Swiss cheese

flour as needed, seasoned with salt and white pepper
3 eggs, well beaten
3 cups dried bread crumbs
1 quart of vegetable oil

- Bring the water and salt to a boil. Add the cornmeal slowly, stirring to prevent lumping. Turn down the fire, stir in the grated cheese, and simmer about 3 minutes.

- Place about 12 egg-sized dollops of hot polenta onto a pan moistened with cold water. When the cornmeal is cool enough to handle, moisten hands with cold water, and shape each portion into a ball. Press a cube of cheese into the center of each ball, wrap the polenta around it, and set aside.
- Heat the oil in a heavy-gauge pan to a temperature of 375°F.
- Dust the balls with flour, dip in egg, and then into the bread crumbs. Deep-fry in the vegetable oil until golden brown, drain, and serve with grated cheese and a side dish of basic tomato sauce.

CHAPTER 6

PASTA AND PIZZA

PASTA Though all grains (cereals), seeds, nuts, and legumes are botanically considered fruits, they are different from other culinary fruits by virtue of a thin and dry layer between the interior of the seed and the outer skin. Grains also have special historical, mythological, and culinary significance. Cereal derives its name from *Ceres,* the Roman goddess of agriculture, and, in addition to pasta, grains make possible beer and bread, both staples in the human diet since the time of ancient Egypt, at about 3000 B.C. The importance of grains as a food staple, and their crucial role in human nutrition and cultural evolution, cannot be overstated. Carbohydrates (starches and sugars), the most abundant organic compounds on earth, are the principle source of energy (up to 80% of the caloric intake in many countries) for all creatures on the planet, including humans.

We generally think of pasta as the quintessential Italian food, yet noodles (from the German *nudel*) were invented in China as early as the first century A.D. and were introduced to the Western world by the Venetian traveler Marco Polo (1254–1324) as a result of his travels to China. One early Chinese writer remarked that common people invented noodles, but learned the best ways to prepare them from foreigners, an indication that this food was invented independently by several cultures. There is good indication that the diet of both India and the Middle East included noodles at some time during the first millennium, and that the Etruscans (pre-Rome) had pasta as well. There is much sense to this idea, since this form of grain-derived food is much easier to produce than bread—no fermentation or baking is required.

The popularity of pasta in modern times dates from the eighteenth century, when mass production by machine was begun in Naples. During the nineteenth century, the use of homemade pasta slowly declined, replaced by the factory version, though commoners took longer to accept what they considered a luxury food. By the 1930s pasta was so prominent in the Italian diet that F. T. Marinetti, author of *Cucina Furista* blamed it for "the weakness, pessimism, inactivity, nostalgia, and neutralism" of his country. Today the per capita consumption of pasta in Italy is 65 pounds a year—more than twice the amount for any other nationality—as compared with about 8 pounds per person in the United States.

There are two basic ingredients in pasta: water and either flour or semolina (the coarsest grade of milled wheat). The harder the wheat, the fewer and smaller the starch grains, and the higher proportion of endosperm. This results in a more continuous and stronger protein matrix. Durum semolina, the strongest variety of wheat, makes for a tough dough, well suited for pasta. Drying is the trickiest step in pasta manufacture. The problem lies in reducing the moisture rate from 25% to 10%. If the noodles are dried too fast, the outer layers will shrink too fast, creating cracks. If the moisture is removed too slowly, airborne bacteria and molds will spoil the dough. Commercial producers allow 15 to 36 hours for drying, beginning with a fast half hour, a slower hour or two, then a very slow day or two, during which time the moisture is fully redistributed.

In pairing pasta with sauces or styles of ingredients, there are few rules. The various cities, towns, and regions of Italy have their own traditional standards, as do cities, towns, and regions in North America. It is perfectly acceptable to create pasta dishes on a daily basis, according to the availability of ingredients, preferences of the guests, the weather, time of the day, and so on. Several of the dishes that follow (Cannelloni, Great Electric Underground Style; Cheese Ravioli, Charlotte Amalie; Fettucine Natalia; Fusilli Jackson; Linguine Leonardo; Mafalda, Bachelor Style; Spinach Linguini Yasamin) were ones I created, based on just these criteria. Yasamin, Leonardo, and Natalia, for example, were co-workers at one place or another, where I, as chef, once prepared a special dish for each of them. By maintaining a record of these creations, I was able to include them as a part of a personal repertoire.

There are, however, certain rules and basic guidelines underlying the creative process and pertaining to the preparation and handling of pasta. These are important.

- Use primarily fresh, local ingredients.
- Unless one is familiar with a maker of locally prepared fresh pasta, a quality dried pasta made from durum semolina (the hard wheat that makes the best pasta), is generally superior. (Fresh pasta also requires as little as 1 minute of cooking time.)
- "One should not indiscriminately sprinkle Parmigiano over everything if all dishes are not to melt into an unappealing sameness," writes Giuliano Buglialli. "Generally, cheese is not used with fish, game, or mushroom sauces—though there are a few exceptions—and rarely in dishes with hot red peppers."
- In the following recipes, the type of grated cheese is not always indicated. This means that the cook's choice applies: feel free to use Parmesan, Romano, pecorino, or even dried Monterey Jack, a California specialty. No matter which variety you select, *always* grate your own.
- Pasta must be cooked in plenty of rapidly boiling, lightly salted water (2 gallons per pound of pasta). It should be

stirred for the first couple of minutes, to prevent the pasta from sticking to itself, until the water returns to a boil.

- Ideally, pasta should be cooked just before it is to be served, not reheated at a later time (large-production restaurants and hotels cannot always afford this luxury).

Olive oil is often added to the water for cooking pasta, based on the supposition that it will prevent the pasta from sticking together. This is a misconception, since the oil floats on top of the water and has little direct interaction with the noodles. The primary reason for adding olive oil is that it prevents the water from boiling over, but this can be prevented by using a pot large enough to allow sufficient space between the water and the top edge of the pot. Perhaps the practice of adding a tablespoon of olive oil to a pot of boiling water is one of many enigmatic little tricks of the trade that add a certain indescribable something to a dish.

Anellini (*anellus:* ring)

Bucatini (*buca:* hole)

Calzone (*calza:* stocking, pants leg)

Cannellone (*canna:* reed, cane)

Capellini, cappelletti (*cappella:* cap, hat; *capello:* hair)

Cavatappi, cavatelli (*Cava, cavus:* hollow)

Conchiglie, conchigliette (*concha:* shell)

Corallini (*coralin:* coral)

Ditalini (*ditale:* thimble)

Farfalle (*farfalle:* butterfly, moth)

Fedelini (*filo:* thread)

Fettuce, fettuccine (*fetta:* ribbon)

Funghini (*funghi:* botanical family that includes mushrooms, truffles, and morels)

Fusilli (*fusus, fuso, fusillo:* spindle)

Gnocchi, gnocchetti (from *gnocco:* knot of a tree, lump)

Lasagna (*lasanum:* cooking pot)

Linguine (*lingua:* tongue)

Lumache (O. E. *sneg:* snail)

Manicotti (*manica:* sleeve)

Mezzani (*mezzano:* middle size)

Orecchiette (*orecchio:* ear)

Panzarotti (*panzarotto:* belly)

Pastina, pastine (*pasta:* dough or paste)

Penne, Pennette, Pennoni (*penna:* feather, wing)

Radittiore (*radiattori:* radiators)

Rigati, rigatoni (*rigato, rigare:* corrugate)

Rigoletti (*righi:* lines)

Spaghetti, spaghettini (*spago:* string)

Spedini (*spiedo:* kitchen spit)

Stellette (*stella:* star)

Taglierini, tagliatelle, tagliolini (*tagliare:* to cut)

Tortelle, tortellini (*tortello:* stuffed pastry)

Trenette (*treno:* train)

Tripolini (*tripodes:* tripod)

Tubetti (*tubulatus:* tubular)

Vermicelli (*verme:* worm)

Ziti (*zito, zita:* bride's macaroni)

············ # *B*AKED ZITI WITH EGGPLANT

(Ziti con Melanzane Grantinati)

1 pound ziti
3 medium eggplants, sliced
  ½-inch thick widthwise
olive oil, salt, and pepper as
  needed

1 recipe tomato sauce (from
  "Cannelloni, *GEU* Style")
¾ pound mozzarella cheese,
  sliced ¹⁄₁₆-inch thick

- Brush the eggplant slices with oil, sprinkle with salt and pepper, and broil until golden brown on both sides.

- Cook the ziti in boiling salted water until al dente. Drain, toss with the tomato sauce, and place in an ovenproof casserole dish. Place the eggplant slices on top, cover with the sliced cheese, and bake at 375°F for 30 minutes, or until the cheese is melted and light brown.

. . . . # *B*UTTERNUT SQUASH RAVIOLI, SAGE BUTTER

1 shallot, minced
1 garlic clove, pressed
1 cup dry white wine
¼ cup minced sage leaves
salt and white pepper to taste
12 tablespoons unsalted butter, soft

1 pound butternut squash, peeled, seeded, and cut into 1-inch pieces
¼ cup Parmesan cheese
¼ pound unsalted butter
pinch of nutmeg
30 wonton wrappers
cornstarch as needed

- Simmer the shallot, garlic, and wine, until reduced by three-fourths. Remove from the fire, and set aside to cool.
- Beat 12 tablespoons of butter along with the reduced liquid, sage, salt, and pepper. Shape the butter into a 1-inch wide cylinder on a piece of wax or parchment paper. Wrap the butter securely, twist or fold the ends shut, and wrap in plastic wrap. Label and refrigerate until ready to use.
- Boil the squash in boiling salted water until tender. Drain until completely dry. Mash the squash, and beat in the cheese, ¼ pound of butter, salt, pepper, and nutmeg.
- Place a half teaspoon of the butternut filling onto the center of a wonton skin. With a small pastry brush, moisten the edges of the skin with water. Place another wonton skin on top, and press the edges together. Trim excess dough from the edge, then place on a plate dusted with cornstarch. Repeat until all the wontons are filled.
- Poach the wontons in boiling salted water for about 1 minute each, or until they float to the surface. Place into a hot sauté pan, and when all the water has evaporated, toss with several slices of the sage butter.

CANNELLONI, GREAT ELECTRIC UNDERGROUND (GEU) STYLE

For the Crêpes

1½ cups flour
4 eggs
pinch of salt
1¼ cups milk
¼ cup grated Parmesan
  cheese

3 tablespoons olive oil
olive oil as needed
6 slices Monterey Jack
  cheese, sliced thin

For the Sauce

¼ cup olive oil
4 garlic cloves, finely sliced
½ cup onions, finely diced
1 tablespoon oregano leaves,
  minced

1½ cups diced tomatoes
  with their juice
1½ cups tomato purée
3 tablespoons tomato paste
salt and pepper to taste

For the Filling

¼ cup olive oil
4 shallots, sliced very thin
6 garlic cloves, pressed
¼ cup dry vermouth
1 pound ground veal
1 cup spinach, finely
  chopped

¼ cup basil leaves, minced
¼ cup capers, drained
the zest of 1 lemon
½ cup heavy cream
salt and pepper to taste

- Beat the flour, eggs, and salt together, until the mixture is a smooth paste. Add the milk, and beat until smooth. Add the cheese and olive oil, blend, and allow to sit for 30 minutes.

- Heat a 6-inch nonstick sauté pan over medium heat. Rub the pan with a cloth or paper towel dipped in olive oil, and pour in enough batter to coat the bottom of the pan (the crêpe should be fairly thin—about 1/16 inch). When the top of the batter is nearly dry, turn the crêpe over, cook another minute, then remove to a plate. Repeat until all the batter is used.

- Sauté the garlic and onions in the olive oil without browning. Add the oregano, tomatoes, salt, and pepper, and simmer for 20 minutes. Adjust seasoning, and set aside.

- Sauté the shallots and garlic in the olive oil without browning. Add the vermouth, and simmer until nearly dry. Remove from the fire, and set aside to cool.

- Place the shallots and garlic in a large bowl, and add the veal, spinach, basil, capers, zest, cream, salt, and pepper. Mix together thoroughly.
- Place a cylindrical roll of filling, about 1 inch in diameter, about ½ inch from each side and slightly off-center on each crêpe, and roll up. Place the crêpes in an ovenproof casserole dish, and top with the sauce. Bake uncovered for 30 minutes. Top the crêpes with the sliced cheese, and bake another 10 minutes.

———— • ————

After the crêpe batter rests for 30 minutes, it will thicken slightly, depending on the degree of moisture in the flour. If it is too thick, thin the batter with additional milk.

Cannelloni can also be made with thin sheets of pasta dough. The crêpe version is unique to San Francisco and certain regions of Italy.

The Great Electric Underground was a restaurant in San Francisco where the author served as chef de cuisine from 1977 to 1979. This dish was a popular favorite that was served weekly as a special (plat du jour).

CAVATAPPI, AMATRICE STYLE

(Cavatappi Amatriciana)

1 pound cavatappi	6 dried hot chile peppers
1 cup bacon, medium dice	1 teaspoon hot chile pepper
¼ cup olive oil	flakes
1 small onion, medium dice	¾ cup tomato purée
6 garlic cloves, pressed	salt to taste

- Render the bacon over medium heat until golden brown. Drain thoroughly, discarding the fat.
- Sauté the onion and garlic in the olive oil, without browning. Add the hot peppers, pepper flakes, tomato purée, and salt. Simmer about 10 minutes.
- Cook the pasta in boiling salted water until al dente. Drain, toss with the sauce, and serve.

CHEESE RAVIOLI, CHARLOTTE AMALIE

2 pounds cheese ravioli	3 tablespoons olive oil
½ cup dry bread crumbs	2 shallots, minced
6 tablespoons unsalted butter	½ cup water

3 tablespoons chicken glaze *(glace de volaille)*, chopped
¼ cup parsley, minced

grated Parmesan cheese
salt and pepper to taste

- Cook the cheese ravioli in boiling salted water until al dente. Drain, cool, and coat with the olive oil.
- Sauté the bread crumbs in 4 tablespoons of butter, until golden brown. Set aside.
- Sauté the shallot in the butter. Add the water and the glaze, and melt. Toss the raviolis in this mixture, add the parsley, and season to taste. Sprinkle the top with the toasted bread crumbs, and serve with the grated cheese.

The word *ravioli* is derived from *rabiole,* meaning "scraps of little value," referring to the leftover food chopped up and wrapped in small pasta pillows by the sailors of Genoa during longer voyages.

Charlotte Amalie is the central township on St. Thomas of the U.S. Virgin Islands. The author created this dish for guests while working as chef de cuisine on a yacht charter.

$\mathcal{C}$ONCHIGLIE WITH BOLOGNESE SAUCE

(Conchiglie alla Bolognese)

2 pounds conchiglie
2 tablespoons olive oil
½ cup pancetta, small dice
4 tablespoons unsalted butter
¼ cup prosciutto, sliced thin, and cut into small dice
1 cup onions, small dice
¼ cup carrots, peeled, trimmed, and grated

½ cup celery, cut into small dice
½ pound ground sirloin
½ pound ground pork
¼ cup dry white wine
2 cups beef or veal stock
3 tablespoons tomato paste
1 cup heavy cream
salt, pepper, and nutmeg to taste

- Sauté the pancetta in the olive oil, until golden brown. Add the butter, prosciutto, onions, carrots, and celery, and cook 10 minutes, until lightly browned.
- Add the ground beef and pork and cook thoroughly, stirring continuously. Add the wine, stock, and tomato paste, blend thoroughly, and simmer 45 minutes.
- Add the cream, season to taste, and serve over the hot pasta.

FARFALLE WITH FOUR CHEESES

(Farfalle ai Quattro Formaggi)

1 pound farfalle
¼ cup grated Parmesan
  cheese
¼ cup grated Romano
  cheese
¼ cup grated pecorino
  cheese

¼ cup grated Asiago cheese
1 cup heavy cream, hot
4 tablespoons unsalted
  butter
½ cup pine nuts or walnuts,
  toasted
pepper to taste

- Cook the farfalle in boiling salted water until al dente. Drain, and toss with the cheeses, cream, and butter. Top with toasted nuts and fresh ground black pepper.

FETTUCCINE NATALIA

1 pound fettuccine
2 tablespoons unsalted
  butter
1 cup mushrooms, medium
  dice
1 cup leeks, well rinsed and
  cut into medium dice
1½ cups heavy cream

1 cup radicchio, cut into
  chiffonade
salt and pepper to taste
2 tablespoons unsalted
  butter, cut into small
  cubes
grated Parmesan cheese as
  needed

- Sauté the mushrooms and leeks in 2 tablespoons of butter for 5 minutes, without browning. Add the cream, and simmer until reduced by half. Add the radicchio, and season to taste with salt and pepper. Add 2 tablespoons of butter, and blend in until fully incorporated. Set aside.
- Cook the fettuccine in boiling salted water until al dente. Drain well, then toss with the sauce, and serve with grated cheese.

FETTUCCINE BARDELLI

1 pound fettuccine
2 tablespoons olive oil
¼ cup prosciutto, thinly
  sliced and minced
4 tablespoons unsalted
  butter
4 garlic cloves, pressed
2 shallots, minced

1 cup mushrooms, sliced
  thin
3 tablespoons basil pesto
½ cup tomato purée
½ cup heavy cream
salt and pepper to taste
grated cheese as needed

- Sauté the prosciutto in the olive oil until golden brown. Add the butter, garlic, shallots, and mushrooms, and cook about 5 minutes. Add the basil and tomato purée, and cook several minutes.

- Add the cream, salt, and pepper, and simmer several minutes.

- Cook the fettuccine in boiling salted water until al dente. Drain, toss with the sauce, and serve with grated cheese.

———————————— • ————————————

Fettuccine Bardelli was created by Charles Bardelli, late chef of Bardelli's, one of San Francisco's oldest restaurants (originally known as Charle's Fashion Restaurant). Bardelli's is still in operation, located on O'Farrell Street in the downtown district.

ℱETTUCCINE WITH ZUCCHINI

1 pound fettuccine
½ cup olive oil
½ cup dry bread crumbs
2 cups zucchini, cut into spears

4 garlic cloves, sliced very thin
salt and pepper to taste

- Sauté the bread crumbs in half the olive oil until golden brown. Set aside.

- Sauté the zucchini in the remaining olive oil until light brown. Add the garlic, and cook several more minutes. Season with salt and pepper, remove from the fire, and set aside.

- Cook the fettuccine in boiling salted water until al dente. Drain, then toss with the zucchini, and top with the toasted bread crumbs.

ℱLORENTINE PASTA ROLLS

1½ cups ricotta cheese
1½ cups cooked chopped spinach, squeezed dry
1 cup onions, finely diced
¼ cup olive oil
8 garlic cloves, finely sliced
½ cup sun-dried tomatoes, reconstituted and finely diced

¼ cup capers, drained
¼ cup basil, minced
¼ cup prosciutto, sliced paper-thin and cut julienne
salt, pepper, and nutmeg as needed
3 sheets fresh lasagna pasta

- Sauté the onions in the olive oil, without browning. Add the garlic, and cook another few minutes. Transfer to a large bowl, and add the rest of the ingredients, except for the pasta. Season to taste with salt, pepper, and nutmeg, and blend thoroughly.
- Cut the pasta sheets in half lengthwise. Place a 1-inch wide line of the filling near one of the long sides of the sheet, about 1 inch from each end. Moisten the edges of the pasta with water, then wrap the pasta firmly around the filling, and roll up. Press the moistened edge in place. Repeat until all the pasta is filled and rolled.
- Poach the pasta rolls carefully in boiling salted water, about 8 minutes. Remove and allow to cool. Cover and refrigerate.
- When fully chilled, slice the rolls in 1-inch wide slices, place on a lightly oiled pan, warm, and serve.

Because making pasta is a time-consuming affair, it is sometimes expeditious to purchase the fresh dough already prepared. For those who wish to make their own, a basic recipe is as follows: 2 cups semolina or high-gluten flour, 2 cups all-purpose flour, 5 eggs, 2 tablespoons olive oil, pinch of salt. Combine all ingredients into a cohesive ball, and knead until smooth. Let rest 20 minutes, then roll out on a floured board to a thickness of $1/16$ inch.

A second option for all stuffed pasta dishes (agnoletti, manicotti, ravioli, tortellini) is to use egg roll or wonton wrappers, available in most Asian markets.

𝒻USILLI JACKSON

1 pound fusilli	1 cup diced tomato
1 cup bacon, cut into medium dice	salt and pepper as needed
2 tablespoons unsalted butter	3 tablespoons olive oil
1 cup asparagus, woody ends removed, and cut on a sharp bias	$1/4$ cup parsley, minced grated Parmesan cheese

- Sauté the bacon over medium heat until golden brown. Drain, discard the fat, and set the bacon aside.
- Sauté the asparagus in the butter for several minutes. Add the tomato, and season with salt and pepper.
- Cook the fusilli in boiling salted water until al dente. Drain well, then toss with the sauce, olive oil, and parsley, and serve with grated cheese.

HAY AND STRAW

(Paglia e Fieno)

½ pound tagliarini
½ pound spinach tagliarini
2 tablespoons unsalted
  butter
½ cup onion, small dice
2 garlic cloves, pressed
¾ cup ground sausage meat
¼ cup prosciutto, sliced
  paper-thin and cut into
  1-inch julienne

1 cup green peas (fresh or
  frozen)
½ cup rich chicken or veal
  stock, hot
salt and pepper to taste
¼ cup olive oil
grated Parmesan cheese

- Blanch the peas (if fresh) in boiling salted water until al dente. Drain and set aside.
- Sauté the onion and garlic in the butter for several minutes. Add the sausage, prosciutto, and peas, and cook several minutes. Season to taste with salt and pepper.
- Cook the tagliarini in boiling salted water until al dente. Drain, and toss with the ham and pea mixture, stock, and olive oil, and serve with grated cheese.

LASAGNA WITH SPINACH AND WILD MUSHROOMS

(Lasagne con Spinaci e Funghi)

2 pounds lasagna noodles
3 tablespoons unsalted
  butter
3 tablespoons flour
3 cups milk, hot
salt, white pepper, and
  nutmeg to taste
½ cup olive oil
1 small onion, finely sliced
6 garlic cloves, pressed
2 cups spinach, cooked,
  drained, and finely
  chopped

¾ cup shiitake mushrooms,
  sliced thin
¾ cup chanterelle mush-
  rooms, brushed clean and
  sliced thin
1 cup button mushrooms,
  brushed clean and
  medium diced
½ cup dry white wine
2 cups ricotta cheese
2 eggs, beaten
¼ cup parsley, minced

2 tablespoons sage leaves,
cut into chiffonade
2 tablespoons basil leaves,
cut into chiffonade

1 pound mozzarella cheese,
grated
½ cup grated Parmesan
cheese

- Cook the lasagna noodles in boiling salted water until al dente. Drain, cool, and set aside.
- Heat the butter, blend in the flour, and cook several minutes without browning. Add the milk and simmer, while stirring continuously, for several minutes. Season with salt and white pepper, strain, and set aside.
- Sauté the onion in half of the olive oil. Add the garlic, then the spinach, and season with salt, white pepper, and nutmeg.
- Sauté the mushrooms in the remaining olive oil over high heat. Add the white wine, simmer until nearly dry, and season with salt and white pepper.
- Preheat an oven to 375°F.
- Coat the bottom of a casserole dish liberally with butter or oil, and cover with a layer of noodles. Cover with a layer of spinach, coated with about half of the sauce, followed by another layer of noodles.
- Blend the ricotta cheese with the eggs and herbs, and spread a layer of this on the noodles. Sprinkle the top of this with the mushrooms, followed by another layer of noodles. Top this with the mozzarella, and a final layer of noodles. Cover this with the sauce, sprinkle with grated cheese, and bake covered for 30 minutes. Remove the cover, and bake another 20 minutes, or until the top is golden brown. Remove from the oven and allow to sit for 20 minutes before serving.

If using aluminum foil to cover the dish for baking, be sure to place a sheet of parchment or wax paper over the pasta first, before covering with foil. Where the foil comes into contact with the lasagna, the acid in the milk, cheese, and so forth, will dissolve the aluminum and leave some on top of the food. (The same applies to tomato-based lasagna.)

Any remaining ingredients can be used to prepare a second, smaller lasagna.

ℒINGUINE LEONARDO

1 pound linguine
1 cup bacon, medium dice
4 tablespoons unsalted
  butter

¾ cup leeks, well rinsed and
  cut into medium dice
¾ cup mushrooms, medium
  dice
grated cheese as needed

- Render the bacon until golden brown. Drain, and discard the fat.
- Sauté the leeks and mushrooms in the butter over low heat, covered, about 10 minutes.
- Cook the linguine in boiling salted water until al dente. Drain, toss with the other ingredients, and serve with the grated cheese.

ℒINGUINE WITH ROCKET

(Linguine con Rughetta)

1 pound linguine
3 tablespoons olive oil
3 tablespoons unsalted
  butter
4 garlic cloves, pressed

2 cups arugula leaves,
  rinsed, dried, and cut into
  2-inch pieces
salt and pepper to taste
grated cheese as needed

- Sauté the garlic in the olive oil and butter for several minutes.
- Cook the linguine in boiling salted water. When it is almost al dente, add the arugula. Drain, toss with the other ingredients, and serve with grated cheese.

ℳAFALDA, BACHELOR STYLE

1 pound mafalda, broken in
  half
¼ cup olive oil
1 cup scallions, thinly sliced
  on the bias

½ cup small-curd cottage
  cheese
salt and pepper to taste
¼ cup dried Monterey Jack,
  grated

- Sauté the scallions in the olive oil. Add the cottage cheese, heat, then set aside.
- Cook the mafalda in boiling salted water until al dente. Drain, toss with the other ingredients, and top with the grated cheese.

$\mathcal{M}$OSTACIOLLI WITH BASIL PESTO

(Mostaciolli al Pesto)

1 pound mostaciolli
the leaves of 1 bunch of
    fresh basil, well rinsed
    and dried
1 cup olive oil
½ cup pine nuts or walnuts,
    toasted
3 large garlic cloves, crushed

salt and pepper to taste
¼ cup grated Parmesan
    cheese
¼ cup grated Romano
    cheese
additional grated cheese as
    needed

- Place the basil, oil, nuts, and garlic in a food processor and purée, using the pulse switch. Add the cheese, blend, season with salt and pepper, then set the sauce aside. (Pesto will taste better if prepared a day before its use.)
- Cook the mostaciolli in boiling salted water until al dente. Drain, leaving a little of the cooking water with the pasta, toss with the pesto, and serve with additional grated cheese.

Pesto is a derivation of "pestle" (from the Italian *pestare*, "to pound"), the grinding tool used with a mortar, in which various herbs and spices are ground into a paste. Any kind of herb or combination of herbs can be ground into a pesto and used in a variety of applications. *Pistou*, a similar preparation, unique to Provence, is an olive oil, garlic, and basil paste that is added to a bean, pasta, or vegetable soup just before serving.

Pasta of the Day, Farmer's Style
(Pasta del Giorno, alla Contadina)

This is more of an approach than an actual recipe, and an item the author has employed frequently in menus past. Similar in style to a Farmer's Omelet or Quiche Maison, in which various ingredients remaining from other dishes are combined in tasteful combinations and incorporated into a pasta dish (or omelet, or quiche), it invites innovation and creates a dish on the menu that is forever changing. The basic ingredients are a pasta, olive oil, cream or stock, garnishes, and seasoning. The choice of pasta may depend on the properties (shape, size, texture) of the other ingredients. Fusilli, for example, by virtue of its corkscrew shape, will tend to hold onto other ingredients in pieces within a sauce. Penne, on the other hand, is so smooth that ingredients will slip and slide when paired with that noodle, so a smooth sauce that coats is preferable. Long pasta, such as spaghetti, fettuccine, or vermicelli, tends to hold ingredients between its strands, though not necessarily when they are picked up with a fork. And, of course, ravioli, cannelloni, or agnolotti completely encase their fillings. All of these things come into consideration when preparing the pasta of the day.

The choice of cream or stock is based on dietary considerations and whether one prefers richness as opposed to the

Since the use of grated cheese should not be combined with dishes containing either seafood or hot chile peppers, a viable alternative is dry bread crumbs moistened with a little olive oil, sautéed or toasted in the oven, then sprinkled on the dish at service.

meaty flavor from a rich chicken, fish, or beef stock. The garnishes may consist of any number of ingredients, including fresh vegetables (artichoke, asparagus, beans, bell peppers, broccoli, green peas, roasted onions, tomatoes, zucchini, etc.), roasted poultry (chicken, duck, pheasant, squab), fish (flaked halibut, salmon, trout, tuna), grilled shellfish (clam, lobster, oyster, shrimp), roasted meat (strips of beef, lamb, pork, veal). Seasoning generally consists of herbs and spices (basil; black, red chile, and white pepper; cilantro; garlic; parsley; sage; etc.). Finally, additional garnishing and/or seasoning ingredients may include anchovies, capers, grated cheese, olives, or toasted bread crumbs.

𝒫ENNE, ANGRY STYLE

(Penne all'Arrabbiata)

1 pound penne
1 recipe tomato sauce (from "Cannelloni, *GEU* Style")
4 dried hot red chile peppers

1 tablespoon hot chile pepper flakes
¼ cup parsley, minced

- Heat the sauce with the addition of the hot chile peppers and flakes. Cook the penne in boiling salted water until al dente. Drain, toss in the sauce, top with chopped parsley, and serve.

𝒫ENNE WITH SUN-DRIED TOMATO PESTO

1 pound penne
3 cups sun-dried tomatoes, soaked in boiling water
1 cup olive paste

8 garlic cloves
1 cup olive oil
¾ cup Romano cheese, grated

- Drain the tomatoes, saving the water for cooking the pasta. Combine the tomatoes, olive paste, garlic, and oil in a food processor, and purée. Blend in half of the cheese, and set the sauce aside.
- Cook the penne in boiling salted water until al dente. Drain, toss with some of the pesto, and serve with the remaining cheese.

PENNE WITH POTATOES, GREEN BEANS, AND BASIL PESTO

(Penne con Patate e Fagiolini Verde al Pesto)

1 pound penne
1 recipe basil pesto (from "Mostaciolli with Basil")
1 cup green string beans, cut into 1½-inch spears (on the bias)

4 medium Red Bliss potatoes, boiled in their jackets, sliced ⅛-inch thick
grated cheese as needed

- Cook the penne in boiling salted water. Just before the pasta is finished cooking, add the string beans. When the pasta is al dente, drain, then toss with half of the pesto. Arrange on a serving platter. Toss the potatoes in the remaining pesto, arrange around the outside edge of the pasta, and serve with grated cheese.

RADITTIORE, TEAMSTER'S STYLE

(Radittiore alla Carrettiera)

1 pound radittiore
½ cup bacon, medium dice
½ cup olive oil
1½ cups button mushrooms, quartered
4 garlic cloves
4 dried hot chile peppers

1 tablespoon hot chile pepper flakes
½ cup dry vermouth
1 tablespoon tomato paste
1½ cups tomatoes, diced
½ cup flaked tuna fish
salt and pepper to taste

- Render the bacon until it just starts to turn light brown. Drain the fat and discard.
- Sauté the mushrooms in the olive oil for 5 minutes. Add the garlic, peppers and pepper flakes, and cook several minutes. Add the vermouth and reduce by half.
- Add the tomato paste, and blend thoroughly. Add the remaining ingredients, and simmer about 5 minutes.
- Cook the radittiore in boiling salted water until al dente. Drain, toss in the sauce, and serve.

$\mathscr{R}$IGATONI WITH WALNUT PESTO

(Rigatoni al Pesto di Noci)

24 cheese ravioli
1 cup walnuts, toasted
1½ cups olive oil
4 tablespoons butter, soft
  (room temperature)

¾ cup grated cheese
salt and pepper to taste
¼ cup parsley, minced

- Place the walnuts, oil, butter, and cheese in a food processor and purée. Season to taste with salt and pepper.
- Cook the ravioli in boiling salted water until al dente. Drain, toss in the pesto, top with chopped parsley, and serve.

$\mathscr{S}$HRIMP AND GINGER RAVIOLI

For the Filling

1¼ pounds 26-30 count
  shrimp, raw, in the shell
¼ cup water chestnuts,
  small diced
2 tablespoons gingerroot,
  grated
2 tablespoons olive oil

2 tablespoons cilantro,
  minced
¼ teaspoon red pepper
  flakes
2 tablespoons soy sauce
60 wonton skins
cornstarch as needed

For the Stock

1 quart water
1 small onion, peeled and
  thinly sliced
1 rib celery, finely chopped

1 bay leaf
1 tablespoon white peppercorns

For the Beurre Blanc

2 shallots, minced
1¼ cups dry white wine
12 tablespoons (1½ sticks)
  unsalted butter, cut into
  ½-inch pieces

2 tablespoons cilantro,
  minced
sprigs of cilantro (for garnish)

- Peel and devein the shrimp. Cut the shrimp into medium dice, and set aside. Simmer the shells in the water, onion, celery, bay leaf, and peppercorns for 20 minutes. Strain and set aside.

- Combine the remaining filling ingredients, except the wonton skins and cornstarch, blend well, and marinate 30 minutes.

- Place a half teaspoon of the filling onto the center of a wonton skin. With a small pastry brush, moisten the edges of the skin with water. Place another wonton skin on top, and press the edges together. Trim excess dough from the edges, then place on a plate dusted with cornstarch. Repeat until all the wontons are filled.

- Simmer the shallots and wine until reduced by half. Beat in the butter, stirring continuously, until fully emulsified. Add the cilantro and set the sauce aside, keeping warm.

- Poach the wontons in the simmering shrimp broth for about 1 minute each, or until they float to the surface. Place on serving plates, top with sauce, and garnish with a sprig of cilantro.

SPAGHETTI, BUCCANEER STYLE

(Spaghetti alla Buccaniera)

1 pound spaghetti
½ cup olive oil
4 garlic cloves, pressed
1 tablespoon red pepper flakes
1 pint tomatoes, peeled and diced
¾ cup raw octopus, medium diced
¾ cup raw shrimp, shelled, deveined, and medium diced
½ cup chopped clams
¼ cup chopped parsley
salt and pepper to taste

- Sauté the garlic and red pepper in the olive oil. Add the tomatoes and fish, and simmer 10 minutes. Add the parsley, and season to taste with salt and pepper.

- Cook the spaghetti in boiling salted water until al dente. Drain, toss in the sauce, and serve.

———————— • ————————

Spaghetti Buccaneer Style *(alla Buccaniera)*, Spaghetti Ditchdigger's Style *(alla Zappatora)*, Penne Angry Style *(all'Arrabbiata)*, and Radittiore, Teamster's Style *(alla Carrettiera)* are all highly spiced dishes, seasoned with an abundance of red chile pepper.

Spaghetti, Charcoal Maker's Style

(Spaghetti alla Carbonara)

1 pound spaghetti	4 eggs, beaten
1 cup pancetta, sliced thin and cut into medium dice	grated Parmesan cheese as needed
3 tablespoons olive oil	freshly ground black pepper

- Render the pancetta in the olive oil until golden brown. (Do not drain off the fat.)
- Cook the spaghetti in boiling salted water until al dente. Drain, toss with the pancetta. Add the eggs, some cheese, and pepper, and toss. Serve topped with additional cheese and pepper.

•

Spaghetti alla Carbonara is the charcoal maker's mainstay, a dish prepared in the Appenine mountains where the charcoal makers retreat for days at a time. There they burn the mountain hardwoods, creating charcoal drawing instruments for the artists of the world. They bring with them essentially nonperishable ingredients, which become a dish they subsist on during their retreats. The black pepper is also intended to imitate flecks of charcoal. Many a restaurant has a tendency to add cream, butter, olives, prosciutto, herbs, and so on—a corruption of the original dish. In such a case, it should ostensibly be given another name.

Spaghetti with Garlic and Oil

(Spaghetti Aglio e Olio)

1 pound spaghetti	1 teaspoon hot red chile pepper flakes
⅓ cup olive oil	
6 garlic cloves, pressed	salt and pepper to taste
4 dried hot red chile peppers	¼ cup parsley, minced

- Sauté the garlic in the olive oil. Add the red peppers and flakes, cook briefly, and set aside.
- Cook the spaghetti in boiling salted water until al dente. Drain, toss in the sauce, top with chopped parsley, and serve.

SPAGHETTI, TEAMSTER'S STYLE

(Spaghetti all Carrettiera)

1 pound spaghetti
½ cup olive oil
3 garlic cloves, pressed
½ pound mushrooms,
  medium dice
½ cup dry red wine
¼ pound ham, medium dice

¼ pound cooked tuna,
  medium dice
1½ cups tomato purée
2 tablespoons tomato paste
salt and pepper to taste
3 tablespoons mixed fresh
  herbs, minced
½ cup dried bread crumbs

- Sauté the garlic in half of the olive oil for several minutes. Add the mushrooms, and cook for several minutes. Add the wine, and reduce until nearly dry. Add the ham, tuna, and tomato ingredients, simmer, and season to taste.
- Sauté the bread crumbs in the remaining oil until golden brown, and set aside.
- Cook the spaghetti in boiling salted water until al dente. Drain, toss in the sauce and herbs, top with the toasted bread crumbs, and serve.

SPAGHETTINI, HARLOT STYLE

(Spaghetinni Puttanesca)

---•---

Pasta Puttanesca got its name from the speed with which it could be made (hence the use of spaghettini, a slightly thinner version of spaghetti, which required less cooking time). This purportedly was a swiftly prepared dish that could be made by a harlot between clients, or by a wife for her husband after an intimate afternoon interlude with her lover.

---

1 pound spaghettini or
  vermicelli
3 tablespoons olive oil
3 garlic cloves, sliced
1 red jalapeño pepper,
  minced
2 cups tomatoes, diced

2 tablespoons capers,
  drained
8 anchovy fillets, roughly
  chopped
½ cup Calamata or Gaeta
  black olives
¼ cup parsley, roughly
  chopped

- Sauté the garlic and red pepper in the olive oil. Add the tomatoes, capers, anchovies, and olives.
- Cook the spaghettini in boiling salted water until al dente. Drain, toss in the sauce, top with chopped parsley, and serve.

SPINACH LINGUINE YASAMIN

1 pound spinach linguine
3 tablespoons unsalted
  butter
1 large shallot, minced
1 cup gin

½ cup celery root, cut into
  fine julienne
½ cup heavy cream
3 sweet Italian sausages,
  grilled or roasted, and
  sliced on the bias

- Sauté the shallot in the butter for several minutes. Add the gin, and reduce by half. Add the celery root and cream, and reduce again by half.
- Cook the linguine in boiling salted water until al dente. Drain, toss in the sauce along with the sausage, and serve.

TAGLIATELLE, GORGONZOLA SAUCE

(Tagliatelle al Gorgonzola)

1 pound tagliatelle
¼ cup olive oil
¾ cup onion, roughly
  chopped
½ cup celery heart, roughly
  chopped
1½ cups milk, hot

8 ounces Gorgonzola cheese,
  crumbled
6 ounces ricotta cheese
2 tablespoons unsalted butter, soft
salt and white pepper to
  taste

Tagliatelle was reputedly invented in 1487 by a Bolognese cook in imitation of the hair of Lucrezia Borgia.

- Sauté the onion and celery in the olive oil for several minutes. Transfer to a food processor or blender, along with the remaining ingredients (except the pasta), and purée.
- Cook the tagliatelle in boiling salted water until al dente. Drain, toss in the sauce, and serve.

PIZZA

The word *pizza* may derive from the Neapolitan pronunciation of the Greek word for flat breads, *pincea,* or it may be related to the Latin *pincere,* meaning "to beat or knead." Pizza originated in Naples, created in 1889 by Rafael Esposito, in honor of Italy's Queen Margherita. She was reportedly pleased with the offering—embellished with tomato, basil, and mozzarella cheese, imitating the colors of the Italian flag.

There are endless versions of pizza dough, so many, in fact, that we have included three variations here. The first is probably the most authentic, but no matter what recipe one follows, these are the most important elements to remember.

- High-gluten or semolina flour is the best, because it has sufficient gluten to render chewy and crispy crust.
- The temperature of the liquid elements should never go beyond 110°F (a higher temperature kills the yeast).
- Knead the dough well, so that the gluten is fully developed.
- After the initial batch of dough is kneaded to a smooth, elastic state, it can be cut up into individual pieces, the size required for one pizza, wrapped securely (airtight) in two layers of plastic, and frozen. Allow the dough to thaw out in a bowl at room temperature overnight, during which time it will rise. Punch it down and allow it to rise again, then roll it out for the pizza.
- As with pasta, there are few rules governing toppings. One can use any combination of ingredients, based on availability, other dishes on a menu, or personal preferences.
- All 3 recipes will yield 2 12-inch pizzas.

 $\mathcal{P}$IZZA DOUGH 1

1 pint water (100°F)
1 cup apple juice (100°F)
1¼ ounces salt
1 ounces sugar
¾ ounce honey
¾ ounce dry yeast

3 pounds (approximately) high-gluten flour
1½ ounces olive oil
olive oil and cornmeal as needed

- Dissolve the yeast, salt, sugar, and honey in the water and apple juice. Add the flour, one cup at a time, and blend thoroughly. Add the olive oil.
- Knead the dough on a floured surface until smooth and elastic. Brush the inside of a bowl with olive oil, place the dough in the bowl, and cover tightly with plastic wrap. Place in a warm place, and allow to rise until doubled in volume (about 1 hour).
- Punch the dough down, reform into a smooth ball, oil the bowl again, and allow to rise again.
- Cut off a portion of the dough and roll out on a floured surface, about ¼-inch thick. Place on a baking sheet sprinkled with cornmeal, top with filling, then bake about 20 minutes in a preheated 450°F oven, or until golden brown.

𝒫IZZA DOUGH 2

1 cup water (100°F)
1 teaspoon salt
¼ ounce granulated yeast (1 envelope)

3¼ cups semolina or high-gluten flour
¼ cup olive oil

- Proceed as in instructions for Pizza Dough 1.

𝒫IZZA DOUGH 3

1 cup water (100°F)
¾ ounce yeast
3 cups high-gluten flour
1 tablespoon salt

½ cup low-fat yogurt
2 tablespoons cornmeal
flour and olive oil as needed

- Proceed as in instructions for Pizza Dough 1.

𝒜LSATIAN PIZZA

1 recipe batch of pizza dough (version 1, 2, or 3)
2 cups sauerkraut, drained
1 cup duck sausage, cut into ¼-inch slices
1 tablespoon caraway seeds

½ cup grated Emmenthaler cheese
olive oil as needed

All of the following pizza recipes involve the same method of preparation. Unless otherwise indicated, simply follow the directions for Alsatian Pizza.

- Preheat an oven to 450°F.
- Divide the prepared dough into two equal portions (or four, or six, for several smaller pizzas), and roll out the prepared dough on a lightly floured board. Place each on a round pizza pan, lightly oiled and lightly dusted with flour and/or cornmeal, and crimp the edges. Top with the filling, and bake 15–20 minutes, or until the edges are golden brown.

𝒜RTICHOKE PIZZA

1 recipe batch of pizza dough (version 1, 2, or 3)
2 cups artichoke bottoms, cut into ¼-inch dice

1 cup artichoke hearts, cut into ¼-inch dice
¼ cup olive oil
the juice of 2 lemons

¼ cup mint leaves, minced
½ cup grated mozzarella
cheese

½ cup grated Parmesan
cheese
salt and pepper to taste

- Combine the artichokes, oil, lemon juice, mint, salt and pepper together in a bowl, and toss. Distribute evenly over the pizzas, then top with the mozzarella and Parmesan cheeses.

CALIFORNIA PIZZA

1 recipe batch of pizza
dough (version 1, 2, or 3)
8 ounces goat cheese, sliced
20 basil leaves, cut into
chiffonade

2 tablespoons cilantro
leaves, minced
salt, pepper, and olive oil as
needed

- Proceed as in instructions for Alsatian Pizza. As a general rule, ingredients are placed on the pizza in the order in which they appear in the recipe.

CLAM PIZZA

1 recipe batch of pizza
dough (version 1, 2, or 3)
2 cups tomatoes, diced
1 cup minced clams

2 tablespoons oregano
leaves, minced
salt, pepper, and olive oil as
needed

- Proceed as in instructions for Alsatian Piza. As a general rule, ingredients are placed on the pizza in the order in which they appear in the recipe.

GARIBALDI PIZZA

1 recipe batch of pizza
dough (version 1, 2, or 3)
2 cups basic tomato sauce
1 cup Gruyère cheese, grated
½ cup Calamata olives,
sliced

½ cup Sicilian green olives,
sliced
12 anchovy fillets
2 tablespoons fresh mar-
joram leaves, minced
¼ cup olive oil

- Proceed as in instructions for Alsatian Pizza. As a general rule, ingredients are placed on the pizza in the order in which they appear in the recipe.

MARGHERITA PIZZA

1 recipe batch of pizza
   dough (version 1, 2, or 3)
1 cup tomato sauce
½ pound mozzarella, grated

½ cup basil pesto (from
   "Mostaciolli with Basil
   Pesto")
salt, pepper, and olive oil as
   needed

- Proceed as in instructions for Alsatian Pizza. As a general rule, ingredients are placed on the pizza in the order in which they appear in the recipe.

MOZZARELLA AND SUN-DRIED TOMATO PIZZA

1 recipe batch of pizza
   dough (version 1, 2, or 3)
½ cup oil-packed sun-dried
   tomatoes, cut into
   julienne (reserve the oil)

⅓ pound mozzarella cheese,
   grated
2 tablespoons minced basil
1 tablespoon minced
   oregano leaves

- Proceed as in instructions for Alsatian Pizza. As a general rule, ingredients are placed on the pizza in the order in which they appear in the recipe.

ONION PIZZA

1 recipe batch of pizza
   dough (version 1, 2, or 3)
¼ cup olive oil
2 cups red onions, sliced
   very thinly lengthwise

4 garlic cloves, pressed
2 tablespoons balsamic
   vinegar
½ cup grated Parmesan
   cheese

- Roll out dough as per instructions for Alsatian Pizza.
- Sauté the onions and garlic in the olive oil for 5 minutes. Add the balsamic vinegar, and simmer another minute. Spread the onions over the pizza dough, and sprinkle with the cheese.

Pissaladière

This Provence specialty, specifically from the region of Nice, is a cousin to pizza. It consists of a sheet of dough, rolled out, and placed on a round pan. It is then covered with a layer of sliced onions lightly caramelized in olive oil, flavored with chopped anchovies, capers pounded into a paste, and black olives, and seasoned with garlic, thyme, and bay leaf. The top is covered with a crisscross pattern of the same dough, rolled out and cut into pencil-thin strips.

CHAPTER 7

$\mathcal{E}$GGS AND $\mathcal{C}$HEESE

EGGS

Eggs are among the most important foods in the human diet, and through history a vast variety of eggs, including those from the duck, ostrich, partridge, peacock (popular among the ancient Romans), pelican, quail, and turtle have been consumed. Hen's eggs, the variety most consumed today, date back to the domestication of wild jungle fowl in India, as early as 2000 B.C. In spite of the recent clamor over saturated fat in the human diet, eggs are a very healthful food, containing all the amino acids, all vitamins except vitamin C, and most essential minerals. It is estimated that as many as 250 billion eggs a year are consumed, and, like all foods, they are an acceptable part of a diet as long as they are eaten in moderation and properly prepared. The method of cooking is significant, since overcooking or excessively browning eggs in butter or oil make them difficult to digest. Poached and soft-boiled eggs are the easiest to digest. The ability to cook an egg properly is a technique taken lightly by some, and, surprisingly, a skill not commonly found among culinarians.

In culinary endeavors, eggs are indispensable. They are used in all areas of the kitchen: as an emulsifier for cold sauces and a liaison for hot sauces; in pasta, shortbread, and cakes; in bread crumb toppings and as a leavener for soufflés; in certain bread doughs and batters; to coat and seal pastries; and in certain drinks. The freshness of an egg is extremely important. Since the shell is porous, an egg begins to lose moisture, its cohesiveness begins to break down, and its flavor deteriorates significantly in its first week of existence. The older the egg, the less its binding and leavening ability, and the less its nutritional value. For the commercial consumer of eggs, it is best to know a local producer, to be sure that one is receiving eggs within a week of their gathering. An Italian proverb says, "Eggs of an hour, bread of a day, wine of a year, a friend of thirty years."

While hot egg dishes are generally considered breakfast items, there are numerous cold egg dishes that fall under the heading of hors d'oeuvres. We have included poached and shirred eggs in this chapter, which can also be served as lunch and supper items, though generally not at formal dinners. As a breakfast item, poached eggs are normally served two per person, shirred eggs two or three per person. As an appetizer, they should be served one per person.

Cold Dishes

The dishes that follow require boiling the eggs until fully cooked (hard-boiled). Begin the eggs in tepid water, with plenty of salt. Bring up to a boil, and continue boiling for 5 minutes. Remove from the fire and allow to sit 15 minutes, then drain, cool in ice water, and peel immediately.

$\mathscr{E}$GGS IN ASPIC

(Oeufs Pochés en Gelée)

4 medium eggs, hard-boiled, peeled	4 large sprigs of dill
¼ pound ham, thinly sliced	1 quart liquid aspic

- Fill four medium ramekins or dariole molds with tempered aspic, and place into an ice-water bath. Allow to set about 10 minutes, then remove from the bath, pour out whatever liquid aspic remains, and reserve. There should remain about a ¼-inch thick layer of jellied aspic on the bottom and sides of the ramekin. If this layer is not thick enough, repeat the process. If the layer is too thick, melt the aspic down, and perform the process again.

- Cut the ham into long triangles, and arrange on the aspic in a ramekin, around the inside of the set, with the short side of each triangle up on the edges. Place a sprig of dill on the bottom, then fill with enough aspic to cover the dill. Continue with the remaining ramekins, and place them in the refrigerator to set.

- Gently place an egg in each ramekin, and carefully fill in the ramekin with the aspic. Place in the refrigerator to set. Put the remaining aspic in a small, clean pan, and place that in the refrigerator to set as well.

- When the aspic in the pan has set, carefully lift it out, place it on a clean cutting board, and cut it into fine dice.

- Dip the ramekins into very hot water for about 5 seconds, then invert onto a chilled plate. Return to the refrigerator once again.

- Transfer the aspics to chilled serving plates, and sprinkle the chopped aspic around each one. Serve with a mayonnaise-based sauce. (See color plate.)

$\mathscr{E}$GGS CASINO

5 eggs, hard-boiled, peeled	4 large barquette shells, baked
½ cup tomato paste	½ cup chicken mousse or finely chopped chicken salad
2 cups liquid aspic, hot	
salt and white pepper to taste	
liquid aspic as needed	12 fat asparagus spears

- Blend the tomato paste, aspic, salt, and pepper together until smooth. Place four of the eggs on a screen over a pan, and nap with the tomato mixture. Refrigerate until the mixture sets. Repeat until the eggs are well coated with the tomato mixture.

- Thinly slice the egg white from the remaining egg, and cut out into geometric shapes. Place in a dish with a little of the aspic, then decorate the eggs. Nap the eggs with two additional coats of aspic, and refrigerate until ready to serve.

- Peel the asparagus, and blanch in boiling water until al dente. Drain, cool, and set aside.

- Spread a little of the mousse or salad on the bottom of each barquette shell. Place a coated egg on top, and serve garnished with the asparagus. (See color plate.)

The undersides of the eggs sometimes do not take to the tomato collée, because it does not have any fat (mayonnaise) in it. While the addition of mayonnaise will solve this, it will also significantly lighten the color of the collée, which is sometimes adjusted with red food color. We prefer to avoid the use of red color and allow the undersides to remain a bit uncoated.

---

*M*ARBLE TEA EGGS

1 quart water
10 eggs, raw, unshelled
2 tablespoons black tea
   leaves
2 pieces of star anise

1 teaspoon Szechwan
   peppercorns
1 tablespoon sliced gingerroot
¼ cup soy sauce

- Combine all the ingredients in a pot and bring to a boil (the eggs should be immersed in the liquid). Turn the fire off. Lift out the eggs, one by one, using a slotted spoon, and place on a cutting board. Tap an egg gently with the back of the spoon, making random cracks all around the shell. Repeat with all the eggs.

- Return the eggs to the liquid, boil another 5 minutes, then remove from the fire. Allow to cool, then refrigerate as is, overnight.

- Remove the eggs from the liquid, remove the shells, and use as desired (stuffed, or as a garnish). They should all have a brown-lined mottled appearance, similar to marble.

STUFFED EGGS, CALIFORNIA

(Oeufs à la Californie)

4 large eggs, hard-boiled, shelled
¼ cup cilantro leaves, minced
mayonnaise as needed
salt and white pepper to taste
alfalfa sprouts as needed
2 radishes, cut in half and sliced very thin

8 very thin green bell pepper spears, about 2 inches long
8 very thin yellow bell pepper spears, about 2 inches long
8 slices Calamata olives
2 cups mixed salad greens
½ cup vinaigrette

- Cut the eggs in half widthwise and remove the yolks. Mash the yolks and cilantro with mayonnaise, salt, and pepper, into a smooth, thick paste.
- Place some alfalfa sprouts into the cavity of each egg half, so that the tops of the sprouts stick out slightly over the edge of the cavity. Fill the egg halves with the paste, using a pastry bag fitted with a round tip. Garnish with a fan of radish slices, 2 pepper spears, and a slice of olive, and serve on a bed of salad greens, tossed in the vinaigrette (mixed California salad greens). (See color plate.)

STUFFED EGGS, FELIX

(Oeufs à la Felix)

6 medium eggs, hard-boiled, shelled
mayonnaise as needed
salt and white pepper to taste
1 tablespoon ham, minced
1 tablespoon gherkins, minced

1 teaspoon shallot, minced
1 tablespoon tarragon, minced
1 tablespoon parsley, minced
1 thin slice of ham
4 paper-thin slices black truffle
2 cups light aspic, warm

- Cut the eggs in half lengthwise and remove the yolks. Mash the yolks with mayonnaise, salt, and pepper into a smooth, thick paste. Add the minced ham, gherkins, shallot, and herbs, and blend in. Fill 8 egg halves with this paste, using a knife dipped in hot water to shape each into a smooth mound.
- Cut the ham, truffle, and remaining egg white into ⅓-inch long

diamond shapes (lozenge). Place on a saucer with a little of the aspic.

- Ladle a line of the truffle cutouts, end to end, across the top of an egg, slightly off-center. Set the egg and ham cutouts next to the truffle cutouts, on the wider side. Repeat a second row if desired. Ladle a coat of aspic over each egg, and place in the refrigerator to set. Ladle a second coat of aspic, refrigerate, and serve on a lettuce leaf cup. (See color plate.)

𝒮TUFFED EGGS, FLORIST STYLE

(Oeufs à la Fleuriste)

4 medium eggs, hard-boiled, shelled
mayonnaise as needed
salt and white pepper to taste
2 carrots, cut into 1 × ⅛-inch julienne

1 red bell pepper, cut into 1 × ⅛-inch julienne
1 medium rutabaga, cut into 1 × ⅛-inch julienne
1 cup green string beans, cut into 1 × ⅛-inch julienne
4 Roma tomatoes

- Remove a thin slice from each end of the tomatoes (so they will stand upright). Cut them in half widthwise, and scoop out the interior pulp (save for another use). Invert and set aside.
- Cut the eggs in half widthwise and remove the yolks. Mash the yolks with mayonnaise, salt, and pepper into a smooth, thick paste.
- Lightly blanch the vegetables in boiling salted water. Drain, cool, and set aside.
- Place the egg halves in the tomato halves, and fill the egg halves with the paste, using a pastry bag fitted with a plain round tube. Insert 4 or 5 julienne strips of each vegetable into the paste, so that they fan out from the center. (See color plate.)

——— • ———

Be careful to add the mayonnaise a little at a time, to avoid making the paste too soft.

_____

Hot Dishes **Poached Eggs.** Poach eggs in water just under the simmering point, slightly acidulated with a little white vinegar or lemon juice. The freshness of the egg is important: the older the egg, the more the albumen will spread in the water before setting. Although the vinegar helps the egg set, it should be a very small amount so that it does not affect the taste. Be sure the eggs are completely drained of water before serving.

Poached Egg, African Style
(Oeuf Poché à l'Africaine)

Poached egg served on a bed of rice pilaf, garnished with slices of crisp bacon, topped with stewed diced tomatoes.

Poached Egg, Algerian Style
(Oeuf Poché à l'Algérienne)

Poached egg served on a tartlet filled with a salpicon of finely diced eggplant, green pepper, pumpkin, and tomato, bound with tomato sauce.

Poached Egg, American Style
(Oeuf Poché à l'Américaine)

Poached egg served on a half tomato seasoned with salt and pepper, broiled, and topped with lobster sauce, garnished with a slice of lobster.

· · · · · · · · · · · · · · · · · · # $\mathscr{P}$OACHED EGG, ARCHDUKE

(Oeuf Poché à la Archiduc)

3 tablespoons unsalted
   butter
½ pound chicken livers,
   well rinsed and cleaned of
   membranes, and finely
   diced
¼ cup cognac

salt, pepper, and paprika to
   taste
8 croutons, toasted and
   buttered
8 large eggs
1 cup chicken velouté
¼ cup heavy cream
¼ cup champagne

- Sauté the chicken livers in the butter until cooked but slightly pink inside. Add the cognac and simmer until almost dry. Season to taste with salt, pepper, and paprika.

- Simmer the velouté and cream until desired thickness is achieved. Finish with the champagne, then strain and set aside, keeping warm.

- Poach the eggs. Place the chicken livers on top of the croutons, place an egg on each, top with the sauce, and sprinkle with paprika.

POACHED EGG WITH ASPARAGUS AND FONTINA

(Asperagi Lessati Sul Crostone)

12 large asparagus spears	grated Parmesan cheese as
4 large eggs	needed
salt and vinegar as needed	4 large baguette slices,
4 thin slices Italian fontina	toasted and lightly
	buttered

- Peel the asparagus, and blanch in boiling salted water until al dente. Drain, cut in half, and arrange on the baguettes.
- Poach the eggs, then place a poached egg on top of the asparagus. Top with a slice of fontina, sprinkle with grated cheese, and glaze (brown under the broiler).

Poached Egg, Baltic Style
(Oeuf Poché à la Baltique)

Poached egg served on an oval crouton, topped with Mornay sauce, garnished with a little caviar.

Poached Egg, Barcelona Style
(Oeuf Poché à la Barcelonnaisse)

Poached egg served on a half tomato seasoned with salt, pepper, and grated cheese, broiled, and topped with small diced green peppers and tomatoes simmered in demi-glaze.

Poached Egg, Bar-le-Duc
(Oeuf Poché à la Bar-le-Duc)

Poached egg served on an artichoke bottom, coated with a tarragon-flavored cream sauce.

Poached Egg, Borgia
(Oeuf Poché à la Borgia)

Poached egg served on a half tomato seasoned with salt, pepper, and grated cheese, broiled, and topped with béarnaise sauce.

Poached Egg, Brazilian Style
(Oeuf Poché à Brésilienne)

Poached egg served on a bed of rice pilaf, topped with tomato sauce with diced green peppers and ham.

Poached Egg, Breton Style
(Oeuf Poché à la Bretonne)

A tartlet shell filled with a purée of white beans, topped with a slice of grilled ham, then a poached egg, followed by demi-glaze seasoned with finely chopped mixed herbs (such as chives, cilantro, parsley, and tarragon).

Poached Egg, Camerani
(Oeuf Poché à la Camerani)

A tartlet shell filled with braised sauerkraut, topped with a slice of grilled ham, then a poached egg, coated with semi-glaze garnished with diced ham.

Poached Egg, Clamart
(Oeuf Poché à la Clamart)

A tartlet shell filled with a creamed purée of green peas, topped with a poached egg, coated with cream sauce.

Poached Egg, Crown Prince Style
(Oeuf Poché à la Dauphin)

A poached egg served on asparagus tips on a toasted buttered crouton, coated with Madeira sauce garnished with diced mushrooms.

Poached Egg, DuBarry
(Oeuf Poché à la DuBarry)

A tartlet shell filled with a creamed purée of cauliflower, coated with Mornay sauce, sprinkled with grated cheese, and glazed.

Poached Egg, Florence Style
(Oeuf Poché à la Florentine)

A tartlet shell filled with finely chopped spinach cooked in butter, seasoned with salt, pepper, and nutmeg, topped with a poached egg, coated with cream sauce, sprinkled with grated Parmesan cheese and glazed.

Poached Egg, Georgette Style
(Oeuf Poché à la Georgette)

A scooped-out baked potato, filled with crayfish tails bound with a little Nantua sauce (cream sauce beaten with crayfish butter),

---

The crayfish is a freshwater crustacean found throughout the world. The average length is 3 to 6 inches, though a crayfish measuring 16 inches in length and weighing 8 pounds was recorded in Tasmania. In the United States, crayfish are variously dubbed crawfish, crawdads, bay crabs, and freshwater lobsters; in Louisiana, they are known as creekcrabs, yabbies, and mudbugs. Though crayfish figure prominently in classical cuisine, in modern times water pollution and overconsumption have depleted what was once an abundant supply.

topped with a poached egg, coated with a little more sauce, sprinkled with grated cheese and glazed.

Poached Egg, Greek Style
(Oeuf Poché à la Greque)

A poached egg served on a slice of seasoned, grilled eggplant, coated with Dutch sauce (Hollandaise).

Poached Egg, Henri IV
(Oeuf Poché à l'Henri IV)

A poached egg on an artichoke bottom, coated with béarnaise sauce.

Poached Egg, Lafayette
(Oeuf Poché à la Lafayette)

A poached egg served on a buttered, toasted crouton, coated with béarnaise sauce, garnished with diced stewed tomatoes.

Poached Egg, Laurent
(Oeuf Poché à la Laurent)

A poached egg served on a slice of smoked salmon on a toasted buttered crouton, coated with cream sauce.

Poached Egg, La Vallière
(Oeuf Poché à la Vallière)

A poached egg served on a tartlet filled with a creamed purée of sorrel, coated with Supreme sauce, garnished with asparagus tips.

Poached Egg, Madrid Style
(Oeuf Poché à la Madrilène)

A poached egg served on a toasted crouton spread with anchovy butter, coated with cream sauce, garnished with diced green olives.

Poached Egg, Menton Style
(Oeuf Poché à la Mentonnaise)

A poached egg served on a tartlet filled with creamed purée of leeks, coated with cream sauce, sprinkled with grated cheese and glazed.

$\mathscr{P}$OACHED EGG, MEURETTE

(Oeuf Poché à la Meurette)

1 cup thick-sliced bacon, cut widthwise into ¼-inch strips	3 cups consommé
	1½ cups demi-glaze
4 large eggs	4 large croutons, toasted and buttered

- Cook the bacon until golden brown. Drain well, discarding the fat, and set aside.
- Poach the eggs in the consommé, drain, then place on the croutons. Top with the sauce and garnish with the bacon.

Poached Egg, Monaco Style
(Oeuf Poché à la Monégasque)

Poached egg served on a half tomato seasoned with salt and pepper and broiled, topped with a tomato sauce seasoned with chopped tarragon and garnished with anchovy fillets.

Poached Egg, New York Style
(Oeuf Poché à la New-Yorkaise)

Poached egg served on a bed of creamed corn, coated with cream sauce.

Poached Egg, Oriental Style
(Oeuf Poché à l'Orientale)

Poached egg served on slices of grilled tomatoes, topped with sliced cucumber cooked in peanut oil, coated with Dutch sauce.

$\mathscr{P}$OACHED EGG, PARMENTIER

(Oeuf Poché à la Parmentier)

3 tablespoons clarified butter	salt and pepper to taste
3 large all-purpose potatoes	4 large eggs
¼ cup heavy cream, hot	unsalted butter as needed

- Peel the potatoes, then grate half of them. Heat the clarified butter in a nonstick pan, and fry the potatoes on both sides until golden brown. Remove from the pan, cut into four squares, and set aside.

There are a number of variations of this dish, all based
on potatoes, since Antoine
Parmentier was significant in
popularizing potatoes as a
food in France during the
late eighteenth century. One
variation consists of a
scooped-out baked potato,
filled with a poached egg,
topped with Mornay sauce
and glazed.

- Cut the remaining potatoes into 1-inch pieces, and cook in boiling salted water until tender. Drain, mash with a fork or mashing tool, blend with the cream, and season with salt and pepper.
- Poach the eggs. Reheat the potato squares, top with mashed potato, then set an egg on top of each square. Place about 3 tablespoons whole butter in a pan, heat until it turns slightly brown (beurre noisette), and spoon a little over each of the eggs.

Poached Egg, Persian Style
(Oeuf Poché à la Persane)

Poached egg served on tomato sauce on a toasted, buttered crouton, garnished with diced ham and finely chopped chives.

Poached Egg, Ritz
(Oeuf Poché à la Ritz)

Poached egg served on a tartlet shell filled with finely diced shrimp bound in shrimp (or cream) sauce, garnished with finely diced green bell peppers stewed in butter.

Poached Egg, Roman Style
(Oeuf Poché à la Romaine)

Poached egg served on a tartlet shell filled with spinach cooked in olive oil and seasoned with anchovy paste and garlic, coated with demi-glaze with a strong presence of tomato.

*P*OACHED EGG, ROQUEFORT

(Oeuf Poché à la Roquefort)

unsalted butter as needed	4 large eggs
4 individual hard rolls	unsalted butter as needed
¼ cup Roquefort cheese, crumbled	

- Preheat an oven to 375°F.
- Slice off the tops of the rolls, and cut out the interiors. Rub the inside of the rolls with a little butter, and bake 8 to 10 minutes, or until golden brown.

- Poach the eggs. Place a tablespoon of Roquefort cheese in each roll, top with an egg, and serve.

Poached Egg, Sully
(Oeuf Poché à la Sully)

Poached egg served on a tartlet filled with creamed chicken, coated with béarnaise sauce.

Poached Egg, Turkish Style
(Oeuf Poché à la Turque)

Poached egg served on a bed of saffron rice pilaf, coated with tomato sauce, and sprinkled with chopped toasted pistachios.

Shirred Eggs. Shirred eggs are eggs baked in a ceramic casserole dish, ramekin, or other ovenproof vessel, along with the appropriate garnish, sauce, or accompaniment of each specific dish. As one-egg appetizers, they can be prepared in a medium-sized ramekin.

Shirred Egg, Carnegie
(Oeuf Cocotte à la Carnegie)

Fill the bottom of a buttered ramekin with mushroom duxelle mixed with finely diced red bell peppers. Top with an egg, salt, pepper, melted butter, and bake.

Shirred Egg, Colbert
(Oeuf Cocotte à la Colbert)

Fill the bottom of a buttered ramekin with a mixture of finely chopped cooked chicken breast, moistened with a little cream and seasoned with salt, pepper, parsley, and thyme. Top with an egg, salt, pepper, and melted butter, and bake.

Shirred Egg, Cuban Style
(Oeuf Cocotte à la Cubaine)

Fill the bottom of a buttered ramekin with finely chopped crab meat, moistened with a little cream and seasoned with salt, pepper, and parsley. Top with an egg, salt, pepper, melted butter, and bake.

Shirred Egg, Diplomat Style
(Oeuf Cocotte à la Diplomat)

Fill the bottom of a buttered ramekin with sautéed sliced goose liver, top with an egg, salt, pepper, melted butter, and bake. Serve accompanied by tomato sauce.

Shirred Egg, Forest Style
(Oeuf Cocotte à la Forestière)

Fill the bottom of a buttered ramekin with diced morels, diced crispy bacon, and minced fine herbs moistened with game demi-glaze. Top with an egg, salt, pepper, some additional demi-glaze, and bake.

Shirred Egg, Gypsy Style
(Oeuf Cocotte à la Zingara)

Fill the bottom of a buttered ramekin with ham, tongue, and mushrooms cut into fine julienne and moistened with a little highly tomato-flavored demi-glaze. Top with an egg, salt, pepper, and a mushroom cap poached in white wine, and bake.

Shirred Egg, Lorraine
(Oeuf Cocotte à la Lorraine)

Set one thick slice of bacon, cooked light brown and cut into 1-inch pieces, in the bottom of a ramekin. Top with an egg, salt, pepper, melted butter, and bake.

Shirred Egg, Magdalena
(Oeuf Cocotte à la Madeleine)

Fill the bottom of a buttered ramekin with finely minced cooked chicken breast bound with a curry-flavored demi-glaze. Top with an egg, salt, pepper, and melted butter, and bake.

Shirred Egg, Marigny
(Oeuf Cocotte à la Marigny)

Fill the bottom of a buttered ramekin with diced ham cooked in butter, and a poached oyster. Top with a little cream sauce, an egg, salt, pepper, a little more sauce, and grated Parmesan cheese, and bake.

Shirred Egg, Mexican Style
(Oeuf Cocotte à la Mexique)

Sprinkel the bottom of a lightly oiled ramekin with tortilla chips broken into slightly smaller pieces. Top with some plain pinto beans, cooked until tender and seasoned with salt, pepper, ground cumin, and Tabasco. Place an egg on top, drizzle with chile oil, and bake. Serve accompanied with Salsa Fresca.

Shirred Egg, Princess Style
(Oeuf Cocotte à la Princesse)

Fill the bottom of a casserole dish with some finely diced asparagus bound with a little cream sauce, top with an egg, salt, pepper, and melted butter, and bake.

Shirred Egg, Provence Style
(Oeuf Cocotte à la Provençale)

Place a little basic Provence-style tomato sauce in a ramekin, top with an egg, salt, pepper, and melted butter, and bake.

Provence-Style Tomato Sauce

3 tablespoons olive oil
4 garlic cloves, pressed
¼ cup onion, finely diced
2 tablespoons basil leaves,
  cut into chiffonade
1 tablespoon thyme leaves,
  minced

2 cups tomato purée
2 tablespoons tomato paste,
  dissolved in ¼ cup rich
  chicken stock
salt and white pepper to
  taste

- Sauté the garlic and onions in the olive oil, for about 10 minutes, over medium fire. Add the herbs, and cook briefly. Add the remaining ingredients, and simmer 30 minutes. Season to taste with salt and pepper.

Shirred Egg, Puerto Rico Style
(Oeuf Cocotte à la Puerto Rico)

Fill the bottom of a casserole dish with some finely diced tomatoes, ham, and asparagus, bound with a little cream sauce. Top with an egg, salt, pepper, and melted butter, and bake.

Shirred Egg, Shepherd's Style
(Oeuf Cocotte à la Bergerie)

Fill the bottom of a casserole dish with some finely chopped cooked lamb and mushrooms sautéed in butter, bound with a little cream, and seasoned with salt and pepper. Top with an egg, salt, pepper, and melted butter, and bake.

Shirred Egg, St. George
(Oeuf Cocotte à la St. George)

Fill the bottom of a casserole dish with some puréed onion cooked in heavy cream until thick. Top with an egg, salt, pepper, and a little cream, and bake.

Shirred Egg, Tosca
(Oeuf Cocotte à la Tosca)

Fill the bottom of a casserole dish with some sour cream, top with an egg, salt, pepper, and a little cream, and bake.

Shirred Egg, Valentine
(Oeuf Cocotte à la Valentine)

Fill the bottom of a casserole dish with some mushroom duxelle moistened with a little tomato sauce. Top with an egg, salt, pepper, and a little chicken velouté, and bake.

Additional Dishes

. . . .

$\mathscr{E}$GGS IN PASTA

(Oeufs au Macaroni)

unsalted butter as needed
½ pound fettuccine or
   tagliarine
½ cup finely diced ham

4 large eggs
salt and pepper to taste
1 cup basic tomato sauce

- Cook the pasta in boiling salted water a little past the al dente stage. Drain well, cool, and set aside.
- Butter four 4-ounce ramekins, and line them radially with the pasta. The strands of pasta should extend beyond the sides of the ramekins by about 1 inch.

- Sauté the ham in butter until lightly browned, then place an equal amount in the bottom of each ramekin. Place a raw egg on top, season with salt and pepper, and dot with a little butter. Bring the strands of pasta back over the top of the egg.
- Place in a hot water bath in a preheated 350°F oven for 8 to 10 minutes. Remove from the oven, run a knife around the inside edge of each ramekin, then invert and serve hot, accompanied by the sauce.

ℳUSTARD PICKLED EGGS

2 dozen large eggs	1 tablespoon coriander seed
2 tablespoons salt	3 to 4 garlic cloves, crushed
1 quart white vinegar	2 bay leaves
1 quart water	2 tablespoons dry mustard
1 tablespoon celery seed	(or Dijon)
1 tablespoon red pepper flakes	4 tablespoons ground turmeric
1 tablespoon black peppercorns	

For red-purple tinted eggs, substitute the turmeric and mustard with 2 cups of beet juice (taken from a can of sliced beets).

- Cover the eggs with warm water, add the salt, and bring to a boil. Simmer 10 minutes. Drain, and cover the eggs with ice and water. Crack and peel the eggs, then set them aside.
- Bring the remaining ingredients to a boil, and pour over the eggs. Marinate refrigerated for 24 hours before serving.

Scotch Woodcock

Square, toasted, buttered crouton, covered with soft scrambled egg, garnished with a crisscross of anchovy fillets and four capers. Serve hot. (See color plate.)

CHEESE

ℬAKED BRIE IN PUFF PASTRY

4 individual 4-ounce brie cheeses	1 Granny Smith apple, cored, cut into ¼-inch thick wedges, and dipped in lemon juice
1 pound puff pastry dough	
1 egg, beaten	
1 cup slivered almonds	4 sprigs mint
2 tablespoons brown sugar	

- Preheat an oven to 400°F.
- Roll the puff pastry out to a thickness of ⅛ inch. Cut eight circles to the exact diameter of the cheese rounds. Cut four strips of pastry, as wide as the cheese's height, about 10 inches long. Place a brie on one round of dough, and place a second on top. Brush the side of the cheese with the egg wash, then wrap a strip of pastry around the cheese, pinching the upper and lower seams together. Repeat this with the remaining cheeses, brush the exteriors with egg wash, place on a lightly buttered baking sheet, and bake until golden brown.
- Toss the almonds with the brown sugar, place on a baking sheet, and bake for 10 to 15 minutes, or until golden brown. Serve the baked brie with the toasted almonds sprinkled on top and garnished with the apple wedges and mint. (See color plate.)

Camembert Fritters

Cut a Camembert cheese into 12 wedges. Dust each with seasoned flour, dredge in beaten egg, coat with dry bread crumbs, and deep fry at 375°F until golden brown.

CHEESE FONDUE, HAMBURG STYLE

Gruyère, one of hundreds of varieties of cheese made in Switzerland, is named after the valley in which it is manufactured. *Swiss* is a generic term, referring to any cheese with the characteristic holes created by the release of carbon dioxide gas by one of the starter bacteria early in the formation of the cheese.

2 cups dry white German or Alsatian wine	1 tablespoon cornstarch
1 pound Gruyère cheese, grated (finely chopped)	pinch of cayenne pepper
	1 fresh baguette, cut into 1-inch cubes

- Place the wine in the fondue pot, and allow to become hot. Toss the grated cheese in the cornstarch and cayenne.
- When the wine is hot (it should be steaming), add the cheese, and stir continuously until smooth and melted. Pierce a baguette cube with a fondue fork, dip in the cheese, and eat. (See color plate.)

CHEESE FONDUE, PIEDMONT STYLE

1 pound Italian fontina, cut into ½-inch pieces	4 tablespoons unsalted butter, cut into ½-inch pieces
1 cup half-and-half	salt and white pepper to taste
1 cup dry white wine	1 fresh baguette, cut into 1-inch cubes
4 egg yolks	

- Place the half-and-half and the cheese in a double boiler, and melt over medium heat while stirring continuously.
- Beat the yolks and wine together, then beat in about half of the cheese mixture in a slow, steady stream. Return to the double boiler, beat in the butter, blend well, season to taste, and serve with the baguette cubes.

•

Fondue is the noun form of the French verb *fondre*, meaning "to dissolve" or "to melt." It is most commonly associated with a cheese sauce that originated in Switzerland, though it also refers to a number of vegetable purées used in many dishes. There are also dessert fondues, one variety consisting of a hot dish of chocolate, kirsch, cream, and brandy, into which cut fruit and pound cake are dipped, then eaten.

CHEESE AND HERB PUDDING

1 tablespoon unsalted butter
18 slices good-quality white bread, crusts removed
¾ cup Gruyère cheese, grated
½ cup sharp white cheddar cheese, grated
½ cup scallions, sliced very thin
4 tablespoons chopped chives

2 tablespoons chopped parsley
2 tablespoons chopped mint
2 tablespoons chopped basil
2 cups heavy cream
2 cups milk
5 large eggs
1 teaspoon salt
½ teaspoon white pepper

- Lightly butter a 4-quart casserole dish, and place a layer of sliced bread on the bottom. Sprinkle the cheddar and half of the herbs on top of this, and cover with another layer of bread. Top with the Gruyère, the remaining herbs, and a final layer of bread.
- Beat the cream, milk, eggs, salt, and pepper together, and pour over the bread. Allow to sit 1 hour. Preheat an oven to 350°F, and bake for 30 to 40 minutes, or until golden brown. Allow to rest about 15 minutes before serving.

Cheese Soufflé Turnovers (Talmouse de Fromage)

Brush a 4 × 4-inch square of puffy pastry lightly with egg wash, place 2 tablespoons of cheese soufflé near one corner, sprinkle with grated Gruyère cheese, and bake until golden brown.

Basic Cheese Soufflé

3 tablespoons unsalted
  butter
6 tablespoons flour
1 cup milk, hot
4 large egg yolks

¾ cup grated Gruyère and/
  or Parmesan cheese
5 large egg whites, beaten to
  a stiff peak

- Melt the butter, and blend in the flour. Cook several minutes, stirring frequently, without browning. Add the hot milk, and stir until completely blended. Simmer, while stirring continuously, until very thick. Set aside, and allow to cool about 15 minutes.

- Add the cheese, and blend thoroughly.

- Add the yolks one at a time, and beat in thoroughly. Add half the beaten whites, and blend in gently, using a rubber spatula. Add the remaining whites, and blend in.

- Pour over the designated dish, and bake in a preheated 375°F oven until puffed up and golden brown.

*G*OAT CHEESE TART WITH LEEKS AND SEASONAL HERBS

½ cup finely diced leek,
  white part only
4 tablespoons butter
1 cup goat cheese
½ cup cream cheese
⅛ teaspoon salt
¼ teaspoon white pepper
1 teaspoon minced fresh
  chives

½ teaspoon each minced
  fresh thyme and tarragon
  leaves
4 large eggs
½ cup sour cream
8 sprigs each, chives, thyme,
  and tarragon

- Preheat an oven to 350°F. Butter an 8-inch tart pan.

- Sauté the leek in 1 tablespoon of the butter for 5 minutes.

- Cream the goat cheese in a small bowl, using an electric hand mixer. Blend in the remaining butter, cream cheese, salt, pepper, and minced herbs until smooth. Add the eggs, one at a time, incorporating each before adding the next. Add the leek and the sour cream.

- Pour the mixture into the prepared pan. Bake 20 to 25 minutes, or until golden brown. Allow to set for roughly 5 minutes before serving.

- Slice the tart into eight wedges, and serve garnished with the chives, thyme, and tarragon.

GREEK CHEESE TRIANGLES

(Tyropetakia)

¾ pound feta cheese, crumbled	2 tablespoons minced parsley
¾ pound cottage cheese	salt and pepper to taste
4 eggs, beaten	15 sheets phyllo dough
2 tablespoons minced dill	melted butter as needed

- Combine the cheeses, eggs, herbs, salt, and pepper, and blend thoroughly.
- Preheat an oven to 375°F.
- Brush one sheet of phyllo lightly with butter. Top this with a second sheet, brush with butter, and top with a third sheet. Cut this into four equal strips, lengthwise. Repeat this process with the remaining phyllo.
- Place a heaping teaspoon of filling about 1 inch from one end of a strip of dough. Fold one corner diagonally over the filling, flush with the side (this will create a 45-degree angle at the top). Continue folding this triangle down the strip, folding and refolding to the end of the strip. Brush with melted butter, and transfer to a baking sheet. Repeat with the remaining dough strips.
- Bake for 10 minutes, or until golden brown, and serve with the sauce.

IOWA BLUE CHEESE TARTE

1 cup flour	2 tablespoons unsalted butter, soft
pinch of salt	pinch of salt
6 tablespoons unsalted butter, cut into ½-inch pieces	pinch of cayenne pepper
1 large egg yolk	2 large egg yolks
¼ cup ice water	4 ounces Maytag Iowa blue cheese, crumbled
	1 cup heavy cream

- Rub the flour, salt, and butter together until the mixture resembles coarse meal. Add 1 egg yolk and the water, and press together into a ball (use additional water if needed). Wrap and refrigerate for 1 hour.
- Preheat an oven to 375°F.
- Roll out the dough on a lightly floured surface, to a thickness of ⅛ inch. Lightly butter five 5-inch round tart shells. Press the dough into the shells, allowing it to rise up slightly above the top of the side of each form. Dock the dough with the tines of a fork, and bake for 10 minutes.
- Beat the butter, salt, cayenne, and two yolks until smooth and creamy. Add the cheese and the cream, and blend thoroughly. Fill the shells, and bake for 12 minutes, or until golden brown.

———————————— • ————————————

For more than two thousand years, the village of Roquefort-sur-Soulzon has produced a blue-veined cheese of the same name. Roquefort cheese is a unique combination of nature, geography, and human effort. Made from the milk of Lacaune sheep, it is cured in 25 naturally occurring caves occupying an area of more than 125 subterranean acres connected by nearly 4 miles of corridors.

In the United States the name Maytag is usually associated with washing machines and the company that has been manufacturing them since the early twentieth century. In the early 1920s, Elmer Maytag, son of the founder of the company, began a dairy division as a hobby. In the late 1930s, his son Frederick expanded the dairy division to include the production of a blue cheese, using a process innovated and patented by the University of Iowa. It is made from the milk of a specially developed herd of Holstein-Frisan cows, grazing on 1,600 acres of pastures spread over five farms in Iowa. Commercial production began in 1941 (when the price of a quart of milk in Iowa was 10¢), and the company continues to produce that cheese today.

𝓛IPTAUER

1 pound cream cheese
½ cup unsalted butter
¼ cup heavy cream
4 tablespoons scallion, very finely sliced

3 garlic cloves, pressed
4 tablespoons chopped cashews, toasted
2 tablespoons capers

2 tablespoons mashed anchovies	½ teaspoon salt
2 tablespoons minced chives	¼ teaspoon white pepper
1 tablespoon paprika	radishes and chopped parsley as needed
1 tablespoon caraway seeds	

- Combine all the ingredients except the radishes and parsley, and blend into a smooth paste. Place on a serving plate or in a bowl, in a domed shape, decorate with sliced radishes, radish rosettes, and chopped parsley, and serve with crisp whole wheat crackers.

———————————— • ————————————

This cheese appetizer originated in Lipto, a county in Hungary, and was known as *Liptoi*. It was made with sour goat cheese blended with paprika, caraway, mustard, capers, chives, and beer. *Liptauer* is the name for the German version of this dish, often simpler than the recipe given here: one part ripe Camembert, one part blend of butter, cream cheese, yogurt, and sour cream, seasoned with paprika and onion. The variations of this dish are unlimited and can be altered to fit one's taste.

——————————————————————

················· ## ℛOQUEFORT CHEESE TART

¾ cup cream cheese, soft	1 tablespoon parsley, minced
¼ cup heavy cream	salt and white pepper to taste
4 eggs	
¾ cup Roquefort cheese, crumbled	1 pound (approximately) puff pastry dough
1 tablespoon tarragon leaves, minced	1 egg, beaten with a little water

- Beat the cream cheese and cream until smooth. Add the eggs, and incorporate completely. Add the Roquefort, herbs, salt, and pepper.
- Preheat an oven to 400°F.
- Roll the puff pastry out to a thickness of ⅛ inch. Line a lightly buttered 10-inch pie or tart shell with the dough. Spread the cheese mixture on the dough, to within ½ inch of the outside edge. Brush this edge with egg wash, place another sheet of

dough on top, and press the edges together. Brush the top with egg wash, and bake 30 to 40 minutes, or until golden brown and puffed up. Cut into wedges and serve.

Soused Camembert

1 bottle dry white wine
1 Camembert cheese
½ cup unsalted butter, soft

1 cup toasted almonds, chopped

- Trim the Camembert of excess mold, pierce it with a knife in several places, place the cheese in a bowl, and pour enough wine over it to cover. Cover, and let sit overnight at room temperature.
- Discard the wine, then mash the cheese with the butter. Shape into a ball, roll in the toasted almonds, and serve with toasted baguette slices.

Welsh Rarebit

½ teaspoon ground mustard
¼ teaspoon cayenne pepper
2 tablespoons Worcestershire sauce
½ cup beer

¾ pound sharp cheddar cheese, grated
8 toast points
paprika as needed

- Simmer the spices with Worcestershire and beer until dissolved. Add the cheese, and continue stirring until melted. Pour this mixture over the toast in a small casserole, sprinkle with paprika, and heat in a hot oven 5 minutes.

———————————— • ————————————

For Welsh Rarebit, Buck, place two poached eggs under or over the cheese; for Welsh Rarebit, Golden Buck, add two slices very crisp bacon; for Welsh Rarebit, Vanderbilt, spread the toast with anchovy butter, top with several slices of hard-boiled egg, and sprinkle the melted cheese with chopped hard-boiled egg.

CHAPTER 8

FINFISH AND SHELLFISH

FINFISH

Cold Dishes

Caviar. From the writings of Aristotle we know that caviar, the salted roe (eggs) of sturgeon and other varieties of fish, was known as far back as ancient Greece. Shakespeare made reference to it in *Hamlet:* " 'Twas caviare to the general [populace]." This delicacy was introduced in France in the 1920s by exiled Russian nobility, and Charles Ritz promoted its popularity by putting it permanently on his hotel menu. Around the turn of this century, sturgeon was plentiful not only in the Caspian Sea, but also in the Black Sea, the Baltic, the North Sea, the Gironde River (France), and in the rivers of North America. Overfishing and pollution have destroyed most of these habitats, leaving the Caspian as the primary source, providing 98% of the world's output. The Soviet Union, once the sole producer of caviar, produces about 1,800 tons a year. In 1953, Iran began processing caviar along its part of the Caspian coast and have added another 180 tons to annual production. (There have been some reports of modern sturgeon farms that remove the roe from females, so that the fish can return to the water and continue to produce for the span of their lifetime—as long as 100 years—but as of this writing, further documentation has not been found.)

The ancestors of Christian Petrossian began processing sturgeon roe into caviar in the Russian town of Baku, long before the Russian revolution. Today, his company (Petrossian, Inc.) is the sole exporter of Russian caviar to the world's markets. The processing technique has evolved over hundreds of years and is considered a great skill. After the roe is removed, it is sieved, washed, graded, and salted. The less salt used in its processing and the younger the roe, the better quality the caviar. *Malossol,* meaning "little salt," is the finest of this kind. There are three sturgeon species from the Caspian used in the production of caviar:

- *Beluga.* The most expensive, produced from the largest sturgeon, weighing from 800 to 2,000 pounds. The eggs are dark gray, firm, and well separated.
- *Osetra.* Smaller, more even-sized eggs, golden yellow to brown, from sturgeon weighing from 200 to 300 pounds.
- *Sevruga.* Very small, light to dark grey eggs from sturgeon weighing 50 to 100 pounds.

Types of Caviar

- Grade 1 is processed as fresh, whole eggs, then shipped and stored under continuous refrigeration at 28° to 32°F. If properly stored, fresh whole (and fresh pressed) eggs have a shelf life of 6 months.

- Grade 2 roe is processed as *fresh pressed* and *pressed pasteurized*. It is literally pressed, losing about 80% of its volume. Pasteurized caviar, which is vacuum packed, has a shelf life of 1 year.

- American caviar—though not caviar in the traditional sense, some varieties have an excellent flavor. (See the list of Specialty Suppliers.)

How to Eat Caviar. Purists maintain that the proper way to enjoy very fine caviar is that the roe be well chilled, eaten with only a bland cracker, potato pancake, or a small Russian-style buckwheat pancake known as a blini, and accompanied by iced vodka or well-chilled champagne. "The caviar may improve the oyster, but the oyster does nothing for the caviar" (Christian Petrossian). In canapé production, since the caviar is used as a garnish combined with other ingredients (sour cream, buttered croutons, smoked and cured fish, hard-boiled eggs, etc.), it is best to use the pressed variety, as it is much stronger flavored. In either case, the use of lemon or lemon juice with any caviar is considered inappropriate.

Caviar Fan

One of the most spectacular ways of serving caviar is to arrange it in the form of a fan. This is made by cutting large slices of pullman bread (a rectangular, unsliced loaf of white bread) into the shape of a fan, ultimately cutting it up into individual croutons. This is not as complicated as it appears, but it is labor-intensive. See Figure 8.1. The template used for the caviar fan pictured in this book measures 17 inches at its widest point; top to bottom it is not quite 11 inches. A template was cut from a medium-weight sheet of paper, known as bristol board (available at art supply stores). The fan was then penciled in, yielding eight sections vertically, more or less, since it fans out from the bottom point; and five sections horizontally, more or less, on a convex curve. The pullman loaf was sliced in half, trimmed of exterior crust, then cut into ¼-inch thick sheets. These sheets were then toasted light brown on both sides. It is important not to overtoast the bread, because then it will break up indiscriminately when cut into the smaller croutons.

Once cooled, the sheets are placed on top of the template and cut to shape the eight vertically fanned-out sections. These long triangular forms are then spread with plain, unsalted, softened butter. Each triangle is returned to the template and cut into five individual croutons. Five varieties of caviar are then spread on each crouton, one variety for each of the horizontal curves. The varieties selected were also arranged in a specific order of color:

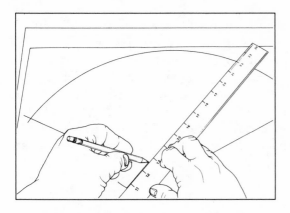

On a piece of bristol board (or other medium-weight paper), draw the outline of a fan.

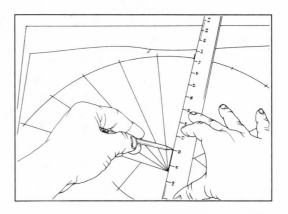

Divide the fan radially into eight equal sections.

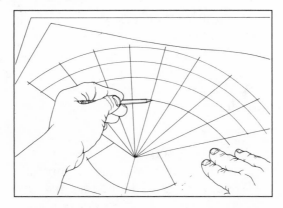

Divide the fan horizontally, as shown, into five sections. Cut out the form at the outside edge, discarding the trim. Place toasted sheets of pullman bread, spread with plain butter, on top of the template, and cut into 40 individual segments. Each segment is then topped with the appropriate caviar, garnished, then reassembled on a platter for service. (Author's note: While this is a tedious exercise, the stunning beauty of the resulting fan is often worth the effort, particularly with a clientele who can appreciate such work.)

Figure 8.1
Cutting template and bread for a caviar fan

lobster roe (red, Maine), Chinook salmon roe (orange, Great Lakes), whitefish roe (light yellow), Tobiko (light green, flying fish, flavored with wasabi), Choupique (black, bowfin).

A central area, running across four of the horizontal sections and three of the vertical sections, was covered with minced hard-boiled egg white. A template representing a Japanese calligraphic character (Harmony), was cut from a sheet of tracing paper. Once the fan was assembled, the paper template was placed over the egg-covered croutons, filled with whitefish roe, then highlighted with Choupique roe (it was piped out with a pastry bag, fitted with a No. 2 round tip). Finally, crêpes were rolled up around a filling of softened cream cheese, sliced on the bias, garnished with a dot of lobster roe and small pieces of blanched leek, and set at the bottom of the fan. (See color plate.)

𝒫OTATO PANCAKES I

1 pound Red Bliss or all-purpose potatoes
4 large eggs
¾ cup half-and-half
3 tablespoons unsalted butter

salt and white pepper to taste
cornstarch as needed
1 cup clarified butter

- Peel the potatoes, and cut into 2-inch chunks. Boil in lightly salted water until tender. Drain and mash, using a mashing tool or a food mill. Add the eggs, half-and-half, and butter, and beat in by hand or with an electric mixer.

- When the potatoes are cool enough to handle, portion out into 2-inch round pieces. Press down into round, flattened cakes, about ⅓-inch thick. Dust with the cornstarch, and sauté in hot clarified butter until golden brown on both sides.

𝒫OTATO PANCAKES II

4 large Red Bliss or all-purpose potatoes, peeled and grated
1 cup Quick Cream of Wheat cereal
4 eggs, beaten

1 cup flour
2 tablespoons parsley, minced
salt and white pepper to taste
clarified butter as needed

- Combine all ingredients except the clarified butter, and blend thoroughly. Shape into 2-inch round circles, and sauté in clarified butter.

*B*LINIS

½ pound buckwheat flour
½ pound all-purpose flour
1 cup warm milk
¾ ounce (1 teaspoon)
  granulated yeast

¼ teaspoon salt
¼ teaspoon sugar
¼ cup sour cream
2 small eggs, beaten
¼ cup heavy cream

- Sift the flours into a large bowl. Dissolve the yeast, salt, and sugar in the milk. Make a well in the flour, add the yeast mixture, and blend thoroughly with the flour. Let sit 30 minutes in a warm place.

- Add the remaining ingredients, and blend thoroughly into a smooth batter. Ladle into 2-inch round pancakes on a pan or griddle greased with the butter, and cook on both sides until golden brown. Serve with caviar and sour cream.

*B*UCKWHEAT PANCAKES WITH CAVIAR

2 cups buckwheat flour
2 large eggs
1 large egg yolk
2 cups milk
2 tablespoons melted butter

salt and pepper to taste
½ cup sour cream
½ cup scallions, sliced very
  thin
1 ounce caviar

- Whip the flour and eggs until smooth. Add the milk, butter, salt, and pepper, and blend thoroughly. Cover, and allow to rest 1 hour.

- Lightly butter a small nonstick sauté pan, and heat over medium flame. Pour in enough batter to just coat the bottom of the pan. When small holes form on the top surface, flip over and cook another 30 seconds. Continue until all the batter is used.

- Place a dollop of sour cream and some scallions on each pancake, slightly off center. Roll the pancake up into a cone, and add ½ teaspoon of caviar on top.

ℒ︎ANCAKES, NORTHERN STYLE

(Crêpes à la Nordique)

1½ cups flour
4 eggs
pinch of salt
1¼ cups milk

3 tablespoons olive oil
olive oil to taste
8 ounces bowfin caviar

- Beat the flour, eggs, and salt together, until they form a smooth paste. Add the milk, and beat until smooth. Add the 3 table-spoons of olive oil, blend thoroughly, and allow to sit for 30 minutes.
- Heat a 6-inch nonstick sauté pan over medium heat. Rub the pan with a cloth or paper towel dipped in olive oil, and pour in enough batter to coat the bottom of the pan (the crêpe should be fairly thin—about 1/16 inch). When the top of the batter is nearly dry, turn the crêpe over, cook another minute, then remove to a plate. Repeat until all the batter is used.
- When the crêpes have cooled, spread them with a thin layer of caviar. Roll up, slice on the bias, garnish with parsley, and serve with a side dish of crème fraîche.

———— • ————

For Pancakes Romanov (*Crêpes à la Romanov*), place the sliced crêpes on a bed of lettuce and add a garnish of minced onion and fennel, and sliced lemon.

————————

ℰSCABECIA

12 whole small fish (such as smelt, herring, anchovy)
salt, pepper, flour, and vegetable oil to taste
1 cup olive oil
½ cup lime juice
¼ cup orange juice
1 small carrot, peeled, trimmed, and sliced thin on the bias

1 small onion, peeled and sliced thin widthwise
2 garlic cloves, crushed
1 bay leaf
2 sprigs dill
1 bunch parsley stems, trimmed and rinsed
¼ cup cilantro leaves, roughly chopped
1 tablespoon black pepper-corns

- Season the fish with salt and pepper, dust with flour, and sauté in the oil until golden brown. Transfer to absorbent paper, then place in a glass bowl.
- Bring the remaining ingredients to a boil, and pour over the fish, Marinate for 24 hours, and serve chilled.

GIN-CURED SALMON, CRANBERRY RELISH

For the Salmon

1 3 to 4-pound side of fresh
   salmon, skin-on, pin
   bones removed
1 cup gin
½ cup salt
¾ cup sugar
1½ tablespoons black pep-
   percorns, crushed

1½ teaspoons mustard
   seeds, crushed
1 cup fresh whole cran-
   berries, mashed
1 orange, sliced very thin
the zest of 1 orange,
   blanched in boiling salted
   water

For the Relish

the zest and juice of 1
   orange
1 tablespoon unsalted butter
6 tablespoons sugar

1 cup dry sherry
1 cup dry white wine
2 cups whole cranberries,
   fresh or frozen

For the Sauce

¾ cup gin
¼ cup juniper berries,
   crushed
1½ cups mayonnaise
½ cup half-and-half

2 tablespoons white wine
   vinegar
¼ cup prepared horseradish
salt and white pepper to
   taste

To Prepare the Salmon

- Combine the salt, sugar, peppercorns, and mustard seeds. Place the salmon skin-side down in a shallow glass casserole dish. Rub ¼ cup of the gin into the salmon flesh, then sprinkle on half of the spice mix. Press the mashed cranberries onto this, and cover with a layer of the sliced orange. Top with the remaining spice mix, and pour on the remaining gin. (The blanched orange zest is for a garnish.)

- Lay a sheet of plastic or wax paper over the salmon, and place another pan, slightly smaller than the first, on top. Weight down, using cans or some other heavy objects. Place this in the refrigerator for 3 days, pouring excess liquid off once each day.

To Prepare the Relish

- Sauté the zest in the butter for 3 minutes. Add the orange juice, sugar, sherry, and wine, and simmer until reduced by half. Add the cranberries and simmer until thick and smooth and the cranberries have all opened. Allow to cool, then cover and refrigerate at least 24 hours before serving.

To Prepare the Sauce

- Simmer the gin and berries for about 10 minutes, then remove from the fire and allow to cool. Strain the gin into a food processor, add the mayonnaise, half-and-half, vinegar, horseradish, salt, and pepper, and purée. Cover and refrigerate at least 24 hours before serving.

To Serve

- Wash the salmon thoroughly in cold water, and pat dry. Slice paper-thin, at a 30-degree angle, using a long, flexible knife. Place several slices of salmon on a serving plate and top with a little of the sauce. Garnish with the blanched zest, a small dollop of the relish to one side, and a sprig of flat-leaf parsley.

—————————————— • ——————————————

Cranberry, the largest species of a number of tart berries native to North America and Europe, is unique to North America. In various parts of the United States smaller varieties are called red whortleberry, partridge berry, whimberry, mountainberry, rockberry, and cowberry. The native clan Wampanoag introduced cranberries to the Pilgrims in the form of pemmican—cranberries crushed with dried venison and bear fat—an important food staple for surviving the rugged New England winters. The colonists called the tart red berries crane berries, because their pink blossoms resembled the head of a crane. In 1677, when the Massachusetts colonists had the audacity to mint their own coins, they shipped ten crates of cranberries, along with some dried codfish and Indian corn, to Charles II, then king of England, in an attempt to appease his wrath. In 1787, James Madison wrote to Thomas Jefferson, gallivanting around France at the time, asking for background information on the constitutional government there, for use at the upcoming Constitutional Convention in Philadelphia. Jefferson supplied the requested information in exchange for a shipment of apples, pecans, and cranberries. During this time, cranberries had become so popular in New England that one Cape Cod village levied a fine of one dollar on anyone found picking more than a quart of them before September 20.

 GRAVLAX

2 boneless salmon fillets, scaled, skin-on	1½ cups sugar
¼ cup brandy	3 tablespoons black peppercorns, cracked
the juice of 1 lemon	½ cup fresh dill, roughly chopped
1½ cups kosher salt	

- Rinse the salmon fillets with cold water, and pat dry. Cut several shallow slits in the skin (to allow the cure to penetrate that side).

- Rub the brandy and lemon juice into the flesh of the fillets, and sprinkle with the pepper. Blend the sugar, salt, and dill together, and pack about half of this mixture onto the flesh of the fillets.

- Place the fillets, flesh side down, in a hotel pan. Sprinkle the remaining sugar/salt/dill mix over the skin. Cover with plastic wrap, then set a second hotel pan on top, and weight down (three No. 10 cans work well). Allow to cure 2 to 3 days refrigerated, pouring excess juice off once daily. (Additional sugar/salt mix may have to be added.)

- Rinse the fillets thoroughly in cold water, and pat dry. Press a small amount of additional cracked pepper and minced dill onto the salmon, wrap and refrigerate until ready to use. (See color plate.)

———————————— • ————————————

Gravlax should be sliced very thin, on a very low angle (about 25 degrees). It can be used for individual canapés, or laid out on a mirror or a platter. It is generally accompanied by a mayonnaise-based mustard and dill sauce, or a Horseradish Sauce (1 cup cream, 1 cups fresh white bread crumbs, 1 cup sour cream, 1 pint prepared horseradish squeezed dry, the juice of 1 lemon juice, salt, and white pepper to taste).

The proportions of salt to sugar varies considerably among culinarians. This recipe includes equal amounts, though they can be adjusted to suit one's taste. The function of the salt is to draw out moisture, effectively curing the fish; the function of the sugar is to sweeten. In the Norwegian style *(Gravlax)*, the ratio is 5 parts sugar to 4 parts salt, along with white peppercorns, brandy, lemon juice, and dill; the Swedish style *(Gravadlax)* consists of nearly all salt, a sprinkling of sugar and white pepper, plenty of dill, and no brandy or lemon. The equal proportions of salt-to-sugar works well, though one is free to experiment with other proportions.

Contemporary innovations include a Tex-Mex version, made by substituting the brandy with tequila, the dill with cilantro, and the pepper with chopped jalapeño peppers; and an Asian or Pan-Pacific version made with brandy, grated ginger, and soy sauce.

SALMON AND SUN-DRIED TOMATO TERRINE

For the Pesto

1½ cups sun-dried tomatoes, packed in olive oil
½ cup olive paste
3 garlic cloves, crushed

6 tablespoons olive oil (drained from the tomatoes)
¼ cup grated Romano cheese

For the Terrine

1 pound all-purpose potatoes
1½ pounds salmon fillet, boneless and skinless, cut into 6 pieces

1 cup dry white wine
1 cup water
1 shallot, minced
1 sprig dill
1 bay leaf

For the Vinaigrette

1½ cups olive oil
½ cup champagne wine vinegar
1 tablespoon Dijon-style mustard
3 tablespoons water

salt and white pepper to taste
2 heads butter lettuce, separated into individual leaves, rinsed, and dried

To Prepare the Tomatoes

- Drain the oil from the tomatoes, and set the oil aside. Combine all the ingredients in a food processor, and blend until puréed. Cover and refrigerate until needed.

To Prepare the Terrine

- Peel the potatoes, then cook in boiling salted water until tender. Drain, cool, then cut into ¼-inch thick slices.

- Bring the wine, water, shallot, and herbs to a boil. Poach the salmon in this liquid, about 10 minutes. Drain, cool, then break up into small flakes.
- Lightly coat the inside of a terrine mold or bread pan with the olive oil remaining from the tomatoes. Cut a piece of parchment paper to fit, and set inside the bottom of the mold. Brush the parchment paper with olive oil.
- Press a layer of salmon onto the parchment paper, about ½-inch deep. Spoon a layer of the tomato paste onto the salmon. Press a layer of the potatoes on top of this, so that the potatoes completely cover the previous layer. Repeat this process two additional times, pressing each layer firmly on top of the previous one. Cover with plastic wrap and refrigerate overnight.

To Prepare the Vinaigrette

- Whip the oil, vinegar, mustard, water, salt, and pepper together.

To Serve

- Arrange a bed of butter lettuce leaves on eight serving plates.
- Run a knife around the inside of the terrine or bread pan. Set the pan in an inch of hot water for 3 seconds, then invert onto a large plate. Tap the top of the mold so that the terrine falls from the form. Dip a knife in hot water, and carefully slice the terrine into eight slices. Place each on a lettuce bed, and drizzle with the vinaigrette.

Pesto is a derivation of "pestle" (from the Italian *pestare*, "to pound"), the grinding tool used with a mortar, in which various herbs and spices are ground into a paste.

ᏚALMON TARTAR, GARNI

1 pound fresh salmon fillet, boneless and skinless
¼ cup olive oil
1 shallot, minced
1 garlic clove, pressed
1 anchovy fillet, minced
1 teaspoon capers
2 tablespoons lemon juice
1 tablespoon minced dill

½ teaspoon green peppercorns, mashed
8 radicchio leaves
1 lemon, cut into 8 wedges, seeds removed
¼ cup salmon caviar
4 sprigs flat-leaf parsley
1 small brioche, sliced ¼-inch thick and toasted

- Mince the salmon very fine. Add the oil, shallot, garlic, anchovy, capers, lemon juice, dill, and mashed peppercorns, and blend. Refrigerate for 2 hours.

- Shape the tartar into four individual round or oval portions, place on serving plates, and garnish with the remaining ingredients.

Hot Dishes

CODFISH CAKES

(Croquettes de Cabillaud)

2 cups cooked codfish, flaked
3 cups freshly mashed potatoes, hot
½ cup scallions, sliced very thin
2 eggs, beaten
1 egg yolk

2 tablespoons dill, minced
1 teaspoon grated gingerroot
2 tablespoons soy sauce
white pepper to taste
4 tablespoons unsalted butter, clarified
lemon wedges and parsley sprigs as needed

- Combine all the ingredients (except the butter, lemon, and parsley) in a large bowl, and blend thoroughly. Shape into round patties, 3 × ½ inches. Fry in the clarified butter until golden brown on both sides. Place on absorbent paper, and place in the oven until all the cakes are fried. Serve with aïoli, rémoulade, or another mayonnaise-based sauce, and garnish with lemon wedges and parsley.

CODFISH QUENELLES, CANTONESE STYLE

(Quenelles de Cabillaud, à la Cantonnaise)

2 tablespoons gingerroot, grated
1 cup saki
¼ cup scallions, finely diced
¼ cup bacon, finely diced
1 pound boneless, skinless codfish, cut into 1-inch pieces
3 egg whites

3 tablespoons soy sauce
¼ cup peanut oil
2 garlic cloves, sliced very thin
1½ cups rich chicken stock
2 tablespoons hoisan sauce
1 tablespoon cornstarch
¼ cup dry sherry

- Place the fish in the freezer for 30 minutes. Simmer the ginger, saki, scallions, and bacon, until about 3 tablespoons of liquid remain. Set aside to cool.
- Place the ginger mixture, fish, egg whites, and soy sauce in a food processor, and purée, using the pulse switch.
- Shape the fish farce into 1-inch balls, slightly flattened on one side, and refrigerate for 1 hour.
- Sauté the fish balls in the peanut oil until golden brown on the flattened side. Remove from the pan, then add the garlic and sauté briefly. Add the sherry, stock, hoisan, and fish balls, and bring to a simmer. Dissolve the cornstarch in the sherry, add to the liquid, and simmer for 1 minute. Serve with a steamed green vegetable.

*F*RIED CATFISH, MUSTARD-PECAN MAYONNAISE

The American bullhead species of catfish can survive out of water for several hours, and the African variety is able to bury itself in mud for months in order to survive rainless periods. Other species have internal air sacs that allow them to breathe while traveling from one pond to another. Since they are scavengers and bottom feeders, they have not been particularly esteemed as a source of food. Farm-raised catfish, however, yield a delicate flesh with few bones.

4 5- to 6-ounce catfish fillets
salt, white pepper, and flour
  as needed
3 eggs, beaten
½ cup cornmeal
½ dry bread crumbs
2 tablespoons unsalted
  butter

¼ cup peanut oil
1 cup mayonnaise
5 tablespoons grainy
  mustard
½ cup toasted chopped
  pecans
the juice of 1 lemon

- Combine the mayonnaise, mustard, pecans, and lemon, and blend thoroughly. Cover and refrigerate until ready to serve.
- Combine the cornmeal and bread crumbs. Season the catfish with salt and pepper, and dust with flour. Dip into the eggs, then coat in the cornmeal mixture.
- Sauté the catfish in the oil and butter until golden brown on both sides. Drain on absorbent paper, and serve accompanied by the pecan mayonnaise.

*P*IKE QUENELLES, LOBSTER SAUCE

(Quenelles de Brochet, Sauce à l'Américaine)

For the Quenelles

1 cup dry white wine
2 shallots, minced

1 pound fresh pike, boneless
  and skinless, cut into
  1-inch pieces

¼ pound unsalted butter, soft

½ cup flour

1 pint heavy cream

4 large eggs

salt and white pepper to taste

1 recipe court bouillon

6 ounces puff pastry dough

For the Sauce

1 shallot, minced

1 cup fish stock

¼ cup mushrooms, roughly minced

2 cups fish velouté

2 tablespoons tomato paste

1 egg yolk

¼ cup heavy cream

3 tablespoons lobster butter, cut into ½-inch pieces

- Preheat an oven to 375°F.
- Roll out the puff pastry to a thickness of ⅛ inch. Using a 3-inch round circle cutter, cut 8 crescent-shaped pieces (fleurons). Brush with egg wash, place on a baking sheet, and bake until puffed up and golden brown. Set aside.

To Prepare the Sauce

- Simmer the shallot, stock, and mushrooms until reduced by three-fourths. Add the fish velouté and tomato paste, and simmer until suitable thickness is achieved. Temper in the egg yolk and cream, beat in the lobster butter, adjust seasoning, and set aside, keeping warm.

To Prepare the Quenelles

- Simmer the wine and shallots until nearly dry.
- Place the pike into a food processor and purée roughly, using the pulse switch.
- Knead the butter and flour together. Add this paste to the fish, along with the shallots, cream, eggs, salt, and pepper into the processor, and pulse until a smooth purée.
- Dip a tablespoon into cold water, and scoop out a heaping spoonful of the mousse. Wet the palm of the opposite hand, and shape the mousse into a smooth oval. Drop the quenelle into the court bouillon (barely simmering).
- Remove the quenelles from the court bouillon, and drain on absorbent paper. Place on serving plates, coat with the sauce, and garnish with the fleurons.

It has been suggested that Lobster à l'Américaine is a misnamed "Lobster à l'Amoricaine," originating in Brittany and so named for the Armorican massif, a mountain mass in the northwesternmost region of France. Brittany is well known for many lobster dishes, given its proximity to the North Atlantic. But Brittany is not known for tomatoes, and until the nineteenth century tomatoes were scarcely known outside the Mediterranean region. All versions of Lobster l'Américaine do include tomatoes, garlic, and olive oil, giving credence to Jules Gouffé's name for this dish—Lobster à la Provençale—as published in his *Le Livre de Cuisine* in 1867. Provence, a southern French region of considerable gastronomic esteem, is known for its abundant use of tomato, garlic, and olive oil. There is speculation that Homard à l'Américaine was created for a distinguished American diner at Noël Peter's, a celebrated dining establishment in Paris, in 1860, while Auguste Escoffier contended that an unnamed cook created Langouste de la Mediterranée at Le Restaurant Français in Nice, exported the Provence-style dish to the United States, then reimported it to France with the names Lobster à l'Américaine.

ᏚHAD ROE, SORREL SAUCE

(Oeufs d'Alose à l'Oseille)

1 shallot, minced
¼ cup (½ stick) unsalted butter
3 tablespoons flour
1 cup fish stock, hot
1 cup heavy cream, hot

1½ cups sorrel leaves, rinsed, stemmed, and roughly chopped
salt and pepper to taste
8 fresh shad roe
½ pound unsalted butter
4 lemon wedges

- Sauté the shallot in the butter for several minutes. Add the flour, blend, and cook several minutes. Add the hot fish stock, blend thoroughly, and allow to simmer for about 15 minutes.

- Simmer the cream until reduced by half. Place the fish sauce, cream, and sorrel in a blender or food processor, and purée. Strain, season to taste with salt and pepper, and set aside.

- Rinse the shad roe gently, then place into a saucepan with ½ pound of butter and simmer, covered, over very low heat, for 10 to 12 minutes, turning once.
- Serve the roe coated with the sauce and garnished with the lemon.

———————————— • ————————————

Shad is a seasonal fish, and is at its fat and succulent best during its spawning season. The best shad is found in the waters of the East Coast of North America, from the Hudson River to the Chesapeake Bay, though related species are found throughout the world. The Hudson River Valley once sported a thriving shad industry—in 1889 more than 4 million pounds were harvested. But by the 1940s, pollution put an end to this industry. In 1973 the folk minstrel Pete Seeger hosted a shad festival in conjunction with the Culinary Institute in Hyde Park, New York. By virtue of Seeger's efforts to identify industries on the Hudson that were discharging waste, the river became sufficiently cleaner and the schools of shad swimming up the Hudson in the spring noticeably increased.

The author participated in this festival and was later apprenticed in nearby Dutchess County where his mentor, Peter Van Erp, frequently served Shad Roe, Meunière: Wrap the roe in strips of bacon that have been blanched in boiling salted water, and secure with toothpicks. Broil on all sides until golden brown. Simmer some dry white wine and minced shallots, and reduce until nearly dry.

Add fresh lemon juice, beat in unsalted butter, finish with minced parsley, and serve with the roe.

SHELLFISH

Cold Dishes

Dungeness Crab Cocktail, California Style

Drop the crab into boiling salted water, return to a boil, cover, remove from the fire, and allow it to sit 20 minutes. Remove the crab from the water, and when cool enough, separate the claws and legs of the creature, and crack with the heel of a knife. Tear off the top shell, and save (scrape off the furry part on the underside of the shell, boil the shell in water with a little vinegar, and save for serving Crab Cardinale). Cut the body into 6 pieces, and serve all with mustard mayonnaise, parsley, and lobster forks (for removing the meat).

𝓛OBSTER COCKTAIL

For the Cocktail

2 1½-pound lobsters	8 butter lettuce leaves
8 fat asparagus	8 lemon slices

For the Sauce

½ cup onion, coarsely chopped	2 tablespoons white Worcestershire sauce
2 garlic cloves	2 tablespoons champagne vinegar
1 tablespoon apple juice concentrate	¼ cup prepared horseradish
1 cup ketchup	salt and cayenne pepper to taste
1 tablespoon tomato paste	
the juice of 2 lemons	

• Purée all of the sauce ingredients in a food processor or blender. Cover and refrigerate until ready to serve.

• Drop the lobster into boiling salted water, return to a boil, cover, remove from the fire, and allow to sit 20 minutes. Remove the lobsters, and when cool enough to handle, remove the claw and tail meat (reserve the bodies for use in other dishes).

• Cut the asparagus into 2½-inch long pieces (reserve the rest of each stalk for soup). Peel them, and blanch in boiling salted water until al dente. Drain, cool, and set aside.

• Arrange the lettuce in four champagne saucers. Divide the lobster meat among the saucers, top with some of the sauce, and garnish each with asparagus and 2 slices of lemon.

———— • ————

Another sauce that can be served with chilled shellfish (clams, crab, lobster, mussels, or oysters) is Raspberry Mignonette (1 cup raspberry vinegar, ¼ cup dry white wine, 1 teaspoon coarsely ground black pepper, 1 shallot minced, 1 teaspoon minced basil leaves, and salt to taste; whip together, and marinate overnight.)

𝓛OBSTER AND SCALLOP MOUSSE

(Mousse d'Homard et Coquilles St. Jacques)

1 tablespoon butter	8 ounces fresh scallops (ocean or bay)
1 shallot, minced	

¼ cup dry white wine
2 tablespoons lemon juice
salt and white pepper to
  taste
1 slice fresh white bread,
  crusts trimmed
1 egg white

2 tablespoons unsalted butter, coarsely chopped
pinch of nutmeg
1 cup heavy cream
1 cup (7 ounces) lobster
  meat, finely diced

- Sauté the shallot and scallops in the butter for 3 minutes. Remove the scallops with a slotted spoon and set aside. Add the wine, lemon juice, salt, and pepper, and simmer until reduced by half.

- Place the bread in a food processor, and pulse until the bread is well shredded. Add the scallops, wine reduction, egg white, chopped butter, and nutmeg, and pulse until fairly smooth. Add the cream in a steady stream, and continue pulsing until well blended. Fold in the lobster meat.

- Butter a mold large enough to accommodate the mousse, and fill with the mousse. Cover with plastic wrap, and refrigerate overnight. To unmold, dip the mold into very hot water, then invert onto a flat cutting surface. Slice, and serve with an appropriate sauce.

SEVICHE, PACIFIC COAST STYLE

1 pound sea scallops
¼ cup lime juice
2 tablespoons lemon juice
salt and white pepper as
  needed
4 blood oranges
¼ cup red bell pepper,
  medium dice
¼ cup green bell pepper,
  medium dice

¼ cup red onion, sliced
  paper-thin
1 green jalapeño pepper,
  minced
2 tablespoons cilantro
  leaves, minced
8 butter lettuce leaves
3 tablespoons chives, minced

- Slice the scallops widthwise into three rounds each, sprinkle lightly wirh salt and pepper, and marinate in the lemon and lime juice overnight.

- Peel the blood oranges, and separate the segments from in between the skin. (See Figure 8.2.) Squeeze out juice from the remaining pulp. Drain the scallops, and combine with the orange segments, orange juice, peppers, onion, and cilantro. Marinate 2 hours, then arrange on the lettuce leaves, and top with the chopped chives.

———— • ————

A blood orange is a small, sweet variety of orange with a rough-textured skin and bright red flesh and juice.

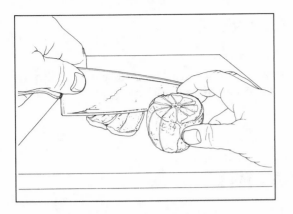

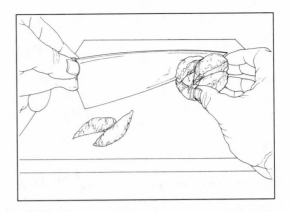

*Slice and remove the ends of an orange
(lime, lemon, or grapefruit).
Slice and remove the skin and pith.*

*Remove the segments by cutting in between the
membranes that separate them. (Squeeze and
reserve the juice from the remaining membranes.)*

Figure 8.2
Cutting the segments from citrus fruit

ʃHRIMP IN BEER

1 pound 12-16 count
   shrimp, shells on
2 bottles beer
1 to 2 cups water
1 teaspoon salt
2 garlic cloves, crushed
1 small onion, thinly sliced
1 bay leaf
½ cup olive oil
½ cup champagne vinegar
½ cup beer

1 shallot, minced
salt, pepper, and Tabasco to
   taste
1 cup mayonnaise
1 tablespoon curry powder
1 tablespoon lemon juice
2 tablespoons water
1 head butter lettuce
6 sprigs parsley
1 lemon, cut into 8 wedges

- Combine the shrimp, 2 bottles of beer, 1 to 2 cups of water, salt, garlic, onion, and bay leaf in a saucepan. Bring to a boil, then turn off and allow to sit 30 minutes. Drain, reserving the shrimp. Peel, devein, and set aside.

- Combine the oil, vinegar, ½ cup of beer, shallot, salt, pepper, and Tabasco in a bowl, and blend. Add the shrimp and marinate refrigerated for 3 hours.

- Combine the curry, lemon, and water, and blend into a smooth paste. Add to the mayonnaise, and blend thoroughly.

- Serve the shrimp on lettuce leaves, with the curry mayonnaise on the side, and garnish with parsley and lemon wedges.

Oysters, Borchardt Style
(Huîtres à la Borchardt)

A raw oyster served on a slice of tomato, topped with a dollop of sour cream, garnished with caviar and a chive spear. (See color plate.)

SHRIMP, DORIA STYLE

(Crevettes à la Doria)

For the Shrimp

½ pound shrimp meat, ¼-inch dice
¼ cup scallions, finely sliced
¼ cup celery, small dice
¼ cup leeks, cut in small dice and cooked in boiling salted water until tender
the juice of 2 lemons
¾ cup mayonnaise
¼ cup chili sauce (or ketchup)

2 tablespoons prepared horseradish, squeezed dry
1 tablespoons minced tarragon
1 tablespoons minced parsley
salt and white pepper as needed
4 large ripe tomatoes

For the Cucumbers

½ hothouse cucumber, sliced very thin
½ cup olive oil
¼ cup champagne vinegar

1 shallot, minced
1 tablespoon dill, minced
salt and pepper as needed

- Combine all of the shrimp salad ingredients (except the tomatoes), blend thoroughly, seasoning to taste with the salt and white pepper. Cover and refrigerate.

- Combine the oil, vinegar, shallot, dill, salt, and pepper, and blend thoroughly. Pour over the cucumber, and marinate for several hours.

- Remove the core and a slice from the bottom of each tomato. Cut in half widthwise, and scoop out the interior (save for another use). Fill the tomato halves with the salad, and garnish with the marinated cucumber.

Shrimp, Modern Style
(Crevettes à la Moderne)

Blend medium-diced cooked shrimp and mayonnaise together, and season with salt and white pepper. Line champagne saucers with a bed of lettuce, top with the shrimp salad, and garnish with a whole shrimp, sliced hard-boiled egg, and sliced lemon.

Shrimp, Newest Style
(Crevettes à la Fin de Siécle)

Place a large shrimp cut in half lengthwise on top of a half lemon, and garnish with parsley.

Hot Dishes

Clams

....

*L*ITTLENECK CLAMS, PROVENÇALE

For the Rouille

1 large red bell pepper
2 red jalapeño peppers
olive oil
2 egg yolks
4 large garlic cloves, pressed

⅓ cup mashed potato
salt and white pepper to
   taste
1 cup olive oil
the juice of 1 lemon

- Preheat an oven to 400°F.
- Rub the peppers lightly with olive oil, and roast on a pan until they begin turning black (20 to 30 minutes). Place in a plastic bag, and seal for 15 minutes. Remove the peppers, and separate the skin and seeds from the flesh.
- Purée the egg yolks, bell pepper flesh, garlic, salt, and pepper in a food processor. Using the pulse switch, add the potato, then the olive oil in a slow, steady stream, alternating with the lemon juice. Adjust the seasoning if necessary, with salt and pepper.

For the Soup

1 pound small Red Bliss
   potatoes, cut in half
2 medium Spanish onions,
   peeled and cut in quarters

1 fennel bulb, trimmed and
   cut into ¼-inch slices
1 red bell pepper, seeded
   and cut in ½-inch strips

olive oil, salt, and pepper
24 littleneck clams
1½ cups dry white wine
2 tablespoons Pernod
2 garlic cloves, crushed
1 bay leaf

1 teaspoon lemon zest
1 cup plum tomatoes, diced
¼ cup cilantro leaves,
    roughly chopped
1 baguette

- Toss the potatoes, onions, fennel, and pepper with olive oil, salt, and pepper. Roast in a 375°F preheated oven for 30 to 40 minutes, or until tender.

- Steam the clams, covered, in the remaining ingredients (except the cilantro), until all the clams are open.

To Serve

- Arrange the roasted vegetables on four individual serving plates, top with the clams, some of the strained broth, and the cilantro. Serve with toasted sliced baguette, spread with the rouille.

Rouille means "rust" in French; this dish is so named because of its reddish tint. It is traditionally served spread on toasted croutons along with bouillabaisse.

Crab

CRAB CAKES, JALAPEÑO BEURRE BLANC

For the Crab Cakes

4 tablespoons unsalted
    butter
3 shallots, minced
¼ cup Pernod
1 tablespoon unsalted butter,
    soft, mixed with 1 table-
    spoon flour
4 ounces sour cream
salt and white pepper to
    taste

1 pound crab meat,
    shredded
4 eggs, lightly beaten
4 cups fresh white bread
    crumbs
1 quart vegetable oil
8 lemon wedges
8 sprigs dill

For the Sauce

3 shallots, minced
2 green jalapeño peppers,
    cut into very fine dice
1 cup dry white wine
¼ cup white wine or cham-
    pagne vinegar

½ pound unsalted butter,
    cut into ½-inch pieces
salt and white pepper to
    taste

To Prepare the Crab Cakes

- Sauté the shallots in the butter. Add the Pernod, and reduce. Add the butter/flour paste, and cook for several minutes, stirring continuously. Add the sour cream, salt, and pepper, blend in, and remove from the fire.
- Add the crab and eggs, and blend in. Shape into eight individual oval or round patties, then roll in the bread crumbs, pressing them on firmly. Cover and refrigerate 1 hour.
- Preheat an oven to 300°F.
- Pour 1 inch of vegetable oil into a cast-iron skillet or heavy-gauge saucepan, and heat to 365°F. Fry the cakes until golden brown on each side. Transfer to absorbent paper, and place in the oven until ready to serve.

To Prepare the Sauce

- Simmer the shallots, peppers, wine, and vinegar, until reduced by three-fourths.
- Add the butter, and incorporate into the reduction by stirring continuously until fully emulsified. Season to taste with salt and white pepper. Serve 2 crab cakes per person, with a little sauce, and garnish with lemon and dill.

Whole butter and uncooked flour kneaded into a paste is a thickening agent (liaison) known as *beurre manié* (*manié* is the past participle of *manier*, meaning "to manipulate," or "knead"). It differs from a *roux* (flour cooked with clarified butter) in that (1) it is prepared without cooking and (2) it is added to a dish during cooking in order to thicken it. It is important to cook the *beurre manié* sufficiently to remove its starchiness.

CRAB CROQUETTES

3 tablespoons unsalted butter
1 shallot, minced
½ cup mushrooms, small dice
¼ cup dry white wine
1½ cups shelled crab claws, cut in half

1 cup very thick béchamel (cream) sauce
3 egg yolks
salt and cayenne pepper as needed
flour, beaten egg, and bread crumbs, as needed

- Sauté the shallot and mushrooms in the butter. Add the wine and crab, and simmer until the wine is evaporated. Add the béchamel, blend, and set aside to cool.
- When the mixture has cooled, blend in the egg yolks and season with salt and cayenne. Refrigerate at least 2 hours. Shape into eight individual cylindrical croquettes, dust with flour, dip in beaten egg, then roll in the bread crumbs, pressing them on firmly. Cover and refrigerate 30 minutes.

If the croquette mixture is not thick enough, add some fresh white bread crumbs, and allow to sit for 30 minutes.

- Preheat an oven to 200°F.
- Pour 2-inch deep vegetable oil in a cast-iron skillet or heavy-gauge saucepan, and heat to 375°F. Fry the cakes until golden brown on each side. Transfer to absorbent paper, and place in the oven until all are ready to serve.

CRAB MOUSSE, GINGER BEURRE BLANC

For the Mousse

1 pound sole fillet, coarsely
    chopped
pinch of cayenne
1 egg
salt and white pepper to
    taste

pinch of nutmeg
1 cup heavy cream
1 pound crab claw meat, cut
    into ¼-inch dice
butter as needed
1 cup Ginger Beurre Blanc

For the Sauce

1 shallot, minced
1 cup dry white wine
1 tablespoon gingerroot,
    peeled and grated

⅓ pound unsalted
    butter, cut into ½-inch
    pieces

- Place the sole, cayenne, egg, salt, pepper, and nutmeg into a food processor, and purée. Add the cream in a steady stream and continue processing until smooth and emulsified.

- Remove the mousse to a large bowl, and fold in the diced crab. Butter eight ramekins, timbales, or dariole molds, and divide the mixture among the molds. Cover each mold with a piece of lightly buttered parchment paper, and set on a rack in a large saucepan or roasting pan. Fill the bottom with about ½ inch water, cover the pan, and steam the molds for 10 minutes. Turn the fire off, and allow to sit for 5 minutes.

- Simmer the shallot, wine, and ginger, until reduced by three-fourths. Add the butter, and stir vigorously until the butter is completely emulsified. Remove from heat and set aside, keeping warm.

- Using a paring knife, carefully loosen the mousses, and invert onto serving plates. Serve with Ginger Beurre Blanc.

Lobster

.... ## *L*OBSTER IN PHYLLO, CAMBRIDGE SAUCE

For the Sauce

2 hard-boiled egg yolks
1 anchovy fillet, mashed
½ teaspoon dry mustard
⅛ teaspoon cayenne pepper
¼ cup champagne vinegar
1 cup peanut oil

1 teaspoon tarragon leaves, minced
1 teaspoon dill, minced
1 tablespoon parsley, minced
1 tablespoon small capers, drained

For the Phyllo

2 tablespoons peanut oil
2 tablespoons scallions, finely diced
2 tablespoons celery, finely diced
2 tablespoons water chestnuts, finely diced
¼ cup heavy cream

½ pound cooked lobster meat, finely diced
the juice of 1 lemon
¼ teaspoon cayenne pepper
salt to taste
12 sheets phyllo dough
clarified unsalted butter as needed

- Beat the yolks, anchovy, mustard, cayenne, and 1 tablespoon of the vinegar into a smooth paste. Add the oil in a slow, steady stream, whipping continuously. Alternate the oil with the remaining vinegar as the sauce thickens. Add the herbs and capers, then cover and refrigerate until ready to serve.

- Sauté the scallions, celery, and water chestnuts in the peanut oil serveral minutes. Add the cream and reduce slightly. Combine the reduction with the lobster, lemon, cayenne, and salt, and blend thoroughly.

- Preheat an oven to 375°F.

- Brush one sheet of phyllo lightly with butter. Top this with a second sheet, brush with butter, and top with a third sheet. Cut this into four equal strips, lengthwise. Repeat the process with the remaining phyllo.

- Place a heaping teaspoon of filling about 1 inch from one end of a strip of dough. Fold one corner diagonally over the filling, flush with the side (this will create a 45-degree angle at the top). Continue folding this triangle down the strip, folding and refolding to the end of the strip. Brush with melted butter, transfer to a baking sheet, and repeat with the remaining dough strips.

- Bake for 10 minutes, or until golden brown, and serve with the sauce.

$\mathcal{L}$OBSTER QUENELLES

(Quenelles de Homard)

1 pound fresh sole or flounder, cut into 1-inch pieces
1 quart heavy cream
2 eggs
2 tablespoons lobster base
2 tablespoons brandy

1½ pounds lobster meat,
 finely chopped
salt and white pepper to
 taste
1 gallon court bouillon

- Place all ingredients into a food processor and purée, using the pulse switch. (Be careful not to overwhip.) Season to taste with salt and pepper.
- Dip a large serving or tablespoon into cold water, and moisten the palm of one hand. Scoop out 1 to 2 ounces of the farce and, using the spoon, shape the quenelle in the palm of that hand. It should be a nicely shaped oval, with no creases or rough spots. Repeat until all of the farce is shaped into ovals. Ease into barely simmering court bouillon, and poach 6 to 8 minutes (depending on their size), and serve with an appropriate beurre blanc or fish-based sauce).

———————————— • ————————————

 A quenelle is a form of dumpling, made from fish, shellfish, veal, game, or poultry. Quenelles are generally served as appetizers, or as a garnish for various classical entrées and soups.

 This farce can be used for making a very fine quenelle, as a stuffing for any dish that calls for a lobster mousse, or steamed in a buttered mold and served as a mousse. It can also be accompanied with any number of fish or shellfish veloutés, beurre blancs, or light tomato sauces.

*L*OBSTER STRUDEL, TOMATO-ARMAGNAC SAUCE

For the Strudel

8 sheets phyllo dough
2 tablespoons unsalted butter
1 garlic clove, pressed
½ cup dry bread crumbs
½ pound fresh spinach, rinsed, steamed, squeezed dry, and finely chopped
6 ounces goat cheese

1 pound lobster meat, medium dice
1 tablespoon basil leaves, minced
pinch of salt and white pepper
clarified unsalted butter as needed
1 egg, beaten with ¼ cup water

For the Sauce

3 tablespoons olive oil
1 shallot, minced
¼ cup Armagnac
1 cup peeled, diced tomato
1 teaspoon thyme leaves

1 teaspoon basil leaves, minced
¼ cup chicken stock
1 tablespoon Armagnac
salt and pepper to taste

To Prepare the Strudel

- Sauté the garlic in half the butter. Add the bread crumbs, season with salt and pepper, and set aside.

- Preheat an oven to 365°F.

- Brush one sheet of phyllo lightly with clarified butter, and place a second sheet on top. Repeat this step until there are four layers of the dough. Place another sheet of dough, overlapping by ½ inch, along the long side of the four-ply buttered sheets. Brush that sheet with butter, top with another sheet of dough then butter. Repeat with the last 2 sheets of dough. Sprinkle on the bread crumbs evenly. Arrange the spinach, cheese, lobster, basil, salt, and pepper in a 3-inch wide strip along the shorter side of the dough. Carefully roll up the dough around the filling, creating a firm cylinder. Fold and pinch the ends shut, then brush the cylinder with the egg wash. Place on a lightly greased pan, and bake 20 to 30 minutes, or until golden brown.

To Prepare the Sauce

- Sauté the shallot in the olive oil. Add ¼ cup Armagnac, and reduce by half. Add the tomato, thyme, basil, and stock, and

Other varieties of shellfish will also work with this recipe, including crab, oysters, and shrimp.

simmer until reduced by half. Purée in a blender or food processor, then return to the fire. Add the remaining Armagnac, season with salt and pepper.

- Slice the strudel carefully into eight slices. Place a portion of the sauce on a serving plate, and top with the sliced strudel.

Mussels

. . . . # MUSSELS WITH SAFFRON AND SNOW PEAS

4 pounds fresh mussels, debearded, scrubbed, and well rinsed
2 cups dry white wine
1 shallot, roughly chopped
1 bay leaf
1 bunch parsley stems, rinsed, trimmed, and tied together with cotton string

pinch of salt
pinch of white pepper
pinch of saffron threads
1½ pounds snow peas
2 ounces (½ stick) unsalted butter

- Steam the mussels in the white wine, shallot, bay leaf, parsley stems, salt, and pepper, until all the shells have opened. Remove the mussels from the shells, discard the shells, and set the mussels aside.

- Simmer the wine broth and saffron until reduced by three-fourths. Strain, and set aside.

- Snip the very ends off the snow peas, gently pulling the thin strings that are attached, and removing them from both sides of the peas. Blanch in boiling salted water for 1 minute. Drain and set aside, keeping warm.

- Bring the broth back to a simmer, and beat in the butter, until fully emulsified. Add the mussels, heat, and remove from the fire. Arrange the snow peas in radial circles, on each of four serving plates. Top with the mussels, and serve.

———————————— • ————————————

Saffron, the world's most expensive spice, is the dried stigmas of a variety of crocus. Its high cost is due to the painstaking labor required to remove the stigmas, flower by flower, as well as the number of stigmas required to yield one pound of saffron—as many as 300,000. Saffron originated in Asia Minor, Italy, and Greece and was cultivated as early as 2000 B.C. Its color, an intense orange-yellow, has long been considered a symbol of royalty. This spice was cultivated in the fifteenth and sixteenth centuries for use in dyes, but that practice waned because of its expense. In modern India, however, it is still used to color ceremonial garments and bridal veils. In the United States, saffron is an important ingredient in Pennsylvania Dutch cookery ("Dutch" is actually a corruption of *Deutch*, in reference to the German origin of these immigrants to Pennsylvania, Ohio, and the Midwest). The family Schwenkfelder introduced saffron to eastern Pennsylvania in the eighteenth century when they emigrated from Germany, transplanting to American soil the business they had pursued in their homeland. Schwenkfelder Kuchen, a saffron-flavored cake, is a dish that survives those earlier days.

Oysters

Angels on Horseback
(Huîtres à l'Anglaise)

Raw oysters wrapped in bacon, skewered with a toothpick, broiled or roasted until golden brown, served on buttered toast points.

*B*EGGAR'S PURSES, AVOCADO SAUCE

For the Avocado Sauce

1 shallot, minced
1 mushroom, finely chopped
2 cups fish stock (or bottled clam juice)
¼ cup dry white wine
¼ cup dry vermouth
1 cup heavy cream

¼ pound unsalted butter, cut into ½-inch cubes
salt and white pepper to taste
1 ripe Haas avocado, peeled and pitted

- Simmer the shallot, mushroom, stock, and wine, until reduced by half. Add the cream, and reduce by half again. Mount with the butter, and season with salt and pepper.

- Purée the sauce with the avocado in a blender. Strain, then return to the saucepan, and bring back to a simmer. Remove from the heat, cover, and keep warm until ready to serve.

For the Purses

8 large egg roll skins (or 8 6-inch square sheets of fresh pasta dough)

8 fresh oysters, poached in a little white wine, drained, and cooled

8 tablespoons crème fraîche or sour cream

8 teaspoons osetra caviar

8 long, thin strips of scallion, blanched briefly in boiling salted water

- Cook the egg roll skins in boiling salted water for 2 minutes. Drain and set aside.
- Place a poached oyster in the center of each egg roll skin. Top with a tablespoon of crème fraîche and a teaspoon of caviar. Pull the edges of the skin up into a little bundle, and tie together with the scallion. Place the purses in a covered steamer for 2 or 3 minutes. Pour 2 ounces of sauce onto each of four serving plates, and place two purses on each plate.

Devils on Horseback
(Huîtres à la Diable)

Raw oysters wrapped in bacon, sprinkled with a little cayenne pepper, piqued with a toothpick, broiled or roasted until golden brown, served on toast points (same as Angels on Horseback, except with cayenne).

Oysters, American Style
Huîtres à l'Américaine)

Oysters poached in white wine court bouillon, returned to the shell, topped with American sauce *(Sauce Américaine)*, garnished with a small slice of cooked lobster tail. (See color plate.)

Oysters, Baltimore Style
(Huîtres à la Baltimore)

Raw oysters on a buttered half shell, sprinkled with dry bread crumbs, grated cheese, and chopped parsley, drizzled with butter and baked until golden brown.

Oysters, Burgundy Style
(Huîtres à la Bourguignonne)

Raw oysters on the half shell, spread liberally with Burgundy-style snail butter (See "Snails, Burgundy Style" on page 296), sprinkled with bread crumbs, baked until golden brown.

Oysters, California Style
(Huîtres à la Californienne)

Raw oysters dusted with seasoned flour, sautéed to light brown, placed in a casserole dish, topped with medium-diced tomatoes and green peppers bound with demi-glaze sauce.

Oysters, Creole Style
(Huîtres à la Creole)

Raw oysters dusted with seasoned flour, dipped in beaten eggs, rolled in cracker crumbs, deep fried, and served on a bed of Creole sauce. (See color plate.)

---•---

Creole cuisine is a unique blend of the French, Spanish, African, Caribbean, and native North American Indian cultures. A Creole sauce is more a thick tomato stew, though for this oyster dish the ingredients will need to be finely diced. Sauté ½ cup each, onion and celery; ¼ cup each, green and red bell pepper; 4 garlic cloves, pressed. Add 3 cups
diced tomatoes, ¼ cup tomato paste, and 1 bay leaf; season to taste with salt and pepper.

Oysters, Delmonico Style
(Huîtres à la Delmonico)

Oysters poached in white wine court bouillon, returned to the shell, topped with béchamel sauce enriched with egg yolks and seasoned with lemon juice.

Oysters, DuBarry Style
(Huîtres à la DuBarry)

Oyster poached in its own juices with a little dry white wine, placed in a baked, scooped-out potato, coated with béchamel sauce, sprinkled with grated cheese, and glazed.

Oysters, Dutch Style
(Huîtres à la Hollandaise)

Buttered individual casserole dish, filled with some peeled asparagus, topped with sliced poached beef marrow and oysters, seasoned with cayenne pepper and lemon juice, sprinkled with bread crumbs and melted butter, and baked until golden brown.

Oysters, Favorite Style
(Huîtres à la Favorite)

Raw oysters on the half shell, topped with a thin slice of peeled and seeded lemon, coated with béchamel sauce, sprinkled with grated cheese, and baked until golden brown.

Oysters, Florence Style
(Huîtres à la Florentine)

Oysters poached in white wine court bouillon, returned to the shell, on a bed of finely chopped spinach cooked in butter, coated with béchamel sauce, sprinkled with grated cheese, and glazed. (See color plate.)

Oysters, Louise Style
(Huîtres à la Louise)

Oysters poached in white wine court bouillon, returned to the shell, topped with béchamel sauce mixed with yellow boletus and beaten with lobster butter, sprinkled with a little cayenne pepper, and baked until hot.

Oysters, Louisiana Style
(Huîtres à la Louisiana)

A bed of cracker crumbs, topped with oysters, sprinkled with diced tomato and diced stewed okra, topped with grated cheese, and baked until golden brown.

Oysters, Manhattan Style
(Huîtres à la Manhattan)

Raw oysters on the half shell, topped with a mixture of finely chopped cooked bacon, green and red peppers, mushrooms, onions, and parsley, and baked.

Oysters, Marshal Style
(Huîtres à la Maréchale)

Raw oysters dusted with seasoned flour, dipped in a basic frying batter, deep-fried, served on lemon slices, garnished with fried parsley.

Oysters, Mornay Style
(Huîtres à la Mornay)

Oysters poached in white wine court bouillon, returned to the shell, topped with Mornay sauce, sprinkled with grated cheese, and glazed.

Oysters, Polish Style
(Huîtres à la Polanaise)

Raw oysters on the half shell, topped with Polonaise mixture (bread crumbs, chopped parsley, and hard-boiled eggs, sautéed in butter), and baked. (See color plate.)

Oysters, Pompadour Style
(Huîtres à la Pompadour)

Oysters poached in white wine court bouillon, returned to the shell, topped with hollandaise sauce, garnished with a slice of truffle. (See color plate.)

Oysters on a Skewer
(Huîtres en Brochette)

Raw oysters wrapped in bacon, place on skewers alternating with mushroom caps, dusted with flour, dipped in beaten egg, coated with bread crumbs, drizzled with butter, baked until golden brown, and served with herb butter.

Oysters, Valparaiso Style
(Huîtres à la Valparaiso)

Raw oysters placed in buttered casserole dishes, topped with medium diced mushrooms and celery sautéed in butter, coated with béchamel sauce, and baked.

Oysters, Victor Hugo Style
(Huîtres à la Victor Hugo)

Raw oysters on the half shell, coated with a mixture of grated horseradish, grated cheese, bread crumbs, drizzled with butter, and baked until golden brown.

Oysters, Virginia Style
(Huîtres à la Virginia)

Raw oysters wrapped in thin slices of Virginia ham, dusted with flour, dipped in beaten eggs, coated with bread crumbs, and deep-fried.

. . . .
*O*YSTER AND SPINACH STRUDEL

3 tablespoons dry white wine
8 large fresh oysters, cut into ¼-inch pieces
4 tablespoons unsalted butter
½ pound fresh spinach, well rinsed, stems removed and discarded

salt and pepper to taste
2 tablespoons unsalted butter, kneaded together with 1½ tablespoons all-purpose flour
½ cup milk, hot
1 package frozen phyllo dough
½ cup melted buter

- Simmer the wine and oysters for 1 minute. Drain, discarding the liquid, and set aside.

- Sauté the spinach in the butter for 3 minutes. Season with salt and pepper. Drain, cool, then chop well.

- Place the milk over a medium flame, and beat in the butter/flour paste, in small pieces, until smooth and lump-free. Simmer very gently for 5 minutes, stirring continuously; strain and set aside.

- Brush a sheet of phyllo very lightly with melted butter. Place 2 more sheets on top of this, brushing each one with butter. Repeat until there are four sets of 3 sheets of buttered phyllo. Cut each set lengthwise into four equal strips.

- Preheat an oven to 350°F.

- Combine the oysters, spinach, sauce, salt, and pepper together in a bowl, and blend. (Mixture should be fairly thick.)

- Place a heaping teaspoon of the filling at one end of a phyllo strip. Fold one corner over the filling, so that the folded-over edge is flush with the side of the strip (this will create a 45-

degree angle). Continue folding the triangle the full length of the strip. Brush with melted butter. Repeat until all the filling is rolled up into triangles.

- Transfer to a lightly buttered baking sheet, and bake for 15 to 20 minutes, or until golden brown.

Scallops

ꟿAUTÉED SCALLOPS, DIJON STYLE

(Coquilles St. Jacques à la Dijonnaise)

For the Potatoes

1½ pounds Red Bliss pota-
toes, peeled and cut into
1-inch pieces
4 tablespoons unsalted
butter

¼ cup half-and-half, hot
4 egg yolks
salt and white pepper to
taste

For the Scallops

2 cups bay or sea scallops
3 tablespoons unsalted butter
1 shallot, minced
¼ cup dry white wine
1 sprig fresh thyme

1 cup crème fraîche or sour
cream
1 heaping tablespoon Dijon-
style mustard
salt and white pepper to
taste

- Preheat an oven to 375°F.
- Cook the potatoes in boiling salted water until tender. Drain, then place in a warm oven until completely dry. Mash the potatoes with a food mill, mashing tool, or electric mixer. (Do not use a food processor; it breaks the potato down into a mass of glutinous, sticky starch.) Add the butter, half-and-half, yolks, salt and pepper, and blend thoroughly. Transfer to a pastry bag with a No. 5 or No. 6 star tube, and pipe out a border on four individual ovenproof casserole dishes.
- Sauté the scallops in the butter for 1 minute. Remove the scallops with a slotted spoon, and set aside. Add shallot, the wine, and the thyme to the pan, and reduce by half. Remove the thyme sprig, then add the crème fraîche and mustard, and bring just to a simmer. Remove from the fire, add the scallops, and season to taste with salt and pepper.
- Divide the scallop mixture among the four casserole dishes, and bake until the potatoes are golden brown.

Scallops are bivalve mollusks found in North America on the Atlantic and Gulf coasts. The edible part is the white abductor muscle that holds the fan-shaped, fluted shells together.

Sautéed Scallops, Garden Style

(Coquilles St. Jacques, Jardinière)

12 baby carrots, tops trimmed to ½-inch length
12 baby zucchinis
12 baby summer squash
12 baby patty pan squash
6 tablespoons unsalted butter
1 shallot, minced

1½ pounds sea or bay scallops
¼ cup dry white wine
2 pinches saffron threads
1 cup heavy cream
salt and white pepper to taste

- Blanch the vegetables briefly in boiling salted water. Set aside.
- Sauté the shallot and scallops in one-third of the butter for 1 minute. Remove the scallops with a slotted spoon, and set aside. Add the wine and saffron, and reduce by half. Add the cream, and reduce by half again. Beat in another third of the butter, until fully emulsified, add the scallops, heat thoroughly, and transfer to an appropriate serving dish.
- Sauté the vegetables in the remaining third of the butter, season with salt and pepper, and arrange around the scallops.

Scallops with Leeks and Endive

(Coquilles St. Jacques aux Poireaux et Endive)

2 tablespoons unsalted butter
1 leek, white part only, cut into 1-inch julienne strips, well rinsed
1 small Belgian endive, bottom trimmed, leaves cut lengthwise into 4 strips each

12 ounces sea scallops
½ cup heavy cream
salt and pepper to taste
1 tablespoons minced chives

- Sauté the leek in the butter for several minutes. Add the endive, and sauté another few minutes. Remove the leeks and endive with a slotted spoon, and set aside. Place the scallops in the same pan, season with salt and pepper, and sauté for 2 minutes. Remove and set aside, keeping warm.
- Add the cream to the pan, and simmer until reduced by half. Return the leeks and endive to the cream, season with salt and

pepper, and simmer several minutes. Place a bed of these vegetables on each of four serving plates. Top with the scallops, and sprinkle with the chopped chives.

SCALLOPS AND VEGETABLES IN COURT BOUILLON

(Coquilles St. Jacques à la Nage)

1 pint sea scallops, cut in half widthwise
4 tablespoons unsalted butter
1 small white onion, peeled, cut in half, and sliced widthwise
1 celery heart, washed, and cut into ¼-inch slices
1 small carrot, peeled, and cut into ¼-inch slices on the bias

1 small leek, white part only, cut into ¼-inch slices
1 bay leaf
1 cup dry white wine
1 cup heavy cream
salt and white pepper to taste
¼ cup chopped parsley

- Sauté the vegetables and bay leaf in half of the butter, over low heat, for 5 minutes. Remove from the pan with a slotted spoon and set aside.
- Add the wine, and simmer until reduced by half. Add the cream, and continue simmering until reduced by half again. Return the vegetables to the pan, and season to taste with salt and pepper. Add the scallops, and simmer 1 minute. Stir in the remaining butter, ladle into four serving bowls, and top with the chopped parsley.

SCALLOPS AND VEGETABLES IN PUFF PASTRY

(Bouchée aux Coquilles St. Jacques, à la Printinière)

¾ pound puff pastry dough
1 egg, beaten
3 tablespoons unsalted butter

1 shallot, minced
¼ cup mushrooms, cut into medium dice
½ cup dry white wine
½ cup fish stock

2 cups heavy cream
salt and white pepper to
    taste
2 tablespoons unsalted
    butter

2 cups fresh seasonal
    vegetables, cut into fine
    julienne (carrot, celery,
    scallion, zucchini, snow
    peas, etc.)
1 pound bay scallops

- Preheat an oven to 375°F.
- Roll out the pastry to a thickness of ⅛ inch. Cut out eight 3-inch rounds, using a circle cutter. Cut out a 2-inch circle from the center of four of the 3-inch circles (save the center cutout circle for another use). Brush the tops of four circles with egg wash, then place the hollowed-out circles on top, and gently press down. Place on a lightly buttered baking sheet, bake until puffed up and golden brown, and set aside.
- Sauté the shallot and mushrooms in 3 tablespoons of butter for several minutes. Add the wine and stock, and reduce by three-fourths. Add the cream, and reduce by roughly half, or until slightly thickened. Season to taste with salt and pepper.
- Sauté the vegetables in 2 tablespoons of butter over low heat until tender, but without browning. Add the scallops, cook for 1 minute. Add the cream reduction and blend thoroughly. Heat the pastry shells in the oven, spoon the scallop mixture into the pastry shells, and serve.

·················· # SCALLOP AND SPINACH TIMBALE

(Timbale des Coquilles St. Jacques et des Épinards)

1 pound sea scallops
the zest of ½ lemon
the juice of 1 lemon
the juice of 1 lime
1 garlic clove, pressed
½ jalapeño pepper, minced
1 shallot, minced

pinch of salt
1½ pounds fresh spinach,
    well rinsed, stems re-
    moved
3 eggs, beaten
butter as needed

- Slice the scallops in thirds, widthwise. Combine with the zest, juices, garlic, pepper, shallot, and salt, and marinate for 24 hours.
- Blanch the spinach briefly in boiling salted water. Drain, squeeze dry, and chop fine. Place in a bowl, add the eggs, and blend thoroughly.
- Preheat an oven to 375°F.

- Butter the interior of four 6-ounce timbale molds. Remove the scallops from the marinade and pat dry. Arrange a layer of scallops on the inside bottom of each mold. Top this with a layer of spinach. Repeat with another layer of scallops, and another layer of spinach.

- Place the timbales in a baking pan, and fill with about 1-inch of boiling water. Place in the oven, and bake for 15 minutes. Remove from the oven, and allow to sit for 10 minutes. Run a paring knife carefully around the inside edge of the timbales, then invert on serving plates. Serve with a *beurre blanc* (see recipe, page 276, for Crab Mousse, Ginger Beurre Blanc) or a side of a mayonnaise-based sauce, accompanied by hot baguette.

Shrimp

*B*EER BATTERED SHRIMP, CHUTNEY SAUCE

For the Sauce

1 cup mango chutney	1 cup fresh or canned
1 cup prepared horseradish, squeezed dry	pineapple chunks

For the Shrimp

16 large shrimp (U-12s), peeled, deveined, tails left intact	1 cup flour
	3 large egg whites
	flour as needed
2 12-ounce bottles of beer	1 quart peanut oil
½ teaspoon salt	4 sprigs flat-leaf parsley

To Prepare the Sauce

- Purée all three ingredients in a food processor. Cover and refrigerate until ready to serve.

To Prepare the Shrimp

- Heat the oil to 365°F in a heavy-gauge saucepan.
- Pour the beer into a mixing bowl, and sprinkle in the salt. Sprinkle in 1 cup of flour, and blend thoroughly. Whip the egg whites to a stiff peak, then fold into the batter.
- Dust the shrimp lightly in the additional flour, then dip into the batter, allowing excess batter to drip off.

Chutney is a corruption of the Sanskrit word *chatni*, meaning "to lick." Chutneys consist of underripe fruits simmered with sugar, vinegar, and aromatics such as chile, garlic, and ginger. They are traditionally made from mango and served with curried dishes, but in recent years many versions have been innovated, with ingredients as varied as pineapple, sun-dried tomato, pears, and tomatillos.

- Carefully place the shrimp into the hot oil, and fry until golden brown on all sides. Remove to a warm oven (200°F) until all the shrimp have been fried.
- Arrange four shrimp on each of four plates, with a paper doily underliner. Serve portions of the sauce in small ceramic or glass ramekins, and garnish with parsley.

.... ## $\mathscr{D}$EVILED SHRIMPS

(Crevettes à la Diable)

1 pound 10-15 count shrimp, shelled and deveined	2 cups dry bread crumbs, seasoned with 1 tablespoon cayenne pepper
1 cup flour, seasoned with salt and pepper	vegetable oil as needed
3 eggs, well beaten	1 cup mayonnaise
	½ cup salsa fresca
	16 parsley sprigs

- Dredge shrimp with flour, shaking off excess. Dip in the egg, coat well, allowing excess to drip off. Dredge in the bread crumbs, making sure each shrimp is well coated.
- Heat the oil to a temperature of 375°F. Preheat an oven to a temperature of 200°F.
- Blend the mayonnaise and salsa together, and transfer to a small serving bowl. Deep-fry the shrimp until golden brown, place on absorbent paper, and put into the oven until all the shrimp are fried. Deep-fry the parsley sprigs. Serve the shrimp accompanied by the sauce and fried parsley.

.... ## $\mathscr{G}$RILLED SHRIMP BROCHETTE

For the Marinade

½ cup olive oil	1 tablespoon cilantro leaves, minced
2 teaspoons rice vinegar	¼ teaspoon salt
2 tablespoons saki (rice wine)	¼ teaspoon white pepper

For the Brochette

16 24-30 count shrimp, shelled and deveined	1 green bell pepper, cut into 8 squares
1 yellow bell pepper, cut into 8 squares	1 red bell pepper, cut into 8 squares
	8 pearl onions, peeled

———— • ————

Shrimp belong to the order Decapoda, which includes any crustacean with five pairs of locomotor appendages (legs), each joined at the thorax (the middle section of their body). Crabs, lobsters, prawns, shrimp, squid, and cuttlefish are all decapods.

- Blanch the pepper squares for 1 minute in boiling salted water. Blanch the onions in the same water, for several minutes.
- Combine all the marinade ingredients, blend thoroughly, and marinate the shrimp and vegetables for several hours. Skewer the shrimp and vegetables on metal or bamboo skewers, and grill or broil about 4 minutes on each side.

𝒫OACHED SHRIMP, SCALLOP MOUSSE

(Crevettes Poché, Mousse des Coquilles St. Jacques)

For the Mousse

1 pound sea scallops
½ pound sole fillet, cut into 1-inch pieces
3 eggs

1 pint heavy cream
salt and white pepper to taste
1 tablespoon clam base

For the Shrimp

8 U-10 shrimp, shelled, deveined, tails left intact

2 cups dry white wine
6 ounces puff pastry dough
1 egg, well beaten

For the Sauce

1 shallot, minced
1 cup fish stock
¼ cup mushrooms, roughly minced
2 cups fish velouté

2 tablespoons tomato paste
1 egg yolk
¼ cup heavy cream
3 tablespoons lobster butter, cut into ½-inch pieces

- Place the scallops and sole in a food processor, and purée coarsely, using the pulse switch. Add the eggs, and a little salt and pepper, and the clam base, and, while pouring the cream in slowly, purée, again using the pulse switch. Scrape down the sides of the processor, and pulse again until the mixture is smooth. (Test the mousse by poaching a tablespoon of it in a little simmering water, and adjust seasoning to taste.)
- Dip a tablespoon into cold water, and scoop out a heaping spoonful of the mousse. Wet the palm of the opposite hand, and shape the mousse into a smooth oval. Carefully wrap the shrimp around the mousse, so that the head of the shrimp wraps around and under the bottom of the oval. Gently press the shrimp into the mousse, set on a plate, and refrigerate. Repeat with the remaining shrimp.

- Preheat an oven to 375°F.

- Roll the puff pastry out to a thickness of ⅛ inch. Using a 3-inch circle cutter, cut eight crescent-shaped pieces. Brush with egg wash, place on a baking sheet, and bake until puffed up and golden brown.

- Simmer the shallot, stock, and mushrooms, until reduced by three-fourths. Add the fish velouté and tomato paste, and simmer until suitable thickness is achieved.

- Beat the egg yolk and cream in a small bowl. Slowly add the velouté, while beating continuously. Return to the saucepan, and stir in the lobster butter. Bring just barely to a boil and set aside, keeping warm.

- Fill a saucepan large enough to comfortably hold the eight shrimp, with the dry white wine and an equal amount of water. Bring to a simmer, carefully set the shrimp in, cover, and poach 8 minutes (there should be enough liquid to just cover the shrimp). Remove the shrimp with a slotted spoon, place on absorbent paper, then place on a platter or serving plates. Top with the sauce, and garnish with parsley and fleurons.

Shrimp sizes are indicated by their count per pound. U-10s (giant or extra colossal), for example, are very large, numbering 10 or less per pound; 10–15s (colossal) are slightly smaller, numbering between 10 and 15 per pound. These are followed by 16–20s (extra jumbo), 21–25s (jumbo), 26–30s (extra large), 31–35s (large), 36–42s (medium large), 43–50s (medium), 51–60s (small), 61–70s (extra small), 70–100 (titi). In Iceland, midgets may run to 150 per pound, and in Holland, to as high as 300 (about the length of the nail on your little finger).

𝒫RAWNS WITH TANGERINE AND RIESLING

2 shallots, minced
2 tablespoons butter
2 tablespoons olive oil
16 large prawns, shelled, de-veined, tails removed
1 cup Riesling wine

juice of 1 tangerine
1 cup heavy cream
salt and pepper to taste
12 sprigs watercress
12 tangerine segments, trimmed and seeded

- Sauté the shallots in the butter and oil for 3 minutes. Add the prawns, and sauté for another minute or two. Remove the prawns and set them aside.
- Add the wine and tangerine juice to the pan, and simmer until almost dry. Add the cream, and reduce by half. Return the prawns and their juices to the pan, bring to a simmer, and season to taste with salt and pepper.
- Arrange the prawns radially on individual serving plates, with the tail ends at the center of the plates. Top with the sauce, and garnish with watercress and tangerine segments.

The term *prawn* is generally used to refer to very large shrimp and to species of freshwater shrimp. Dublin Bay prawns, however, are actually small, spiny lobsters, as are the Italian scampi—making the name of the dish Shrimp Scampi, already redundant, a misnomer as well. It seems that on the East Coast of the United States a shrimp is called a shrimp, while on the West Coast the same item is called a prawn. In either case, shrimp and/or prawns are found in ocean waters all over the planet. The world's richest shrimp waters are in the Gulf of Mexico, and the United States is the largest consumer—about 500 million pounds a year, of which 80 million pounds are supplied to New York City alone.

𝒮HRIMP WONTONS, PLUM CHUTNEY

For the Chutney

2 oranges, peeled, segments removed, and cut into medium dice
½ cup orange juice
3 tablespoons sugar
1 tablespoon gingerroot, grated
2 tablespoons dried currants

¼ teaspoon ground cloves
1 teaspoon curry powder
¼ cup water
½ cup apricot preserves
2½ pounds fresh freestone plums, pitted and cut into ½-inch pieces

For the Wontons

3 tablespoons peanut oil
1 scallion, finely diced

½ stalk celery, peeled and finely diced

1 teaspoon gingerroot, grated
2 tablespoons cilantro
1 pound cooked shrimp, peeled, deveined, and cut into fine dice
1 teaspoon cornstarch, dissolved in ½ cup cold dry sherry

2 tablespoons soy sauce
1 tablespoon hoisan sauce
black pepper to taste
40 4 × 4-inch wontons (or egg roll skins)
10 cilantro sprigs
vegetable oil as needed

- Simmer all of the chutney ingredients, except the plums, for 30 minutes. Add the plums, and simmer another 30 minutes. Cool, cover, and refrigerate until ready to serve.

- Sauté the scallion, celery, and ginger in the oil for several minutes. Add the cilantro and shrimp, and heat. Add the sherry, soy and hoisan sauces, and pepper, and simmer until thick. Remove from the fire, and allow to cool.

- Draw an imaginary line diagonally across a wonton skin. Place a small teaspoon of filling in the center, to one side of the imaginary line. Dip a finger in water, and moisten the edges of the skin. Fold over into a triangle, pressing the edges together.

- Grasp the two broadest corners of the wonton with the thumb and forefinger of each hand. Moisten one of the corners, turn them both up, and press the two corners together. Repeat with the remaining skins.

- Preheat an oven to 200°F, and heat the vegetable oil (2 inches deep) in a havy-gauge pot to 360°F. Deep-fry the wontons until golden brown. Place on absorbent paper, and hold in the oven until all the wontons are fried. Serve accompanied by the chutney and cilantro sprigs. See Figure 8.3.

Snails

SNAILS, BURGUNDY STYLE

(Escargots à la Bourguignonne)

12 small Red Bliss potatoes
2 tablespoons unsalted butter
4 garlic cloves, pressed
1 shallot, minced
1 cup dry red wine

½ pound unsalted butter, cut into ½-inch pieces
1 tablespoon tarragon leaves, minced
salt and pepper to taste
24 select snails, well rinsed

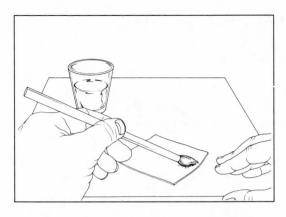

Brush the edges of a wonton skin with water.

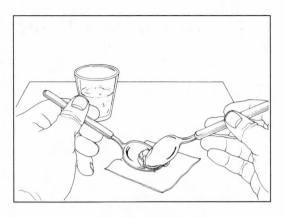

Place the filling slightly off center.

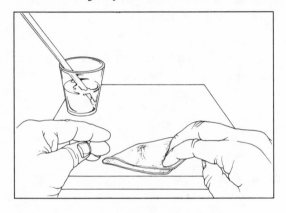

Fold the wonton over diagonally, and press the edges together.

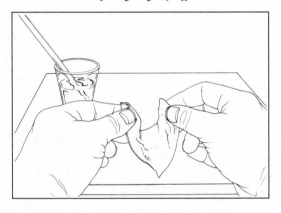

Grasp the two ends of the wonton, along the diagonal fold, moisten lightly with water, then turn up and press together.

Figure 8.3
Folding wontons

—————— • ——————

An *escargotière* is a metal or ceramic dish, with six concave indentations on the bottom, designed specifically for baking escargot. If these are unavailable, a very small slice can be removed from the bottom of each potato so that it will sit up in a casserole or baking dish.

- Cut the potatoes in half, and scoop out the center of each half with a Parisienne scoop (store the scooped-out potato pieces refrigerated, immersed in water, and save for another use). Blanch the potato halves in boiling salted water until tender, but still firm—do not overcook! Drain, cool, and set aside.

- Preheat an oven to 375°F.

- Sauté the garlic and shallot in 2 tablespoons of butter for several minutes, without coloring. Add the wine, and reduce by half. Beat in the butter pieces until fully emulsified. Add the tarragon, season with salt and pepper, and set aside.

- Place the potato halves in *escargotières*, and place a snail in each. Fill each potato with sauce, then bake for 20 minutes. Serve with a side of any remaining sauce and a hot baguette.

Snails, Dutchess Valley Style

(Escargots à la Vallée Duchesse)

24 select snails
2 cups dry white wine
2 shallots, finely chopped
1 bay leaf
½ teaspoon juniper berries
½ pound unsalted butter, soft

1 shallot, minced
3 garlic cloves, pressed
2 tablespoons chopped parsley
3 tablespoons Pernod
salt, pepper, and nutmeg to taste

- Bring the wine, shallots, bay leaf, and juniper berries to a boil. Pour over the snails, and marinate 1 hour.
- Preheat an oven to 375°F.
- Whip the remaining ingredients until smooth. Place the snails in an *escargotière*, top each with the butter, and bake 20 minutes.

Mixed Seafood Dishes

Leghorn Fish Stew

(Cacciucco alla Livornese)

¼ cup olive oil
½ cup onions, small dice
4 garlic cloves, thinly sliced
1 teaspoon sage, minced
2 bay leaves
1 cup dry white wine
2 tablespoons tomato paste
1 cup fish stock or clam juice
1 tablespoon lemon zest
salt and pepper to taste
½ pound squid, cut into ½-inch rings
4 littleneck or cherrystone clams

6 U-16 count shrimp, peeled and deveined
1 pound two varieties of fish—cod, haddock, halibut, mackerel, or sea bass—boneless and cut into 1-inch pieces
½ pound sea scallops, cut in half widthwise
¼ cup flat-leaf parsley, minced
16 sices baguette, spread with garlic butter and toasted

- Sauté the onions and garlic in the olive oil, without browning, about 10 minutes. Add the herbs, wine, tomato, stock, lemon zest, salt, and pepper, blend thoroughly, and simmer 10 minutes.

- Add the squid, and simmer 10 minutes. Add the clams and shrimp, and simmer 5 minutes. Add the remaining fish, and simmer 5 more minutes. Add the scallops and simmer covered, for 3 minutes. Adjust seasoning, top with the parsley, and serve with the garlic croutons.

MONTEREY BAY CIOPPINO

¼ cup olive oil
2 shallots, sliced
6 garlic cloves, sliced
1 green bell pepper, ½-inch dice
1 red bell pepper, ½-inch dice
2 large ripe tomatoes, peeled, ½-inch dice
3 tablespoons tomato paste
½ teaspoon oregano leaves, minced
1 tablespoon basil leaves, minced
2 tablespoons parsley, minced
salt and pepper to taste

2 live Dungeness crabs, cleaned, top shell removed, trimmed of inedible parts, and cut into 1-inch pieces
2 pounds mussels, cleaned and debearded
½ pound 16–20 count shrimp, shell on
4 cups dry white wine
6 ounces sea bass fillet, cut into 1-inch pieces
6 ounces sea scallops
6 ounces halibut fillet, cut into 1-inch pieces
2 tablespoons parsley, minced

- Sauté the shallot, garlic, and peppers in the olive oil for 5 minutes. Add the tomato, paste, herbs, salt, and pepper, and blend thoroughly. Add the crab, mussels, shrimp, and wine, then cover and simmer 5 minutes. Add the sea bass and halibut, and simmer another 3 minutes. Add the scallops, simmer 1 minute, remove from the fire, and allow to sit 5 minutes. Ladle into large soup bowls, topped with the parsley.

SEAFOOD SAUSAGES WITH MUSTARD SAUCE

(Saucisse de Mer à la Dijonnaise)

1 shallot, minced
½ cup dry white wine
6 ounces boneless, skinless cod, cut into ½-inch pieces

6 ounces boneless, skinless salmon, cut into ½-inch pieces
8 ounces sea or bay scallops
1 tablespoon dill, minced

1 tablespoon parsley, minced
salt and pepper to taste
½ cup heavy cream
24 inches fresh lamb sausage
  casings
1 shallot, minced
½ cup fish stock

1 cup dry vermouth
1 cup heavy cream
2 tablespoons grainy Dijon-
  style mustard
1 tablespoon chives, minced
salt and white pepper to
  taste

- Place the cod, salmon, and scallops in the freezer for 30 minutes. Simmer the shallot and wine until nearly dry. Place the fish, herbs, salt, pepper, and shallots in a food processor and purée, using the pulse switch. Incorporate the cream, using the pulse switch.

- Fill a pastry bag fitted with a large (No. 6) round tube with the fish farce. Slide one end of the sausage casing over the tube, and carefully pipe in the farce. When they are filled, twist the casing at roughly 4-inch intervals. Poach the sausage in barely simmering court bouillon for 10 minutes. Remove and set aside, keeping warm.

- Simmer the shallot, stock, and vermouth until reduced by two thirds. Add the cream, and continue simmering until thick. Add the mustard and chives, and season to taste. Serve the sausages accompanied by the sauce.

CHAPTER 9

POULTRY AND MEAT

POULTRY

....

*B*RAISED CHICKEN LEGS, GREEK STYLE

(Kota Yahni)

12 chicken legs
salt and pepper as needed
¼ cup olive oil
1 cup onion, small diced
6 garlic cloves, pressed
1 cup dry white wine
1 cup chicken stock

1 cup tomato purée
2 tablespoons tomato paste
6 sprigs oregano
½ cup basil leaves, roughly
    chopped
4 sticks cinnamon
½ teaspoon ground nutmeg

- Sauté the chicken in the olive oil until light brown on all sides. Remove and set aside. Add the onion and garlic, and cook briefly. Add the remaining ingredients, blend well, and bring to a boil. Return the chicken to the pan, cover, and simmer for 30 to 40 minutes. Adjust seasoning with salt and pepper, and serve with rice pilaf or orzo (a small pasta in the shape of rice).

....

*B*UFFALO CHICKEN WINGS

4 garlic cloves, pressed
¼ cup Tabasco or hot chile
    pepper sauce
salt and pepper to taste
16 chicken wings
1 cup mayonnaise
½ cup sour cream

½ cup blue cheese,
    crumbled
3 tablespoons parsley,
    minced
2 stalks celery, cut into large
    julienne

—— • ——

The chicken wings can also be deep-fried in plain vegetable oil, at the same temperature. Buffalo Wings were innovated in 1964 by Teresa Bellissimo at the Anchor Bar in Buffalo, New York. For further details of the historic event, the reader may wish to consult "An Attempt to Compile a Short History of the Buffalo Chicken Wing," the second chapter in *Third Helpings,* by Calvin Trillin (Penguin Books, 1983).

- Cut the wings into three separate joints, saving the outer segment for stock. Combine the garlic, hot sauce, salt, pepper, and chicken wings, and marinate several hours.
- Preheat an oven to 375°F.
- Combine the mayonnaise, sour cream, blue cheese, and parsley, and blend thoroughly. Cover and refrigerate until ready to serve.
- Place the chicken wings on a baking sheet, skin side up, and roast for 30 to 40 minutes, until golden brown. Serve with a side dish of the sauce, accompanied by the celery.

CAJUN FRIED CHICKEN LEGS

12 chicken legs
2 tablespoons salt
¼ cup Tabasco sauce
1 pint milk
1 cup flour

1 cup dry bread crumbs
1 tablespoon salt
1 tablespoon cayenne pepper
vegetable oil as needed

- Pour the salt and Tabasco sauce over the chicken legs, and rub them vigorously. Add the milk, cover, and marinate overnight.
- Preheat an oven to 375°F.
- Drain the chicken and pat dry. Combine the flour, bread crumbs, salt, and pepper, and dredge the legs in this mixture. Deep-fry in a heavy-gauge pan at 365°F until golden brown. Continue baking in the oven for another 15 minutes.

CHICKEN ENCHILADA, SALSA VERDE

For the Enchilada

2 pounds boneless and skin-less chicken thigh and breast meat
1 large onion, medium dice
3 cups water
1 garlic bulb, cloves peeled and thinly sliced
1 cup cilantro leaves, coarse-ly chopped

1 teaspoon ground cumin
½ teaspoon salt
¼ teaspoon cayenne pepper
24 6-inch flour tortillas
1½ cups Monterey Jack cheese, grated
1 cup sour cream
6 sprigs cilantro

For the Salsa Verde

12 large tomatillos, skin and core removed, and quar-tered
1 large onion, coarsely diced
6 garlic cloves, pressed
3 green jalapeño peppers, stems removed, coarsely chopped

the poaching liquid from the chicken
1 cup tortilla chips, crushed
1 cup cilantro leaves, finely minced
salt and white pepper to taste

- Simmer the chicken and onion in the water until the chicken is fully cooked. Remove the chicken, reserving the liquid, and cut into small julienne. Place in a bowl with the garlic, cilantro, and seasoning, and blend well. Divide among the tortillas, and roll up. Place in a baking pan, cover, and set aside.

- Simmer the tomatillos, onion, garlic, and peppers in the poaching liquid until the tomatillos are very soft. Add the crushed chips and simmer until they are soft. Transfer to a blender or food processor, add the cilantro and purée, and adjust seasoning with the salt and pepper.
- Preheat an oven to 350°F.
- Ladle some of the salsa onto the enchiladas, and bake for 20 minutes. Top with the grated Monterey Jack, and return to the oven for 5 minutes. Place on serving plates, top with sour cream, and garnish with cilantro.

CHICKEN GALLI-CURCI

2 tablespoons butter
1 shallot, minced
2 tablespoons flour
2 cups milk, hot
1 bay leaf
1½ cups heavy cream
2 cups cooked chicken breast, medium dice

salt, white pepper, and nutmeg to taste
2 cups cooked spinach, finely chopped
1 small sweet potato, baked in the skin, peeled, and cut into ½-inch thick slices

- Sauté the shallot in the butter without browning. Add the flour, and cook for several minutes, also without browning. Add the hot milk and bay leaf, and blend thoroughly. Add the cream, and simmer for 5 minutes, stirring continuously. Season to taste with salt, pepper, and nutmeg, and strain.
- Divide the sauce in half, and add one half to the chicken, and the other half to the spinach. Heat both, and adjust seasoning.
- Arrange a border of creamed spinach around the outside edge of a serving plate. Place the chicken in the center, and top with a slice of sweet potato.

─── • ───

Hans Brandt was the venerable and eccentric maître d'hotel at L'Orangerie, a classic French restaurant on O'Farrell Street in San Francisco that closed its doors in the mid-1980s. Hans taught me this dish during my stint as chef there, and claimed that he was one of only a handful of people who knew the dish—created for Amelita Galli-Curci, a turn-of-the-century diva, on one of her trips to San Francisco. He may have been correct, since I have, as of this writing, been unable to find the dish in any book.

CHICKEN QUENELLES, GINGER BEURRE BLANC

(Quenelles de Volaille au Beurre Blanc de Gingembre)

For the Quenelles

2 shallots, minced
1 cup dry white wine
1 bay leaf

1 pound boneless, skinless chicken breast, cut into 1-inch pieces

2 tablespoons butter
2 tablespoons flour
salt and white pepper as
  needed
3 eggs

1 cup heavy cream, very
  cold
salt and white pepper to
  taste
court bouillon as needed

For the Beurre Blanc

½ cup dry white wine
3 tablespoons grated ginger
1 shallot, minced

½ pound unsalted butter,
  cut into ½-inch pieces

- Place the chicken in the freezer for 30 minutes. Simmer the shallots, wine, and bay leaf until nearly dry. Discard the bay leaf, and allow to cool.

- Place the chicken, shallots, butter, and flour in a food processor and purée, using the pulse switch.

- Season with salt and white pepper, then add the eggs, one at a time, and incorporate, still using the pulse switch. Add the cream in a slow, steady stream, again using the pulse switch. Take out a small portion of the farce and poach in the court bouillon; taste, checking for seasoning.

- Moisten a tablespoon and the palm of one hand with cold water. Scoop out a heaping tablespoon of the farce, and shape into a smooth oval in the moistened palm. Place in barely simmering court bouillon. When all the quenelles have been made, cover the court bouillon and remove from the fire.

- Simmer the wine, ginger, and shallot until reduced to about 2 tablespoons. Add the butter, and stir continuously until fully incorporated. Drain the quenelles completely, and serve topped with the beurre blanc.

CHICKEN TERRINE WITH WILD MUSHROOMS

1 bunch watercress leaves,
  stems removed and
  minced
1 cup mayonnaise
the juice of 1 lemon
2 tablespoons unsalted butter
1 shallot, minced

½ pound shiitake mush-
  rooms
½ cup dry vermouth
1 pound boneless, skinless
  chicken breasts, cut into
  ½-inch pieces
2 eggs
1 cup heavy cream

1 tablespoon thyme leaves,
  minced
salt and white pepper to
  taste

butter as needed
4 sheets dried nori
8 sprigs watercress
24 baguette slices, toasted

- Combine the watercress leaves, mayonnaise, and lemon, and blend thoroughly. Cover and refrigerate until ready to serve.
- Place the chicken in the freezer for 1 hour.
- Sauté the shallot and mushrooms in 2 tablespoons of butter for several minutes. Add the wine, and reduce until nearly dry.
- Place the chicken, eggs, and thyme in a food processor and purée, using the pulse switch. Pour in the cream in a slow, steady stream and incorporate, using the pulse switch. Season with salt and pepper, and fold in the mushrooms.
- Preheat an oven to 300°F.
- Butter a 1-quart terrine or pâté mold. Brush the sheets of nori lightly with water, and line the inside of the mold with the nori (where the nori is pieced together, overlap the seams). Fill the mold with the farce, cover with nori, then cover with buttered parchment paper (or a butter wrapper). Place in a hot water bath, and bake for 50 minutes. Allow to cool, then refrigerate overnight.
- Dip the terrine mold into very hot water, invert the mold on a plate, and remove the terrine. Serve with the baguette slices and a side of sauce, and garnish with the watercress.

———— • ————

Nori is a dried seaweed, rich in vitamins, that is used for wrapping sushi; it can be found in most Asian grocery stores.

————————————

· · · · · · · · · · · · · · · · · ·

𝒞HICKEN WINGS IN BEER BATTER, CHUTNEY SAUCE

1 cup mango chutney
1 cup prepared horseradish,
  squeezed dry
1 cup fresh or canned
  pineapple chunks
16 single chicken wings (upper wing joint)

1 12-ounce bottle of beer
½ teaspoon salt
1 cup flour, seasoned with
  salt and pepper
1 egg white
peanut oil as needed
4 sprigs flat-leaf parsley

- Place the chutney, horseradish, and pineapple in a food processor and purée. Cover and refrigerate until ready to serve.
- Place the oil in a heavy-gauge saucepan, to a depth of 3 inches, and heat to 375°F. Preheat an oven to 200°F.
- Pour the beer into a mixing bowl, and sprinkle in the salt. Sprinkle in the flour, and blend thoroughly until there is a

thick, smooth batter. Whip the egg white to a stiff peak, then fold into the batter.

- Make a cut around the circumference of the narrow end of the chicken wing, so that the skin is separated from the end joint. Using the knife, scrape the skin and meat down to the opposite (the fatter) end, so that it is all balled up at that end and hanging off the end of the bone. Dust the balled-up meat and skin with flour, shake off the excess, and dip in the batter. Allow the excess to drip off, then deep-fry until golden brown. Place on absorbent paper, and hold in the oven until all the wings are fried. Serve with a side dish of the chutney sauce, garnished with parsley. See Figure 9.1.

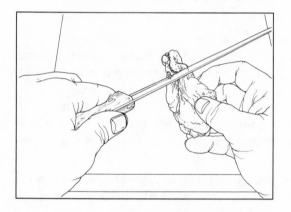

Sever the skin and meat around the smaller end of the wing.

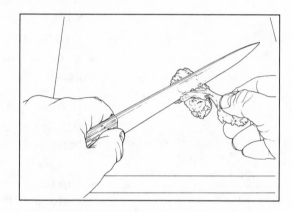

Holding the smaller end of the wing, scrape down the meat and skin from the bone.

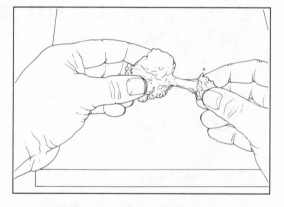

Ball up the meat and skin at the end, dust with flour, batter, or bread as required, then deep-fry.

Figure 9.1
Preparing chicken wings for deep-frying

CREAMED CHICKEN TENDERLOINS WITH PEARS AND BELGIAN ENDIVE

(Poulet à la Crème de Poires et Endive)

3 cups chicken stock
4 ripe pears (any variety)
12 chicken tenderloins, trimmed of tendon, and lightly pounded

2 cups heavy cream
salt and pepper to taste
2 heads Belgian endive, cut into ½-inch pieces

- Peel the pears, setting the peel aside. Cut the pears into quarters lengthwise, then remove and discard the core.
- Poach the pears in simmering chicken stock until tender. Remove, and continue reducing the stock. Purée the pears in a blender or food processor.
- Place the peelings and chicken into the broth and season lightly with salt and pepper. Simmer 5 minutes, then remove the chicken and set aside, keeping it warm. Continue simmering the stock.
- Simmer the cream in a saucepan until reduced by half. Add the pear purée, some of the reduced stock, and season to taste with salt and pepper.
- Place a bed of endive on each of four serving plates. Top with the chicken tenderloins, and coat with sauce. Garnish with fresh watercress.

GOOSE LIVER CROQUETTES

(Croquettes de Foie Gras)

1 pound goose liver
3 tablespoons unsalted butter
3 tablespoons flour
1 quart hot chicken stock
salt and pepper to taste
¼ cup cream
3 egg yolks

1 cup flour, seasoned with salt, pepper, and ground fennel
4 eggs, beaten with 3 tablespoons heavy cream
3 cups dry bread crumbs
vegetable oil as needed
2 cups Madeira sauce

- Poach the goose liver covered, in the chicken stock for 15 minutes. Remove and allow to cool. When cool enough to handle, cut into ¼-inch dice.

- Reduce the stock by three-fourths (to about 1 cup). Knead the butter and flour together into a smooth paste, and beat into the stock. Add the cream, season with salt and pepper, and simmer about 5 minutes, stirring continuously. Strain, dab the top of the sauce with a little butter (to prevent formation of a skin), and set aside to cool.

- Knead the butter and flour together into a smooth paste, and beat into the hot stock. Add the cream, season with salt and pepper, and simmer until thick (about 5 minutes). Strain, dab the top of the sauce with a little butter (to prevent formation of a skin), and set aside to cool.

- When the sauce mixture has cooled, beat in the yolks, one at a time, until fully incorporated.

- Combine the diced liver and the sauce, and blend together. Refrigerate covered, for about 1 hour.

- Heat the vegetable oil (enough to be 2 inches deep) in a heavy-gauge pot, to a temperature of 365°F.

- Scoop out 2-ounce portions of the liver mixture, shape into balls, and dust with flour. Dip in the beaten eggs, and then coat thoroughly with the bread crumbs. Fry, until golden brown on all sides, and serve with the Madeira sauce.

$\mathcal{G}$OOSE LIVER MEDALLIONS, RUSSIAN STYLE

(Médallions de Foie Gras, à la Russe)

1 pound goose liver
1 recipe basic court bouillon
½ pound puff pastry
egg wash as needed

2 ounces osetra or sevruga
   caviar
1 cup Madeira-flavored
   aspic, chilled until firm,
   and finely diced

- Preheat an oven to 375°F.
- Roll out the puff pastry on a lightly floured board, and cut into triangles, 1 inch wide at the bottom and 2 inches long. Dock with a fork, brush with egg wash, place on a baking sheet, and bake until puffed up and golden brown. Set aside to cool.
- Trim the liver of any blood vessels, and poach covered, in the court bouillon for 15 minutes. Remove and allow to cool completely. When cool, cut into small bite-size, pyramid-shaped pieces, and arrange on a bed of aspic. Garnish with the puff pastry triangles, topped with a small portion of caviar.

Foie gras is the enlarged liver of a goose or duck, created by overfeeding the bird. This is a tradition that dates back to the ancient Romans, who used figs for fattening. In modern times the birds are fattened with corn. A fattened goose liver weighs 1½ to 2 pounds; fattened duck liver 11 to 14 ounces. (The record for goose liver is 4½ pounds.) Many Americans consider the technique barbaric, but in France (foie gras is also produced in Austria, Czechoslovakia, Hungary, Israel, and Luxembourg), it is considered something of an honor for the bird. The selected birds are treated with great respect and are neither penned up nor physically abused in any way. Charles Gérard, in *L'Ancienne Alsace Table* wrote: "The goose is nothing, but man has made of it an instrument for the output of a marvelous product, a kind of living hothouse in which there grows the supreme fruit of gastronomy." Fresh foie gras has traditionally been unavailable in the United States, since the Department of Agriculture prohibits the import of raw (fresh) foie gras. Today, however, there are several producers in the United States (two are listed in the list of Specialty Suppliers).

*R*OAST QUAIL, MUSTARD SAUCE

(Caille Rôti, Dijonnaise)

4 tablespoons unsalted butter
4 quail
1 shallot, minced
½ cup cognac
3 tablespoons Dijon-style mustard
¾ cup heavy cream

salt and white pepper to taste
4 slices of bread, toasted, trimmed of crusts, and cut diagonally in half, lengthwise
8 sprigs watercress

- Preheat an oven to 425° F.
- Lightly season the inside cavity of each quail with salt and pepper. Fold the wing tips back under the body of each quail, and make an incision in the bottom of each bird, just inside its tail. Insert the ends of the drumsticks into this incision.
- Rub the quails with a little of the butter, place in the oven, and roast for 10 minutes. Turn the temperature down to 375°F, and continue roasting for 20 minutes. Remove from the oven and set aside.

- Sauté the shallot in the remaining butter. Add the cognac, and reduce by three-fourths. Add the jelly, mustard, and cream, blend thoroughly, and simmer until thick. Season to taste with salt and pepper. Place the quails back in the oven for about 5 minutes, then serve on the toast points, topped with the sauce and garnished with watercress.

——————— • ———————

Commercially grown currants, native to Northern Europe, were brought to this country in colonial times. In France, black currants, though extremely sour, are grown for production of jams and jellies, as well as a popular dessert beverage, *cassis*. A *Kir* is also a popular beverage, consisting of dry white wine or champagne (in this case, called a *Kir Royale*) poured over a tablespoon of cassis in the bottom of the glass. It was named for Felix Cannon Kir, French resistance fighter who lost his life during World War II. Red currant jelly is also an important ingredient in Cumberland jelly, an accompaniment to game. Fresh red and white currants can occasionally be found in specialty markets during summer months and are excellent eaten with a little sugar and cream.

*R*OAST QUAIL, WILD RICE STUFFING

(Caille Rôti, Farcis au Riz Sauvage)

For the Quail

½ cup wild rice
2 tablespoons unsalted
  butter
1 shallot, minced
1 scallion, finely sliced
½ cup mushrooms, finely
  diced

½ cup cognac
2 tablespoons parsley,
  minced
4 barrel-boned fresh quail
clarified butter as needed
8 sprigs watercress

For the Sauce

2 tablespoons unsalted
  butter
⅓ cup chicken livers,
  trimmed of membranes,
  well washed in cold
  water, and roughly
  chopped

1 large shallot, minced
¼ cup dry white wine
¾ cup chicken stock
1 cup heavy cream
salt and white pepper to
  taste

- Preheat an oven to 425°F.
- Cook the wild rice in boiling lightly salted water until tender. Drain and set aside.
- Sauté the shallot and the scallion in the butter. Add the mushrooms, cook several minutes, then add the cognac and simmer until nearly dry. Add the wild rice and parsley, and remove from the fire.
- Lightly season the inside cavity of each quail with salt and pepper. Fold the wing tips back under the body of each quail, and place the stuffing in the cavity. Close the cavity, using two toothpicks, and secure with cotton twine. Sauté the quails in the butter until lightly browned on all sides. Place in the oven, and roast for 20 minutes.
- Sauté the livers and shallot in the butter for 3 minutes. Remove the livers with a slotted spoon, and set aside. Add the wine and stock to the pan, and simmer until reduced by two-thirds. Add the cream and chicken livers, and simmer until reduced again by half. Transfer to a blender, and purée. Strain, return to the fire, bring to a boil, and adjust seasoning. Remove the toothpicks from the quail, serve with the sauce, and garnish with watercress.

.... # $\mathscr{R}$OAST STUFFED CHICKEN LEGS

(Jambonneau de Volaille)

12 chicken thighs
1 quart chicken stock
2 tablespoons butter
2 shallots, minced
½ cup dry white wine
1 cup finely ground veal
½ cup finely ground pork
¼ cup dry bread crumbs, soaked in ½ cup heavy cream
oil as needed
½ cup leek, well rinsed and cut into small dice
1 rib celery, cut into small dice

1 small carrot, peeled, trimmed, and cut into small dice
1 small onion, peeled and cut into small dice
3 garlic cloves, crushed
2 tablespoons flour
1 cup dry white wine
1 bay leaf
4 sprigs thyme
1 bunch parsley stems, trimmed and rinsed
1 cup heavy cream
salt and pepper as needed
olive oil as needed

- Bring the chicken stock to a simmer. Remove the leg bones from the chicken thighs by making a single incision the length of each leg. Add the bones to the stock. Remove all tendons from the thighs, season lightly with salt and pepper, and set aside.

- Preheat an oven to 375°F.

- Sauté the shallots in the butter. Add the wine and simmer until nearly dry. Combine the shallots, ground meat, and bread crumbs, and season with salt and pepper. Stuff the chicken thighs with this mixture and carefully roll up, securing each leg with a toothpick. Brush the legs lightly with oil, place in a roasting pan on a bed of the chopped vegetables, and roast for 20 minutes.

- Push the legs to one side, and sprinkle the flour in the pan, blending it with the hot oil in the bottom of the pan. Add the stock, wine, and herbs, and continue roasting another 20 minutes.

- Remove the legs from the pan, place on an ovenproof platter, turn the oven off, and place in the oven. Pour the contents of the roasting pan into a saucepan. Add the cream and simmer, reducing until it reaches the desired thickness. Strain, degrease the top of the sauce, and season to taste with salt and pepper. Remove the toothpicks from the chicken legs *(very important!)* and serve with the sauce.

Jambonneau, literally "little ham," is the French term for the knuckle end of a ham or pork leg. It also refers to a stuffed leg of chicken, since it resembles the shape of the former.

················

SAUTÉED BABY CHICKEN, CHINA STYLE

(Poussin à la Chinoise)

12 medium shiitake mushrooms, stems removed	1 tablespoon unsalted butter
4 12-ounce baby chickens, split along the back, breast bones removed	2 garlic cloves, minced
	1 tablespoon finely julienned gingerroot
salt and pepper as needed	1½ cups chicken stock
	1 tablespoon soy sauce

- Preheat an oven to 400°F. Arrange the mushroom caps in groups of 3 in a roasting pan.

- Season the chickens lightly with salt and pepper, then sauté in the butter, skin side down, until lightly browned.

- Place a chicken, skin side up, on each of the sets of mushroom caps, and rub the top surface of each with garlic and ginger. Roast for 15 minutes.

- Place the roasting pan on top of the stove, and add the stock and soy sauce. Simmer for 2 minutes.

- Serve 1 chicken per person, with 3 shiitake mushrooms and some of the broth spooned over it.

Sonoma Foie Gras with Chanterelles and Cider Sauce

1 shallot, minced
2 tablespoons unsalted butter
½ cup apple cider
2 tablespoons golden raisins
¼ cup dry white wine
1 tablespoon curry powder
1½ cups heavy cream
salt and white pepper to taste
1 bunch spinach, stems removed and well rinsed
3 tablespoons unsalted butter

20 medium shiitake mushrooms, cut into 4 strips each
20 medium oyster mushrooms, cut into 4 strips each
20 medium chanterelle mushrooms, cut into 2 or 3 pieces each
½ pound foie gras, thinly sliced
flour as needed

- Sauté the shallots in the butter for several minutes. Add the cider, raisins, wine, and curry, and simmer until reduced by half. Add the cream and reduce until desired thickness is achieved. Season to taste with salt and pepper and set aside, keeping warm.
- Sauté the spinach in one tablespoon of the butter until wilted. Set aside.
- Sauté the mushrooms in one tablespoon of the butter for 3 minutes. Set aside.
- Dust the foie gras slices lightly in flour. Sauté in the remaining butter, a minute on each side.
- Place the spinach in the center of each of four serving plates, and top with the sliced foie gras. Arrange the mushrooms around the outside of this, and nap with the sauce.

BEEF AND PORK

Barbecued Spareribs

1 pound pork ribs, cut in half lengthwise
1 cup tomato ketchup

¼ cup dark brown sugar
3 tablespoons orange marmalade

2 scallions, sliced paper-thin
1 garlic clove, pressed
1 tablespoon grated gingerroot
1 tablespoon soy sauce

¼ cup water
2 tablespoons red chile paste
the juice and zest of one
   lemon
¼ cup parsley, minced

- Place the ribs into boiling lightly salted water, bring to a boil, drain, and rinse well in cold water.
- Combine the remaining ingredients in a stainless steel bowl, and blend thoroughly. Add the ribs, coat well with the marinade, cover, and refrigerate for 2 days. Roast in a preheated 350°F oven for 1 hour, turning frequently.

———————————— • ————————————

Although cooking over charcoal is one of the most ancient of cooking methods, the barbecue method is of American origin, associated with the conquest of the Western regions of North America and subsequently exported to Europe. The origin of the word may be the Haitian *barbacoa*, meaning "grill," or the French *de la barbe à la queue* (from the beard to the tail), referring to the method of roasting an entire animal on a large spit.

ℬEEF IN BEER

(Boeuf à la Bière)

4 tablespoons unsalted
   butter
3 cups onions, thinly sliced
3 pounds beef top round,
   trimmed of fat and gristle,
   cut into 3 × 2 × ½-inch
   strips

1 cup flour, seasoned with
   salt and pepper
3 cups dark beer
½ cup red wine vinegar
¼ cup tomato purée
2 tablespoons Dijon-style
   mustard
salt and pepper to taste

- Sauté the onions in the butter, stirring frequently, for about 10 minutes. Remove the onions with a slotted spoon, and set aside.
- Dust the beef with the seasoned flour, shake off the excess, and sauté in the same pan as the onions. Add the beer, onions,

vinegar, tomato, mustard, salt, and pepper. Blend thoroughly, and simmer, covered, about 30 minutes, or until the beef is tender.

*P*ORK TART, GREAT ELECTRIC UNDERGROUND STYLE

For the Dough

1½ pounds flour
1 pound unsalted butter

2 eggs in a 1-cup measure, the remainder filled with ice cold water
1 egg, well beaten

For the Filling

1 pound boneless pork loin
salt, pepper, and oil as needed
½ cup seedless green grapes
½ cup pineapple, cut into ¼-inch dice
½ cup golden raisins
½ cup brandy

½ cup rutabaga, cut into ¼-inch dice
1 cup chicken velouté sauce
¾ cup heavy cream
¼ cup brandy
salt and white pepper to taste

- Rub the flour and butter together until it resembles coarse meal. Add the eggs and water, and press the dough together without kneading. Cover and set aside.

- Preheat an oven to 400°F.

- Season the pork with salt and pepper, and sear in a pan with the oil over high heat until well browned. Place in the oven and roast for 30 minutes, or until medium rare. Remove and allow to cool.

- Heat ½ cup of brandy and pour over the raisins. Allow to sit 30 minutes, then drain, discarding the brandy. Blanch the rutabaga in boiling salted water until al dente. Drain and set aside.

- When the pork cools down to warm, cut it into ¼-inch dice.

- Combine the pork, grapes, pineapple, raisins, rutabaga, velouté sauce, cream, ¼ cup brandy, salt, and white pepper. Spoon this mixture into medium-sized ovenproof casseroles.

- Roll out the dough on a lightly floured board to a thickness of ¼ inch. Cover the casseroles with the dough, and brush with

———— • ————

The Great Electric Underground was a restaurant in San Francisco where the author served as chef de cuisine from 1977 to 1979. This dish was a popular favorite that was served occasionally as a special *(plat du jour)*. Much to the chagrin of its employees and patrons, the restaurant closed its doors forever in 1988.

egg wash. Cut out a small floral or geometric forms from the dough, place one on top of each casserole, and brush that with egg wash. Bake at 350°F until the tops are golden brown.

Sausage Fritters

(Beignets de Porc)

3 cups flour, sifted
½ tablespoon baking powder
1½ cups warm water
¼ cup olive oil

¾ pound pork sausage meat, cooked
3 tablespoons mixed herbs, minced
salt and pepper as needed
vegetable oil as needed

- Sift the flour and the baking powder into a mixing bowl. Add the water and oil, and blend thoroughly. Remove to a lightly oiled bowl, cover, and place in a warm area. Allow to rest 30 minutes.

- Heat vegetable oil (1-inch deep) in a heavy-gauge or cast-iron skillet to a temperature of 365°F.

- Combine the sausage and the herbs, and season to taste with salt and pepper.

- Divide the dough into 1-ounce pieces. Roll them into smooth balls, then flatten. Place a small portion of the sausage on each round, moisten the edges of the dough with water, then seal the dough around the filling. Roll the fritters into smooth spheres. Fry in the oil until golden brown, drain, and serve.

Sausages with Dried Fruit Compote

2 pounds sweet Italian sausage
1 cup sugar
2 cups dry champagne
1 cup red wine vinegar
1 stick cinnamon
¼ teaspoon ground cinnamon
4 cloves

½ lemon, sliced very thin
the zest of half an orange
½ pound pitted prunes, cut in half
½ pound dried apricots, cut in half
½ pound sultana raisins
½ pound dried figs, cut in half

- Simmer all the syrup ingredients, except the dried fruit, for 5 minutes. Add the fruit, and continue to simmer for 5 minutes. Remove from the fire and allow to cool.

- Grill, broil, or sauté the sausages, and serve with a side of the sweet and sour fruits.

Stuffed Zucchini

(Zucchine Ripiene)

¼ cup olive oil
3 garlic cloves, pressed
3 tablespoons onion, minced
4 ounces ground lean pork
4 ounces ground lean beef
4 ounces ground prosciutto (fat and lean)
¼ cup dry bread crumbs, mixed with 3 tablespoons water

¼ cup grated pecorino cheese
2 large eggs, beaten
salt and pepper to taste
pinch of nutmeg
4 pounds medium zucchini
1 pint chicken stock, hot

- Sauté the garlic and onion briefly in the olive oil. Add the meat and sauté until fully cooked. Add the remaining ingredients (except the zucchini and stock), blend thoroughly, and season to taste.

- Preheat an oven to 375°F.

- Cut the ends from the zucchini, and hollow out using a vegetable peeler. Fill with the stuffing mixture, using a pastry bag, then place in a casserole dish, and add the stock. Cover and bake 15 to 20 minutes, or until tender. Cut the zucchini into 1-inch thick slices and serve.

Veal Kidneys Armagnac

(Rognons de Veau à l'Armagnac)

4 small veal kidneys, trimmed of skin and blood vessels, well rinsed, and cut into ¼-inch slices
2 shallots, minced
4 tablespoons unsalted butter
1 cup Armagnac

1 cup Madeira sauce
2 tablespoons unsalted butter, cut into small pieces
2 tablespoons parsley, minced
4 slices of bread, toasted, trimmed of crusts, and cut diagonally in half

- Sauté the kidneys and shallot in the butter over high heat for 3 minutes. (The kidneys should still be slightly pink inside.)
- Remove the kidneys with a slotted spoon, and set aside. Add the Armagnac, and reduce by half. Add the Madeira sauce, and reduce again until slightly thickened. Return the kidneys to the sauce, add the butter, and beat in. Serve on the toast points, sprinkled with the parsley.

MOUSSES AND PÂTÉS

.... *C*HICKEN LIVER PÂTÉ

1 pound chicken livers, trimmed of connecting membranes
½ cup dry white wine
¼ cup brandy
salt and pepper to taste
pinch of nutmeg

6 tablespoons unsalted butter, cut into about 12 pieces
1 cup heavy cream
unsalted butter as needed
1 bunch watercress
1 cup Madeira or Cumberland sauce

- Marinate the livers in the wine for 1 hour, then drain.
- Coarsely purée the livers, brandy, salt, pepper and nutmug, in a food processor. Using the pulse switch, add the butter, a few pieces at a time, and purée. Add the cream in a steady stream until fully incorporated.
- Butter eight ramekins, timbales, or dariole molds. Divide the mousse mixture among the molds, cover with a piece of lightly buttered parchment paper, and set on a rack in a large saucepan or roasting pan. Fill the bottom with about ½-inch water, cover the pan, and steam the molds for 10 minutes. Turn the fire off, and allow to sit for 15 minutes.
- Using a paring knife, carefully loosen the mousses, and invert onto serving plates. Serve with Madeira sauce, or a side of Cumberland sauce, and garnish with fresh watercress.

Cumberland Sauce

1 cup currant jelly
½ cup port wine
1 minced shallot
1 tablespoon orange zest

1 tablespoon lemon zest
1 teaspoon grated gingerroot
pinch of cayenne

- Blanch the zest in boiling salted water, and drain. Simmer the remaining ingredients for 10 minutes, add the zest, cool, cover, and refrigerate until ready to serve.

· · · · · · · · · · · · · · · · · ·

*C*HICKEN LIVER MOUSSE

2 pounds chicken livers, trimmed of connecting membranes
1 small onion, finely chopped
2 garlic cloves, pressed
4 ounces unsalted butter
¼ teaspoon ground cumin
¼ teaspoon allspice
1 tablespoon anchovies, mashed

6 ounces unsalted butter, soft
¼ cup Madeira wine
salt and white pepper to taste
unsalted butter as needed
1 cup light aspic
1 bunch watercress
1 baguette, sliced and toasted

- Sauté the livers, onion, and garlic in 4 ounces of butter, for 7 minutes. Set aside and allow to cool.
- Place the liver mixture in a food processor, along with the spices, anchovies, 6 ounces of soft butter, and wine, and pulse until smooth. Season to taste with salt and pepper.
- Lightly coat the inside of a fancy domed mold (such as a bombe mold) with butter, then fill with the mousse. Cover and chill overnight.
- Dip the mold in very hot water for about 10 seconds, then invert onto a rack over a pan. Coat with aspic, and serve garnished with watercress and toasted baguette slices.

———— • ————

Madeira is a fortified wine originating on the island of the same name off the coast of Portugal. Madeiras are named after the grapes from which they are produced: Sercial is the driest, Verdelho is nutty and mellow, Boal and Malmsey are sweet and full-bodied. Madieras of exceptional vintage years can last a century or more in the bottle.

Aspic is a crystal-clear, highly gelatinous meat jelly, used to coat various appetizer items both for flavor and to prevent drying. A fairly good powdered version is available in gourmet markets and can be improved by using sherry, Madeira, or brandy instead of water. After the aspic has been heated to liquid form, it is *tempered* by placing it in a bowl, set in ice water, and stirred until it is just barely tepid. It should be slightly viscous, though liquid enough to flow freely over the mousse. After each coating, the mousse is placed in the refrigerator, allowing that coat to gel. Repeat the coats until a thin layer of aspic has formed over the mousse.

CHICKEN LIVER AND MUSHROOM MOUSSE

½ pound chicken livers, trimmed of connecting membranes and coarsely chopped
¼ pound unsalted butter
1 medium onion, coarsely chopped

3 cloves garlic, crushed
¾ cup mushrooms, coarsely chopped
¼ cup brandy
pinch of nutmeg
salt and pepper to taste

- Sauté the livers, onion, garlic, and mushrooms in the butter, until the livers are fully cooked. Set aside and allow to cool.
- Place this mixture in a food processor, along with the brandy, nutmeg, salt, and pepper, and pulse until smooth. Adjust seasoning.
- Lightly coat the inside of a domed mold (such as a bombe mold) with butter, then fill with the mousse. Cover and chill overnight.

DUCK SAUSAGE, RHUBARB COMPOTE

For the Compote

2 tablespoons unsalted butter
1 shallot, minced
2 cups rhubarb stalks, cut into medium dice
½ cup sultana (golden) raisins

¼ cup sugar
¼ cup dry white wine
the zest and juice of 1 lemon
1 teaspoon gingerroot, grated

For the Sausage

1 pound boneless and skinless duck breasts, cut into ½-inch pieces
½ pound ground pork
¼ cup craisins (dried cranberries)

2 tablespoons mint leaves, roughly chopped
salt and pepper to taste
6 pieces pork caul, approximately 5 × 5 inches
cornstarch and vegetable oil as needed

- Sauté the shallot and rhubarb in the butter for several minutes. Add the remaining compote ingredients, and simmer for 30 minutes. Remove from the fire, cover, and refrigerate until ready to serve.

- Place the duck and the pork in the freezer for 1 hour, then put into a food processor along with the craisins, mint, salt, and pepper and, using the pulse switch, purée. Shape the ground meat into six equal patties, and wrap in the pork caul. Dust with cornstarch and sauté on both sides in the vegetable oil, until golden brown. Place on absorbent paper, and hold in the oven. Serve with warm or room-temperature compote.

The French term *charcuterie* (from the French *chair,* meaning "meat," and *cuite,* meaning "cooked") refers to various smoked, ground, and/or preserved meat products, made primarily from pork. These dishes are as old as cooking itself, though a *porcella* law, which governed the rearing, feeding, slaughtering, and preparing of pork, dates back to ancient Rome. In Paris, in 1475, a separate job classification was designated to permit *maîtres charcutiers-saucissier-boudiniers* the right to sell cooked and prepared items made from pork flesh and offal. The term *sausage* (from the Latin *salsicia* and *salsus,* meaning "salted") refers to various mixtures of ground, seasoned meat (generally pork and/or beef), stuffed into pig, sheep, or lamb casings (intestines), or enclosed in caul fat (in French known as a *crépinette*), the thin membrane surrounding a pig's stomach. Sausage mixtures can also be formed into patties, floured or breaded, and grilled, sautéed, or deep-fried. Germany boasts the greatest variety of sausages, but many countries produce hundreds of regional varieties. In France, varieties of sausage are called *saucisse* (usually small and fresh) or *saucisson* (usually large, and smoked or dried).

SWEETBREAD MOUSSE

1 pound sweetbreads	¼ teaspoon white pepper
¼ cup cognac	pinch of nutmeg
¼ cup dry vermouth	1 teaspoon lemon juice
2 tablespoons basil pesto	2 egg whites
¼ teaspoon salt	1 cup heavy cream

- Break up the sweetbreads into small pieces, removing most of the connective membranes. Marinate in the cognac and vermouth for 3 hours.
- Remove the sweetbreads from the marinade, and purée in a food processor with the pesto, salt, pepper, nutmeg, and lemon

juice. Add the egg white and pulse, while adding the cream. Continue pulsing until smooth and completely puréed.

- Butter four or five ramekins, timbales, or dariole molds, and fill with the mousse. Cover each form with plastic wrap, wax paper, or buttered parchment paper, place on a rack over simmering water, and steam for 15 minutes. Allow to sit for another 10 minutes, then remove. Slide a paring knife around the mousse inside the mold, invert, and place on a serving plate. Serve with a rich brown sauce (e.g., Madeira, Périgordine, or Zingara), garnished with fresh watercress.

This mousse can be used as a stuffing or for making quenelles.

𝒱ENISON PÂTÉ

1 pound pork belly, cut into 1-inch cubes
2 pounds pork shoulder, cut into 1-inch cubes
2 cups lean venison, cut into 1-inch cubes
4 slices bacon, cut into 1-inch pieces
½ cup chicken livers
½ teaspoon white pepper
1 teaspoon salt
1 teaspoon paprika

½ teaspoon ground cloves
1 sprig thyme
1 tablespoon sugar
½ cup brandy
½ cup Madeira
3 eggs
½ cup mango chutney
2 pounds sliced fat back
1 pork tenderloin, well trimmed, and cut in half lengthwise
½ pound thinly sliced ham

- Marinate the cubed meats, the bacon pieces, and the chicken livers for 24 hours in the spices, sugar, brandy, and Madeira.

- Season the tenderloin pieces with salt and pepper, and grill, sauté, or broil, until fully cooked. Set aside to cool. When cool, wrap both pieces into a long cylinder with the ham, and set aside.

- Drain off excess liquid, and put the marinated meats through the large-holed plate of a meat grinder. Add the eggs and chutney, and grind again, through the fine-holed plate.

- Preheat an oven to 300°F.

- Line a terrine or pâté mold with fat back. Fill half full with the farce, and place the wrapped tenderloin lengthwise down the center of the mold. Fill with the remaining farce, and cover with fat back. Place in a water bath, and bake for 2 hours.

- Remove from the oven, and allow to cool. Refrigerate overnight. When ready to serve, dip the mold into hot water, invert, and remove the pâté. Slice, serve with cornichons, a plain lettuce salad, toasted sliced baguette, and a side of Cumberland sauce.

CHAPTER 10

VEGETABLE DISHES

$\mathcal{V}$egetables have taken a fundamental place in cookery, ever since an unnamed ancestor tossed a handful of aromatic roots into a cauldron of boiling meat and verjuice. Today we may take for granted their availability and variety, but we can never underestimate their value in both fine cooking and nutrition.

Fiber, an indigestible material made up primarily of cellulose and (in fruits) pectin, is what gives vegetables structure, shape, and firmness. Applying heat (cooking) softens this structure, and, although some nutritional loss is inevitable, cooking enhances the color, flavor, and character of all vegetables; however, excessive cooking destroys their texture, flavor, color, and nutrients. While the method of cooking vegetables is based on gastronomic criteria, the duration of cooking time is directly related to fiber content: spinach and tomatoes, for example. have very little fiber; carrots and turnips have considerably more; and other varieties have varying degrees of fiber in their parts (e.g., broccoli flowers versus stems, asparagus tips versus stalks).

Pigments are compounds that give vegetables their color: *flavones* (light yellow) in potatoes, onions, and cauliflower; *anthocyanins* (blue-red) in red cabbage, beets, and red kale; *carotenoids* (yellow-deep red) in carrots, red peppers, tomatoes, corn, winter squash, rutabaga, and sweet potatoes; *chlorophyll* in green vegetables. Different pigments react differently to heat and acidity, and this must be taken into consideration when cooking.

Vegetables are divided botanically into six groups: (1) *fungi* (morel, mushroom, and truffle); (2) *roots* (beet, radish and turnip, carrot and parsnip; (3) *tubers* (potato, sweet potato, water chestnut, and yam); (4) *leaf and stem* (asparagus, leek, and onion; cabbage and brussels sprouts; lettuce, endive, and dandelion; bamboo shoot; celery; rhubarb; spinach; watercress); (5) *flowers* (broccoli and cauliflower, artichoke); (6) *fruits* (botanical fruits considered culinary vegetables) (cucumber, pumpkin, and squash; beans and peas; eggplant, pepper, and tomato; avocado; corn; okra; olive).

All vegetables should be washed prior to cooking. The peelings and assorted trimmings should be placed in a stockpot, covered with cold water, and simmered for about 2 hours. The resulting stock is excellent for blanching vegetables, cooking potatoes and pasta, as a base for soups, and as an all-purpose fond wherever a lightly flavored liquid is preferred in place of water. After peeling, most vegetable varieties (roots, tubers, and flowers) should be stored in cold water before they are used for cooking. Leaf and stem varieties (leek, cabbage, brussels sprouts, lettuce, celery, spinach, watercress, etc.) must be washed several times because of the presence of soil and sand, and, on occasion, insects. In the event that a vegetable is cooked without peeling (potatoes, carrots, beets), it should be well scrubbed with a stiff brush (reserved only for this purpose).

Cold Dishes

Agoursi
(Ogourzi)

Peeled cucumber sliced very thin, sprinkled with salt, allowed to drain, rinsed and dried, blended with sour cream and minced dill.

....

ALLIGATOR PEAR COCKTAIL

(Avocado Cocktail)

1 cup ketchup
3 tablespoons white Worcestershire sauce
¼ cup mayonnaise
3 tablespoons heavy cream
the juice of 1 lemon

salt and white pepper to taste
2 ripe Haas avocados
8 butter lettuce leaves
8 slices of lemon

- Combine the ketchup, Worcestershire, mayonnaise, cream, lemon, salt, and white pepper, and blend thoroughly. Cover and refrigerate until ready to use.
- Peel and seed the avocados, and cut into ½-inch dice.
- Place 2 lettuce leaves in each of four champagne saucers. Divide the avocado among the four, top with the sauce, and garnish with a twisted lemon slice.

Native to Central America, avocados are extremely high in fat (30%) and contain protein, minerals, and vitamins A through K.

....

ARTICHOKES ORIENTAL STYLE

(Artichauts à l'Orientale)

16 medium artichokes
½ cup olive oil
1 cup dry bread crumbs
3 garlic cloves, pressed
1 tablespoon gingerroot, grated
1 teaspoon lemon zest

1 tablespoon mint leaves, cut into chiffonade
1 tablespoon cilantro leaves, minced
the juice of 3 lemons
salt and pepper to taste
1 cup dry white wine

- Slice off the top ½ inch of each artichoke and the stem (discard tops and stems). Using a pair of sharp shears (scissors), trim and remove any damaged leaves near the stem, and snip off the tops of the remaining leaves. Spread open the leaves, and scoop out the furry part of the choke, using a Parisienne scoop.

- Combine half the olive oil with the bread crumbs, garlic, ginger, lemon zest, mint, cilantro, 2 tablespoons of the lemon juice, salt, and pepper, and blend well. Stuff the artichokes with this mixture, closing the leaves over the stuffing.
- Preheat an oven to 375°F.
- Place the artichokes in a casserole dish, and drizzle with the remaining oil and lemon juice and the wine. Bake covered for 20 to 30 minutes, or until tender. Allow to cool, then refrigerate overnight. Serve chilled or at room temperature.

Artichoke Bottoms, Dieppe Style
(Fonds d'Artichaut à la Dieppoise)

Artichoke bottoms filled with a mound of finely diced poached mussels and shrimp, bound with a little mayonnaise, and garnished with chopped parsley.

Artichoke Bottoms, DuBarry
(Fonds d'Artichaut à la DuBarry)

Artichoke bottoms filled with a mound of small cauliflower flowerettes blanched in boiling salted water until al dente, coated with mayonnaise thinned with a little vinegar, and garnished with chopped parsley.

Artichoke Bottoms, President Style
(Fonds d'Artichaut à la Président)

Artichoke bottoms filled with a mound of finely diced chicken bound with mayonnaise, topped with a slice of hard-boiled egg and a thin slice of truffle, and glazed with aspic.

Beetroot Squares
(Caisses de Betteraves)

Roast some large beets in a preheated 400°F oven, with a little water in the pan, for about 1 hour, or until tender when pierced with a toothpick. Remove and allow to cool. Cut the beets into uniform 1-inch square cubes, and marinate one hour in vinegar. Scoop out the top of each beet cube, using a Parisienne scoop, and fill with a salad consisting of finely diced capers, gherkins, egg whites, and anchovies, marinated in mustard vinaigrette. Sprinkle the top with sieved egg yolks. (See color plate.)

Beets, native to the coasts of western Europe and North Africa, have been eaten by humans since the days prior to recorded history. They contain as much as 10% carbohydrate by weight, mostly in the form of sucrose, 1.5-2% protein, iron, and calcium. In the eighteenth century, a white variety was cultivated for sugar production. Beets are classified as having a (1) round root, (2) flat-roundish root, or (3) long root (up to 12 inches long). Varieties include Crosby's Egyptian, Burpee Red Ball, Early Wonder, Detroit Dark Red, Burpee's Golden, Dark Red Massy, Dark Red Globe Early, and Dark Red Turnip-Rooted Egyptian.

California Apples
(Pommes à la Californienne)

Remove the tops and scoop out the interiors of medium Gravenstein or Granny Smith apples (or any preferred variety). Douse in a lemon bath, drain well, then fill with finely diced chicken and celery bound with mayonnaise, seasoned with lemon juice, fresh herbs, salt, and white pepper. Set the tops back in place, pipe out a rosette of butter (mashed into a smooth paste with finely minced herbs) onto each top, and serve well chilled. (See color plate.)

*C*ELERY ROOT RÉMOULADE

(Celeriac Rémoulade)

2 medium celery roots	salt and white pepper to
the juice of 4 lemons	taste
1 cup rémoulade sauce	

- Bring about 1 quart of lightly salted water to a boil.
- Peel the celery, then cut into a long, fine julienne, using a Japanese mandolin. Place the celery in a bowl, pour the lemon juice, over the celery, and enough boiling water to cover. Allow to sit 15 minutes. Drain thoroughly, and allow to cool.
- Blend the rémoulade sauce with the celery, adjust seasoning with salt and white pepper, and allow to marinate overnight. Serve on a bed of lettuce, garnished with parsley sprigs.

This very simple and elegant dish can be prepared with any variety of mayonnaise-based sauce.

Celeriac, also called German or turnip-rooted celery, has a starch-storing root, with long green stems and minimal development of its leaves. The best-known varieties are Verona and Alabaster.

Celery, Housewife Style
(Céleri à la Bonne Femme)

Peeled celery, sliced very thin on the bias, combined with sliced cooked potatoes, bound with mustard-mayonnaise.

Celery Stuffed with Roquefort
(Céleri Roquefort)

Peeled celery cut, on a sharp bias, into 1-inch long diamond-shaped pieces, then stuffed with a paste made with Roquefort cheese, cream cheese, and butter, seasoned with white Worcestershire sauce and paprika. (See color plate.)

In California this dish is commonly found at catered affairs, and the manner of presentation is often startlingly dramatic. When each variety of vegetable is relegated to its own serving plate or platter, it can be arranged in striking geometric patterns. The height of each of these is often varied, with the use of attractive risers (or risers covered with a tablecloth). Innovative materials are often used for platters, such as 1-foot square Plexiglass (a plastic material), in a broad range of colors—an effective and attractive way to present a fairly low-cost item.

In ancient Greece, celery was made into a crown and placed on the head of a victorious athlete. The Romans did the same thing much later, believing it would protect them from hangovers, and in Plutarch's time celery was used as a funeral wreath. Its first recorded use as a food was in France in 1623. A member of the carrot family, celery consists of a bunch of petioles, or leaf stalks, and is rich in mineral salts, vitamins, and iron. It also has diuretic properties, making it a natural remedy for kidney ailments. In Chinese medical practice, consumption of 4 ounces of raw celery per day is known to alleviate high blood pressure. Cultivars include Stuffed White Pascal, Giant Pascal, American Stuffed White, Fordhook, Golden Self-Blanching, Verona, and Alabaster.

Chilled Asparagus, Aurora

Peel 24 fat asparagus, and blanch in boiling salted water until al dente. Thin some mayonnaise with a little lemon juice, and ladle onto four serving plates, or a serving platter. Thin some tomato paste with some of the water used to blanch the asparagus, transfer to a plastic squeeze bottle, and squeeze out a spiral on the mayonnaise. Run a toothpick out from the center in eight equidistant lines, then run the toothpick in toward the center, in between the other lines. Arrange the asparagus on top of sauce. See Figure 10.1.

Crudités, Herb Mayonnaise
(Crudités, Sauce Verte)

An assortment of raw vegetables, attractively arranged and served with an herb mayonnaise. Some of the vegetables are improved by brief blanching in boiling salted water: broccoli, cauliflower, string beans, yellow squash, and zucchini. Other varieties are better left raw: bell peppers, celery, cucumber, radishes, and scallion.

Cucumbers, Danish Style
(Concombres à la Danoise)

Scooped-out cucumber boats, 2 inches long, filled with a paste made of smoked salmon and cream cheese, seasoned with horseradish, and garnished with hard-boiled egg. (See color plate.)

CUCUMBERS, SWEDISH STYLE

(Concombres à la Suédoise)

1 large hothouse cucumber	¼ cup mayonnaise
1 cup marinated herring fillets, drained	the juice of 1 lemon
	1 teaspoon dill, minced
¼ cup red onion, finely diced	salt and white pepper to taste
¼ cup celery, finely diced	12 sprigs dill

- Combine the herring, onion, celery, mayonnaise, lemon, dill, salt, and pepper, and blend thoroughly. Set aside.
- Cut the cucumber widthwise into 1½-inch lengths. With a Parisienne scoop, scoop out the cucumber, about 1 inch deep, and within ¼ inch of the outside edge. Fill the cucumbers with the salad, and garnish with a dill sprig.

A native of India and tropical Asia and cultivated since 2000 B.C., the cucumber was introduced to France in the ninth century and to England in the fourteenth. From the

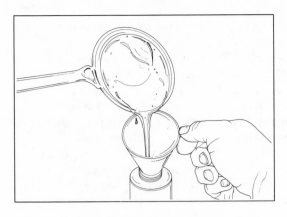

Pour the thinned and seasoned tomato paste
into a plastic squeeze bottle.

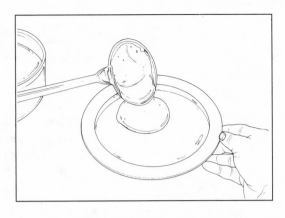

Ladle the thinned mayonnaise
onto a serving plate.

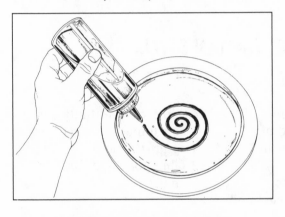

Carefully squeeze out a spiral line
of the tomato paste.

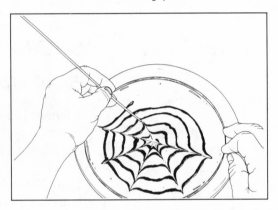

Run a toothpick or skewer from the center out,
in eight equidistant radial lines.

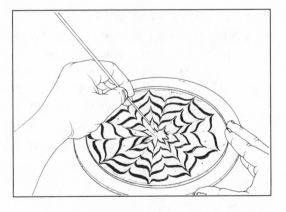

Run the toothpick from the outside in, through
the center of each section. Arrange the prepared
asparagus on top, and serve.

Figure 10.1
Sauce painting (Chilled Asparagus, Aurora)

Middle Ages through the eighteenth century, cucumbers were considered unhealthful, and "hard of Digestion, because they continue long in the Stomach" (Dr. Lemery). Samuel Johnson (1709–1784) wrote, "A cucumber should be well-sliced, dressed with pepper and vinegar, and then thrown out." Early cultivars, such as Russian and Holland Yellow, have disappeared because of agricultural methods geared toward monoculture. One ancient variety—Paris Green—still exists, and newer varieties include Victory, Ohio MR 17, Sunnybrook, Pioneer, Marketeer, West Indian Gherkin, Straight Eight, Marketmore 70, China (Kyoto), and Mariner.

$\mathscr{F}$ENNEL ROOT, ITALIAN STYLE

(Fenouil à l'Italienne)

4 fennel bulbs, trimmed of stalks, bottom, and any dark spots, and cut in half
¼ cup olive oil
1 cup dry white wine
1 medium onion, peeled and thinly sliced

4 garlic cloves, thinly sliced
1 cup tomatoes, diced
4 sprigs thyme
2 tablespoons parsley, minced

- Preheat an oven to 375°F.
- Blanch the fennel bulbs in boiling salted water for 2 minutes. Drain and place cut side down in an oiled casserole dish. Drizzle with the olive oil, and sprinkle with salt and pepper. Add the remaining ingredients, except the parsley, cover, and bake 30 to 40 minutes, or until tender. Remove from the oven, allow to cool, and refrigerate overnight.
- Serve the fennel chilled or at room temperature, sprinkled with the parsley.

$\mathscr{H}$UMMUS

2 cups cooked garbanzo beans
¾ cup sesame tahini
the juice of 3 lemons

6 garlic cloves, pressed
¼ cup olive oil
1 teaspoon salt
¼ teaspoon white pepper

- Purée all ingredients in a food processor, using the pulse switch. Serve with vegetable crudité, with toasted pita bread slices, or as part of another appetizer.

𝓛EEKS VINAIGRETTE

(Poireaux Vinaigrette)

4 medium leeks, white part
  only
1½ cups olive oil
½ cup champagne vinegar
2 garlic cloves
2 tablespoons Dijon-style
  mustard

½ cup parsley leaves, roughly chopped
water as needed
salt and black pepper to
  taste

- Place all the ingredients except the leeks in a blender, and purée. Adjust seasoning, and set aside.
- Remove the roots from the leeks, and discard. Split the leeks lengthwise, into quarters, up to 1 inch from the root end, leaving them attached. Rinse the leeks well in cold water, then blanch in boiling salted water until tender. Drain, cool, and set aside.
- Complete the two cuts in the leeks, dividing each leek into quarters. Arrange on a serving plate, and coat with the vinaigrette. (See color plate.)

———————————— • ————————————

This is a good all-purpose cold sauce, because it is made to one's taste—and because the parsley emulsifies the sauce, which will stay that way up to 12 hours. To reemulsify, simply place in a covered jar and shake well.

The Vegetables Vinaigrette dish pictured with the leeks in the color plate is prepared with the same vinaigrette. Select some seasonable vegetables, such as broccoli, carrots, cauliflower, white turnip, yellow bell pepper, zucchini. Blanch lightly (firmly al dente), drain, cool, and toss in the vinaigrette.

MARINATED MUSHROOMS, GREEK STYLE

(Champignons à la Greque)

1 cup button mushrooms
1 cup shiitake mushrooms
1 cup chanterelle mush-
  rooms
the juice of one lemon

1 quart (approx.) cold water
1 package of fresh enoki
  mushrooms

For the Marinade

1 cup olive oil
1 cup white wine vinegar
1 cup water
salt and white pepper to
  taste
4 garlic cloves, crushed

1 shallot, thinly sliced
2 sprigs rosemary
2 sprigs thyme
2 sprigs oregano
1 bay leaf

For the Service

8 Boston lettuce cups
4 red cabbage leaf cups

16 Belgian endive leaves
¼ cup chopped parsley

- Trim the very bottom portion of the stems of the button, shiitake, and chanterelle mushrooms, and discard. Rinse these mushrooms in the cold water and lemon juice. Pat dry. Cut the shiitakes into julienne, and the chanterelles into ½-inch pieces.
- Combine all of the marinade ingredients in a saucepan, and bring to a boil. Add the mushrooms, simmer for 1 minute, then turn off the fire and allow to cool to room temperature. Cover and refrigerate overnight.
- Arrange the butter lettuce leaves on four individual plates, place a cabbage leaf in the center, and four endive leaves on each plate. Place the marinated mushrooms on the cabbage leaves, garnish with the enoki mushrooms and chopped parsley.

———— • ————

This marinade can be used to marinate numerous other vegetables: artichoke bottoms and hearts, celery, fennel, bell peppers, summer squash, zucchini, and so forth.

SAUERKRAUT

2 heads white cabbage   salt as needed

- Cut the cabbages in half, removing and saving the outer green leaves, and removing the cores. Slice as thinly as possible, rinse, and drain.
- Line the bottom of a stone crock (OK to substitute a stainless steel or glass container) with the outer cabbage leaves. Place a 1-inch deep layer of cabbage on top of this, and sprinkle lightly with the salt. Repeat this with layers of cabbage alternating with the salt until the container is full. Cover with a final layer of cabbage leaves, and set a wooden board or a plate on top of the cabbage. Press down firmly until the juice that has drained from the cabbage rises above the plate. Place a heavy weight (a stone is the usual choice) on top, so that the plate remains below the level of the juice. Place in a cool spot (basement) for 3 to 6 weeks, and marinate. At the end of 3 months, remove any moldy cabbage from the top, and refrigerate the sauerkraut until needed.

Sauerkraut is an extremely healthful dish, and can be eaten as is or used in numerous Alsatian and German dishes. Typically served with pork, smoked pork, sausages, and apples, it is also cooked with Alsatian wine and accompanied with smoked salmon, salt cod, monkfish, or fish sausages.

VEGETABLES VINAIGRETTE

¾ cup pearl onions
¾ cup zucchini, cut into medium julienne
¾ cup yellow squash, cut into medium julienne

¾ cup carrot balls (cut with small end of Parisienne scoop)
¾ cup broccoli flowerettes
¾ cup cauliflower flowerettes

For the Vinaigrette

3 cups olive oil
1 cup champagne vinegar
2 garlic cloves, peeled
1 tablespoon Dijon-style mustard

salt and pepper to taste
½ cup parsley leaves, well rinsed
¼ cup water

- Blanch the vegetables individually, in boiling salted water, until al dente. Remove, cool, drain thoroughly, and set aside.
- Combine all the vinaigrette ingredients in a blender, and purée. Adjust seasoning with salt and pepper.
- Pour the vinaigrette over the vegetables, and allow to marinate several hours before serving.

Both the variety of vegetables and the seasoning ingredients in the vinaigrette can be adjusted according to preference and seasonal availability of ingredients.

Hot Dishes

Ardennes Potatoes
(Pommes à l'Ardennaise)

Baked potatoes scooped out, restuffed with mashed potato flavored with egg yolks, butter, finely diced ham, and mushrooms, seasoned with salt, pepper, nutmeg, and parsley, sprinkled with Parmesan cheese, and baked until golden brown.

ARTICHOKES, DEVIL STYLE

(Fonds D'artichaut à la Diable)

8 medium artichokes
the juice of 2 lemons
1 cup flour
1 teaspoon baking powder
pinch of salt
1 tablespoon clarified butter
1 cup warm water (approximately)

1 large egg white
flour seasoned with salt and cayenne pepper as needed
1 quart vegetable oil
8 parsley sprigs
salt and cayenne pepper as needed

- Trim the bottom of the stem and the tougher outer leaves of each artichoke, and discard. Cut lengthwise into quarters, remove the furry choke, and blanch in boiling salted water with the lemon juice. Drain, cool, and set aside.

- Sift 1 cup of flour and the baking powder into a bowl. Add the salt, butter, and water, and blend thoroughly. Allow to sit 30 minutes, then adjust thickness of the batter if necessary.

- Heat the vegetable oil in a heavy-gauge pan to a temperature of 375°F. Preheat an oven to 200°F.

- Beat the egg white to a stiff peak, and fold into the batter. Dust the artichoke quarters in the seasoned flour, shake off the excess, then dip in the batter, allowing the excess to drip off. Deep-fry the artichokes until golden brown, and hold in the oven until all are cooked. Sprinkle with salt and cayenne pepper, and serve garnished with fried parsley sprigs.

*A*SPARAGUS, VERGÉ SAUCE

32 jumbo asparagus,
    trimmed to 5-inch lengths
    and peeled
1 cup crème fraîche or sour
    cream

4 tablespoons Dijon-style
    mustard
the juice of 1 lemon
4 tablespoons minced chives

- Blanch the asparagus in lightly salted simmering water until al dente. Drain and set aside, keeping warm.
- Combine the remaining ingredients, except the chives, in a small saucepan, over medium heat. Bring just to a simmer, and remove from the fire. Arrange the asparagus on individual plates, top with the sauce, and garnish with chives.

*A*SPARAGUS AND MORELS IN CREAM SAUCE

(Asperges et Morels à la Crème)

32 jumbo asparagus,
    trimmed to 5-inch lengths
    and peeled
1 shallot, minced
½ cup dry white wine
1½ cups heavy cream
salt and white pepper as
    needed

2 tablespoons unsalted
    butter
12 large fresh (or dried)
    morels
2 tablespoons unsalted
    butter, cut into 1-inch
    pieces
2 tablespoons parsley,
    minced

- Simmer the shallot in the wine, and reduce to 2 tablespoons of liquid. Add the cream, and reduce by half, or until thick. Season to taste with salt and white pepper.
- Rinse the morels well in cold water. (If using the dried variety, soak in boiling hot water for 30 minutes, drain, and rinse.) Slice the morels widthwise into ¼-inch pieces, and sauté in 2 table-spoons of butter. Add the cream, bring to a boil, and beat in the butter pieces. Set aside, keeping warm.
- Blanch the asparagus in lightly salted simmering water until al dente. Drain, place on individual serving plates, top with the sauce, and sprinkle with the parsley.

ℬAKED STUFFED ONIONS

(Oignons Blanc Farcies)

4 large white onions
unsalted butter as needed
2 shallots, minced
2 garlic cloves, pressed
¾ cup ground pork
¼ cup chicken livers, finely
  chopped

1 tablespoon chives, minced
1 tablespoon tarragon leaves,
  minced
1 tablespoon parsley, minced
1 tablespoon mint, minced
salt and pepper to taste
4 small slices Italian fontina

- Slice off the tops and bottoms of the onions, blanch briefly in boiling salted water, then set aside.
- Sauté the shallot, garlic, and pork in butter until cooked. Add the chicken livers, herbs, salt, and pepper, blend in, and remove from the fire.
- Preheat an oven to 350°F.
- Scoop out as much of the interior of the onions as possible, and stuff with the pork mixture. Rub the outside of the onions with butter, place in a baking dish with a little water, and bake for 45 minutes. Place the cheese on top during the last 5 minutes of cooking.

The concentric layers of an onion are the swollen bases of the previous year's leaves and contain food reserves for the following year's growth, when the plant will flower. Native to a broad region stretching from Israel to India, the onion has been cultivated at least since 3000 B.C. In ancient Egypt, the onion was so highly valued that it was an object of worship, and Robert Courtine called it ". . . the truffle of the poor." Henrik Ibsen (1828–1906) and others have used the onion as a metaphor for superficiality and emptiness—"Life is like an onion: you peel back the layers, and cry a little."—yet the center of the onion contains two bud stems from which the second year's growth arises. Spanish onion varieties include Yellow Sweet Spanish, Nutmeg, Ebenezer, Stuttgarter, Buccaneer, Yellow Globe Hybrid, and Yellow Utah; red varieties include Red Bermuda, Ruby, and California Early Red; and white varieties include Crystal White Wax, White Sweet Spanish, Milan Coppery, and White Portugal. Green onions (also scallions, or spring onions) are picked when young, before they form a bulb. Varieties include White Sweet Spanish, White Portugal, Japanese Bunching, Southport White Bunching, and Evergreen Long White Bunching.

*B*RAISED RED CABBAGE

....

1 large head red cabbage,
  cored and shredded
¼ cup olive oil
2 Granny Smith apples,
  peeled, cored, and finely
  chopped

½ cup basalmic vinegar
½ cup chicken stock (or
  water)
¼ cup brown sugar
salt and pepper as needed

- Sprinkle the cabbage with salt and pepper, and sauté in the olive oil for 5 minutes. Add the apples, vinegar, stock and brown sugar. Cover and simmer for 45 minutes, or until tender.

———————————— • ————————————

Brassica oleracea, the original wild cabbage and a member of the mustard family, is native to central and western Europe and the Mediterranean. The salty, sunny climate of the Mediterranean made it difficult to retain water. Consequently, wild cabbage developed a thick cuticle and water-storing leaves characteristic of desert plants, yet its ability to thrive in cold climates made it popular in eastern Europe. Sauerkraut, pickled cabbage, may have been brought to Europe by the Tartars from China. One of the single most healthful vegetables, its health-giving properties have been written about throughout history. Varieties are classified as follows: *black cabbage* (Tuscany Black), with stems sometimes reaching a height of 6 to 7 feet, used mostly as livestock feed; *brussels sprouts*, small numerous lateral buds along the main stem of the cabbage plant; *savoy cabbage*, with a short stem and crimped leaves; *head cabbage* (common cabbage), with smooth, pale green leaves and compact head; *kohlrabi*, globe-shaped, with a fleshy swollen stem; *cauliflower*, an unripe hypertrophied inflorescence; *broccoli*, similar to cauliflower, but with small individual flowers making up the head. Other varieties of cabbage include kale, bok choy, and Chinese cabbage.

Varieties of Savoy cabbage include Savoy King, Chieftain Savoy, Vanguard, Perfection Drumhead, Asti, and Iron Head. Head, or common cabbage varieties, are categorized by season and color. Early season cultivars include Copenhagen Market, Market Victor, Market Topper, Early Jersey, Wakefield, Earliana, Golden Acre, and Stonehead Hybrid; midseason: O-S Cross, Harris Resistant Dutch, Market Prize, King Cole, and Roundup; late, or winter: Danish Ballhead, Green Winter, Premium Flat Head, Surehead, and Danish Roundup; red, or purple: Red Acre, Ruby Ball, and Red Head. Other brussels sprouts cultivars include Jade

Cross Hybrid, Long Island Improved, Green Gem, and Cats-kill; broccoli cultivars are De Cicco, Calbrese, Waltham 29, and Green Comet; and cauliflower cultivars include Super Snowball, Snowball A, Clou, White Horse, Igloo, Jet Snow, Purple Head, Burpeeana, and Self-Blanche.

.... *B*RUSSELS SPROUTS, MIKADO SAUCE

(Choux de Bruxelles, Mikado)

1 pound brussels sprouts	juice of one lemon
3 large egg yolks	1 cup clarified butter
3 tablespoons tangerine juice	the zest of one tangerine,
pinch of salt	blanched
pinch of cayenne pepper	

- In a stainless steel bowl, over a saucepan of barely simmering water *(bain marie)*, beat the yolks, tangerine juice, salt, and cayenne pepper with a whip until thick (about 5 minutes).

- Remove from the heat, lift up the bowl, and place a clean, damp towel over the top and down under the saucepan. Set the bowl on top of the saucepan, over the cloth, and pour the butter in a slow, steady stream while beating continuously. As the mixture thickens, alternate the butter with some of the lemon juice. Continue until all of the butter and lemon juice are emulsified. Adjust the thickness of the sauce by beating in warm water. Add the zest, and set aside in a warm area until ready to use.

- Trim the ends from the bottoms of the sprouts, and discard, along with any loose leaves. Cut very large sprouts in half, lengthwise. Cook all in lightly salted boiling water until al dente. Drain, then transfer to serving dishes. Serve with a side of the Mikado sauce.

.... *C*ELERY ROOT GRATIN

1 garlic bulb, cloves peeled and sliced in half lengthwise	1 large onion, cored removed, and sliced lengthwise very thin

olive oil as needed
½ cup dry white wine
1 pound celery root, peeled and sliced ¹⁄₁₆-inch thick
1 pound Red Bliss potatoes, peeled and sliced ¹⁄₁₆-inch thick

½ cup heavy cream
½ cup milk
salt and white pepper to taste

- Preheat an oven to 375°F.
- Sauté the garlic and onion in olive oil, about 5 minutes, without coloring. Add the white wine and reduce by half. Season with salt and pepper.
- Lightly oil a deep 8-inch pie dish with olive oil. Layer the potatoes, and sprinkle with salt and pepper. Add a layer of celery root, followed by the garlic and onions. Mix the cream and milk together, and pour over all. Cover with parchment paper, then foil, and bake for 30 minutes. Then uncover and continue baking until the potatoes are tender.

ℱRIED OKRA, PECAN MAYONNAISE

¾ cup mayonnaise
¼ cup grainy Dijon-style mustard
½ cup toasted pecans, chopped
the juice of 1 lemon
salt and white pepper to taste
1 pound large okra

1 cup flour, seasoned with salt, pepper, and ground cumin
4 eggs, well beaten
1 cup dry bread crumbs
1 cup cracker meal
1 tablespoon fillet gumbo
vegetable oil as needed

Okra is a native of tropical Africa and was cultivated by the Egyptians in the twelfth century A.D. Brought to the southern United States in the eighteenth century, it has been cultivated there ever since. In culinary usage, okra is valued for a mucilaginous substance that thickens soups, sauces, and stews.

- Combine the mayonnaise, mustard, pecans, lemon juice, salt, and white pepper, and blend thoroughly. Cover and refrigerate.
- Pour lightly salted boiling water over the okra, and allow to sit 10 minutes. Drain and dry.
- Combine the crumbs, cracker meal, and gumbo. Dust the okra with the flour, dip in the eggs, and coat with the bread crumb mixture.
- Heat the oil (1-inch deep), in a heavy-gauge pan, to a temperature of 375°F. Preheat an oven to 200°F.
- Deep-fry the okra until golden brown, transfer to absorbent paper, and hold in the oven until all are fried. Serve accompanied by the mayonnaise, and garnish with parsley.

.... ## GARLIC MASHED POTATOES

8 large Red Bliss potatoes,
   peeled and quartered
1 garlic bulb, peeled
1 teaspoon salt

¼ pound unsalted butter
½ cup half-and-half, hot
salt and white pepper to
   taste

- Boil the potatoes and garlic in salted water until the potatoes are fully cooked. Drain and mash with a ricer or mashing tool. Blend in the butter and half-and-half, and season to taste with salt and pepper. Set aside until ready to serve.

.... ## GRILLED SHIITAKE MUSHROOMS, MISO SAUCE

2 tablespoons sake
2 tablespoons soy sauce
1 tablespoon sugar
1 shallot, minced
½ cup dry white wine
16 medium shiitake mush-
   rooms, stems removed
   (retain)

2 cups heavy cream
2 tablespoons light miso
   paste
1 teaspoon soy sauce
white pepper to taste
4 large sprigs cilantro

- Dissolve the sugar in the sake and 2 tablespoons of soy sauce, and marinate the mushrooms in this mixture for 1 hour.
- Simmer the shallot, wine, and mushroom stems until reduced by half. Add the cream, miso, 1 teaspoon of soy sauce, and pepper, and simmer until desired thickness is achieved. Strain and set aside, keeping warm.
- Grill, broil, or sauté the mushrooms about 3 minutes on each side. Remove to serving plates, top with the sauce, and garnish with the cilantro.

Grilled Vegetables, California Style

Grilling vegetables is a practice that arose in the late 1970s in an effort by the culinary world to expand into different cooking styles, as well as a marketing effort to highlight "new" culinary trends. Grilling is neither new nor unique to California. The same can be said of the "nouvelle cuisine" that came out of France at this time, hawking a lighter style of classical French cuisine. Archestratus, a wandering Greek poet and gastronome, lay down the guidelines for nouvelle cuisine in the fifth century B.C. The introduction of "mesquite grilled" meat and fish (the mesquite is imported from Mexico), however, led to grilling all manner of food items. In addition to mesquite, other woods were experimented with, including alderwood, hickory, and cuttings from grapevines, and orange and lemon trees. The use of such woods adds an interesting rustic flavor.

Since we continue to avoid highly saturated fats in our diets, in favor of a healthier low-fat diet, the innovative use of plant-derived foods is a welcome addition. Virtually any variety of vegetable can be grilled (or roasted), including carrots, fennel, leeks, mushrooms, onions, bell peppers, potatoes, summer and patty pan squash, zucchini, and so on. They need only be trimmed of ends, seeds (and, in some cases, skin), washed well, brushed with olive oil, seasoned with salt and pepper, then placed on a grill. On the grill, they can be lightly browned ("marked"), then finish cooking in a hot oven. (See color plate.)

·············· $\mathscr{M}$USTARD GREENS, YANKEE STYLE

1 medium onion, finely diced
3 slices thick bacon, cut into julienne
1 very large bunch mustard greens, rinsed, stems removed, and roughly chopped

½ cup water
2 tablespoons chicken glaze (*glace de volaille*)
salt and pepper to taste

• Render the bacon until golden brown. Add the onions, cover, and sweat 5 minutes over medium heat, stirring frequently. Add the mustard greens, cover, and sweat another 5 minutes. Add the water, glaze, salt, and pepper, and simmer 30 to 40 minutes, or until tender.

·············· $\mathscr{O}$KRA, AMERICAN STYLE

(Gombos à l'Américaine)

1 pound okra
¼ cup olive oil
1 cup onions, small dice
6 garlic cloves, sliced thin
1 cup tomatoes, diced

pinch of saffron threads
1 bay leaf
¼ teaspoon cayenne pepper
2 sprigs thyme
the juice of 2 lemons

- Trim the tops and bottoms from the okra. Pour boiling salted water over the okra, and allow to sit 30 minutes. Drain and set aside.
- Sauté the onions and garlic in the olive oil. Add the remaining ingredients, and blend well. Add the okra, cover, simmer 30 to 40 minutes, and serve with rice pilaf.

$\mathcal{R}$ATATOUILLE

....

½ cup olive oil	6 garlic cloves, pressed
1 large onion, peeled and cut into large dice	2 cups diced tomatoes
	¼ cup tomato purée
1 green pepper, cut into large dice	¼ cup chopped basil
	¼ cup chopped tarragon
2 medium zucchini, cut into 1½ × 1½-inch julienne	1 bay leaf
	4 sprigs fresh thyme
1 medium eggplant, peeled and cut into 1½ × 1½-inch julienne	salt and pepper to taste

- Sauté the onion in the olive oil about 5 minutes. Add the pepper, zucchini, and eggplant, and continue cooking. Add the garlic, and cook briefly. Add the tomatoes, the purée, herbs, salt, and pepper. Cover and simmer 15 to 20 minutes. Remove the bay leaf and thyme before serving.

———————————————— • ————————————————

Ratatouille is a vegetable stew originating in Nice; its name is derived from the verb *touiller,* meaning "to stir" or "mix." It is found throughout southern France and is often served as an accompaniment to roasts or braised fish, or as an omelet filling. In Provence, ratatouille is generally cooked to a puréed consistency; the minimally cooked version here is reflective of the author's style. In the United States it is often served as a vegetarian main course and is sometimes baked with a Parmesan–bread crumb crust. Variations may include anchovies, Japanese eggplant, fennel, mushrooms (wild and cultivated), olives (black and green), red bell pepper, patty pan squash, and so on.

ROMAN-STYLE SPINACH

¼ cup sultana raisins
¼ cup olive oil
1 cup scallions, finely sliced
¼ cup pignolias (pine nuts)
6 garlic cloves, thinly sliced

2 large bunches spinach, very well rinsed, stems removed
salt and pepper to taste

- Pour boiling water over the raisins, and allow to sit 15 minutes. Drain and set aside.
- Drop the spinach into boiling salted water, and cook for 1 minute. Drain, cool, and squeeze dry.
- Sauté the scallions in the olive oil for several minutes. Add the pignolias and garlic, and continue cooking until the nuts are golden brown. Add the spinach and raisins, blend well, and season with salt and pepper.

Spinach is indigenous to southwestern Asia, or possibly Persia, and was introduced in Europe by the Moors at about 1000 A.D. Widespread cultivation began only after the eighteenth century, but today spinach is cultivated the world over. It has been said that an indication of a great chef is his or her ability to create excellent spinach dishes. This versatile vegetable is used in dishes as diverse as croquettes, omelets, pasta, puddings, salads, soufflés, soups, and tarts. Spinach is one of the most healthful foods, containing vitamins A, B, C, E, and K, oxalic acid, and some iron (though not quite as much iron as has been generally believed).

SPINACH FRITTERS

¼ cup olive oil
½ cup onion, finely diced
5 garlic cloves, pressed
3 cups cooked, chopped spinach, squeezed dry
½ cup heavy cream
2 cups dry bread crumbs
6 eggs, beaten

¼ pound unsalted butter, melted
½ grated Parmesan cheese
salt and white pepper to taste
flour, beaten eggs, and bread crumbs as needed

- Sauté the onion in the olive oil, without coloring, about 5 minutes. Add the garlic, and cook briefly. Add the spinach and cream, blend, and remove from the fire.
- Add 2 cups of bread crumbs, eggs, butter, cheese, salt and pepper, and blend thoroughly. Allow to cool, then roll into 1-inch balls, and refrigerate for 1 hour.
- Dust the balls with flour, dip in beaten eggs, then roll in bread crumbs. Bake (or deep-fry in oil) in a preheated 375°F oven for 15 to 20 minutes.

Spinach with Madeira Wine
(Épinards au Madère à la Germaine)

Blanch, squeeze dry, and purée some fresh spinach. Sauté some sliced mushrooms in butter and Madeira wine, combine with the spinach, add heavy cream, and season with salt, white pepper, and nutmeg. Bake until bubbly, top with croutons.

SPINACH TIMBALE

1 pound spinach, rinsed and
  stemmed
2 eggs, beaten
1 tablespoon unsalted butter,
  kneaded into a paste with
  1 tablespoon flour

1 cup milk, hot
salt, pepper, nutmeg to taste
3 tablespoons grated Parmesan cheese

Timbale is derived from an Arabic word, *tahbal*, meaning "drum" and referring to a small cup. Traditionally, a guest entering a host's home was offered a small cylindrical cup filled with an aperitif beverage. Today, in the culinary field, *timbale* refers to both the small 2 to 3-inch slope-sided cylinder and the hot or chilled savory dish prepared therein.

- Blanch the spinach in a small amount of lightly salted water. Drain, squeeze dry, and mince. Add the beaten eggs and blend.
- Preheat an oven to 375°F.
- Beat the butter/flour paste into the hot milk and simmer about 5 minutes, stirring continuously (it will be fairly thick). Strain the sauce into the spinach, blend thoroughly, and season to taste with salt, pepper, and nutmeg. Add the cheese and blend.
- Butter four to six ramekins or timbale molds. Fill them with the spinach mixture, cover each with a small circle of buttered parchment paper, then place in a baking pan. Fill the pan about 1-inch deep with boiling water. Bake for 15 minutes, then remove and allow to sit 10 minutes. Run a knife around the inside edge of each timbale, invert, and serve.

STUFFED GRAPE LEAVES

(Dolmades)

1 cup long grain white rice
3 tablespoons olive oil
1 medium onion, finely
   chopped
3 garlic cloves, minced
½ cup dried currants (or
   raisins)
¼ cup pine nuts
2 cups chicken stock (or
   water)

2 tablespoons chopped
   parsley
2 tablespoons chopped mint
salt and pepper to taste
1 jar grape leaves
¼ cup olive oil
the juice and zest of one
   lemon

- Rinse the rice thoroughly in cold water and drain.. Sauté the onion in the olive oil, over medium heat, until transparent. Add the rice, garlic, currants, and pine nuts, and sauté briefly. Add the chicken stock, herbs, salt, and pepper. Blend well, cover, and simmer for 15 minutes. Set aside and allow to cool.

- Lay out one or two grape leaves, and place a tablespoon of the rice in the center. Repeat until all of the rice is used. Roll up firmly (like a burrito), and place in a saucepan or casserole. Pour the olive oil, lemon juice, and zest, over the stuffed grape leaves. Cover, bake for 20 minutes in a 350°F oven, and serve hot or cold.

SWEET AND PUNGENT BRAISED CABBAGE

4 slices bacon, cut into
   ¼-inch dice
1 medium onion, cored and
   sliced very thin lengthwise
4 tablespoons brown sugar
⅓ cup cider vinegar
1 teaspoon dry mustard, dissolved in ½ cup vinegar

1 small head white cabbage,
   sliced very thin
2 Granny Smith apples,
   peeled, quartered, cored,
   and sliced very thin
1 teaspoon grated gingerroot
salt and pepper to taste

- Render the bacon in a sauté pan over a medium flame. Add the onion and cook 5 minutes. Add the remaining ingredients, cover, and simmer 30 minutes. Adjust seasoning and serve.

𝒯OMATOES, ALGERIAN STYLE

(Tomates Algerienne)

4 large ripe tomatoes
salt, pepper, and olive oil as
  needed
1 small onion, finely diced
1 medium eggplant
4 garlic cloves, pressed

½ cup dry white wine
1 tablespoon tomato paste
2 tablespoons parsley,
  minced
¼ cup dry bread crumbs

- Slice the tops from the tomatoes, and scoop out the pulp (reserve for another use). Sprinkle the interiors with salt and pepper, and set aside.
- While the onion is being sautéed in olive oil, peel the eggplant and cut into 1-inch cubes. Add the eggplant to the onions, and cook several minutes. Add the garlic, wine, and tomato paste, cover and simmer 15 to 20 minutes, or until the eggplant is very soft. Remove from the fire, stir in the parsley, and season to taste with salt and pepper.
- Stuff the tomatoes with the eggplant mixture, top with bread crumbs, and bake 10 minutes.

𝒯OMATOES CLAMART

(Tomates Clamart)

4 large ripe tomatoes
1½ cups heavy cream
1 cup potatoes, peeled, and
  roughly chopped

2 cups green peas
2 shallots, minced
salt and white pepper to
  taste

- Slice the tops from the tomatoes, and scoop out the pulp (reserve for another use). Sprinkle the interiors with salt and pepper, and set aside.
- Preheat an oven to 350°F.
- Simmer the potatoes in the cream until they are completely cooked. Add the peas and shallots, and simmer until tender. Remove from the fire, and purée in a food mill. Season to taste with salt and pepper.
- Fill a pastry bag with the purée and stuff the tomatoes. Bake 15 minutes, and serve.

Tomates Clamart is often served as a garnish for roasted or grilled beef, or as part of a bouguetière garnish.

TOMATOES, DUTCH STYLE

(Tomates à la Hollandaise)

4 large ripe tomatoes
4 tablespoons unsalted
    butter
2 shallots, minced
2 cups cooked spinach,
    squeezed dry and finely
    minced

salt, pepper, and nutmeg to
    taste
1 cup Dutch (hollandaise)
    sauce

- Slice the tops from the tomatoes, and scoop out the pulp (reserve for another use). Sprinkle the interiors with salt and pepper, and set aside.
- Preheat an oven to 350°F.
- Sauté the shallots and spinach in the butter until warm. Season to taste with salt, pepper, and nutmeg. Stuff the tomatoes with the spinach, and bake 20 to 30 minutes. Serve accompanied by the Dutch sauce.

TOMATOES HUSSAR

(Tomates à la Hussarde)

4 large ripe tomatoes
¼ cup olive oil
2 shallots, minced
1½ cup mushrooms,
    medium dice
¾ cup ham, finely diced

2 tablespoons parsley,
    minced
2 tablespoons dry bread
    crumbs
salt and pepper to taste

- Slice the tops from the tomatoes, and scoop out the pulp (reserve for another use). Sprinkle the interiors with salt and pepper, and set aside.
- Preheat an oven to 350°F.
- Sauté the shallots and mushrooms in the olive oil for about 5 minutes. Add the ham, parsley, bread crumbs, salt, and pepper, and remove from the fire.
- Stuff the tomatoes with the mushroom mixture, and bake 20 to 30 minutes.

The term *hussar* refers to a horseman of the Hungarian light cavalry, which originated in the fifteenth century.

*Y*AMS WITH CHESTNUTS AND RUM

(Yams aux Marrons, Flambé à la Fort-de-France)

3 pounds yams
1 cup chestnut purée
1 cup raisins
1 cup dark rum

½ cup dark rum
the juice of 3 limes
unsalted butter as needed

- Boil the yams until tender, but still firm in the center. Drain, cool, peel, and cut into ¼-inch slices.
- Bring 1 cup of rum and the raisins to a boil. Remove from the fire and set aside.
- Butter a glass pie or casserole dish. Arrange the sliced potatoes in the dish, then spread the chestnut purée evenly on top of them. Pour the rum and raisins mixture and the lime juice over the purée. Bake for 45 minutes, or until golden and bubbly.
- Heat the remaining rum, pour over the top, bring to the table, and flame.

CHAPTER 11

SALADS

A salad is a dish of raw or cooked food items, seasoned and dressed with a sauce. Ideally, classic and traditional salads should be prepared in their traditional mode. Caesar Salad, for example, a commonly corrupted dish, was created by a hotel maître d' of the same name in Mexico City in the 1940s. When the ingredients for a dish served at a large banquet failed to arrive, Caesar innovated a dish with available ingredients, adding a bit of flair by directing his dining room captains to prepare and serve the dish at table-side. In order to respect the tradition of this dish, it should be prepared at table-side, with ingredients as close to the original as possible. Any major variance from the original salad should be qualified with a different name.

Salads are divided into the following categories (the boundaries between these categories are not absolute):

Tossed Green: for example, Caesar Salad; Salade de Laitue; Tossed Garden Salad, Vinaigrette.

Marinated: for example, Celery Root Rémoulade; Mushrooms à la Greque; Leeks Vinaigrette, Potato/Pasta Salad; Cole Slaw; Waldorf Salad.

Composed: for example, Salade Niçoise; Cobb Salad; Shrimp/Crab Louis; Chef's Salad.

SALAD SAUCES

Salad sauces are derived from two *mother* sauces: vinaigrette and mayonnaise. A true basic vinaigrette, also referred to as *French dressing,* consists of three parts oil, one part vinegar, salt and pepper. The type of oil used in a salad sauce depends on the dish, as well as the culinary practitioner's style. Olive oil is the most commonly chosen, both for its unique flavor and for its nutritional advantages—it is high in mono-unsaturated acids, which have been found to help regulate both harmful and beneficial cholesterol levels. *Extra virgin* olive oil, the first pressing of the olive, is the strongest in flavor and color (some varieties will coagulate under refrigeration). Because it is strong (and more expensive than other grades), extra virgin is recommended for use in its uncooked state—in salad sauces, drizzled over a finished dish, or as an accompaniment to bread served at the beginning of a meal. Subsequent pressings are lighter, thus better suited for cooking, and are bottled as *extra virgin, virgin, super fine,* and *pure.* Other oils used in salads are almond, avocado, corn, grape seed, hazelnut, peanut, poppy seed, safflower, sunflower, and walnut.

Vinegar dates back to the early days of the Roman Empire. Diluted with water, it was a common drink among Roman legionnaires. The word *vinaigre,* literally "sour wine," is a combination of *vin* ("wine," from the Latin *vinum*), and *aigre* ("sour," from the Latin *acer,* meaning "sharp"). A vinegar merchants corporation was formed in Orléans in 1394 and became the center of wine production in France. More than sour wine, vinegar is a fermented product, its production requiring nearly as much care as wine fermentation, though less time. White or red wine is fermented in oak barrels, using a *mother,* a strain of bacteria that consumes the alcohol in the wine and excretes acetic acid. Fermentation requires roughly 6 months. This step is followed by a careful filtering of the vinegar, then adjustment of the acid content (roughly 6% in the finished product) by the addition of water and/or wine. The *Orléans method* is the name applied to the careful fermentation process, whereas the *German method* refers to industrially produced vinegar, which uses a short distillation method requiring 1 to 3 days. The differences in flavor, character, and aroma between the two, of course, are significant.

Vinaigrette

Basic vinaigrette can be augmented in innumerable ways to create an infinite number of variations. While there exist specific sauce variations with specific names, there is no limit to innovations. For example, a vinaigrette intended for a salad having an Asian character might include ginger and oyster sauce; a salad in the style of New England might include dried cranberries; and a salad with a Cajun quality might include abundant cayenne pepper. Mayonnaise-based sauces may also be varied to complement a vast array of culinary styles.

· · · · · · · · · · · · · · · · ·

*B*ASIC VINAIGRETTE

(French Dressing)

1 cup olive oil	⅛ teaspoon salt
⅓ cup red or white wine vinegar	⅛ teaspoon white pepper

- Combine the ingredients in a bowl, and blend thoroughly with a wire whip.

ℰMULSIFIED VINAIGRETTE

3 cups olive oil
1 cup champagne vinegar
2 garlic cloves, peeled
1 small shallot, peeled and
  chopped
1 tablespoon Dijon-style
  mustard

½ teaspoon salt
¼ teaspoon pepper
½ cup parsley leaves, well
  rinsed
½ cup water

- Place all the ingredients in a blender, and purée. Adjust seasoning with salt and pepper.

ℂILANTRO-LIME VINAIGRETTE

1 cup olive oil
¼ cup champagne vinegar
¼ cup lime juice
1 jalapeño pepper, seeds removed and roughly chopped

½ cup cilantro leaves, well
  rinsed and dried
½ cup mint leaves, well
  rinsed and dried
½ teaspoon kosher salt
½ teaspoon black pepper

- Purée the ingredients in a blender. Cover and refrigerate until ready to use.

Mayonnaise

ℬASIC MAYONNAISE

3 egg yolks
½ teaspoon dry mustard
3 tablespoons lemon juice

1 pint olive oil
salt and white pepper to
  taste

- Beat the yolks, mustard, and 1 tablespoon of the lemon juice in a stainless steel bowl, using a wire whip.
- Add the oil in a slow, steady stream, whipping continuously. Alternate the oil with the rest of the lemon juice as the sauce thickens.
- Season to taste with salt and white pepper.

———————— • ————————

There are several stories of the origin of mayonnaise.
One tells of its creation by the chef to the duc de Richelieu,

French cardinal and statesman, in honor of the duke's successful capture of Port Mahon on the island of Minorca on June 28, 1756. The sauce was subsequently dubbed *Mahonnaise*.

Antoine Carême claimed that the word was derived from *manier*, a French verb meaning "to stir":

Some people say mayonnaise, others mahonnaise, still others bayonnaise. It makes no difference that vulgar cooks should use these words, but I urge that these three terms never be uttered in our great kitchens and that we should always denominate this sauce with the epithet, magnonaise.

Other etymologists relegate the origin of mayonnaise to Bayonne, France, the original name being *Bayonnaise*. *Moyeu* was Old French for "middle" and consequently referred to the middle of an egg—the yolk. *Bayonnaise* eventually combined with *moyeu*, they say, evolving into the name we currently use for this cold, egg yolk-emulsified sauce.

Robert Sokolov, author of *The Saucier's Apprentice*, adds to the confusion with a theory of his own:

"It seems to me improbable that no one has yet proposed a fourth solution to the problem. Since most sauces are named after places *(Béarnaise, Hollandaise, Piémontaise, Anglaise)*, it is logical that mayonnaise refer to one also. Unfortunately, there is no town of Mayonne; however, there is a city at the western edge of Normandy, called Mayenne. Who is to say that mayonnaise did not begin as mayennaise?"

Mayonnaise Variations

....

 AïOLI

4 to 6 large garlic cloves, split in two	pinch of white pepper
2 egg yolks	⅓ cup mashed potato
pinch of salt	the juice of ½ lemon
	1 cup olive oil

• Pound the garlic in a mortar until it is a smooth paste. Add the yolks, salt, pepper and potato. Continue pounding, while adding the oil in a slow, steady stream. Intersperse with the lemon juice. When the oil is completely emulsified, adjust the seasoning with salt and pepper.

———————————— • ————————————

The word *aïoli* is a combination of *ail* ("garlic") and *oli* (Provençale dialect for "oil"). Léon Daudet (1867–1942), one of the greatest gastronomes of his time, contended that the culinary use of garlic achieved its peak of perfection in aïoli. Frédéric Mistral who founded the journal *L'Aïoli* in 1891, wrote: "Aïoli epitomizes the heat, the power, and the joy of the Provençale sun."

GREEN GODDESS DRESSING

1 cup mayonnaise
1 garlic clove, pressed
3 tablespoons mashed
   anchovy
3 tablespoons minced chives
1 tablespoon lemon juice

3 tablespoons tarragon
   vinegar
½ cup heavy cream
⅓ cup chopped parsley
salt and pepper to taste

- Combine all ingredients and blend thoroughly.

HERB MAYONNAISE

½ cup mayonnaise
¼ cup half-and-half
2 tablespoons white wine
   vinegar

1 teaspoon each, minced
   basil, parsley, and
   tarragon
salt and white pepper to
   taste

- Combine all ingredients and blend thoroughly. Season to taste with salt and white pepper.

MUSTARD-PECAN MAYONNAISE

1 cup mayonnaise
5 tablespoons grainy
   mustard

½ cup toasted chopped
   pecans
the juice of 1 lemon

- Combine all ingredients and blend thoroughly. Cover and re-frigerate until ready to serve.

RUSSIAN MAYONNAISE

1 cup mayonnaise
1 tablespoon Dijon-style
   mustard
¾ cup ketchup or strained
   chile sauce

2 tablespoons white wine
   vinegar
3 tablespoons osetra, sevruga, or choupique caviar

- Combine all the ingredients, except the caviar, and blend thoroughly. Ladle over the appropriate salad, and garnish with the caviar.

.... 𝒯HOUSAND ISLAND MAYONNAISE

1 cup mayonnaise
1 cup strained chile sauce or ketchup

½ cup green and red bell pepper, cut into 1-inch julienne

- Combine all ingredients and blend thoroughly.

VEGETABLE SALADS

.... 𝒜LEXANDER SALAD

(Salade Alexander)

1 cup ham, cut into 1-inch julienne
1 cup celeriac, cut into 1-inch julienne
2 Belgian endives, cut widthwise into ¼-inch strips
1 cup olive oil
½ cup white wine vinegar
salt and pepper to taste
½ cup mushrooms, cut into ¼-inch dice, blanched in white wine, drained, and cooled

2 large russet potatoes, peeled, sliced, and blanched until tender but firm
2 small Granny Smith apples, thinly sliced and immersed in lemon juice
2 large beets, baked, peeled, cut in half, and thinly sliced
½ cup mayonnaise (optional)

- Marinate the ham, celeriac, and endive in the oil, vinegar, salt, and pepper.
- Arrange the potatoes, overlapping, in a circle on each of four salad plates. Arrange a second circle of the apples (drained), followed by a circle of beets.
- Drain the ham, celeriac, and endive, add the mushrooms, and arrange in the center of each circle. Top with a dollop of mayonnaise (optional). (See color plate.)

American Salad
(Salade Américaine)

Sliced tomatoes and potatoes on a bed of lettuce, topped with celery and whole-kernel corn tossed in emulsified tomato vinaigrette, garnished with sliced onion rings and halves of hard-boiled eggs.

$\mathcal{A}$RIZONA SALAD

1 head butter lettuce
1 heart romaine lettuce, cut into chiffonade
2 Red Bliss potatoes, boiled al dente, peeled, and sliced ¼-inch thick
1 cup scallions, sliced very thinly on the bias

1 cup diced tomatoes
3 hard-boiled eggs, quartered
1 cup mayonnaise
¼ cup lemon juice
¼ cup chopped parsley

- Arrange a base of butter lettuce, and top with the romaine. Arrange the potatoes and tomatoes on top of this. Blend the mayonnaise and lemon juice together thoroughly, and nap over the salad. Garnish with the eggs and parsley.

Bagration Salad
(Salade Bagration)

Two artichoke bottoms filled with blanched celery and ditalini (or other small pasta) cooked al dente, bound with a little mayonnaise, accompanied by sliced poached chicken breast, garnished with hard-boiled eggs and watercress or parsley, drizzled with mayonnaise thinned with a little vinegar or lemon juice. (See color plate.)

$\mathcal{B}$LACKSMITH SALAD

3 pints mesclun salad mix
1 cup shaved pecorino cheese

1 cup olive oil
½ cup balsamic vinegar
salt and pepper to taste

- Toss the greens, cheese, oil, and vinegar together. Season to taste with salt and pepper.

Mesclun refers to a mix of seasonal salad greens, which may include arugula, butter lettuce, frisée, limestone, mâche, radicchio, and others.

Café Anglais Salad
(Salade Café Anglais)

Sliced morels blanched in white wine, drained and cooled, and poached shrimp bound in mayonnaise, served on a bed of lettuce, garnished with shaved truffle.

The Café Anglais was originally established in Paris in 1802, named in honor of the peace treaty of Amiens between England and France. In 1822, Paul Chevreuil purchased the café and made it into a very fashionable restaurant. Adolphe Dugléré (1805–1884) took over the kitchens in 1866 and brought it to the gastronomic heights that made it one of the most enduring establishments until the early twentieth century. His Dinner for Three Emperors was served to Alexander II and his son (the Russian emperor and his successor, Alexander III), Wilhelm I (emperor of Prussia), and Otto Von Bismarck (chancellor of Germany). The menu remains an excellent example of the style of haute cuisine of that era. Among the dishes Dugléré created, which remain well known today, were *Anna Potatoes, Filet de Sole Dugléré,* and *Soufflé à l'Anglaise.*

CALIFORNIA SALAD

4 butter lettuce hearts, quartered
2 Belgian endives, bottoms removed and quartered lengthwise
12 fat asparagus, cut to 4-inch lengths, peeled, and blanched al dente

1 large ruby red grapefruit, segments separated from skin and seeds
1 orange, peeled, sliced, and seeded
8 sprigs mustard blossoms
1 cup olive oil
½ cup champagne vinegar
salt and pepper to taste

- Arrange a bed of lettuce hearts and two endive quarters, then arrange the remaining ingredients on top. Beat oil, vinegar, salt, and pepper, and drizzle over the top.

California Salad was designed by Peg and John Powers, proprietors of The Nut Tree in Vallejo, California. It was served to donors at a fundraising event, Bay Area Culinary Traditions, A Food Symposium, in May 1983, for their contributions of time and effort on behalf of the DeYoung Museum, San Francisco. This salad is typical of the innovative cuisine that is still evolving in California. Mustard blossoms may not be readily available in all areas of the United States throughout the year, so substitutions must be left to the discretion of the chef.

CHAPON SALAD

. . . .

———— • ————

Chapon Salad is typically prepared at table-side, and was once quite popular. The bread is intended to give just a hint of garlic flavor.

————————

sufficient salad greens for
   four servings
1 heel of stale baguette
2 cloves garlic, pressed

1 cup olive oil
½ cup champagne vinegar
salt and pepper to taste

- Rub the heel of bread with the garlic. Place the greens and bread in a salad bowl, and toss. Beat the oil, vinegar, salt, and pepper together, and toss. Remove the bread and discard, and serve the salad.

DAKOTA SALAD

1 head butter lettuce
2 cups cabbage, shredded
   very thin
½ cup minced parsley,
   tarragon, and mint
½ cup mayonnaise
½ cup sour cream
½ cup low-fat yogurt

¼ cup white wine vinegar
salt and white pepper to
   taste
½ cup carrot, cut into very
   fine julienne
1 cucumber, peeled, seeded,
   and sliced very thin

- Combine the cabbage, herbs, mayonnaise, sour cream, yogurt, and vinegar, and blend thoroughly. Season to taste with salt and white pepper, and allow to marinate 4 hours.
- Prepare a bed of butter lettuce leaves. Top with the cabbage, and garnish with carrot and cucumber.

Danticheff Salad
(Salade Danticheff)

Medium-diced celeriac and potatoes, bound in lemon mayonnaise and chopped chervil, served in artichoke bottoms, garnished with asparagus tips, sliced truffle, and chopped chervil.

GERMAN-STYLE POTATO SALAD, BEER VINAIGRETTE

2 pounds small Red Bliss
   potatoes
½ cup red onions, sliced
   paper-thin

2 tablespoons chopped
   chives
½ cup olive oil
1 shallot, minced

1 tablespoon Dijon-style
mustard
3 tablespoons chopped
parsley

salt and pepper as needed
¼ cup white wine vinegar
½ cup beer

- Cook the potatoes in lightly salted boiling water until tender but firm. Drain, peel, and slice ¼-inch thick.
- Place the olive oil, shallot, mustard, parsley, salt, and pepper in a blender, and purée. Bring the vinegar and beer to a boil, and add to the vinaigrette.
- Toss the potatoes and onions with the vinaigrette, and garnish with the chives.

GREENSBORO SALAD

1 head green leaf lettuce,
rinsed and torn into bite-
size pieces
1 English cucumber,
5 inches long, sliced
paper-thin
1 cup mushrooms, medium
dice

1 cup vidalia onions, sliced
paper-thin
1 cup olive oil
½ cup red wine vinegar
2 tablespoons chopped
parsley
salt and pepper to taste
1 cup feta cheese, crumbled

- Beat the olive oil, vinegar, parsley, salt, and pepper together. Pour over the mushrooms and onions, and marinate 1 hour.
- Toss the greens, cucumber, and marinating mix together. Arrange on chilled plates, and top with the feta.

HEARTS OF PALM, CARNELIAN

1 head butter lettuce
4 palm hearts
1 grapefruit, sections separated from skin and seeds
1 ripe Haas avocado, peeled,
seeded, and cut into 8
wedges with a serrated
knife

8 strips pimento, 2 × ¼
inches
1 cup olive oil
½ cup champagne vinegar
salt and pepper to taste

- Wash the palm hearts, and cut in half lengthwise. Beat the oil, vinegar, salt, and pepper together, and marinate the palm in this for 1 hour.

- Remove the outer leaves (discard), and arrange a bed of butter lettuce leaves on each of four plates. Place the palm hearts side by side in the center. Place 2 grapefruit sections in the center of the palm halves, and top with a cross of pimento strips. Place two wedges of avocado along the outside of the palm halves, and drizzle with the vinaigrette. (See color plate.)

𝓘SABELLA SALAD

¼ cup olive oil
2 cups eggplant, large dice
1 cup red bell pepper, medium dice
½ cup dry white wine
2 cups cooked rice
2 medium zucchini, medium diced and blanched al dente
½ cup cooked lima beans

1 cup diced tomatoes
1 cup cucumber, peeled, seeded, and medium diced
½ cup olive oil
the juice of 1 lemon
1 tablespoon chopped oregano
1 tablespoon chopped basil
2 garlic cloves, crushed
salt and pepper to taste

- Sauté the eggplant and pepper in the olive oil, covered, about 5 minutes or until the eggplant is soft. Add the white wine, simmer another few minutes, then remove from the fire, drain, and set aside.
- Beat the oil, lemon, herbs, garlic, salt, and pepper together. Combine all ingredients, and adjust seasoning. Cover and marinate overnight before serving.

𝓙ASPER SALAD

3 medium pears, ripe, but firm
pinch of salt
black pepper to taste
2 teaspoons sugar
¼ cup champagne vinegar
¼ cup peanut oil
2 cups celeriac, cut into fine julienne
the juice of 2 lemons

3 tablespoons mayonnaise
2 tablespoons champagne vinegar
salt and white pepper to taste
1 large (or 2 small) head red leaf lettuce, rinsed, dried, and torn into bite-size pieces

- Peel and core the pears. Toss with the salt, pepper, sugar, ¼ cup vinegar, and oil, and marinate 1 hour, refrigerated.

- Pour the lemon juice and 2 cups of boiling water over the celeriac. Allow to sit 10 minutes, then drain and cool.
- Add the mayonnaise, 2 tablespoons vinegar, salt, and pepper to the celeriac, and blend thoroughly.
- Drain the liquid from the pears onto the lettuce, and toss. Arrange the lettuce on each of four plates. Top with the pears and the celeriac.

JERSEY SALAD

1 head romaine lettuce
1 head escarole
1 cup emulsified vinaigrette
½ cup ketchup
1 cucumber, peeled, seeded, and cut into fine julienne

1 green bell pepper, cut into fine julienne
4 scallions, cut into fine julienne
4 large radishes, sliced paper-thin
12 Calamata olives

- Discard the outer leaves of both lettuces. Separate the romaine into very large leaves, the escarole into smaller pieces, rinse, dry, and chill. Prepare a base of romaine leaves, and arrange the escarole on top.
- Blend the vinaigrette and ketchup together, and add enough to the cucumber, bell pepper, and scallions to lightly coat. Place this in the center of the lettuce, garnish with radishes and olives, and drizzle additional sauce as needed.

MARYLAND SALAD

1 head butter lettuce
1 cup crab meat claws, shell off
1 cup 20-24 count cooked shrimp, split lengthwise

1 cup diced tomatoes
1 cup green bell pepper, cut into fine julienne (1 inch)
1½ cups Thousand Island dressing

- Arrange a base of butter lettuce, top with the crab, shrimp, tomatoes, and green peppers, and nap with the dressing.

Pretty Helen Salad
(Salade Belle Hélène)

A mound of blanched celery root cut into julienne, bound with a little mayonnaise, surrounded by a circle of baked beets, sliced and cut into crescents, and slices of Calamata olives, sprinkled with toasted walnuts, and garnished with watercress or parsley. (See color plate.)

ℛICHMOND SALAD

1 small head romaine lettuce
1 heart of escarole
1 heart of butter lettuce
1 cup string beans, frenched, blanched al dente
1 large beet, boiled in the skin until tender, peeled, and sliced ⅛-inch thick

3 hard-boiled eggs, whites minced and yolks sieved
½ cup scallion, sliced paper-thin
1 cup olive oil
½ cup red wine vinegar
salt and pepper to taste

Frenched string beans refers to cutting the beans lengthwise into two or three pieces. These are actually an imitation of the young miniature vegetables, the *printinière*, available in the spring.

- Tear up the greens into bite-size pieces. Rinse, drain, and chill.
- Arrange the lettuce in a bed. Toss the string beans and sliced beet in the oil, vinegar, salt, and pepper, and place on top of the lettuce. Garnish with the eggs and scallion.

ℛOMAINE SALAD, BOHEMIAN STYLE

For the Vinaigrette

1 cup olive oil
¼ cup lime juice
¼ cup champagne vinegar
1 jalapeño pepper, split and seeded
¼ cup cilantro leaves, stems removed, rinsed, and coarsely chopped

¼ cup mint leaves, stems removed, rinsed, and coarsely chopped
½ teaspoon kosher salt
½ teaspoon black pepper

For the Salad

1 head romaine lettuce, cut into 2-inch pieces
1 ripe avocado, peeled and cut into ½-inch dice
1 cup jicama, cut into very fine julienne

4 ripe Italian plum tomatoes, ¼-inch slices
2 ounces goat cheese
½ cup walnut pieces, toasted

- Place all of the vinaigrette ingredients in a blender, and purée. Refrigerate until ready to use.
- Toss the avocado, jicama, and tomatoes with the vinaigrette. Arrange on top of a bed of romaine. Garnish with goat cheese and walnuts, and drizzle additional vinaigrette on top.

SOUTHERN CROSS SALAD

1 head romaine lettuce
2 Belgian endives
1 bunch watercress
1 ripe Haas avocado

4 palm hearts
1 cup olive oil
½ cup white wine vinegar
salt and pepper to taste

- Remove the outer leaves of the romaine, and discard (or save for Cream of Lettuce Soup). Cut the remaining lettuce into ½-inch pieces. Remove the bottoms of the endives, and cut into ½-inch pieces. Remove the leaves of the watercress. Wash all the three varieties of greens in cold water, drain, and chill.

- Peel the avocado, and cut into 12 wedges.

- Rinse the palm hearts well, and drain. Cut in quarters lengthwise.

- Toss the romaine, endive, and watercress in the oil and vinegar, and season with salt and pepper. Arrange on four individual chilled plates. Place the palm hearts in the center of the base, and garnish with the wedges of avocado. Drizzle with additional oil and vinegar, and top with freshly ground pepper.

TABBOULEH

2 cups bulgar wheat
3 bunches parsley, leaves
 only, rinsed and minced
1 bunch mint, leaves only,
 rinsed and minced
2 large vine-ripened tomatoes, peeled, seeded, and
 diced

½ cup olive oil
½ cup lemon juice
salt and white pepper to
 taste

Reserve the parsley and mint stems for use in stock, sauce, or soup.

- Cover the wheat with 2 quarts cold water and allow to soak 3 hours. Drain, and add the remaining ingredients. Marinate overnight, refrigerated. Serve with roasted pita bread wedges.

TOMATOES, ANDALUSIAN STYLE

(Tomates Farcies Andalousienne)

4 ripe medium tomatoes
3 tablespoons olive oil
¼ cup green pepper, finely
 diced

¼ cup onion, finely diced
1 cup cooked rice
salt and pepper as needed

| ¼ cup mayonnaise, thinned with 2 tablespoons lemon juice | 4 2 × ¼-inch julienne strips of green pepper |
| | 8 ¼-inch circles of green pepper |

- Slice the top from each of the tomatoes, and scoop out the pulp (reserve for another use). Sprinkle with salt and pepper, and invert on absorbent paper.
- Sauté the pepper and onion in the olive oil for several minutes, without browning. Remove from the fire, and blend with the rice.
- Stuff the tomatoes with the rice, top with the mayonnaise, and garnish with a strip of green pepper down the center, and two green pepper circles on either side.

Tomatoes, Rumanian Style (Tomates Farcies Roumaine)

Tomatoes stuffed with rice pilaf mixed with diced tomatoes and green peppers stewed in olive oil and lemon, garnished with a thin slice of peeled and seeded lemon.

Tomatoes, Waldorf Style (Tomates Farcies Waldorf)

Tomatoes stuffed with finely diced apple, celery, and toasted chopped walnuts, bound in a little mayonnaise, garnished with sliced apple and a toasted walnut. (See color plate.)

FISH SALADS

AVOCADO GOURMET

(Coeur d'Avocat, Gourmet)

1 head romaine lettuce	8 parsley sprigs
2 ripe Haas avocados	½ cup mayonnaise
2 cups titi shrimp	½ cup Dijon-style mustard
1 large ripe tomato, cored and cut into 8 wedges	¼ cup half-and-half

- Remove the outer leaves of the lettuce, remove the core, and cut into chiffonade.
- Cut the avocados in half, and remove peel and seed.

- Blend the mayonnaise, mustard, and half-and-half until smooth.
- Place a bed of lettuce on each of four chilled plates. Press the shrimp into a 4-ounce scoop, and place on top of the cut side of each avocado half. Place the avocados on the bed of lettuce. Garnish with 2 tomato wedges, nap the shrimp with the sauce, and garnish with parsley.

BANKER'S WELCOME SALAD

2 celery hearts, 4-inches long
1 cup white wine vinegar
1 cup dry white wine
2 cups water
1 bay leaf
1 teaspoon salt
1 teaspoon peppercorns
1 ripe tomato, cut into 8 wedges

½ ripe Haas avocado, peeled, cut widthwise with a serrated knife
1 cup titi shrimp
12 Dungeness crab claws, shell removed
8 parsley sprigs
1 cup olive oil
½ cup white wine vinegar
salt and pepper as needed

- Poach the celery hearts in the vinegar, wine, water, bay leaf, salt, and pepper until tender. Remove from the fire, and allow to cool.
- Place the chilled celery hearts in the center of each of four chilled plates. Place the tomato, avocado, shrimp, and crab in individual arrangements around the celery. Beat the vinaigrette ingredients together, and drizzle over the salad.

CAESAR SALAD

1 garlic clove, crushed
3 garlic cloves, pressed
1 teaspoon Dijon-style mustard
4 anchovy fillets
the juice of half a lemon
2 tablespoons wine vinegar
1 teaspoon white Worcester- shire sauce
pinch of salt

pinch of pepper
1 large egg, immersed in a cup of warm water (cod- dled)
1 cup olive oil
1 large head romaine lettuce
1 cup garlic croutons
½ cup grated Parmesan cheese

- Remove the exterior leaves and cut and remove the base of the romaine. Split the remaining leaves lengthwise, then cut into

1-inch pieces. Rinse well in cold water, drain, dry, and chill.

- Rub the interior of a wooden salad bowl with the crushed garlic clove. Discard.

- Place the 3 cloves of garlic, mustard, anchovy, lemon juice, vinegar, Worcestershire, salt, and pepper into the bowl. Mash thoroughly using the tines of a fork. Crack the egg, discard the white, and add the yolk to this mixture. Add the olive oil in a slow, steady stream, and blend thoroughly.

- Add the romaine, croutons, and cheese, and toss thoroughly. Transfer to serving plates, and top with freshly ground black pepper.

•

Caesar Salad was created by a maître d' of the same name, in the mid-twentieth century at a hotel in Mexico City. It was created out of necessity, since certain ingredients for a menu salad had failed to arrive. To honor the true origin of the salad, it should be prepared at table-side, in view of the dining guests. This particular recipe was adapted from the personal recipe of Peter Stahl, maître d'hôtel at the Clift Hotel, San Francisco, 1977.

CAULIFLOWER SALAD, PARTENOPEAN STYLE

1 pound cauliflower flowerettes, blanched in boiling salted water	2 heaping tablespoons capers, drained
½ cup olive oil	12 anchovy fillets, split lengthwise
3 tablespoons balsamic vinegar	6 hard-boiled eggs, cut into quarters, lengthwise
pinch of salt	12 Calamata olives
pinch of pepper	

- Place the cauliflower in a mixing bowl. Add the oil, vinegar, capers, salt, and pepper, and toss. Marinate 1 hour, tossing every 15 minutes.

- Arrange the cauliflower on a serving platter. Crisscross the anchovies on top, and garnish with the eggs and olives.

Dumas Salad
(Salade Dumas)

Mussels poached in white wine, served on a bed of diced potatoes dressed with simple vinaigrette, and garnished with truffle.

Dutch Salad
(Salade Hollandaise)

Flaked cooked salmon, diced potatoes, and sliced (or diced) gherkins on a bed of lettuce, garnished with hard-boiled eggs and asparagus, seasoned with oil and lemon juice, sometimes garnished with a little caviar. (See color plate.)

Empire Salad
(Salade à l'Empire)

A composed salad consisting of sliced poached sturgeon, sliced tomatoes and cucumbers, green beans, cauliflower flowerettes, diced artichoke bottoms, green peas, asparagus tips, and dressed with simple vinaigrette.

FREELANCER'S SALAD

There is a significant philosophy, within the culinary craft, of working with ingredients according to local market availability. In the same spirit, the cuisinier adheres to the dictum "Necessity is the mother of invention," and this approach has produced many a fine innovation. The Freelancer's Salad is one such creation, originated by the author and made with ingredients on hand.

2 cups broccoli flowerettes, blanched and chilled
1 cup celery, medium diced
1 cup zucchini, medium diced, blanched and chilled
1 small bunch spinach, stemmed, well rinsed and dried

1 cup scallions, sliced paper-thin on a sharp bias
¾ cup mayonnaise
¾ low-fat yogurt
6 anchovy fillets, minced
salt and pepper to taste

- Blend the mayonnaise, yogurt, and anchovies together thoroughly. Combine the broccoli, celery, and zucchini, and mix with the sauce. Season to taste with salt and pepper.
- Arrange a bed of spinach leaves on salad plates, place the vegetables on top, and garnish with the scallions.

FIRE ISLAND SUMMER SALAD

2 pounds mussels, scrubbed and debearded

½ cup dry white wine
2 garlic cloves, crushed

2 pounds small Red Bliss
  potatoes
1 bunch broccoli, cut into
  flowerettes
1 cup mayonnaise
3 tablespoons Dijon-style
  mustard

1 shallot, minced
2 tablespoons capers,
  drained
½ cup chopped parsley
salt and pepper to taste

- Steam the mussels in the white wine and garlic, covered, until all shells are open. Set the mussels aside and discard the rest.
- Cook the potatoes in lightly salted boiling water until tender, but slightly firm. Drain and set aside. Blanch the broccoli in boiling salted water until al dente. Drain and set aside.
- Combine the remaining ingredients, except the parsley, blend thoroughly, and season to taste with salt and pepper.
- Slice the potatoes into ¼-inch thick slices. Arrange them around the edge of a platter. Arrange another circle of the broccoli flowerettes inside the potatoes. Drizzle half the sauce over the potatoes and broccoli. Toss the mussels in the remaining sauce, place them in the center, and top with chopped parsley.

Grand Duchess Salad
(Salade Grand-Duchesse)

Mixed diced vegetable salad bound in simple vinaigrette, garnished with strips of poached sole fillet, shrimp, anchovies, and cucumbers.

ℋEARTS OF PALM, EDWIN THROWER

1 head butter lettuce
8 large palm hearts, well
  rinsed and drained
½ cup olive oil
½ cup red wine vinegar
1 ripe tomato, cut into 8
  wedges
12 large rings (slices)
  Bermuda onion

1 cup mayonnaise
1 tablespoon Dijon-style
  mustard
¾ cup ketchup or strained
  chile sauce
2 tablespoons white wine
  vinegar
3 tablespoons osetra caviar

- Marinate the palm hearts in the oil and vinegar for several hours. Remove, and split in half lengthwise.

- Combine the mayonnaise, mustard, ketchup, and vinegar, and blend thoroughly.
- Arrange a bed of lettuce on each of four chilled plates. Place the palm hearts in the center, and arrange 3 rings of onion on each. Ladle about 2 ounces of sauce across the center of the palm, garnish the top of the sauce with caviar, and place 2 wedges of tomato at the edges of the sauce.

$\mathscr{L}$OBSTER SALAD, EAST BAY LODGE

2 1½-pound live lobsters
16 asparagus spears
½ cup scallions, finely sliced
½ cup celery, small dice
½ cup leeks, cut in small dice and cooked in boiling salted water until tender
the juice of 3 lemons
1 cup mayonnaise
¼ cup chile sauce
2 tablespoons prepared horseradish, squeezed dry

2 tablespoons minced tarragon
2 tablespoons minced parsley
salt and white pepper as needed
1 head butter lettuce, rinsed and separated into leaves
4 hard-boiled eggs, cut in quarters lengthwise
12 golden cherry tomatoes
4 sprigs flat-leaf parsley

- Immerse the lobsters in boiling water. Bring to a full boil, cover, remove from the fire, and allow to sit 20 minutes.
- Remove the top 2-inch length of each asparagus spear, peel, and set aside. Cut the remaining stalk into ¼-inch pieces, only as far as the beginning of the woody part of the spear. Blanch the asparagus, spears and dice, in boiling salted water until al dente. Drain and set aside.
- Remove the lobsters and drain. Crack the shells, arms, and tails, and remove the meat. Cut this into ¼-inch dice.
- Combine all the ingredients, except the asparagus spears, lettuce, eggs, tomatoes, and parsley sprigs, and blend thoroughly. Season to taste with salt and white pepper.
- Arrange a base of lettuce leaves on four chilled plates. Divide the salad among the four plates. Garnish with the asparagus spears, egg quarters, tomatoes, and parsley sprigs.

This salad has been slightly updated from one that was served throughout the summer season for a Sunday buffet at the East Bay Lodge, a restaurant in Osterville, Massachusetts, in the 1970s.

Monaco Salad
(Salade Monégasque)

A bed of sliced cooked potatoes, topped with flaked poached whitefish, garnished with diced artichoke bottoms and tomatoes, and Niçoise olives, dressed with mustard-anchovy vinaigrette.

ℳushroom Salad, Gourmet Style

1 cup olive oil
½ cup white wine vinegar
salt and pepper to taste
1 cup mushrooms, washed
  and sliced
1 cup oyster mushrooms,
  medium dice
1 cup chanterelles, washed
  and medium dice
12 artichoke hearts,
  blanched and halved
1 cup celery, cut into fine
  julienne
4 Roma tomatoes, cored and
  quartered

16 24-30 count shrimp,
  peeled, deveined, and
  poached
1 head butter lettuce, rinsed
  and leaves separated
2 radicchio leaf cups
1 cup mayonnaise
the juice of 2 lemons
1 tablespoon minced parsley
1 tablespoon minced
  tarragon
1 tablespoon minced cilantro
1 tablespoon minced chives

- Whip the oil, vinegar, salt, and pepper together, add the mushrooms, and marinate 1 hour.
- Combine the mayonnaise, lemon juice, and herbs, and blend.
- Place a bed of lettuce on four individual serving plates. Drain the mushrooms, and place in the center of the lettuce inside a radicchio cup. Arrange the artichokes, celery, tomatoes, and shrimp around the mushrooms in concentric circles, and serve with a side of the herb mayonnaise.

Paris Salad
(Salade Parisienne)

A half tomato, topped with a slice of hard-boiled egg topped with a dollop of mayonnaise, garnished with cooked string beans, some peas and carrots blanched and tossed in a little vinaigrette, a heart of butter lettuce, and a little cooked diced lobster. (See color plate.)

ℛoman Rice Salad

(Insalata di Riso, alla Romana)

1½ cups long grain white
  rice
2½ cups water
1 cup white navy beans,
  soaked in water overnight

1 tablespoon chopped basil
  leaves
1 tablespoon chopped
  marjoram leaves

2 tablespoons chopped
  parsley
½ cup dried bread crumbs
4 garlic cloves
1 teaspoon red chile pepper
  flakes

1 cup olive oil
½ cup red wine vinegar
1 head butter lettuce
12 green olives
12 anchovy fillets

- Cook the rice in the water until all the water has been absorbed. Boil the beans in 1 quart of water until tender (about 1 hour). Drain the beans and blend with the rice, along with the bread crumbs and the herbs.

- Combine the garlic, pepper, oil, and vinegar in a blender, and purée. Pour this over the rice, and blend. Season to taste with salt.

- Serve the rice on a bed of lettuce leaves, garnished with green olives wrapped with anchovies.

·················· SACHA SALAD

1 head butter lettuce, rinsed
  and separated into leaves
12 1-ounce slices fresh
  salmon
1 English cucumber,
  3 inches long, sliced very
  thin
1 cup snow peas, ends
  trimmed, blanched briefly
  in boiling salted water
1 cup olive oil
¼ cup red wine vinegar
¼ cup lemon juice
salt and white pepper as
  needed

½ cup carrots, cut into
  ¼-inch spheres (using a
  small noisette scoop) and
  blanched al dente
½ cup garbanzo beans,
  cooked
½ cup fresh green peas,
  blanched briefly in boiling
  salted water
½ cup sunflower seeds,
  toasted
½ cup ¼-inch square
  croutons

- Season the salmon with salt and pepper, and grill or sauté briefly on both sides. Set aside.

- Beat the oil, vinegar, lemon, salt, and pepper together. Pour over the carrots and beans, and marinate 1 hour.

- Arrange a bed of lettuce on each of four chilled serving plates. Arrange the salmon, cucumber, and snow peas on top of the lettuce, in individual sections. Top with the marinated carrots and beans, and garnish with peas, sunflower seeds, and croutons.

Squid Salad, Capri Style

(Insalata di Capri)

¼ cup scallion, very finely sliced	2 tablespoons water
¼ cup celery, medium dice	6 garlic cloves, pressed
¼ cup carrot, medium dice	2 tablespoons basil, minced
¼ cup red bell pepper, medium dice	salt and pepper as needed
1½ cups olive oil	1 pound squid
½ cup lemon juice	1 bunch curly endive
	2 lemons, cut into 8 wedges each

- Blanch the diced carrot in boiling salted water for several minutes, until tender but firm.
- Remove the cartilage from the squid body, and the inner part of the tentacles. Slice the body into ¼-inch thick slices, and cut the tentacles into ½-inch pieces. Blanch in boiling salted water, with a little white wine, until fully cooked. Drain, cool, and set aside.
- Beat the olive oil, lemon juice, water, garlic, basil, salt, and pepper in a bowl.
- Marinate the squid, scallion, celery, and carrot in the marinade, and refrigerate overnight.
- Cut the endive into 1-inch pieces, and arrange as a bed on one large platter or four individual serving plates. Place the marinated salad on top, and garnish with lemon wedges.

Stuffed Lettuce, Genoa Style
(Laitue à la Genoise)

Minced hard-boiled eggs, anchovies, capers, and chopped parsley, bound with a little mayonnaise, wrapped in butter lettuce leaves that have been rinsed, dried, and trimmed of excess stem, then sprinkled with finely diced red bell peppers and cooked beets, and garnished with parsley sprigs.

Stuffed Lettuce, Indian Style
(Laitue à l'Indienne)

Finely diced lobster and anchovies, bound with a little curry mayonnaise, wrapped in butter lettuce leaves that have been rinsed, dried, and trimmed of excess stem, served with a side of chutney.

Endive (curly-leafed) and escarole (broad-leafed) are native to India and were known in ancient times. Like dandelion, they are more bitter than other lettuces. In France, *cichorium endiva* was used as a medicinal plant and not considered as a food until the fourteenth century. Dandelion has been cultivated off and on throughout history, usually as a novelty or for emergency as a green vegetable.

Lettuce is a member of the daisy family, the second largest family of flowering plants. Today's lettuce varieties are all related to an ancestor native to Asia, Europe, and northern Africa. Lettuce contains vitamins A and C, riboflavin and thiamin, much water, virtually no calories, 1% protein, and 2–3% carbohydrates. Butter-head varieties include Buttercrunch, Bibb, Summer Bibb, White Boston, Dark Green Boston, and Matchless; Crisp-head (iceberg) varieties include Great Lakes, Iceberg, Imperial 44, Mesa 659, Ithaca, and Fulton; Leaf (curly) varieties include Grand Rapids, Green Ice, Salad Bowl, Oak Leaf, Ruby, Slobolt, and Greenhart; romaine varieties include Cos, Parris Island, Paris White, Dark Green Cos, and Mammoth Giant White.

$\mathcal{T}$ARPON SPRINGS GREEK SALAD

For the Hummus

1 cup garbanzo beans, soaked in water overnight
1 cup sesame tahini
6 garlic cloves, pressed
¼ cup olive oil
1 teaspoon salt
¼ teaspoon white pepper

For the Salad

1 head iceberg lettuce
2 cups potatoes, sliced ¼-inch thick and boiled al dente
2 ripe tomatoes, cored and cut into 6 wedges each
1 cucumber, peeled, seeded, and cut into large julienne
1 ripe Haas avocado, cut into 8 wedges
1 cup feta cheese, crumbled
1 green bell pepper, cut into rings
1 medium beet, boiled skin-on until tender
4 anchovy fillets
12 Calamata olives
4 scallions, cut into 2-inch lengths and quartered lengthwise
1½ cups olive oil
¾ cup white wine vinegar
salt and pepper to taste

To Prepare the Hummus

- Boil the beans in 2 quarts lightly salted water until tender. Drain and cool.
- Place the beans and remaining ingredients in a food processor and purée. Adjust seasoning with salt and pepper.

This salad derives its name from Tarpon Springs, a Greek fishing village on the west coast of Florida near the city of Tampa.

To Prepare the Salad

- Remove the outer leaves of the lettuce, and arrange a bed on a large platter. Cut the remaining lettuce into chiffonade, and place this on top of the bed. Arrange the remaining ingredients (including the hummus), in individual sections, on top of the lettuce. Drizzle with oil and vinegar, and season with salt and pepper.

Tomatoes, Baltic Style
(Tomates Farcies Baltique)

Tomatoes stuffed with finely diced potatoes, herring, apples, onions, and gherkins, bound with a little mayonnaise, garnished with a gherkin fan.

Tomatoes, Genoa Style
(Tomates Farcies Genoise)

Sliced tomatoes, topped with green pepper julienne marinated in garlic vinaigrette, garnished with anchovy fillets.

Tomatoes, Hotel Plaza Style
(Tomates Farcies Hôtel Plaza)

Half tomatoes topped with mashed sardines flavored with a little ketchup and mayonnaise, garnished with finely diced green peppers and green olives.

Tomatoes, Lucullus Style
(Tomates Farcies Lucullus)

Tomatoes stuffed with finely diced chicken, celery, capers, and toasted chopped hazelnuts bound with a little mayonnaise, garnished with sliced hard-boiled eggs, anchovy fillets, and black olives. (See color plate.)

Tomatoes, Mirabeau Style
(Tomates Farcies Mirabeau)

Tomatoes stuffed with finely diced celery, anchovies, and minced truffles, bound with a little mayonnaise, garnished with anchovy fillets.

$\mathcal{T}$OMATOES, MONACO STYLE

(Tomates Farcies Monégasque)

6 large ripe tomatoes
½ cup celery, medium dice
½ cup carrots, medium dice
½ cup green peas
½ cup celery root, medium dice
½ cup cauliflower, cut into ¼-inch flowerettes
½ cup broccoli, cut into ¼-inch flowerettes
1 cup mayonnaise
the juice of one lemon
salt and white pepper to taste
1 8-ounce piece of fresh tuna, blanched and chilled

- Blanch all of the vegetables, except the celery, in lightly salted boiling water until al dente. Drain and set aside to cool.
- Blend the mayonnaise with the lemon juice, then blend in with the vegetables and the celery. Season to taste with salt and pepper.
- Remove the cores and slice the tops from the tomatoes, then scoop out the pulp (reserve the pulp for other uses). Fill each tomato with the salad, place the lid on, and top with a slice of tuna. (See color plate.)

Tomatoes, Northern Style
(Tomates Farcies Nordique)

Half tomatoes filled with caviar, topped with a slice of hard-boiled egg and a crisscross of anchovy fillet, garnished with a dollop of tartar sauce.

Tomatoes, Paris Style
(Tomates Farcies Parisienne)

Sliced tomatoes on a bed of lettuce, topped with blanched diced celery root, flavored with minced anchovy, chervil, chives, and shallots marinated in a little vinaigrette.

Tomatoes, Polish Style
(Tomates Farcies Polonaise)

Tomatoes stuffed with finely diced herring, celery, onion, and minced dill, bound in a little mayonnaise, garnished with a piece of herring and a sprig of dill. (See color plate.)

TUNA AND GRILLED EGGPLANT SALAD, PACIFIC RIM STYLE

8 1-ounce slices ahi tuna
2 tablespoons sesame oil
¼ cup rice wine vinegar
¼ cup soy sauce
3 dried red Thai chile peppers, coarsely chopped
¼ cup lemon grass, minced
4 Japanese eggplants

peanut oil, salt, and pepper as needed
2 cups daikon radish, peeled and cut into long ¹⁄₁₆-inch strands
½ cup minced cilantro leaves

The best way to cut the daikon is with a Japanese-style mandolin, a tool designed for slicing vegetables with three different blade attachments. This mandolin can be found in most Asian food markets.

- Combine the oil, vinegar, soy, peppers, and lemon grass, and blend well. Coat the slices of tuna, and marinate 3 hours.
- Cut the eggplants into ¼-inch thick slices, on a *very sharp* bias. Brush with peanut oil, sprinkle with salt and pepper, and grill or sauté until golden brown.
- Arrange a bed of the daikon strands on each of four individual plates. Arrange the eggplant slices around this bed, top with two slices of tuna, and sprinkle with the chopped cilantro.

POULTRY SALADS

AMAGANSETT DUCK SALAD, CORNBREAD CROUTONS

4 boneless duck breasts (preferably Long Island duck)
¼ teaspoon parsley, finely minced
¼ teaspoon ground sage
¼ teaspoon ground thyme
¼ teaspoon cayenne
¼ teaspoon cumin
¼ teaspoon paprika
¼ teaspoon black pepper
2 tablespoons vegetable oil

1 cup stale cornbread, cut into ¼-inch cubes, toasted until brown and crispy
1 bunch arugula
1 head green leaf lettuce
1 head curly endive
¾ cup olive oil
¼ cup red wine vinegar
½ teaspoon Dijon-style mustard
salt and pepper to taste

- Preheat an oven to 375°F.
- Combine the herbs and spices, and dredge the duck breasts in them. Heat the vegetable oil in a hot sauté pan, and brown the breasts on both sides. Place on a baking sheet, and roast for 8 minutes.

- Tear the greens into bite-size pieces, rinse well, drain, and pat dry.
- Combine the olive oil, vinegar, mustard, salt, and pepper, and blend well. Toss the greens in this vinaigrette, and arrange on individual serving plates. Cut the duck breasts very thinly across the grain, on an angle, place on top of the greens, and top with the cornbread croutons.

CALIFORNIA GRILLED QUAIL AND WATERCRESS SALAD

4 barrel-boned fresh quail
salt, pepper, and olive oil as needed
5 ounces goat cheese
1 tablespoon minced parsley
1 tablespoon minced tarragon

1 tablespoon minced cilantro
8 slices of baguette, toasted
1 shallot, minced
1 cup orange juice
½ cup basalmic vinegar
2 tablespoons chicken glaze
2 bunches watercress

- Preheat an oven to 375°F.
- Rinse the quail and pat dry. Coat lightly with olive oil, and season with salt and pepper. Place in a hot sauté pan, brown lightly on both sides, and place in the oven for 15 minutes. Remove and set aside.
- Mash the goat cheese with the herbs until smooth. Spread on the toasted baguette slices, and set aside.
- Simmer the shallot, orange juice, and vinegar until reduced by half. Add the chicken glaze, blend thoroughly, and set aside to cool.
- Divide the watercress among four serving plates. Cut the quails in half, and place two halves on top of the watercress. Drizzle the warm sauce over the salad, and garnish with the baguette slices.

CHICKEN SALAD, MEDITERRANEAN STYLE

For the Chicken

2 6-ounce chicken breasts, boneless and skinless

1 cup dry white wine
1 cup water

1 small onion, quartered
2 garlic cloves, crushed
2 sprigs thyme

1 bay leaf
pinch of salt
pinch of pepper

For the Salad

1 cup string beans, ends
  trimmed, cut in half, and
  split
½ cup finely grated celery
  root
¼ cup capers, drained
2 tablespoons tarragon
  leaves, minced

½ cup mayonnaise
2 tablespoons walnut oil
3 tablespoons basalmic
  vinegar
pinch of saffron
salt and white pepper to
  taste

For Serving

8 large butter lettuce leaf
  cups
8 small radicchio lettuce leaf
  cups
1 ripe tomato, cut into 8
  wedges

2 hard-boiled eggs, cut into
  4 wedges each
16 Calamata olives

- Bring the poaching ingredients to a boil, add the chicken breasts, simmer for 5 minutes, then turn off the fire and set aside for 10 minutes. Drain, pat dry, and cut the chicken across the grain (widthwise) into ¼-inch strips.
- Blanch the string beans in boiling salted water until al dente. Drain, cool, and set aside.
- Bring the vinegar and saffron just to a boil, and set aside to cool.
- Combine the mayonnaise, oil, vinegar, salt, and pepper, and blend well. Add the chicken, string beans, celery root, capers, and tarragon, and blend thoroughly. Place a bed of butter lettuce, topped with the radicchio leaves, on four individual plates. Place a mound of the chicken salad in the center, and garnish with tomato, egg, and olives.

.... # *C*OBB SALAD

2 medium heads romaine
  lettuce

2 8-ounce chicken breasts,
  skinless and boneless

6 slices thick bacon
3 eggs, hard-boiled
2 large tomatoes
1 medium cucumber

1 cup crumbled blue cheese
1 cup olive oil
⅓ cup white wine vinegar
salt and pepper to taste

- Slice the romaine into 1-inch wide pieces. Rinse in cold water, drain, wrap in paper towels, and refrigerate until ready to use.
- Poach the chicken in lightly salted water. Drain, pat dry, and cut widthwise into a thin julienne.
- Roast or pan-fry the bacon until brown and crispy. Pat dry and mince.
- Press the egg yolks through a screen sieve, and finely mince the whites.
- Core the tomatoes, and cut into medium dice.
- Peel and seed the cucumber, and cut into medium dice.
- Divide the romaine lettuce among four clear glass bowls. Arrange the chicken, bacon, egg yolks, egg whites, tomatoes, cucumber, and blue cheese, in sections on top of the lettuce. Beat the olive oil, vinegar, salt, and pepper, and serve on the side.

Imperial Salad
(Salade Imperiale)

Poached chicken cut into julienne strips, asparagus tips, and green beans, arranged on a bed of lettuce, garnished with truffle, and dressed with simple vinaigrette.

SONOMA FOIE GRAS WITH MIXED GREENS

½ cup olive oil
¼ cup champagne vinegar
salt and pepper to taste
1 bunch arugula
1 head butter lettuce
1 head red leaf lettuce
1 small head radicchio

8 ½-inch thick wedges brie cheese
¼ cup vegetable oil
8 1-ounce slices Sonoma foie gras
12 ¼-inch thick slices of baguette, toasted

- Combine the oil, vinegar, salt, and pepper in a bowl, whip vigorously, and set aside.
- Preheat an oven to 350°F.
- Tear all of the salad greens into bite-size pieces. Rinse well in cold water, drain, wrap in paper towels, and refrigerate.

- Place the brie wedges on a baking pan, and place in the oven for about 5 minutes.
- Heat the vegetable oil, and sauté the foie gras for about 10 seconds on each side, or until slightly browned. Remove to absorbent paper.
- Toss the salad greens in the vinaigrette, and arrange on salad plates. Place 2 slices of foie gras, and 2 wedges of cheese on top of each salad. Serve with the toasted baguette.

Tomatoes, Nana Style
(Tomates Farcies Nana)

Tomatoes stuffed with finely diced chicken and toasted chopped walnuts, bound with a little mayonnaise, served on a bed of lettuce, topped with a little mayonnaise thinned with vinegar.

MEAT SALADS

Princess Salad
(Salade Princesse)

Broiled or grilled veal kidneys, finely diced. Diced celery and red bell peppers, marinated in mustard vinaigrette then drained. Served on a bed of lettuce, garnished with asparagus tips and sliced cucumber, seasoned with a sauce of mustard and mayonnaise thinned with lemon juice.

ROAST BEEF SALAD, THAI STYLE

¾ pound medium-rare roasted beef tenderloin, cut into ¼ × 2-inch julienne
½ cup fish sauce (nam-pla)
½ cup lime juice
2 tablespoons sugar
4 garlic cloves, pressed
1 teaspoon dried red chile pepper flakes
1 head butter lettuce
2 limes, sliced very thin

- Combine the fish sauce, lime juice, sugar, garlic, and red pepper flakes, and marinate the beef in this for 3 hours.
- Tear the lettuce into bite-size pieces, rinse in cold water, drain, pat dry, and refrigerate until ready to serve.
- Drain excess marinade from the beef. Arrange on a bed of lettuce, and garnish with the sliced lime.

Swedish Salad
(Salade Suédoise)

A composed salad consisting of sliced boiled beef, cooked potatoes and beets, apples, herring fillets, and raw oysters arranged in sections, garnished with anchovies, gherkins, capers, and quartered hard-boiled eggs, and dressed with mustard-paprika vinaigrette.

GLOSSARY

aiguillettes: Long, thin slices of poultry, game breast, or fish fillet, cut on the bias.

à la carte: In kitchen parlance, any dish that is prepared at the time it is ordered. Also *à la minute* and *à la command*.

al dente: Literally, "to the tooth" or "to the bite," this term is used to describe pasta and vegetables cooked until they are tender but not mushy. They should be somewhat firm and resilient when bitten into.

aspic: An ultraclarified, strong-flavored stock made from meat, poultry, game, fish, or shellfish, with a high gelatin content, giving it a translucent quality when chilled. Aspic is used to coat numerous dishes prepared in the garde manger department, including canapés, centerpieces, and a variety of sliced items arranged on mirrors for buffet service. It is also a medium in which various *timbales* are prepared (such as *oeufs en gelée*) and can be cut into numerous shapes and used as a garnish for buffet items.

attereau: A hot hors d'oeuvre consisting of raw or cooked pieces of offal, seafood, or vegetables, threaded onto a metal or wooden skewer, dipped into a reduced sauce, coated with bread crumbs, and deep-fried.

bain marie: A vessel of hot water, used for maintaining the heat of a smaller vessel, containing soup, sauce, or some other food item, within the larger vessel. May refer to small vessels placed in a steam table, and can also be used for chilling, placing a cold container into a larger one filled with ice and water.

bard: To place slices of fat back or bacon over a roast (usually game items such as partridge, pheasant, and boar), helping to keep it moist during roasting.

barquette: A small boat-shaped mold, measuring from 2 to 4-inches in length, used to bake a pastry shell for use as a canapé base.

batonnet: A large julienne, measuring $\frac{1}{4} \times \frac{1}{4} \times 2\frac{1}{2}$–3 inches. From the French *bâton*, meaning "stick."

blanch: To place a food in boiling salted water, stock, or other liquid, in order to cook it partially, set its color, or facilitate peeling.

boil: To cook a food in water or other liquid at 212°F. A full rolling boil is essential for cooking some foods (such as pasta), but undesirable for cooking others (such as stocks).

bouchée: A small bite-size pastry case made from *pâte feuilleté* (puff pastry), into which any of various fillings are placed, then served as an hors d'oeuvre or as a garnish to a larger dish. Attributed to Marie Leszcynska, queen to Louis XV. In contemporary times, bouchées are also fashioned from numerous farinaceous foods, such as wonton skins and tortillas.

bouquet garni: A collection of herbs and spices, tied together in a bundle with cotton twine and added to a stock, soup, sauce, or stew, to impart the flavor of those herbs and spices to the dish it is simmered with. A standard bouquet garni consists of parsley stems, bay leaf, thyme, and peppercorns. Variations on this are limitless, depending on an individual's style and the dish in which it is used. Loose herbs and spices can be added within a tea ball, or can be tied up in a large leek leaf.

braise: To cook a food item by dry heat method (sauté), and moist heat method (simmer in liquid). Typical braised dishes, which are tough or fibrous yet flavorful, include pot roasted beef, brown and white stews, and braised celery.

brunoise: French term for a very small dice, measuring approximately ⅛-inch square.

caisse: Literally, a "case" in which hors d'oeuvres, small entrées, and pastries are served. A holdover from earlier classical eras, and not commonly used in contemporary cookery nomenclature. The word refers to the form itself, as well as the pastry or bread form created to hold all manner of dishes.

caramelize: To cook sugar or another food in a sauté pan or saucepan over direct heat long enough to allow the sugar, or the sugar in the food, to begin to brown. Caramelizing imparts a brown color and a nutty flavor to the finished dish.

chaud-froid (pronounced show-fwa, literally "hot-cold sauce"): A brown, green (herb), red (tomato), or white colored sauce that is prepared hot and served cold. It is typically used as a base coating for pieces of meat, poultry, fish, or game, which are then decorated in elaborate fashion, coated with aspic, and served on a buffet table with other cold food items.

chiffonade: A leafy vegetable (such as lettuce, basil leaves, radicchio, etc.) cut into shreds, approximately ⅛-inch wide, and used as a salad base or as a garnish.

china cap (chinoise): A cone-shaped strainer, with a single handle extending from the wide end of the strainer. China caps come in three basic varieties, in reference to the size of their perforations: large *(chinoise gros)*, small *(chinoise fin)*, and very fine (bouillon strainer, or *chinois mousseline*).

clarified butter: The butter fat remaining after whole butter is simmered, evaporating the milk solids (the equivalent of skim milk).

compound sauce: A finished sauce fashioned from a foundation (mother) sauce as a base, augmented with other specific ingredients, including reductions; aromatic vegetables, herbs, and spices; garnishes; and various liaisons. Also called a small sauce, or a compound derivative.

court bouillon: A liquid medium used for poaching various forms of meat, fish, poultry, quenelles, and vegetables. The ingredients vary, depending on the item poached, but generally include water, wine, and aromatics (mirepoix, herbs, and spices).

croustade: A small farinaceous vessel, made from hollowed-out bread, pastry, mashed potato (Duchess potato mixture), or rice. The vessel is usually deep-fried or baked, then filled with a stew, soup, purée, or other viscous dish.

crouton (from Old French *crouste*, and Latin *crusta*, meaning ("crust"): A small, crisp piece of toasted or fried bread, used as a base for canapés, or as a garnish for various soups.

crudité: Raw vegetables cut into interesting and uniform pieces, served with a cold sauce as an hors d'oeuvre.

debeard: To remove the fibrous strands extending from the hinged side of a fresh mussel. Mussels use these strands to attach themselves to shoreline rocks.

deep-fry: To fry a food item by immersing it in hot fat.

deglaze (déglacer): To pour a liquid into a sauté or roasting pan, apply heat, and remove particles of food remaining in the pan after sautéing or roasting. This liquid may consist of wine, brandy, juice, or stock and is used to augment the flavor of stocks or sauces.

dock: To puncture a rolled-out pie, tart, or puff pastry dough, using the tines of a fork (or a special rolling tool), to prevent the dough from rising during baking.

drum sieve: A circular metal frame, open on one side and covered with a screen on the other. Used for sifting flour and other dry ingredients, as well as for pressing mousses and various farces through, with the help of a rubber spatula, as a final step in puréeing. Pressing mousses, pâtés, and other finely puréed preparations through a sieve eliminates remnants of sinew or elements not fully puréed.

egg wash: Beaten whole egg, sometimes with water or milk added, that is brushed onto a pastry exterior. When the pastry is baked, the egg browns slightly, resulting in a glossy, golden-brown veneer.

emulsion: Two or more liquids that do not naturally come together, slightly thickened with the aid of an emulsifying agent. This agent—notably the fat in eggs and butter, the starch in flour and cornstarch, the protein in gelatin, or the chlorophyll in parsley—creates a molecular suspension of minute drops of oil or fat within another liquid. Typical culinary emulsions include hollandaise sauce, mayonnaise, and certain vinaigrettes.

en papillote: Literally, "in paper," a method of cooking fish and poultry, combined with wine and aromatics, in which the flavors of the ingredients *marry* together.

faggot (pronounced "feh-go"): Literally, "a bundle of sticks," this term refers to a collection of fresh herbs and spices tied up into a bundle; also called *bouquet garni*.

farce (forcemeat): A finely ground, seasoned paste of meat, game, poultry, fish, or shellfish, raw or cooked, used as a stuffing for a ballotine, gallantine, or roulade, or as the main body of a pâté, terrine, sausage, or quenelle. The French term *farce* (from *farcir*, meaning to stuff), which also connotes a prank or practical joke, comes from an earlier practice (probably dating to ancient Rome) of playing a joke on one's guests by filling a hen, fish, or some other animal with an unexpected filling.

fine herbs: A mixture of finely minced fresh herbs, traditionally parsley, chervil, tarragon, and chives. In actual practice, it may consist of any assemblage of herbs—parsley plus three others.

fleuron: A small crescent-shaped savory pastry, cut from puff pastry dough *(pâte feuilleté)*, used as a garnish for certain fish dishes (when accompanied by a sauce), or as a decorative element on a pastry-covered pie, tarte, pâté, or terrine.

flowerettes: Cauliflower or broccoli, cut into ¼ to ½-inch pieces.

foie gras: Literally, "fat liver," the fattened liver of geese or duck, prepared in various ways.

fold: Generally with the help of a rubber spatula, to combine gently two foods, one being highly whipped. This method of blending allows the whipped product to retain its whipped-in air. It is most often associated with soufflés.

fond: Literally "base," or "bottom," this is a French term for stock, as well as the caramelized particles remaining in a cooking vessel after roasting or sautéing.

food mill: A straight-sided or conical container with a perforated bottom and a curved flange attached to a crank, which rests in the center of a perforated plate at the bottom. The crank is manually rotated, pressing a soup or sauce through one of three different sizes of perforated plates. With the advent of food processors, this ingeniously simple device has fallen on hard times, but it can still be a tremendous aid in puréeing soups and sauces.

garlic press: A small hand tool, designed to purée garlic, one peeled clove at a time.

glaze (glace de viande): A 90% reduction of a meat, poultry, game, or fish stock.

gratiner (also *au gratin;* English: to glaze): A technique in which the top of a food item is sprinkled with a mixture of buttered bread crumbs and/or cheese, then placed under a broiler and lightly browned.

hors d'oeuvre: Literally, "outside of the main piece." This is a small course served before the main course.

julienne: A designated rectangular-shaped vegetable cut, generally used for garnishes, measuring from ⅛ × ⅛ × 1 inch to ¼ × ¼ × 2 or 3 inches, or any food cut into strips. A large julienne is also referred to as *bâtonnet* (little stick).

lard: Larding is a technique in which a strip of pork fat is inserted into a piece of meat, game, or poultry, using a "larding needle," in order to add moisture and flavor during roasting or braising. In modern times, other items have been inserted, including compound butters, herbs, vegetables, and truffles.

large dice (jardinière): A designated vegetable cut, measuring approximately ⅓ to ½-inch square.

lozenge: Diamond-shaped cut, often used for canapé bases, but also for meat, fish, poultry, game, and vegetables.

medium dice (macedoine): A size of vegetable cut, measuring approximately ¼-inch square.

mince: To chop a spice, herb, or vegetable very fine.

mirepoix: A mixture of celery, carrot, and onion, commonly used for flavoring a stock or sauce.

mise-en-place: From the verb *mettre*, "to place." In culinary parlance this phrase is translated to mean "a place for everything, and everything in its place." It refers to the importance of being well organized and well prepped, so that kitchen production can move smoothly, and all problems can be handled in the heat of peak production.

mother sauce (sauce de mère): One of five foundation sauces, originally formulated by Antoine Carême and later revised by August Escoffier. Also called *leading,* or *foundation* sauce.

mount (monter au beurre): From the French verb *monter,* "to lift," this term refers to the technique of incorporating butter into a sauce or soup just before it is served. Stirring in butter in small pieces creates an emulsion that slightly thickens the liquid and improves or "lifts" the flavor of the final product. *Montée* is the past participle of the verb *monter; mount* is the colloquial American equivalent.

nap: To coat a food with a hot or cold sauce.

offal: Edible internal organs (and some external parts) of an animal, considered by some to be gastronomically superior to other edible parts. They include bone marrow, brains, ears, feet, heart, kidneys, liver, sweetbreads (thymus gland), tongue, and tripe (stomach lining).

pan fry: To fry a food item in a saucepan or sauté pan in a small amount of fat.

Parisienne scoop: Commonly known as a melon baller, this tool creates spherical garnishes from fruits and vegetables.

pastry thermometer: a high-range thermometer, particularly useful in pastry work, as well as for determining and maintaining the correct temperature when deep-frying a food item.

paupiette: Literally, "little package," referring to a rolled fish fillet, bundle of julienned vegetables tied together with scallion greens and so forth.

peasant style (paysanne): A common term for both a style of cooking, and a method of cutting food ingredients. As a cooking style, it is characterized by a robust and spontaneous approach, based on available

ingredients and/or refashioned leftovers, often including root vegetables (potatoes, carrots, and turnips) and cabbage. As a cutting technique, it refers to *mirepoix* cut into approximately 1-inch size uneven pieces, then used as an aromatic, as well as an integral ingredient in various dishes.

poach: To cook very gently in simmering liquid, at between 180° and 200°F.

ramekin: An ovenproof, round, ceramic dish, in which individual custards, shirred eggs, and soufflés are prepared. Side portions of cold sauces, compotes, salsas, and so forth, are also served in ramekins. Their size varies with the application: smaller ones (about 2 ounces) are used for side dishes, medium ones (4 to 6 ounces) for eggs dishes and custards, and larger ones (6 to 8 ounces) for soufflés.

red chile pepper paste: A spicy purée of exceptionally hot chile peppers, blended with oil, found in Asian and Hispanic food markets. It affords an easily available and consistent condiment to use in recipes that call for this kind of flavoring.

reduce: To decrease the volume of a sauce or stock by simmering or boiling, thus increasing its flavor and thickness.

render: To melt bacon, fat back, chicken fat, or other fat by cooking it in a heavy-gauge pan over medium heat.

ricer: A two-armed hinged press, with a solid plate on one arm and a perforated plated on the other, designed for mashing boiled potatoes.

roasting pan (plaque à rôtir): A large rectangular metal pan, deeper and heavier than a baking (sheet) pan, used for roasting meats and poultry.

sachet: A small piece of cheesecloth (muslin) tied into a small bag, containing herbs and/or spices for flavoring a stock or court bouillon.

salpicon: A small dice of one or more ingredients, bound with any number of sauces: cold (mayonnaise), brown (Bordelaise, Madeira, Perigordine, etc.), white (Lyonnaise, Mousseline, Newburg, etc.), or tomato (Amatricianna, Bolognese, Napolitana, etc.).

saucepan (sautoir): A heavy-gauge round cooking vessel with vertical sides and a single handle.

sauté: To cook food in a small amount of fat or oil. From the French verb *sauter*, meaning "to jump."

sauté pan (sauteuse): A round cooking vessel with sloping sides and a single handle.

scallop: Though most often associated with the connector muscle of one variety of bivalve mollusk, this word also refers to a slice of meat, game, poultry, or fish, pounded very thin, then cooked. The French word for this is *escalope;* the Italian, *scallopine*.

shallot (eschallote): a unique aromatic vegetable, a separate variety of the onion family, and an essential ingredient in finished sauces. The name is derived from Ascalon, an ancient Palestinian port, and it is believed that shallots were cultivated as early as the middle of the eighth century. Their flavor is subtler than onion, with a hint of garlic. They are also served raw in salads and grilled or roasted as an accompaniment to scores of dishes. Because of their ancient and Middle Eastern origins, shallots are also used frequently in Vietnamese, Chinese, Indian, and Creole cookery.

skillet: A heavy-gauge cast-iron pan with a single handle. Sometimes called a Griswold pan, it can be placed in the oven, thus doubling as a roasting pan.

skim (dépouiller, pronounced *day-pou-yay*): Literally, "to skin, to skim," a technique in which the top of a simmering stock, soup, or sauce is skimmed of fat and impurities. (The substance removed is known as *dépouillage.*)

small dice (brunoise): A designated vegetable cut, measuring approximately ⅛-inch square.

socle: A container for food made out of food. Examples are cucumbers scooped out for use as canapés, apples and tomatoes scooped out and filled with salad, and small rolls scooped out for use as croustades.

stockpot (marmite): A large pot, taller than wide, with straight sides and two opposing handles near the top edge. In French, a stockpot is called a *fait-tout,* (literally, "do-all") in reference to its many uses. A stockpot can also come with a spigot attached near the bottom, which can expedite the careful removal of a stock, particularly a consommé.

sweat: To sauté gently, covered, so that the ingredients sautéed exude moisture, which does not evaporate, effectively steaming these ingredients in their own moisture.

temper: To combine two liquids, one hot and the other cold, by slowly blending the hot liquid into the cold one. By gradually raising the temperature of the cold liquid, the two can be combined without adversely affecting either liquid. Applies to the incorporation of final liaisons, in the making of *chaud-froid* and mayonnaise collée, crème anglaise, pastry cream, as well as to melting chocolate.

whip (fouet): Sometimes referred to as a "whisk," it consists of several strands of stainless steel wire, in various thicknesses, bent into loops and held in place with a metal handle. The very heavy, stiff wire whips are commonly called "French whips"; the lighter, more flexible ones are "piano wire whips"; and the even lighter, large bulbous type are known as "balloon whips." All are indispensable in a well-equipped kitchen, used for beating liaisons into sauces, blending baking batters, and whipping air into various foods (such as heavy cream and egg whites).

white pepper: Black pepper that has been soaked in water, then rubbed to remove the skin and thin outer pulp. White pepper is preferred over black pepper in some dishes because of its lighter color. Dedicated cooks often keep two pepper mills, one filled with black pepper, the other with white, and each labeled accordingly.

zest: The outermost skin of a citrus fruit, excluding the pith (the underlying white part of the skin). It is shaved off with a zester, a five-holed tool specifically engineered for that purpose, or with a sharp paring knife or vegetable peeler. Zest contains the essential oils of the fruit and is used as both a flavoring agent and a garnish.

SPECIALTY SUPPLIERS

For information on specialty food items that may be difficult to obtain, contact the following organizations.

Asian Ingredients: Epicurean International, Inc., P.O. Box 13242, Berkeley, CA 94701; (510) 268-0209. For catalog on premium imported Thai cooking ingredients. Seth Jacobsen, contact person.

Aspic: Haller Foods, P.O. Box 422483, San Francisco, CA 94142; (415) 588-3192. Wholesale supplier of powdered aspic and other specialty items. Hans Haller, contact person.

Berries: The Oregon Caneberry Commission, 712 NW 4th Street, Corvalis, OR 97330; (503) 758-4043. For information on, and recipes using, blackberries, boysenberries, caneberries, loganberries, marionberries, and their availability in various forms. Jan Marie Schroeder, contact person.

Oregon Department of Agriculture, 121 SW Salmon Street, Suite 240, Portland, OR 97204-2987; (503) 229-6734. For information on other unique products, write for catalog.

Books and Tools: J. B. Prince, 29 West 38th Street, New York, NY 10018. Carries unique and hard-to-find culinary tools, books, and smallwares. Write and request current catalog.

Caviar: Carolyn Collins Caviar, P.O. Box 662, Crystal Lake, IL 60014; (312) 226-0342. Producer of a line of North American caviars. Carolyn Collins, contact person.

Cheese: Laura Chenel's Chevre, 1550 Ridley Avenue, Santa Rosa, CA 95401; (707) 575-8888. Producer of an exceptionally fine line of goat cheeses. Laura Chenel, contact person.

Maytag Dairy Farms, Inc., Box 806, Newton, IA 50208; (800) 258-2437. Call for the closest retail source of Maytag Blue cheese.

Cutlery: Russell Harrington Cutlery, Inc., 44 Green River, Southbridge, MA 01550; (508) 765-0201. Write for catalogs and information on where to purchase cutlery and tools.

Eau de Vie: Clear Creek Distillery, 1430 Northwest 23rd Avenue, Portland, OR 97210; (503) 248-9470. Producer of several fruit brandies, including an exceptional pear brandy. Stephen R. McCarthy, contact person.

Foie Gras: Sonoma Foie Gras, P.O. Box 2007, Sonoma, CA 95476; (707) 938-1229. Producers of an exceptional goose liver. Junny Gonzalez, contact person.

Commonwealth Enterprises, Ltd., P.O. Box 49, Airport Road, Mongaup Valley, NY 12762; (914) 583-6630. One of the first U.S. producers of duck foie gras and related products.

Olive Oil: For information on olive oil, telephone 1-800-232 OLIVE.

Vinegar: Kimberly Wine Vinegar Works, 290 Pierce Street, Daly City, CA 94015; (415) 755-0306. Produces several varieties of exceptionally fine vinegars and olive oils. Ruth Robinson, contact person.

INDEX
••